Engaged Buddhism in Japan

Volume 1

An Engaged Buddhist History of Japan from the Ancient to the Modern

Jonathan S. Watts

for my *kalyanamitra* in INEB,
who are always asking questions about
the Japanese and their unique form of Buddhism

ENGAGED BUDDHISM IN JAPAN
Volume 1
An Engaged Buddhist History of Japan from the Ancient to the Modern
Jonathan S. Watts

Published by
The Sumeru Press Inc.
PO Box 75, Manotick Main Post Office,
Manotick, ON, Canada K4M 1A2

Copyright © 2023 by Jonathan S. Watts

ISBN 978-1-896559-91-9

Cover: Japanese Buddhist monk's semi-formal *kesa*, 17th century
Courtesy of the RISD Museum, Providence, RI.

All rights reserved. No part of this book may be reproduced, stored in a retrieval system, or transcribed in any form or by any means—electronic, mechanical, photocopying, recording, or otherwise—without the prior written permission of the publisher.

LIBRARY AND ARCHIVES CANADA IN PUBLICATION

Title: Engaged Buddhism in Japan / Jonathan S. Watts.
Names: Watts, Jonathan S., 1966- author.
Description: Includes bibliographical references and index. |
Contents: Volume 1. An engaged Buddhist history of Japan from the ancient to the modern
Identifiers: Canadiana 20230153135 | ISBN 9781896559919 (v. 1 ; softcover)
Subjects: LCSH: Buddhism—Japan—History. | LCSH: Buddhism and social problems—Japan. | LCSH: Buddhism—Social aspects—Japan.
Classification: LCC BQ676 .W38 2023 | DDC 294.3095209/034 dc23

For more information about The Sumeru Press visit us at sumeru-books.com

Contents

Volume 1:
An Engaged Buddhist History of Japan
from the Ancient to the Modern

Introduction: Axialization and the Potential of
Socially Engaged Buddhism 7

Part I

The Historical Struggle of Buddhism to Axialize Japan
in the Pre-Modern Era

1 Buddhism's Entry into Japan and the Nara Period (646–794) .. 27

2 Esoteric Buddhism as Socio-Political Ideology
   in the Heian Period (794–1185)............................ 43

3 Buddhist Axialization in the Kamakura Period (1185–1333)... 61

4 Religio-Ideological Conflict and the Rising of the Masses
   in the Muromachi Period (1333–1558) 89

5 The Brahmanistic and Confucian Turns of Buddhism
   in the Tokugawa Era (1603–1868)........................... 99

Part II

Archaic Modernity and the Foundations
of Socially Engaged Buddhism in Prewar Japan

6 Archaic Continuity across the Tokugawa and Meiji Periods ...121

7 The Meiji Buddhist Enlightenment 135

8 Axial Challengers: Buddhist Socialism and the *Lotus Sutra*
   in the Taisho and Early Showa Periods 155

9 Descent into Holy War and the Conversion (*tenko*) to
   Imperial Way Buddhism 183

Part III
Defining Peace and Internationalism in the Liberal Utilitarian State: Socially Engaged Buddhism in Postwar Japan

10 The Sudden Turn Towards Peace in the 1940s and the Question of Principled Social Change. 199

11 The *Lotus Sutra*, Confrontational Buddhism, and Social Protest in the 1950s 205

12 Responsibility and Autonomy in Japanese Social Ethics in the 1950-60s. 221

13 Confronting the Past and Defining a New Buddhist Internationalism in the 1970s-80s. 239

14 Towards a Global Buddhist Civil Society in the 1980s-90s 267

Conclusion

The Promise of Principled Protest
and the Buddhist Resolution to Modernity 281

Afterword

Towards an Autonomous Buddhist Social Ethics
and a Dharmic Civil Society 297

Appendices

Works Cited 313

Index 325

Note: Our standard style for non-English text unless otherwise noted is Sanskrit, Chinese character, Japanese.

Introduction

We begin with a vignette: In April 2010, the International Network of Engaged Buddhists (INEB) held its 1st East Asian sub-network conference in Tokyo through the fledgling new Japan Network of Engaged Buddhists (JNEB) formed in late 2009. The theme was "Buddhism Confronting the Suffering of Contemporary Society" (現代の苦悩と向き合う仏教 *gendai-no kuno-to mukiau bukkyo*). It was a small but fairly typical gathering of Buddhists from South Korea, Taiwan, and Japan. It was also typical that after the first two days, the participants from South Korea and Taiwan expressed their astonishment at the state of Japanese Buddhism: seeing the priests in the causal clothing of any common Japanese citizen instead of their monastic robes; discovering that most had outside jobs to make income to support their wives and children; and gawking at their appetite for meat and alcohol during the evening group dinners.

What was and perhaps is most surprising is that even Buddhists from Japan's nearest neighbors, who share the same core East Asian Mahayana tradition, are not aware of the now-common reality of Japanese Buddhism.[1] Yet as the conference progressed, the Koreans and Taiwanese were also exposed to the unique skills of a new generation of Japanese Socially Engaged Buddhists. They listened to stories by priests of their intense work with suicidal citizens and the bereaved families of those who had killed themselves, and they took part in a project run by priests to wander the streets of Tokyo feeding the homeless while proving emotional support. In the end, they were filled with a new respect for these typically laicized priests, who were atypical in their commitment to engage in people's suffering. In turn, they reflected critically on their own national traditions, remarking that because of their monastic vows and appearance, monks and nuns find it difficult to, or simply cannot, connect so directly and intimately with lay people and their worldly problems.

---

1 Conversely, while serious Japanese Buddhists are aware of the particular situation of their tradition, many common Japanese are surprised to find out that Buddhist monks in other countries live by the strict code of the ancient *vinaya* system.

Various aspects of this vignette have been continually recreated over the past 150 years: first, when Japanese priests began to travel the world after the 260+ year ban on international travel by the Tokugawa military government was lifted at the opening of the Meiji era in 1868; then, after the end of World War II with the deepening secularization and marginalization of traditional Buddhism and the emergence of major lay Buddhist denominations on the global stage.

Japan has always been a mystery rolled into a conundrum for the West, but it has also been difficult to understand for other Asians despite many of the common cultural and religious traditions, and continues to be so. Attempting to unfurl this mystery from a Buddhist standpoint, for those on the outside looking in, is the first goal of Volume I of this two-volume work. The second goal, for those on the inside looking out, is to propose the role of Buddhism, specifically a Socially Engaged Buddhism, as an essential part of post-modern Japanese society in the new millennium that can reconcile its unique culture with the challenge of finding its role *within* the greater civilizational order of Asia and the wider global system.

This latter goal will be presented in two parts. The second half of Volume I comprises a history of Socially Engaged Buddhism in Japan in the modern era since the advent of the Meiji era. Volume II comprises five case studies presenting new areas of dynamic Socially Engaged Buddhist activism that have emerged in the 21st century.

An Archaic Culture Adrift in Post-Modernity

While the opening half of this first volume will look into the deeper historical roots of Japan's struggle to fit into the civilizational process of Asia, the touchstone, especially in terms of modern Socially Engaged Buddhism, is Japan's re-opening of its borders and entry into the modern global system in 1868 with the Meiji Restoration (明治維新 *Meiji Ishin*). The term "Restoration" here is not a mistranslation. Unlike the English, French, and Russians who literally killed off their divinely-sanctioned royal autocracies, Japan recreated theirs, fusing it with a unique interpretation of the modern nation state under the "archaic" symbols of their emperor and his polity (国体 *kokutai*). Even after the emperor's renunciation of his divinity at the end of World War II and his marginalization from the daily life of the average citizen, this archaic sense of Japanese collectivity and uniqueness as *kokutai* fueled its rapid economic expansion. Today, however, this once deeply cohesive social system is crumbling amidst economic and social decline along with epidemic levels of suicide and psychological disease that began to appear in the late 1990s.

In fact, the millennium serves as a perfect cut-off point between the postwar Japan of economic and social revitalization and a new era marked by economic stagnation, social "dis-ease" (Skt. *dukkha* 苦 *ku*), and human "disconnection" (無縁 Jp. *mu-en*). Except for two brief periods from 1993–96 and 2009–2012, the conservative Liberal Democratic Party (自由民主党 *Jiyu-minshu-to*) has maintained its domination over the Japanese political process as the ruling party since 1955. This domination, however, masks an even deeper entrenchment of power in the elite bureaucracy formed in the first decades of the Meiji, which continues to steward the LDP and all sectors of society though the time-honored division of authority and power.

As the economy turned ever downward into the late 1990s and early 2000s, LDP politicians, specifically Prime Minister Koizumi Junichiro 小泉 純一郎 (2001–2006), sought to dislodge these bureaucrats from their entrenched seats of power and launch a series of neoliberal economic policies to enable Japan to compete better globally. One of the most far reaching of these initiatives was the liberalization of the labor market. This led to the end of Japan's famous system of corporate paternalism and lifetime employment—and a subsequent jump in part-time employment from 15.3% in 1984 to 33.7% in 2009, and 38.3% by 2019.[2]

The effect of these economic policies is perhaps best evidenced in Japan's sudden jump in suicide rates during this time, from 24,391 in 1997 to 34,427 in 2003, remaining at 30,000+ per year until 2012. While suicide rates increased across all demographics, the group at highest risk was clearly middle-aged men in their 50s who bore the direct brunt of this neoliberal turn.

The new decade of the 2010s marked a shift in popular opinion and social activism, with the removal of the LDP from power in 2009 by the Democratic Party of Japan (DPJ) and the development of a strong civil disobedience movement opposed the resumption of nuclear power after the Fukushima disaster in 2011. However, after the DPJ's complete failure to dislodge the bureaucracy as the central governing system, the LDP returned to power under Abe Shinzo 安倍晋三 (2012–2020), who became the longest-tenured prime minister in Japan's modern history.

---

[2] The Issue and Situation of Irregular Employment (「非正規雇用」の現状と課題 *"Hiseiki Koyo"-no Jotai-to Kadai*). Japan Ministry of Health, Labor, and Welfare. https://www.mhlw.go.jp/content/000830221.pdf

His socio-cultural policies included the most serious threat to date to revise Japan's famous postwar constitution, by legalizing a pro-active military and re-articulating the nature of human rights as collective rather than individual.[3] His economic policies exacerbated the growing gap between rich and poor by raising consumption taxes that further marginalized the growing pool of non-regular or part-time employment, and led to increasing levels of poverty among single parents and children. The Abe administration's economic policies also remained loyal to Japan's long-established construction-centric development paradigm. Examples of this include his, and previous LDP regimes, continual push for nuclear energy development even after the Fukushima disaster, while squandering the competitive advantage Japan held in solar technology in the 1990s.[4]

The continual emphasis on highly centralized economic development was also tragically witnessed in the spent political will and finances for hosting the Olympics in 2020–21. This not only occurred in the midst of the government's late delivery of the COVID vaccine and the specter of the Olympics becoming a super-spreader event amidst an unprotected citizenry—to the point the usually quiet Japanese Emperor Naruhito publicly expressed concern only a month before their staging. The Olympic movement also occurred amidst the deeper backdrop of the expiration of relief subsidies for the people living in the areas of Northeast Japan still affected by radioactive fallout and the great tsunami of 2011.

Two decades into the new millennium, life in Japan has become increasingly precarious economically. Meanwhile, vast electoral apathy and no competitive alternative national party with a new vision for Japan bode poorly for any imminent resolution to these crises. The following chart[5] gives a more comprehensive view of the social

---

3   This latter re-interpretation of rights is epitomized in the Act on the Protection of Specially Designated Secrets (SDS) (特定秘密の保護に関する法律 *Tokutei Himitsu-no Hogo-ni kansuru Horitsu*) passed in 2013, which can put normal citizens in prison for up to five years for publishing any information deemed important to national security. Repeta, Lawrence & Jones, Colin P.A. "State Power versus Individual Freedom: Japan's Constitutional Past, Present, and Possible Futures". In *Japan: The Precarious Future*. Eds. Frank Baldwin & Anne Allison (New York University Press, 2015), pp. 304-328.

4   Fairley, Peter. "Can Japan Recapture Its Solar Power?" *MIT Technology Review* December 18, 2014. https://www.technologyreview.com/s/533451/can-japan-recapture-its-solar-power/

5   This chart and the following one on the problems of Japanese Buddhism were developed initially and then updated from a survey done in 2006 by the International Buddhist Exchange Center (IBEC) at Kodosan of key academics,

crises in Japan in the 21st century in lieu of a lengthy assessment here:

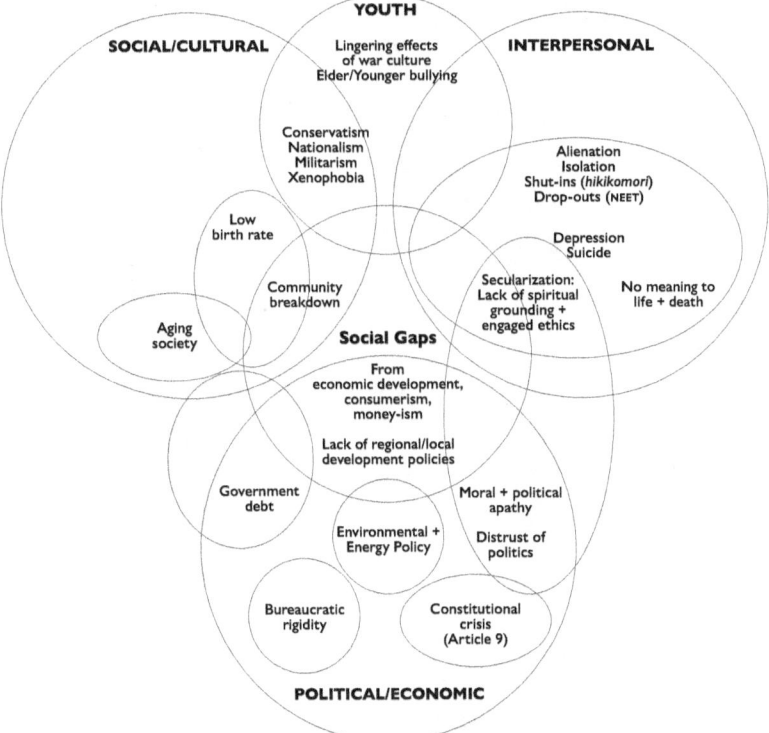

Matrix of Social Problems in Japan

An essential question for this book is: As a "religion" focused on the alleviation of suffering (*dukkha*), its First Noble Truth, can Buddhism offer any means to overcome these critical challenges facing Japan today? In order to answer this and to also unfurl the mysteries of Japanese Buddhism and culture in general, we must take a hold of the First Noble Truth to examine the present problems of Japanese Buddhism itself, as conceptualized in the graphic on the next page:

---

civil society activists, media members, and priests involved in social issues and Buddhism.

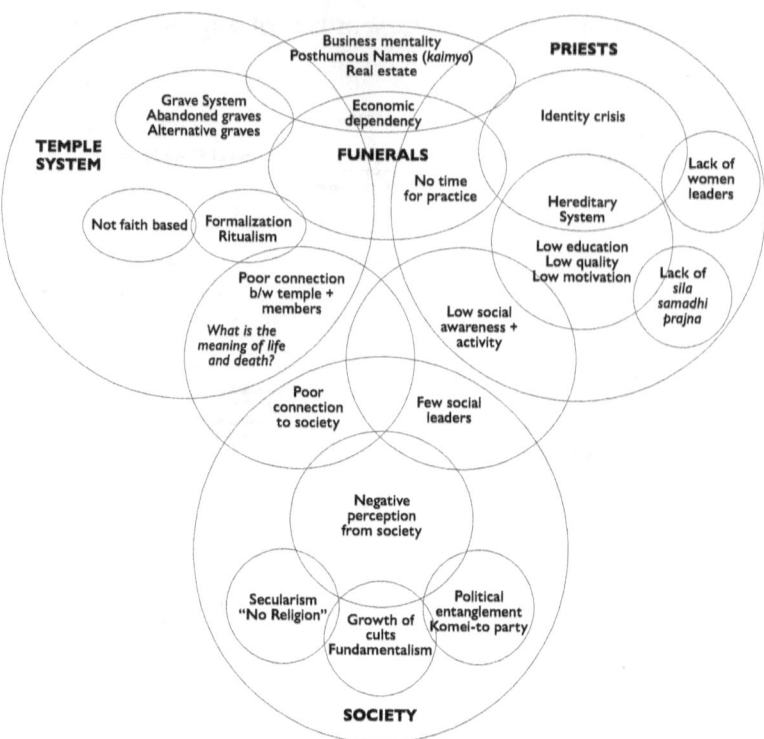

Matrix of Buddhist Problems in Japan

Contemporary Japanese Buddhism finds itself deeply mired in an identity crisis that is the fruit of its ongoing negotiation with modernity since Japan opened its borders to the West in the mid 19th century. The changing demographic landscape of modern Japanese society has increasingly marginalized Buddhist temples and priests from their central roles in the nexus of traditional, rural community life. In the mass shift of the population to urban eras after World War II, many Japanese abandoned their traditional family temples in the countryside. Curiously, the traditional denominations were unable to coordinate the transfer of temple membership to affiliated denominational temples in these urban areas, which for some denominations is due to the lack of such temples in these areas. While there have been a number of attempts at internal reform and restructuring, few of these efforts have led to any substantive change in the nature of traditional Japanese Buddhism,[6] which maintains its style of ancestor veneration based

---

6   Covell, Stephen G. *Japanese Temple Buddhism: Worldliness in a Religion of Renunciation*. (Honolulu: University of Hawai'i Press, 2006).

around funerals and memorial services, or what is now pejoratively dubbed as Funeral Buddhism (葬式仏教 soshiki bukkyo).

The increasing modernization and professionalization of social institutions (such as schools, hospitals, and even funeral homes), and the subsequent loss of social roles for priests, coupled with outdated forms of monastic education based on the study of ritual and doctrine, has meant that priests are no longer regarded as public intellectuals and opinion leaders in Japanese society. In sum, most Japanese Buddhist priests themselves will admit that the Japanese Buddhist world is very inward-looking and lacking in confidence to confront mainstream society.

Indeed, it is the Japanese Buddhist "priest"[7] who has perhaps undergone the greatest change and is under the greatest threat since the beginning of modernization in the Meiji era. As with the original community modeled around the Buddha himself and as with the variety of other national forms of Buddhism in Asia, traditional Japanese Buddhist sects were built around a charismatic, male, monastic founder (宗祖 shuso). These founders were celibate practitioners who went forth from their homes on a religious quest and came to profound insights through arduous training and spiritual exploration. The first notable exception in Japan was Shinran, the founder of the Jodo Shin Pure Land sect 浄土真宗, who paved the way for the modern Japanese priest by marrying and having children. However, even he began as a celibate monk at the headquarters of the Tendai sect 天台宗 on Mt. Hiei, later trained under the strict guidance of Honen (founder of the Jodo Pure Land sect 浄土宗 who maintained the monastic *vinaya* until his death), and certainly devoted his entire life to serious and intense spiritual exploration.

It is unrealistic to compare the rank-and-file priest of modern

---

7   Except for some small exceptions, the Buddhist tradition is overwhelmingly made of up celibate monastics (monks and nuns), and so there is no linguistic term in traditional Buddhist culture to differentiate a celibate monastic from a non-celibate one. On the other hand, English with its cultural grounding in Christianity has the distinction between the term "monk" as a cloistered celibate focused on intensive and strict religious practice and the term "priest" as an ordained religious professional living a more laicized life among the people that may include marriage and the consumption of meat and alcohol. In this way, we use "monk" and the honorific "Venerable"" to distinguish celibate Buddhist monks in the mainstream Buddhist monastic tradition, while using "priest" and the honorific "Reverend" to refer to the fully ordained yet laicized Japanese Buddhist religious professionals. These terms are used to denote distinction and have no implied sense of evaluation of the quality of either group.

Japan with these great founders. However, the lives of the founders are held aloft by each sect as the template upon which contemporary priests are to model their spirituality and practice. Amidst a very small number of exceptions, the typical modern priest is not celibate and does not live in a manner substantially different from a typical Japanese man. He marries, chooses his own clothes that often conform to the latest trends, eats a diet of his own choice, and generally consumes in any way he wishes. Around 80 percent of all priests in Japan today did not "go forth from the home" (Skt. *pravrajya* 出家 Jp. *shukke*) into the monkhood as a form of spiritual quest. Ironically, they were "born into the home" of the Buddhist temple family (寺族 *ji-zoku*), which is now in its fourth to sixth generation of priestly fathers and their wives since its standardization in the Meiji era. As for their religious vocation, the average priest performs a morning chanting service for 30-40 minutes, while the rest of the day is spent attending to the largely ritual duties of conducting funerals and memorial services for parishioners. Outside of the large training centers, which house a small minority of monks, the time spent for serious spiritual development is severely limited by both the institutional demands of maintaining a temple and the lifestyle (outside work, family, hobbies, and consumptive habits) of the priest.

This point then reflects on the present normative social role of the Buddhist priest. With the advent of modern, secular culture in Japan, the Buddhist priest is no longer valued for his traditional roles; either as exemplar of spiritual insight or as community leader (school teacher, doctor, mortician, counselor, or mobilizer of community projects). Rather than consult a local priest, who may have little to offer outside the rote doctrine they have learned in divinity school, modern Japanese now turn to literature, therapists, and a variety of New Age pundits for their spiritual-emotional needs. In turn, they also have a wide variety of modern secular institutions which provide the services that the temple once did. Within the last two decades or so, funeral companies have increasingly encroached upon the priest's last domain of activity. Funeral companies now are present in the hospital to greet the bereaved and offer a full set of services for the deceased and mourning families, including locating a suitable priest for the funeral. In this age of specialization, the Buddhist priest seems to do one thing, and one thing only, rituals and memorial services for the deceased. In turn, many Japanese when they see a black-robed monk have a visceral feeling of "death" rather than, for example, a feeling of "sacred" or "venerable".

In this way, the modern Buddhist priest finds himself in a deep identity crisis. On the one hand, there is the normative spiritual role model of the sect founder. Due to the structure of his experience from being born into the temple and inheriting his position to his fundamental ritual duties—which he must perform to keep his temple running and provide for his family—he has neither the proclivity nor the space to live up to these normative monastic standards. On the other hand, the priest has been circumscribed out of the variety of social roles that he used to perform in the past. As such, it is not surprising that society holds him in low esteem for he neither conforms to a spiritual ideal nor fulfills a deeply meaningful social role. In the estimation of many, he has become *bozu-marumoke*, a money-grubbing ritualist.[8]

With such freedom of lifestyle and such low social expectations, a Japanese Buddhist priest actually has a number of identities from which to choose. The usual, default identity is to confine himself to his ritual activities, serve his parishioners, and provide for his family and temple—a sort of Buddhist-styled Japanese "salary man". A second identity is to attempt to revive his spirituality and pursue a more monastic lifestyle. In contemporary Japan and Japanese Buddhist society in particular, this is virtually impossible unless he decides to abandon his temple and renounce a family. A third identity is to attempt to redefine his temple and his own activities through engaging in a variety of social activities—some of which are more focused on cultural entertainment than engagement in the problems of society. This identity is being increasingly pursued by some priests as they acknowledge the deep marginalization of temples and priests from mainstream society. However, this identity is fraught with the dangers of upsetting parishioners who do not wish for priests to do anything other than their ritual duties. Thus, it can endanger his and his own family's livelihood if he takes on activities that may or may not improve the standing of the temple.

The identity crisis of the Buddhist priest clearly reflects on the broader institutional crisis of traditional Japanese Buddhism, which continues to struggle in trying to define itself in the modern era. Outside of the Jodo Shin Pure Land sect, which has long acknowledged and supported its priests to marry, the other traditional sects' persistence on modeling its priests on the life of their founders imposes

---

8   This point reminds us of the Buddha's famous words in the *Vasettha Sutta* of the *Sutta Nipata* in the Pali Canon, "Know well that whoever among humans makes a living by priestly craft is a ritualist, not a *Brahmin* [i.e., a well-regarded religious person]." (Sn 3.9:618)

an impossible double identity on modern priests and their temples. Perhaps it is true that Japanese Buddhism needs to redevelop a strong lineage of monks focused on training in insight as with larger proportions of the monastic orders in other Buddhist countries. However, the core of the problem is not exactly this lack of spiritual discipline and training, but more the double standard which the sects impose on their members and attempt to portray to society.

Still today, the wives of priests are not directly acknowledged within the official rules or central power structures of the traditional sects. Without their agency, the sects are missing a precious resource for redefining and reviving themselves in modern society. Indeed, the persistent patriarchy and lack of meaningful roles for women in most Japanese Buddhist denominations fuels the image of Buddhism as an outdated and unmeaningful participant in contemporary Japanese life.[9] Since Japan's opening up to the modern world in the Meiji Restoration, Japanese Buddhists have tried to resolve these problems, principally in establishing new lay Buddhist organizations, such as Soka Gakkai and Rissho Kosei-kai. However, these groups miss the spiritual depth that highly accomplished monks and nuns offer to a complete Buddhist community, normatively defined as the four assemblies of lay and monastic men and women. Without the embodiment of the teachings and their attainment in the monastic Sangha, these denominations have found themselves having to elevate their founders and successors as a kind of royal family, sometimes bordering on the cultish.

This inability to confront the disjuncture between the past and the present is further evidenced in the way Buddhist institutions engage in society. Their deep complicity with the agendas of Japanese imperialism and the subsequent moral and spiritual bankruptcy by the end of the war created a deep distrust in traditional religion, both Shinto and Buddhist, in postwar Japan. In this period, traditional Japanese Buddhism has mirrored the government's missteps in expressing remorse for this history, which has contributed to its inward-looking nature and inability to act as leaders in society. Buddhist denominations in general refrain from taking vocal leadership roles in pressing political issues,

---

9 One positive outcome of the low birth rate in Japan is that due to the dearth of male successors to the many inherited positions in Japanese society, including Buddhist temples, we are starting to see a new generation of Japanese female priests succeeding their fathers as temple abbots and potentially paving the way for a new style of temple management. One prominent lay Buddhist denomination, Rissho Kosei-kai, will soon install as their third president, Niwano Kosho, the granddaughter of the founder Niwano Nikkyo.

as witnessed in the extended silence to the government's compromised response to the Fukushima nuclear disaster and to the Abe administration's push to alter Japan's constitution. Rev. Okano Masazumi 岡野正純, the President of the Kodo Kyodan Buddhist Fellowship 孝道教団,[10] comments on this issue.

> Even if the (denomination's) parliament decides to view the Fukushima problem without linking it to the war-time issue, it may still be difficult to build a consensus. What may typically happen is *paralysis by analysis*. One MP may insist that, "The government is saying that the problem is under control, and this kind of accident will never happen in the future. Why should we make a critical statement, if that is so?" Another MP may point out that, "We know that some of our parishioners work within and on the edges of the nuclear power industry. If we make a critical statement, we will end up harming them." These kinds of discussions were actually repeated in and out of the parliament sessions of some denominations. Discussions like these only breed confusion, not decision. If this is the state of the highest decision-making body, one can easily imagine that it will tend to keep the status quo rather than take on new challenges.[11]

The one prominent exception to this lack of civic and political engagement is the controversial Soka Gakkai lay denomination, which established the Komei-to political party that has been a coalition partner to successive LDP administrations since the beginning of the millennium. Soka Gakkai is an estranged member of the Japanese Buddhist community for their history of converting away members from other denominations. They do not belong to any of the current pan-Buddhist or pan-religious federations in Japan, where religious groups from a wide variety of backgrounds share perspectives and engage in basic forms of cooperation. Their present leader, Rev. Ikeda Daisaku 池田大作, has not been seen in public for years, and the

---

10 The Kodo Kyodan is a unique denomination. It is a new, lay denomination in the style of Rissho Kosei-kai, yet it is recognized as an offshoot of the Tendai sect, thereby maintaining membership in the Japan Buddhist Federation (全日本仏教会 *Zen Nihon Bukkyo-kai*) of traditional sects.

11 Okano, Masazumi. "Afterword". In *Lotus in the Nuclear Sea: The Promise of Buddhism in the Nuclear Age*. Ed. Jonathan S. Watts (Yokohama: International Buddhist Exchange Center IBEC, 2013), p. 231.

Komei-to has become increasingly non-resistant to the nationalistic agendas of the LDP.[12]

Political engagement remains an extremely sensitive issue amongst religious organizations in Japan, all of which were deeply compromised during World War II. Most Buddhist orders in Japan took well over fifty years after the war ended to declare their errors in pro-actively contributing to the imperial cult that fueled Japanese nationalism. While the typical Japanese citizen is far from a flag waving nationalist and holds vague conceptions of international peace, the fear that Japan could easily slip into old patterns of cultural exceptionalism and aggressive nationalism fuels suspicions and counter nationalist sentiments in the volatile region of East Asia. While Japanese Buddhist denominations have spent vast sums of money on "peace activities" (*heiwa-katsudo*), the ritualized manner of these initiatives and their inability to act as progressive social voices on critical social issues keeps them on the margins of mainstream consciousness.

Axialization and the Potential of Socially Engaged Buddhism in Contemporary Japan

The world-renowned Japanese scholar of Vedic, Hindu, and Buddhist texts, Nakamura Hajime 中村元 (1912–1999), illuminates here one of the core issues in Japan's struggle to negotiate its archaic cultural outlook with the demands of a now intimately globalized world:

> Those who observed the moral confusion in Japan immediately after World War II may be led to doubt the proposition that the Japanese in the past were moralistically inclined…. Little difference seems to be discoverable between traditional and recent Japanese morality. The difference seems to lie rather in the fact that what was considered to be morally tenable in Japan's "closed-door" past became untenable under rapidly changing worldwide social and economic conditions to which Japan is adapting itself. The traditional concepts of honesty as loyalty to the clan and emperor is applicable only to the conduct of man as a member of the particular and limited human nexus

---

12 "New Komeito's Role as Partner to the Right Leaning LDP Led Government". *Japan Times* September 24, 2014. https://www.japantimes.co.jp/opinion/2014/09/24/editorials/new-komeitos-raison-detre/#.W9qgdJP7RaR

to which he belongs; it is not applicable to the conduct of man as a member of human society as a whole.[13]

This inability to reconcile with the past leads to an inability to move forward into the future with a holistic vision for national development. Now that Japan has attained its economic miracle and seen it fall, can we see the emergence of qualitatively new sorts of values, practices, and systems that break from the failed ones formulated as Japan entered the modern age? Addressing this question will be a central theme of the second volume.

It is clear that economic development is not enough as Japan began to experience social decline in several areas from the end of the last century. Yet the LDP can only seem to recycle old policies of industrial, construction-driven capitalism and Japanese cultural exceptionalism. The result, as seen in so many social sectors, is a terrible intermediate state in which Japan has lost the depth of its traditional life systems while incorporating already-outdated and ill-fitting American or European systems. It is not surprising then to see that this lack of vision and the problems which have been created by development (environmental degradation, class disparity, community breakdown) have resulted in high rates of depression, suicide, social reclusion, bullying, and violent crime, especially among the young.

For Japan to successfully confront the future, it needs to integrate its material and spiritual selves. Socially Engaged Buddhists in such places as Sri Lanka, Thailand, and Bhutan[14] have developed critiques of mainstream economic development and have offered concrete alternatives for a holistic vision of development (開発 *kaihotsu*)[15] that have been translated into Japanese and could offer a valuable resource for this endeavor. However, as seen above, Japanese Buddhism has been too institutionally and spiritually adrift to draw on the progressive stands of either its ancient traditions or these new Socially

---

13   Nakamura, Hajime. *Ways of Thinking of Eastern Peoples India-China-Tibet-Japan*. Revised English Translation. Ed. Philip P. Wiener. (University of Hawaii Press, 1964), p. 521.

14   Such as the Sarvodaya Shramadana movement in Sri Lanka, the Thai development monk movement in Thailand, and the Gross National Happiness movement in Bhutan.

15   Nishikawa, Jun. "The Choice of Development Paradigms in Japan after the 3/11 Fukushima Nuclear Disaster". In *This Precious Life: Buddhist Tsunami Relief and Anti-Nuclear Activism in Post 3/11 Japan*. 2nd Edition. Ed. Jonathan S. Watts. (Yokohama: International Buddhist Exchange Center, 2012/2016), pp. 87-104.

Engaged Buddhist streams in other countries in order to to engage in this endeavor. In order to awaken this potential—the way of the Third and Fourth Noble Truths—we must return to the first challenge of unravelling the mysterious character of Japanese Buddhism and culture; that is, an investigation of the various causes and conditions of this situation—the Second Noble Truth. For this investigation, we will begin with perhaps the core conundrum of Japanese Buddhism as articulated again by Nakamura Hajime:

> Although Buddhism has been the flesh and blood of Japanese culture for more than the past ten centuries, the people by and large still regard it as "an imported system of thought." In this respect, our attitude differs from those of Western nations in regard to Christianity and from those of southern Asiatic nations in regard to Buddhism. As for those nations, universal world religions are conceived to be such integral parts of their own culture that they are linked to the formation of respective norms themselves. But for the Japanese, in contrast, such a conception is totally absent.[16]

If the above observation came from a foreign writer, it might be construed as a misguided observation of Japanese exceptionalism. As part of a monumental analysis of Indian, Tibetan, Chinese, and Japanese culture in *Ways of Thinking of Eastern Peoples* by the foremost Japanese Buddhist scholar of the 20th century, it deserves long and thoughtful inquiry. Taken with the earlier quote by Nakamura on the "closed-door morality" of Japan as inapplicable to a larger civilizational system, it leads us into a cultural comparison between Buddhist and world civilizations as a whole. What is it that makes Japan so unique, not even within the global system of civilizations, but just within its own Buddhist and even East Asian Buddhist socio-cultural systems?

An initial clue comes in the concept of "axialization" first developed by the German-Swiss philosopher Karl Jaspers in *The Future of Mankind* (1961) and then further developed by the Israeli sociologist S.N. Eisenstadt. Among Eisenstadt's numerous writings on this subject, his immense *Japanese Civilization* is an attempt to answer the vast mysteries of Japanese historical development in comparison to other civilizations. In keeping with Jaspers, Eisenstadt defines axi-

---

16 Nakamura. *Ways of Thinking of Eastern Peoples*. p.489.

alization as a process that occurred from around 500 BCE to the 1st century CE, and even up to the rise of Islam, in certain key locations of highly developed human civilization—such as China, India, Greece, and Mesopotamia—in which "new types of ontological visions, [and] conceptions of a basic tension between the transcendental and mundane orders, emerged and were institutionalized."[17] Eisenstadt further explains that this tension between the transcendental and mundane gave rise to attempts to reconstruct the mundane world (human personality as well as socio-political and economic orders) according the transcendental vision. In this way, *the mundane order was perceived as incomplete, inferior, unsatisfactory, or polluted and "in need of being reconstructed according to the principles of a higher ontological or ethical order that bridged the chasm between the transcendental and the mundane orders."* The activators of this reconstruction emerged from among "autonomous, relatively unattached 'intellectuals', such as prophets or visionaries." Their visions or teachings ultimately *transformed into the basic "hegemonic" premises of their respective civilizations,* becoming institutionalized as the dominant orientations of both the ruling and many secondary elites, fully embodied in their respective centers or subcenters (e.g., the Mosaic law in ancient Israel, the Pauline vision in Christianity, Confucian metaphysics in China, Shakyamuni Buddha's ethics of mind in India).[18]

Eisenstadt and other scholars contend that although Japan did develop a sophisticated philosophical and aesthetic discourse while undergoing continuous institutional and cultural change from both within and from foreign influences, it has yet to fully axialize. Eisenstadt points out that, "The central axis of differentiation between the historical experience of Axial civilizations and that of Japan lies in the strength of the tendency towards *the ideologization of changes* and struggles in different social and institutional areas."[19] He does not imply that Japan has not undergone vast changes in its history but, rather, that many new and varied activities were incorporated *without ideological struggle* and without a principled reconstruction of the essential boundaries of Japanese collectivity and its central symbols such as the emperor.[20] Nakamura echoes this sentiment in the following:

---

17 Eisenstadt, S.N. *Japanese Civilization: A Comparative View*. (London: University of Chicago Press, 1996), p. 13

18 Ibid., p. 13.

19 Ibid., p. 420.

20 Ibid., p. 421.

> The inclination to regard as absolute a limited specific human nexus naturally brings about a tendency to disregard any allegedly universal law of humanity that every man ought to observe at any place at any time. Instead, the standard of the evaluation of good and evil is identified here with the consideration of the appropriateness or inappropriateness of conduct judged solely by reference to the particular human nexus to which one happens to belong.[21]

Eisenstadt feels that while Buddhism and Confucianism provided transcendental visions or ideologies beyond these boundaries, they were eventually Japanized—like other foreign systems of universal thought that came into Japan such as Western liberalism and Marxist socialism—and subsumed within this archaic thought system of Japanese exceptionalism.[22]

A typical example of this distinction is how the Church in Europe became a state unto its own while creating loyalties and schisms that superseded national and ethnic ones. Eventually, this order gave way under the universal, secular principles of human rights, democracy, and socialism that led to the assassinations of divinely ordained monarchs in places like England, France, and Russia. The Chinese, while basing themselves on the much less transcendental vision of Confucianism, still sought to bridge the gap between an ideal, principled (if not transcendental) order and the mundane through the proper management of the state. Unlike the Japanese emperor, if the Chinese emperor did not follow the principled norms of Confucian ethics and violated the Mandate of Heaven through corrupt governance, revolt and regime change were seen as a just response. In Japan, the emperor is a living descendent of the gods who created Japan, and an act of revolt, much less regicide, has been historically seen as an act of defiance against one's own parents, kin, or "tribe" (族 zoku). In this way, while there were numerous dynastic changes in China over its history, the Japanese have maintained a single unbroken succession of their royal house with 125 emperors since its inception in 660.[23] Eisenstadt crystalizes these points as:

---

21 Nakamura. *Ways of Thinking of Eastern Peoples*. p. 393
22 Eisenstadt. *Japanese Civilization*. p. 423.
23 Eisenstadt points out that this was one of the main barriers to Confucianism being fully adopted by the Japanese. Eisenstadt. *Japanese Civilization*. pp. 256, 289.

There did not develop in Japan the emphasis on a *principled* discontinuity between different regimes or "stages" of institutional change. Nor did there develop any strong conception of such changes and breaks as constituting steps in the unfolding of historical programs or cosmic plans with possible eschatological implications. In principle, no new modes of legitimization were connected with such changes. The assumed mythical continuity of the imperial symbolism—often fictitious but continuously emphasized—was crucial in this respect. The bases of legitimization—especially those rooted in the symbolism of the emperor—were continuous and could not be dismantled or changed. The epitome of this emphasis on (a reconstructed) continuity could be seen in the totally new construction of the emperor system under the Meiji regime.[24]

In conclusion, Eisenstadt echoes Nakamura's comments that Japan has never seen itself "as part of a broader civilization, as sharing basic premises and identity with other societies."[25] This leads us to question whether Japan, despite its highly developed social and cultural forms, is indeed a civilization, since the one major distinction between it and the other civilizations we have mentioned is its almost total ethnic and linguistic homogeneity. If we define "civilization" as *the binding together of multiple ethnicities with various languages, cultural customs, and religious or spiritual outlooks through an appeal to universal—but not necessarily transcendental—values to enrich human and perhaps all sentient life amidst a dynamic interplay of diversity*, then it is possible to call Europe, the Middle East, the Indian subcontinent, and even greater China all civilizations, but it is rather untenable to denote the single nation and people of Japan as a civilization unto its own. It is important to keep this definition of civilization in mind, specifically when we explore Japan's attempts in its modern imperial era to define its own civilization, within which all of Asia would encompassed through the "civilization and enlightenment" (文明開化 bunmei kaika) movement.

Based on the above analysis, the challenge of Buddhism to offer contemporary Japan a means of "transcending" the schism between its archaic past and present paralysis seems daunting, if rather impossible. Yet the recent activities of Socially Engaged Buddhists in Japan indicate a new potential—along with a variety of recent social shifts,

---

24　Ibid., p. 424.

25　Ibid., p. 15.

like the growth of numerous localized civic works and the increase of long-term foreign residents creating a new level of diversity. As we will investigate in Volume II, these activities are promoting and embodying a variety of civilizational values, such as: cross-denominational, ecumenical network-building as well as partnership with secular social organizations; direct engagement with the suffering of common people without agendas towards conversion; and the articulation of a wider social ethic of concern beyond the limited social nexus that Nakamura identified to the bodhisattvic concern for "all sentient beings" (衆生 *shujo*).

In turn, we are seeing a reinvigoration of the Buddhist priest as "sacred" not through a reclamation of the ancient monastic *vinaya* but a revival of the bodhisattva vows upon which Japanese Buddhism was first created. For Volume I, however, we must re-ask the question, "Can Buddhism as a religious system—or more fundamentally, a mode of thought and way of life—provide the universal and axial modes of praxis (which are at the same time indigenous after 1500 years of historical development within the country) to support Japan to face its ongoing confrontation with modernity and globalization as well as its present social crises? For Buddhism to offer such resources, a critical reconstruction of its history along such axial contours is essential, for as we will see, Buddhist history, like the history of so many other religions, is rife with de-axial regressions into ethno-centric, clannish nationalism.

Part I

The Historical Struggle of Buddhism to Axialize Japan in the Pre-Modern Era

1

Buddhism's Entry into Japan and the Nara Period (646-794)

Context and Beginnings: Japan's Pre-axial Clan Society

Buddhism was introduced into Japan in the mid 6th century from Korea through a political alliance with the Baekje, one of the three kingdoms competing for power on the Korean peninsula. The particular form of the Buddhism of the Baekje was strongly influenced by the southern school of Chinese Buddhism as well as direct transmissions from India. By this time, Buddhism was entering its second millennia of historical development, after having served as the civilizational foundation of Ashoka's empire in the 3rd century BCE, undergone major changes and development in the Mahayana reform movement that spread into Central Asia in the early Common Era, and then being further digested by the rich civilization of China up to its transmission into Korea and Japan in the middle of the 1st millennium CE. Needless to say, the task of Japanese culture—still in its formative stage of development—to digest this massive and highly developed civilizational movement was daunting.

In the mid 6th century, according to the renowned Japanese scholar Kuroda Toshio,[1] Japan existed as an "ancient autocratic state" (古代専制国家 *koda-sensei kokka*) ruled by local chiefs and powerful

---

1   Kuroda Toshio 黒田俊雄 (1926-1993) was one of the more radical and influential Japanese Buddhist scholars of the 20th century. He is known especially for his expertise in medieval Japanese history and his defining work on the esoteric *ken-mitsu* system (顕密体制 *ken-mitsu taisei*) and structure of medieval Japanese Buddhism. His work is seminal for going beyond the confines of traditional Buddhist scholarship by interpreting how teachings and doctrine also reflected the political and sociological systems of medieval Japan. In this way, he can be compared to his Indian contemporary D.D. Kosambi (1907-1966), whose penetrating historical analysis serves as a foundation for many of this volume's comparisons with Indian Buddhism and society.

families, often referred to as clans (氏 *uji*)². Nakamura Hajime³ notes that, "Under the ancient clan system, the early Japanese were devout ancestor-worshippers and diligent observers of family devotions conducted in compliance with [what we would call today as] Shintoism.... Large and small clans, related by blood, having common ancestors and occupations, set up a deity which the entire clan worshipped as their tutelary deity or *ujigami* 氏神."⁴ This eventually led to the concept of state as an aggregation of families.⁵ Nakamura further notes that in contrast to the Chinese Confucian moral code that stresses joint family ownership and blood lineage, the Japanese have understood "family" on more patriarchal terms and based on the concept of "household" (家 *ie*) so that non-blood relations can be adopted as full heirs even if they are of lower social status.⁶ This "ancient autocratic state" of controlled communities and a hierarchical power structure built from local families up to the emperor extended through to the emergence of the medieval state in the 9ᵗʰ century during the Heian Era.⁷

In this way, Buddhism with its universal ethics, its call to transcend the world, and its central figures who had renounced clan and family, did not find an easy congruence with indigenous Japanese culture. Shakyamuni's resignation to the genocide of his Shakyan tribe at the hands the Kosalans without lifting a hand in combative defense would be unthinkable in Japanese culture—nor perhaps to the nationalistic Buddhisms of Southeast Asia. Buddhism thus had to enter Japan through this clan structure, first finding patronage through the powerful Soga, a clan with strong links to the Korean peninsula and an appreciation of the new religion. Thus, from the beginning,

---

2   Kuroda, Toshio. "The Development of the *Kenmitsu* System as Japan's Medieval Orthodoxy". Trans. by James C. Dobbins. In *Japanese Journal of Religious Studies*. 1996. Vol. 23, No.3-4. pp. 236-39.

3   Nakamura Hajime 中村元 (1912-1999) is probably the most important and influential Buddhist scholar in modern Japan. An expert in Sanskrit and Pali, he is best known in Japan for making the first and still definitive translation of significant parts of the Pali *Tripitaka* into Japanese. Through his long career at Tokyo University, he published more than 170 monographs and 1,000 articles, both in Japanese and in Western languages, including his seminal work on Indian, Chinese, Tibetan, and Japanese thought, entitled *Ways of Thinking of Eastern Peoples* (東洋人の思惟方法 *Toyo-nin-no shi-i hoho*).

4   Nakamura. *Ways of Thinking of Eastern Peoples*. p. 417.

5   Ibid., p. 418.

6   Ibid., p. 420.

7   Kuroda. "The Development of the *Kenmitsu* System as Japan's Medieval Orthodoxy". p. 237.

Buddhism becomes a faith tied to the maintenance of ancestral cults and practiced through prayers for welfare in this world and the next.[8] While Shakyamuni was not unsupportive of the family system, there is little to nothing in the early tradition of practicing ancestor worship, a religious practice in India more closely identified with Brahmanism and its emphasis on maintaining caste purity.[9] As such, the early Japanese adopted Chinese Buddhist teachings that the Chinese had already adapted themselves to their own indigenous conception of filial piety, such as compassion (慈悲 *jihi*) between child and parent rather than towards all sentient beings—expressed by the famous Japanese Zen teacher Bankei 盤珪 (1622–1693) as "the Unborn Buddhahood transmitted from parents to child." Also, in this earliest period, the Bon Festival was instituted during the Suiko era (592–628) to express gratitude to the ancestors of the seven preceding generations.[10] This festival is based on the *Ullambana Sutra* (盂蘭盆經 *Urabon-kyo*) popular in the Mahayana East Asian tradition for its teaching on filial piety.[11] In Japan, it has become the most important Buddhist festival and holiday in the calendar year.

While it has been commonplace for Buddhism to be adapted to the specific cultural traditions of each country, the Japanese had a particularly daunting task in assimilating the massive work of the Indian, Central Asian, and Chinese developments of Shakyamuni's original and radical insights. Carl Becker, a renowned Buddhism and Japanese cultural expert at Kyoto University, sums up the challenge facing the early Japanese in their importation of Buddhism:

> The problem was there was so much there, and it was so rich. The Mahayana Canon was so huge that even if Ennin 圓仁 [794–864, the saecond patriarch of the Tendai sect] understood it and brought it all back to Mt. Hiei, the average Japanese, who was still having trouble mastering

---

8   Kasahara, Kazuo. *A History of Japanese Religion*. Trans. Paul McCarthy & Gaynor Sekimori. (Tokyo: Kosei Publishing, 2001), p. 61.

9   As we will see later on, "purity" is a central concept in the maintenance of caste bonds in India and the maintenance of clan and family bonds in Japan.

10 Nakamura. *Ways of Thinking of Eastern Peoples*. pp. 421, 424.

11 In the *Ullambana Sutra*, the Buddha's disciple Maudgalyayana saves his deceased mother from the realm of hungry ghosts (Skt. *preta* 餓鬼 *gaki*) by transferring the merit accrued from making a large offering to the monastic community. This story is found in the Theravada tradition in the Petavatthu (lit. "Ghost Stories") of the *Khuddaka Nikaya* of the Pali Canon, but Maudgalyayana is replaced with the Buddha's disciple Shariputra.

Chinese characters and still thinking in the ancient vernacular (*Yamato kotoba*), was not capable of grasping all of Buddhism in their lifetime. It's like bringing Emmanuel Kant and the Enlightenment to the pygmies or the Papua New Guineans. The very language and thought structure of the Yamato vernacular in the 9th century was incapable of expressing or formulating the 1,000 years of deep philosophy that was already there in Chinese Buddhism. This was not the fault of the Japanese—the language gap was just too great. The way the Japanese went about addressing this was by picking and choosing.[12]

Nakamura further elaborates on this point noting that:

It is important to note that the Japanese frequently misinterpreted the original Chinese texts. This misinterpretation of the sources for the transmission of Chinese thought is one of the most significant phenomena in the history of Japanese thought. The Japanese translators of these Chinese writings would, knowing that the Chinese language has no rigid grammar, make very free interpretations of Chinese texts, adding ideas of their own for their own purposes. It was natural that the more studious and disinterested monastic Buddhist scholars in Nara, the ancient capital of Japan, and Mt. Hiei, a center of Buddhist studies, were able to read and write Chinese with accuracy because their own thought conformed to Chinese ways of thinking. This, however, was not the case with the preachers who propagated Buddhist thought to the Japanese people. The closer to the Japanese public the mind of the preacher was, the greater was his deviation from the Chinese source texts.[13]

---

12 Becker, Carl. B. "Embracing the Pure Land Vision: Coming to Grips with Dying through Living". In *Never Die Alone: Death as Birth in Pure Land Buddhism*. Eds. Jonathan S. Watts & Yoshiharu Tomatsu. (Tokyo: Jodo Shu Press, 2008), p. 65.

13 Nakamura. *Ways of Thinking of Eastern Peoples.* p. 348.

Pre-Axial Clan Culture Problem #1: Axial Dialectic vs. Mystical Ritualism

So, what then did the Japanese choose from the Buddhist tradition? And what is specific to their ethnic character that would lead to such choices? Nakamura points out the tendency towards what he calls the "limited social nexus" of Japanese society (i.e., the clan and household system) and the stress on inter-personal and non-individual relations, which leads Japanese towards intuitive and emotional forms of communication rather than towards ones based in the logic of a universal understanding of humanity and the world. In the Japanese language, there is the well-known tendency towards vagueness and assumed points in communication with the frequent dropping of subjects and objects. As such, the Japanese language has never been a good medium for expressing philosophical concepts and has depended on the use of Chinese characters in combination to develop such concepts.[14]

When Buddhist logic (因明 *inmyo*) was introduced to Japan around 661, it was used primarily as a technique of oral expression in question and answer sessions (問答 *mondo*) at meetings of teachers and students or among monks, rather than as a subject in itself. It became institutionalized within the Nara period in the Hosso school 法相宗 that focused on the Yogacara teachings (瑜伽行派 *Yuga-gyo-ha*). However, with the rise of esoteric Buddhism in the 9th century and the marginalization of the Hosso by new rival schools like the Tendai 天台宗, it eventually deteriorated into a ritualized and formalized system of etiquette fitting the aristocratic culture of Heian Buddhism.[15] While Tibetan esoteric Buddhism has maintained the great Indian tradition of logic and debate as centered in the Madhyamaka teachings—a competing strand of thought to the Yogacara in the early Mahayana—this did not transmit well into Chinese and Japanese culture.

Another influence of the esoteric tradition in Japan was that logic became a field of study that was transmitted orally in a secret transmission to disciples and thus kept from the public with many masters disseminated their writings secretly. Later on, the Soto Zen sect 曹洞宗 developed a tradition called *kirigami*, manual-like texts (or sometimes just a single sheet of paper) that record Soto teachings secretly handed down from master to disciple. This secretive transmission of teaching reflects more the attitude of the teachers of the

---

14   Ibid., pp. 531-35.
15   Ibid., pp. 543-45.

Vedic *Upanishads* and their closed communities,[16] which the Buddha rejected even on his death bed by re-affirming to Ananda that he had not held anything back in proclaiming his teachings. Contemporary Soto scholar, Hakamaya Noriaki 袴谷憲昭—one of the founders of the Critical Buddhism (批判仏教 *Hihan Bukkyo*) movement—has also noted that these practices form the basis of Japanese Buddhism's tendency towards social discrimination.[17]

Thus, from this earliest period, Buddhism had to adapt to cultural tendencies towards intuitive and faith based spirituality through prayer, ritual, and exorcism for "this worldly benefit" (現世利益 *gense riyaku*). Early Japanese saw Buddhism as offering practical benefit as part of the adoption of Chinese and Korean continental culture[18] and the creation of a new state system under the unifying power of an absolute ruler, the emperor. In this way, Buddhist prayers for imperial power and protection of the state were developed from the Chinese along with a variety of apocryphal sutras also originating in China.[19] The adoption of Hindu gods from India is another example of the pick-and-choose method the Japanese took towards the vast spiritual worlds of the Asian continent. By the Heian era, Hindu gods—such as Mahakala (大黒天 Daikokuten) worshipped as a god of commerce and prosperity, Vaisravana (毘沙門天 Bishamonten) worshipped as the god of fortune in war, and Sarasvati (弁才天/弁財天 Benzaiten) worshipped as the god of financial fortune—were imported and took a central place in the spiritual lives of Japanese.

In this way, Nakamura notes that, "The Japanese have much in common with the Brahmanists of ancient India…in regarding sin as a kind of material entity, which could easily be purged by means of a ritual of purification."[20] As we move forward, it is important to note how Shakyamuni often harangued Brahmin priests for the emptiness of their Vedic rituals, while he rationalized and ethicized Brahmanistic ritual concepts. Brahmanism with its emphasis on ancestral rites

---

16 Watts, Jonathan S. "Karma for Everyone: Social Justice and the Problem of Re-ethicizing Karma in Theravada Buddhist Societies". In *Rethinking Karma: The Dharma of Social Justice*. Ed. Jonathan S. Watts. (Bangkok: International Network of Engaged Buddhists, 2014), pp. 19-20.

17 Hakamaya Noriaki. "Thoughts on the Ideological Background of Social Discrimination". Trans. Jamie Hubbard. In *Pruning the Bodhi Tree: The Storm over Critical Buddhism*. Eds. Jamie Hubbard & Paul L. Swanson. (Honolulu: University of Hawaii Press, 1997), pp. 341-42.

18 Kasahara. *A History of Japanese Religion*. p. 47.

19 Nakamura. *Ways of Thinking of Eastern Peoples*. p. 578.

20 Ibid., p. 518.

(*sraddha*) focused on relationships in the life of the householder, yet remained constrained to such a limited social nexus by its sexism, classism, and domination by a priestly class. In contrast, the Buddha articulated morality (*sila*) into several different ethical systems for different types of communities[21] in what marks the full ethicization and universalization of the Vedic and *shramana* cultures of India.

Pre-Axial Clan Culture Problem #2:
Purity of Mind vs. Purity of Form and Karmic Determinism

This similarity with Brahmanism in viewing sin, taint, or impurity as something that can be purged by ritual purification leads us into further important parallels with Indian religion and Buddhism's response to it. There is an essential distinction to be made here between sin and taint or impurity. The latter can be defined as the breaking of community standards or taboos, which may or may not be considered universally moral or ethical outside of that community. The response to such transgression is purification and ritual to re-establish purity and harmony between the human world and the natural or cosmic world. Vedic Brahmanism is the classical example of this type of religious outlook with its wide variety of taboos based around a religiously sanctioned fourfold class society. This class or caste system is based on a descending level of purity from the Brahmin priests themselves down to the lowest Sudra worker class and on outward to the Untouchable class, which is not even considered part of the system.

Up until the time of B.R. Ambekdar's Buddhist revival in the 1930s, such Untouchables were not allowed to drink from public wells, although animals could. When Ambedkar led the Mahad Satyagraha movement to drink from a community well in Maharashtra in 1927, the response by the Brahmin community was to re-purify the well using cow's milk, curd, clarified butter, cow-urine, and cow-dung. In this way, we see that the logic and standards of non-axial and insular or "tribal" communities do not follow a form of logic or ethics that can be considered universal or commonly agreed upon by communities outside of it.

On the other hand, the concept of sin can be described as the breaking of universal, transcendent truths and their moral and ethical

---

21 For example, the guidelines for a moral king (*dhamma-raja*) in the *Cakkavatti Sutta*, for the householder in the *Singalovada Sutta* (D. iii. 180–93), and for republican congresses in the *Mahaparinibbana Sutta* (D.ii.74). See Watts. "Karma for Everyone". p. 31

norms (such as killing, stealing, lying, adultery) that are commonly found in numerous civilizational religions that exist across a variety of nations and cultures, such as Islam, Buddhism, and Christianity. The response to such transgression requires confession and punishment or repentant acts. These acts focus not as much on a ritual resetting of purity but on a change in the transgressor's attitude and conscience. Indeed, sin in Christianity and *dukkha* and bad karma in Buddhism are not seen as afflictions of the present material world (i.e., impurity) but as essential taints inborn to the human condition. Therefore, their expiation or resolution is not found in an act of physical purification but in an act of psychological or spiritual transformation, which lays the foundation for the final resolution of this human dilemma at the time of death (i.e., gaining eternal Heaven or achieving nirvana, upon which birth and death ends).

Like Christ's axialization of the tribal mentality of early Judaism, Buddha axialized the Vedic tradition by rejecting not only the Bhramanistic emphasis on physical purity—such as by begging for leftover food from commoners and accepting Untouchables in the monastic community as equals. He also rejected the Upanishadic emphasis on taint as a material entity afflicting the soul that requires extreme asceticism and self-mortification.[22] Thus, instead of relying on ritual or physical purification, the Buddha taught the cleansing of mental impurity or "affliction" (*klesha* 煩悩 *bonno*) through the balanced system of the Three Trainings (Skt. *trisiksa*) of ethics/virtue (*sila*), meditation (*samadhi*), and learning/wisdom (*prajna*). As we will see, this has major ramifications for developing moral and ethical standards that are truly inclusive and do not create graded groups of insiders and outsiders.

The Japanese national character has been deeply defined by these clannish characteristics, though Brahmanism's use of ritual has a more otherworldly bent in the restoration of the transcendental cosmic order. Japan's physical isolation as an island nation, as well as the isolation of communities even within Japan's mostly mountainous landscape, created a limited social nexus in which ritual purity became the standard for re-establishing harmony with the only "other", the natural order. This forms much of the essence of Japanese Shinto and its sacralization of the natural world through an endless designation of gods (神 *kami*). This tradition of establishing harmony through acts of ritual focused on transforming taint into purity continues on in contemporary Japan in new ways. For the foreign visitor, one is always

---

22 Ibid., pp. 18-19.

struck by the immaculate cleanliness of the country and attention to physical impurity, such as the wearing of surgical masks on the train to prevent the spread of germs and the fastidious habit of mothers removing their toddler's shoes before they stand up on the seats.

This is evidenced in the Buddhist world where the traditional Zen monastic practice of temple labor (作務 *samu*) has been adopted by temples of all denominations to become more of a fastidious cleaning of the temple than the fundamental labor of growing crops and manually repairing buildings as in traditional Zen contexts. On a deeper level, notions of *kega-re* (taint or impurity) have informed Japanese morality since the beginning, eventually leading to the creation of its own Untouchable caste known as *burakumin* 部落民 in the medieval period. Such orientations have informed modern forms of social discrimination against those who threaten the purity of a family's, community's, or even the nation's gene pool, such as the mentally ill, homosexuals, the homeless, and those afflicted with nuclear radiation (被爆者 *hibaku-sha*) from Hiroshima, Nagasaki, and Fukushima.

The purpose here is not to paint the Japanese as a backward, immoral people on an isolated island in the Pacific. No one can dispute the refinement of their culture, which has led to the debate that Japan could even be a civilization unto its own. The purpose here is more about understanding the motivations behind certain behaviors and where pitfalls may occur in choosing such behaviors. Unlike culture in the axialized religious world where sin is a consciousness or awareness that a universal evil has been done, in Japan there is more of a shame consciousness in having disrupted the group harmony. Nakamura explains that morality is thus understood in a restructured sense to the norms of the group and not to a universal norm. Hence, there can be a strong sense of moral self-reflection within the limited context of human relationships but no larger critical spirit on the norms of the group in relation to the world.[23] This leads back to Nakamura's quote in the Introduction about the moral confusion in Japan after World War II. With the defeat of the entire nation and the bankruptcy of their core culture as expressed and warped in Imperial Shinto, what was the standard by which to remake society? Adopt the norms of the new conquering clan (the United States) or slowly reboot their archaic cultural nexus? This question will be taken up in detail in the latter half of the volume. However, suffice to say here, it would seem that Buddhism could offer a third or Middle Way.

---

23 Nakamura. *Ways of Thinking of Eastern Peoples*. p. 518.

In this way, the classical notion of the rag-wearing Buddhist monk walking barefooted across the countryside and across communities proclaiming a universal value system was not going to be any easy fit in Japan. Indeed, many of the classical aspects of the Buddhist monastic *vinaya*, such as prohibitions on hard labor, were transformed upon its entry into China. The great Chinese Chan (Zen) master Baizhang Huaihai 百丈懷海 (720–814) famously said, "A day without work is a day without food 一日不做一日不食."—a motto that helped begin the tradition of Chan/Zen monks growing their own food and laboring over the upkeep of their own temples. In Japan, the Ritsu school 律宗, based on the observance of the monastic *vinaya*, was one of the first six schools of Japanese Buddhism during the Nara period. Unlike in China where such schools were integrated as part of a complete monastic practice, the Ritsu school became a specialized sect in Japan that quickly declined with the infusion of esoteric Buddhism in the Heian period and never regained a strong foothold. Furthermore, the ideal of the wandering Buddhist monk as "home-leaver" (Skt. *pravrajita* 出家者 *shukke-sha*) was difficult to establish in this early period as monks and nuns were literally state appointees with official study curriculums that forbade them to leave temples and teach the common people.[24]

Again, while the monastic *vinaya* was not an important part of the newly imported Buddhism, it did not mean that Buddhists or Japanese in general followed no moral code. As we will see, more essential Japanese moral values—such as goodness, righteousness, ritual propriety, humility, filial piety, brotherhood, loyalty, trustworthiness, sincerity, and virtue[25]—were developed in Buddhist contexts. As Buddhism adapted to these Japanese norms, so did the Shinto tradition take up challenges posed by the new continental religion. As Nakamura notes, "Shinto, in the process of its development as religion, advanced from the cleanness of the body to the idea of cleanness of spirit. This 'internal cleanness' was expressed by moral virtues of 'sincerity' and 'honesty'."[26]

The essential point for understanding the role of the monastic *vinaya* in Japan, especially for those coming from the classical

---

24 Kasahara. *A History of Japanese Religion*. p. 47.

25 As quoted from *The Collected Works of Motoori Norinaga* (1730-1801), the systematizer of the National Learning (国学 *Koku-gaku*) movement which de-emphasized Confucian and Buddhist thought and sought to revive the study of Japanese classics in the Tokugawa era. In Matsumoto, Shiro. "Buddhism and the Kami: Against Japanism". Trans. by Jamie Hubbard. In *Pruning the Bodhi Tree*. p. 367.

26 Nakamura. *Ways of Thinking of Eastern Peoples*. p. 572.

Theravada tradition, is that its maintenance was never an essential means for gaining transcendence from the world of suffering (*dukkha*) or liberation from bad karma under the Three Trainings of *sila-samadhi-prajna* (戒定慧 *kai-jo-e*). Unlike Indian culture, the Japanese see the world as inherently sacred, filled with gods, and not defiled, so that there is no need to transcend it. Furthermore, the emphasis on impurity of conduct rather than affliction of character entailed proper ritual and led to an emphasis on purity of faith—a trend in the larger East Asian Mahayana tradition that runs counter to the emphasis on stoic meditation and penetrating wisdom in the Southeast Asian Theravada tradition. In this way, the role of the monastic vis-à-vis the laity is not as a "field of merit" (Skt. *punya-ksetra* 福田 *fuku-den*) gained from the practice of the Three Trainings by which to attain a favorable rebirth. Rather, the monastic becomes a priest-as-ritualist who can reset community harmony through prayers for this worldly benefit, exorcism of impurities, and, most essentially, maintaining ancestral bonds through funerary and memorial rites—the ancestral realm being the only other possible world after death, a topic which will be discussed in more detail later.

On the larger socio-political level, the great Buddhist monarch of India, Ashoka (r. 270–232 BCE), formed the precedent that subsequent Theravada nations followed of interfering in the monastic Sangha to maintain its *vinaya* and tapping into its transcendental qualities to help legitimize the state. However, in Japan, the *vinaya* was irrelevant, so the state used the esoteric rituals of national well-being performed by the monastic Sangha to sacralize its power. While sacralization of political power and authority were essential in both cases, the mechanisms were quite the opposite with the state being sacralized as the protector of the Sangha in the former and the state being sacralized through the protection of the Sangha in the latter.

Potentials and Pitfalls:
Buddhism as Social Ethics or State Ideology?
Shotoku's Universalist Leanings and the Grafting to State

Having covered two major pitfalls in the introduction of Buddhism into Japan, it is time to turn to one of the potentials that Buddhist axialization offered Japan's emerging culture. As mentioned, Buddhism first came to Japan in the mid 5th century through relations with the imperial family under Emperor Kinmei 欽明天皇 (r. 539–71) and the Korean imperial family. The Soga Clan was the first to promote

Buddhism and fought other clans, who opposed it as a threat to the indigenous spiritual system upon which their rule was sanctified. It was under the rule of Empress Suiko 推古天皇 (r. 592–628) that Buddhism began to be propagated as a national religion and the first critical Buddhist reformer takes the stage in the Empress's nephew, the Regent Prince Shotoku 聖徳太子 (574–622)—a figure akin to Ashoka to the Japanese for his creation of a kind of Buddhist statecraft. As regent to the imperial throne, he played a critical role in the creation of Japan's first proper nation-state system, specifically through the *Seventeen Article Constitution*, in which he introduced and assimilated a number of key Buddhist ideas. Unlike his successors, Shotoku appears to have been less interested in the ritualistic aspects of Buddhism to protect the state than in a practical ideology to unify and guide Japan's clan riven society[27]—what we might consider a civilizational or axial impulse.

The *Seventeen Article Constitution* (十七条憲法 *Ju-shichi-jo kenpo*)[28] was less of what we would consider today as a document composed of basic laws and statutes. It was more a text focusing on morals and ethics based in the continental cultures of Buddhism and Confucianism to guide government officials and the running of the state under the supreme authority of the emperor. While the Buddha had articulated the normative model of the "moral-king", the *dharma-raja*, based in natural and ethical law (*dharma*) and the Chinese themselves held concepts of ethical rule and the possibility of righteous rebellion (as expressed by Mencius), these concepts were untenable to the Japanese ideal of the emperor as an emanation of the divine ancestors of the nation. As Nakamura points out, "The absence of a critical spirit based on universal human reason was too often in the past a conspicuous characteristic of the Japanese way of thinking, and this uncritical attitude appears in the way of thinking which reveres the living emperor as divine."[29] Again drawing on parallels with Brahmanism, he notes, "The idea of emphasizing the prestige and benevolence of the ruler appears in India in the Brahmanistic legal codes, but Buddhists universally rejected it."[30] It is also interesting that he notes the Japanese emperors who were the most devout Buddhists tended to downplay their divine status and often took some form of Buddhist ordination.[31]

---

27 Kasahara. *A History of Japanese Religion*. p. 59.
28 http://afe.easia.columbia.edu/ps/japan/shotoku.pdf
29 Nakamura. *Ways of Thinking of Eastern Peoples*. p. 474.
30 Ibid., p. 474.
31 Ibid., p. 480.

Shotoku's introduction of the Three Treasures of Buddha, Dharma, and Sangha as well as the understanding of dharma as a universal law that *could* even transcend the emperor is the first critical Buddhist contribution to the *Seventeen Article Constitution*. In the Second Article, Shotoku writes: "Sincerely revere the Three Treasures, viz., the Buddha, the Dharma, and the Sangha, which constitute the final ideal of all living beings and the ultimate foundation of all countries. Should any age or any people fail to esteem this truth? There are few people who are really vicious. They will all follow it if adequately instructed. How can the crooked ways of humans be made straight unless we take refuge in the Three Treasures?"[32] In his other major work, *Commentary on Three Sutras* (三教義書 *Sangyo-gi-sho*), Shotoku writes, "The Law [*dharma*] is the norm of all living creatures; the Buddha is in fact the Law embodied, which being united with Reason becomes Sangha. So, according to this way of teaching, everything converges on the one fundamental principle called the Law."[33] We see here clearly Shotoku's embrace of a civilizational ethic that could go beyond Japanese culture and possibly could form a bridge with the other cultures. However, his emphasis on following imperial command in the following Third Article highlights the tension between Buddhist law (仏法 *buppo*) and imperial law (王法 *obo*) that comes to the fore often in the history of Japanese Buddhism and to a lesser extent in the overall history of Japan, which is generally dominated by the latter.

A second key Buddhist aspect to Shotoku's thought is his emphasis on it as a practical way of living. In contrast to the highly ritualistic forms of esoteric Buddhism that came to dominate Japan in the Heian period, Shotoku attempted to present Buddhism within a concrete, secular social life, while emphasizing the Mahayana bodhisattva ideal of serving people's needs now.[34] In keeping with the Japanese and East Asian emphasis on the sanctity of this world, Shotoku chose three sutras for guiding the nation in his *Commentary on Three Sutras* that are all lay in orientation: the *Vimalakirti Sutra*, the *Lotus Sutra*, and the *Srimala Sutra*[35]. In this commentary, he indicates there

---

32   Ibid., p. 413.

33   Ibid., p. 394.

34   Ibid., p. 498.

35   The *Srimala Sutra* (勝鬘經 *Shoman-gyo*) is also a key text in the *tathagata-garbha* and buddha-nature tradition which forms the basis for the teaching of innate enlightenment (本覚 *hongaku*). *Hongaku* became the dominant feature of Heian Era esoteric Buddhism and ultimately the entire Japanese Buddhist

is no difference in value between the sacred and profane, the religious and secular, and venerating the Buddha and showing compassion to a beggar.[36] Here we see the beginnings of a critical aspect of Japanese Buddhism that remains predominant to this day, the elevation of the lay Buddhist path. While the corruption of the monastic order as a beacon to committed, intensive Buddhist practice continues to be an ongoing problem in Japanese Buddhism, the opposite side of this shadow is the ownership of the tradition taken by Japanese lay Buddhists. The lack of an empowered lay sangha is not only an important issue in the transcendentalized Theravada traditions of Southeast Asia and Sri Lanka; it was also an important factor in the final decline of Buddhism in India in the 10th century CE.

A third essential aspect of Shotoku's dharma is the teaching of "repaying or returning benefits" (報恩 ho-on), another concept that is somewhat foreign to the Indian and Theravada Buddhist traditions and appears to be another innovation of the Chinese. The term on 恩 is analogous to Sanskrit terms such as *upakara* and *prasada* and can be translated as "kindness", "service", or even "compassion". In Chinese Buddhism, it was defined in terms of the practice of the four types of on (四恩 shi-on) towards parents, all sentient beings, rulers, and the Three Treasures. In this East Asian context, we can see how the classical form of Buddhist service towards the universal objects of sentient beings and the Three Treasures shifted to the more clannish objects of one's own parents and the ruler of one's own nation/clan. In this way, the connotation of *on* becomes more of a feeling of gratitude, obligation, and piety to elders and those higher in the social hierarchy.[37] For Shotoku, *on* became a key moral concept to fuse together Buddhist ethics and East Asia's more indigenous ethics of loyalty to parents, elders, and authority.[38] In this way, *on* becomes one of the essential foundations for Japanese morality and ethical reflection[39] and was generally an important concept for Japanese sectarian founders from Kukai in the Heian era up to Nichiren in the Kamakura era, who

---

tradition as well as the object of contemporary criticism as a doctrine of authoritarianism and social discrimination.

36 Kasahara. *A History of Japanese Religion.* p. 59.
37 See the terms *on* 恩 and *shi-on* 四恩 in the *Digital Dictionary of Buddhism.* http://www.buddhism-dict.net/ddb/
38 Nakamura. *Ways of Thinking of Eastern Peoples.* p. 427.
39 According to Ichikawa Hakugen in Victoria, Brian. *Zen at War.* (New York: Weatherhill, 1997), p. 173. & Davis, Winston. *Japanese Religion and Society: Paradigms of Structure and Change.* (Albany: State University of New York Press, 1992), pp. 18-19.

further linked them to the Mahayana ideas of karma, the unity of self and other, and the bodhisattva ideal.

The more classical sense of service in Buddhism is expressed in the term of *dana* (布施 *fu-se*), one of the *paramitas* or practices of ethical perfection. While it can denote not only generosity but also service to others, Nakamura feels that as it is applied in a universal way, it is a concept alien to Japan since Japanese terms for giving always denote reciprocal action based on rank or social status.[40] Both Nakamura and the famous postwar Zen social critic, Ichikawa Hakugen 市川白弦, feel that Shotoku was ultimately more devoted to the pair of emperor and parents than the pair of sentient beings and the Three Treasures found in the teaching of *on*. Hakugen lists the teaching of *on* as sixth of the twelve historical characteristics that make Japanese Buddhism receptive to authoritarianism. He highlights this point through the Third Article of the *Seventeen Article Constitution*: "If you receive an imperial command, it must be obeyed without fail. The sovereign is heaven, and imperial subjects are the earth.... Should the earth seek to overthrow heaven, there will only be destruction."[41]

The First Article also introduces one of the most hallowed concepts of Japanese culture, "harmony" (和 *wa*), stating in short: "Harmony is to be valued, and an avoidance of wanton opposition to be honored.... [When] there is concord in the discussion of business, right views of things spontaneously gain acceptance. Then what is there which cannot be accomplished!" There are some who feel "harmony" is a Buddhist concept, such as in the "six ways that Buddhist practitioners should live in harmony and be sensitive and caring towards each other" (六和敬 *roku wa-kyo*),[42] yet this also appears to be an innovation made by the Chinese tradition. This First Article along with the Third buttress the Second on revering the Three Treasures, highlighting the syncretic character of the *Seventeen Article Constitution* as a mix of Buddhist, Confucian, and Japanese sentiments. While they are seen as the foundations for Japanese morals and social ethics, postwar Buddhist social critics like Ichikawa, as well as Hakamaya Noriaki and Matsumoto Shiro of the Critical Buddhism movement, feel Shotoku's constitution forms the basis of Japanese totalitarianism and the spiritual bankruptcy of 19th and 20th century

---

40 Nakamura. *Ways of Thinking of Eastern Peoples*. p. 426.

41 Victoria. *Zen at War*. pp. 172-3.

42 六和敬 *roku wa-kyo* in the *Digital Dictionary of Buddhism*. http://www.buddhism-dict.net/ddb/

Japanese imperialism.⁴³

The syncretic nature of Shotoku's constitution expresses the tensions and ongoing negotiation of importing Buddhism's axial teachings into the still very clannish social context of early Japan. It is not long after Shotoku's death that we see a shift away from Shotoku's use of Buddhism as a social ethic to it as a means to build up and protect the state.⁴⁴ Emperor Shomu 聖武天皇 (r. 724–49) appears to have become a devout Buddhist and attempted to instill Buddhist values, such as the non-harming of animals and the six fasting days of each month, through the establishment of state monasteries (国分寺 *kokubun-ji*) and nunneries (国分尼寺 *kokubun-ni-ji*). Yet in the face of a number of health epidemics and worsening relations with Korea, Shomu needed to show Buddhism's ability to protect and bring prosperity to the nation. Thus, he also instituted prayers at these provincial state temples for the protection and welfare of the state, using the *Golden Light Excellent King Sutra* (金光明最勝王經 *Konkomyo saisho-o-kyo*).⁴⁵ Such apocryphal Chinese Mahayana texts exalting the divine nature of the monarch (i.e., as "god-king", *deva-raja*) fit the Japanese cultural context more smoothly and developed in tandem with esoteric Buddhist rites for the protection and prosperity of the nation.⁴⁶

Buddhism, however, had proved its resiliency over the previous millennium in its numerous geographical migrations and mutations into various cultures—a hallmark of its axial civilization character. Amidst tight control over the ordination and lifestyles of the monastic Sangha, there were Japanese who picked up the itinerant and revolutionary spirit of dharma, seeking out places to cultivate themselves secretly in the vast mountain ranges of Japan. The quasi mythical character En-no-Gyoja 役行者 (634–707, literally "the Ascetic En") was one of the first of such wandering holy men called *hijiri* 聖. Usually persecuted by the authorities, they became popular in the provinces for healing powers and teaching the common people. With the concurrent development of lay-sponsored temples called *chishiki-ji* 知識寺 (lit. *mitra-vihara*, "temple of spiritual friends") in the provinces, Buddhism began to make its way into the heart of the Japanese landscape.

---

43 Matsumoto. "Buddhism and the Kami: Against Japanism". In *Pruning the Bodhi Tree*. p. 363.

44 Kasahara. *A History of Japanese Religion.* p. 60.

45 Ibid., pp. 65-66.

46 Nakamura. *Ways of Thinking of Eastern Peoples.* pp. 436-38.

2

Esoteric Buddhism as Socio-Political Ideology in the Heian Period (794–1185)

Potentials for Axialization: The Emergence of Wandering Ascetics (*Hijiri*)

The Heian period marks a major shift in Japanese culture in several ways. Firstly, the capital was moved from Nara to Kyoto (then known as Heian-kyo), and while the emperor remained as the figurehead of the state, Japan was increasingly run by the powerful Fujiwara clan. This separation of authority rested in the emperor and power in the Fujiwaras marked the early development of a particular governing style, which still endures in Japan and will become a key point of reference in the latter part of this volume. In many ways, this period resembles the breakdown of the local tribal republics of the Buddha's time and the consolidation of northeast India under the imperial systems of the Kosalans and Maghadhans. In Japan, it was the breakdown of the aforementioned "ancient autocratic state" consisting of various local clans and chiefs, with consolidation under the Fujiwara.[47] Concurrently, there was also the breakdown in the spiritual authority of these clans and of the state-sponsored Buddhism of the Nara period. As Kuroda Toshio points out, a peasant class based in independent, small-scale farming rose in this period and rejected the system of spiritual sanctification based on the thaumaturgy (magic, performing of miracles) of these clans and the state.

This was a "liberation and elevation of the human spirit," not in outright rebellion but in a raising of consciousness and the creation of independent economic means that did not rely on magical devotion to the emperor.[48] Again, the parallels of this shift to India at the Buddha's time are striking, with the rise of new agricultural and

---

47 Kuroda. "The Development of the *Kenmitsu* System as Japan's Medieval Orthodoxy". p. 236.

48 Ibid., p. 238.

economic classes that became receptive to other forms of spirituality than Brahmanism. There were new spiritual movements like Jainism and, of course, Buddhism that did not make them cower under the power of the Brahmin class and its wasteful requisitioning of cattle and other animals without payment for Vedic sacrifices (Skt. *yajna*).[49]

We see in the *Nihon Ryoi-ki* 日本霊異記—an early history of the condition of religion and the common people in the late 8th and early 9th centuries—the emergence of wandering holy men (*hijiri*), like the new wandering Buddhist monk of 5th century India, and their appeal to the new provincial culture of this period. Two of the greatest such *hijiri* to emerge from the early Heian were Saicho 最澄 (767–822), the founder of the Tendai sect, and Kukai 空海 (774–835), the founder of the Shingon sect 真言宗. At the age of eighteen upon receiving full ordination at the great Nara temple Todai-ji 東大寺, Saicho turned his back on the establishment and began a period of ascetic practice in the forests of Mt. Hiei, on the outskirts of present-day Kyoto. While devoting himself to the intense practice of a *hijiri*, he also self-identified as "the greatest of fools (凡 *bon*)" and as "precepts-violating Saicho".[50] Kukai, as well, turned his back on a career as a high-ranking civil servant with advanced expertise in Confucian studies, to pilgrimage through the island of Shikoku. Although a great ascetic with profound experiences, he was not even ordained as a novice until 804, at the age of 30.[51] In this way, the founding of the Tendai and Shingon Sanghas signified a more progressive assertion of spiritual independence and agency by the common people. According to Kuroda, it added a second way to evaluate the human condition beyond the worldly designations of high and low class to the more spiritual designations of sagely (*sho/sei*) and unenlightened (*bon*).[52]

This designation of "unenlightened, common person, or fool" (Skt. *prthag-jana* 凡夫 *bonbu*), however, was not a denigration as in the Indian and Theravada traditions. Rather, it became the focus of the spiritual potential of the common person as emphasized in the later Mahayana, especially Pure Land, tradition. We see this in Saicho's assertion that all sentient beings have buddha-nature in his debate with Tokuitsu 徳一, a monk of the Nara based Hosso school,

---

[49] Kosambi, D. D. *Ancient India: A History of Its Culture and Civilization.* (Cleveland: Meridian Books, 1969), p. 102.

[50] Kasahara. *A History of Japanese Religion.* pp. 73-74.

[51] Ibid., pp. 98, 101, 107.

[52] Kuroda. "The Development of the *Kenmitsu* System as Japan's Medieval Orthodoxy". p. 245.

who emphasized the existence of *icchantika* (一闡提 *issendai*) as those who have fallen too far to be redeemed.[53] Kukai, as well, emphasized the "inseparability of the sage and the unenlightened".[54] This new Mahayana spirit of Heian Buddhism becomes a perennial feature of Japanese Buddhism going forward, especially in the later Pure Land movement, and mirrors the spiritual democracy and egalitarianism of Shakyamuni's ministry in ordaining women and outcastes.

Full spiritual egalitarianism, however, was not to be accomplished in the Heian period. These *hijiri* were often feared as much for their magical powers as they were revered for their ties to the people. In the *Nihon Ryoi-ki*, karma is explained less as an empowering means of ethical action to change one's life and more as a kind of karmic determinism explaining fortune, misfortune, "the inescapability of karmic effects (現報 *genpo*)", and one's position in the new varieties of class division. This inescapability fueled a fear of karma and led to an explanation of the Three Treasures as having thaumaturgic powers that could save people and deliver them from the fearful powers of the authorities and even the emperor.

This pattern of historical development mirrors the rise of the ascetics of the *Upanishads* who rejected Brahmanical ritual means to salvation in favor of ascetic practice yet still held beliefs in material karmic determinism.[55] The full ethicization and axialization of the Indian tradition had to await the Buddha's teaching of karma as "intentional ethical action" available to all persons and all classes, not an elite group of either ritualists or ascetics. Similarly, the *hijiri* developed spiritual independence from the Nara Court and its state-controlled Buddhism yet still held a sort of power over the common person with the powers that came from their elevated ascetic practices. In Japan, Kuroda sums up this period by noting that the common people still maintained "a certain weakness…an inability to assert their spiritual independence or to conceive of themselves as active agents."[56]

Still, this is one of the few periods in Japan when the universal and axial teachings of Buddhism or dharma (*buppo*) were seen to supersede indigenous values and the imperial law (*obo*). Kuroda further

---

53 Kasahara. *A History of Japanese Religion*. p. 78.

54 Kuroda. "The Development of the *Kenmitsu* System as Japan's Medieval Orthodoxy". p. 247.

55 Watts. "Karma for Everyone". pp. 18-19.

56 Kuroda. "The Development of the *Kenmitsu* System as Japan's Medieval Orthodoxy". p. 246.

notes a kind of positive disintegration[57] of society in parallel with the time of the Buddha. Previously, thaumaturgy had been "submerged in a natural, localized community structure." However, it had now taken on "a generalized and trans-local character, linking it broadly to the good or ill fortunes of individuals caught up in the process of urbanization as the ancient community structure disintegrated."[58]

From Universalism to the Buddhist State

From the *hijiri's* travels through the mountains and villages of provincial Japan, we return to the centers of power in the old capital of Nara and the new capital of Heian-kyo (Kyoto). The ruling class was in a state of crisis regarding their own existence, reflected in the political intrigues and secret plots of the mid-8th to 10th centuries and the decline of numerous aristocratic families. As Kuroda points out, it was no longer possible to dwell comfortably in the all-encompassing state of the ancient era. Perhaps for the first time in Japanese history, an "objective" consideration of the state became necessary, along with a new political ideology and new religious concepts to legitimize and mediate it.[59] In tandem with the emerging presence of Buddhist teachings and practices as a trans-local, if not universal, force, the concept of the "spiritual protection of state" (鎮護国家 *chingo kokka*), in which Buddhism played a central role, became increasingly important. In the "spiritual protection of state", the state is protected by a complex entity (Buddhism) located outside of it—unlike earlier visions of "the sacred state" (神政国家 *shinsei kokka*) or later ones of Japan as "the land of the gods (*kami*)" that saw the ruler as a god (i.e., *deva-raja*) and the state itself as inherently sacred.[60]

This new conception is somewhat similar to Indian and Theravada attitudes towards Buddhism in seeing the transcendental and universal power of Buddhism as a means to legitimize a specific regime and the rule of the state as an entity in a world of other states. Both Ashoka in India and the Theravadin kings of Southeast Asia sought

---

57 Watts, Jonathan S. "The 'Positive Disintegration' of Buddhism: Reformation and Deformation in the Sri Lankan Sangha". In *Rethinking Karma*. pp. 92-105.

58 Kuroda. "The Development of the *Kenmitsu* System as Japan's Medieval Orthodoxy". p. 254.

59 Ibid., p. 240.

60 Rambelli, Fabio. "Religion, Ideology of Domination, and Nationalism: Kuroda Toshio on the Discourse of *Shinkoku*". In *Japanese Journal of Religious Studies*. 1996. Vol. 23, No.3-4. p. 409.

to co-opt the spiritual authority of the monastic Sangha as a means of legitimization. *Chingo kokka* appears to be a similar development, yet it was used by not only the state but also the new Tendai and Shingon sects to legitimize themselves vis-a-vis the social and political order.

Indeed, while Saicho and Kukai might have been against the incomplete Mahayana vision of the Nara schools and the "ancient autocratic state", they eventually showed a great interest in cultivating relations with the new powers at Heian-kyo and in the creation of what they may have viewed as a true Mahayana State under *chingo kokka*. In 804, both of them became part of a government-sponsored study tour of China, which allowed them to bring significant new esoteric teachings back to Japan and led to Kukai becoming the official transmitter of esoteric Buddhism in Japan.[61] Saicho's successors Ennin, Enchin, and Annen more fully developed Tendai esotericism (台密 *tai-mitsu*) to rival that of Shingon (東密 *to-mitsu*), even declaring it to supersede the *Lotus Sutra*, considered the core of Tendai teaching.[62] Ennin and Enchin also developed close ties with the Fujiwaras and other nobility, who sought their esoteric rites for use in political warfare. After 809, Kukai himself became close to Emperor Saga and other aristocrats, and unlike Saicho, became close with the Nara schools who sought him out to develop their own competitive form of esotericism called *nan-mitsu* 南密. By the middle of the Heian period, the Tendai and Shingon sects were dominated by the sons of nobles who had ordained and brought their political intrigues into the precincts of the sacred Mt. Hiei and Mt. Koya, eventually leading to a variety of armed conflicts involving ordained and quasi-ordained monastics.

Kuroda makes an essential point about this shift from the Fujiwara regency (967–1068) to the Insei government[63] in the latter part of 11th century as featuring not only an ideological tension between imperial law (*obo*) and Buddha law (*buppo*) but also a parallel structural tension between the political power base in Kyoto and the new political power bases at the three main Buddhist centers of Nara, Mt. Hiei, and Mt. Koya.[64] This tension is first expressed in the

---

61 Kasahara. *A History of Japanese Religion*. pp. 75–77.

62 Ibid., pp. 80, 85.

63 *Insei* 院政 means literally "temple administration" and refers to rule by retired emperors who adjudicated between the Fujiwaras and the rising warrior class from cloistered temples. A retired emperor who entered a Buddhist monastic community became a "cloistered emperor" (太上法皇 *Daijo Ho-o*). This marks a further stage in the Japanese governing system of separating authority (in this case, the present emperor) with power (the *insei* emperor).

64 Kuroda. Toshio. "The Imperial Law and the Buddhist Law". Trans. Jacqueline

8th century when the concept of the "origin and manifestation" (本地垂迹 *honji-suijaku*) developed, in which Japanese gods (*kami*) came to be regarded as manifestations of buddhas and bodhisattvas—even in the cases of the great Sun Goddess Amaterasu 天照大神 as the Buddha Mahavairocana, and the deity Hachiman 八幡大神 as the Bodhisattva Avalokiteshvara.[65] It is later expressed during the period of the Insei system (1086–1156) when retired emperors remained in power from their cloistered residences within Buddhist monastic communities.

As such, the term *obo-buppo* signifies the joining of these two major factions into one national ruling system, not just as an ideological force but also as a structural system. From an ideological standpoint that sees the potential for Buddhism to act as an ethical and civilizational force, the actual role of the dharma as *buppo* in this period seems suspect. As noted above, the esoteric Buddhism of this period, while containing a Mahayana spirit, was still overly focused on thaumaturgy rather than the social and political ethics of the Buddha's standards for the "moral king" (*dharma-raja*) and for republican assemblies.[66] In this way, we need to turn our attention to some of the key teachings of Heian esoteric Buddhism.

The Rise of Esoteric Buddhism as a Socio-Political Ideology

The Heian period, covering most of the 9th to 12th centuries, is part the rise of esoteric or Vajrayana Buddhism throughout Asia: the great Srivijaya empire based in Sumatra (8th–12th cent.) that featured the building of the Borobudur complex in central Java in the 9th century; the entry and flowering of Vajrayana Buddhism in Tibet from the 8th century onward; the establishment of the Angkor Empire in Cambodia in the 9th century and the building of Angkor Wat in the 12th. The Vajrayana tradition has come under scrutiny within Buddhism itself due to its heavy influence from other Indian religious forms like Saivism, including a number of unorthodox practices, such as ritualized sex and the consumption of alcohol and meat. However, its development, especially by the Tibetans, of spiritual insight coupled with high-level

---

I. Stone. In *Japanese Journal of Religious Studies*. 1996. Vol. 23, No.3-4. pp. 275-76, 280.

65 *Honji-suijaku* is a concept developed from Chinese Tiantai's (Tendai) interpretation of the *Lotus Sutra* that taught of the Eternal Buddha as origin and his manifestations. Williams, Paul. *Mahayana Buddhism: The Doctrinal Foundations*. (London: Routledge, 1989), p. 156. *Suijaku* 垂迹 in the *Digital Dictionary of Buddhism*. http://www.buddhism-dict.net/ddb/

66 Watts. "Karma for Everyone". p. 31

Mahayana ethics cannot be disputed. Indeed, it is said to have pacified Tibetan culture from an amalgam of constantly warring clans to a theocracy built around the first precept of non-harming.

Kuroda Toshio has posited that the distinctive form of Japanese esoteric Buddhism, called the *ken-mitsu* system (顕密体制 *ken-mitsu taisei*), provided a highly elaborate dharma (*buppo*) that not only unified all of Buddhism in the Heian Period but also created the ideological foundation for the social and political order. The *ken-mitsu* system is a fusing of the supposedly more straightforward or exoteric teachings (顕 *ken*)—found in the *Flower Garland Sutra* (Skt. *Avatamsaka Sutra* 華厳經 *Kegon-kyo*), the *Lotus Sutra* (Skt. *Saddharma Pundarika Sutra* 法華經 *Hokke-kyo*), and the *Great Wisdom Sutras* (Skt. *Prajnaparamita Sutra* 般若經 *Hannya-kyo*)—with the more complex or profound esoteric teachings (密 *mitsu*)—found in the *Mahavairocana Sutra* (大日經 *Dainichi-kyo*) and the *Vajrashekhara Sutra* (金剛頂經 *Kongocho-kyo*). While Shingon was more focused on the esoteric teachings, Tendai created a distinctive hybrid system based on Saicho's original vision of the Mahayana that brought together the *Lotus Sutra*, esotericism, meditation, and precepts (円密禅戒 *en-mitsu-zen-kai*) with an emphasis on the harmonization of the first two.[67] Kuroda emphasizes that this brand of esotericism was distinctively Japanese and different from original Indian Buddhist esotericism.

> Prayers and thaumaturgic methods representing degenerate applications of esoteric practices were prevalent even within the original sphere of esoteric ritual. These prayers and thaumaturgic methods included practices aimed at producing rain, safeguarding childbirth, healing diseases, defeating enemy countries, subjugating rebels, and attaining bliss in this world and the next, and it was widely assumed in society that such things represented the original purpose of the esoteric Buddhist teachings.[68]

He further notes,

> Such activities should not be seen as representative of the original, standard form of esoteric Buddhism, for they were tinged with superstitious qualities that differ from

---

67 Kuroda. "The Development of the *Kenmitsu* System as Japan's Medieval Orthodoxy". pp. 250-51.

68 Ibid., p. 252.

the fundamental thought of Buddhism. They were closer in character to Japan's ancient religious asceticism.⁶⁹

As the supposed benefits of such practices fed the interests of the ruling Heian aristocracy, Tendai found itself bending its doctrine more deeply to such esoteric forms. Shingon, as well, became increasingly focused on demands to provide practical benefits through such acts of ritual magic.⁷⁰

As important as these esoteric practices were to the Heian era, perhaps the greater legacy of this period for the development of Japanese Buddhism and subsequent forms of social ethics is the teaching of "original enlightenment" or "innate enlightenment" (本覚 *hongaku*). In short, *hongaku* means that since all sentient beings are endowed with buddha-nature, one is innately or already enlightened. As such, one must simply awaken from one's present state of delusion, perhaps spontaneously or suddenly, rather than tread the long path of numerous rebirths to gain the state of enlightenment attained by Shakyamuni and other great monastic practitioners. This concept of *hongaku*, of which there is no Indian Sanskrit equivalent, along with "the womb of the Tathagata" (Skt. *tathagata-garbha* 如来蔵 *nyorai-zo*) and buddha-nature (仏性 *bussho*) are predominantly developed in the East Asian tradition through the *Treatise on the Awakening of Mahayana Faith* (大乗起信論 *Daijo kishin-ron*), a seminal text dating from the 6th century in China. In Japan, this teaching is first emphasized by Kukai and is central to his emphasis on "attaining Buddhahood in this very body" (即身成仏 *sokushin jobutsu*)—a central tenet to the larger Vajrayana tradition. While Saicho did study the *Awakening of Mahayana Faith*, innate enlightenment was not a teaching he directly addressed. As a later development under Enchin and Annen, it marks the high point of the *ken-mitsu* system in Tendai during the Insei period in which the present world is absolutely affirmed and rituals are performed for "this-worldly benefit" (*gen-se riyaku*).⁷¹

At face value, *hongaku* seems to embrace the Mahayana emphasis on the equality of all, rejecting the transcendentalization of nirvana as a state only realizable by the greatest of ascetics. However, Kuroda and other postwar Buddhist social critics, like those in the Critical Buddhism movement, have noted that *ken-mitsu* Buddhism's

---

69   Ibid., p. 252.

70   Kasahara. *A History of Japanese Religion*. p. 111.

71   Kuroda. "The Development of the *Kenmitsu* System as Japan's Medieval Orthodoxy". p. 262-64.

"uncritical acceptance of everything" and desire to appeal to the state and the masses allowed it to become "the ideology of the medieval establishment".[72] Furthermore, this world-affirming tendency of *hongaku* was "more commonly interpreted as an authoritarian discourse that legitimated social hierarchy and the entrenched system of rule."[73]

Hakamaya Noriaki argues that *hongaku* as part of the larger *tathagata-garbha* tradition is based in a monistic view of reality[74], in which True Mind is eternal, permanent, and pure. Contemporary critics as well as traditional ones, such as the Madhyamaka schools of Tibet, have seen this concept as a kind of essentialism, an eternal essence or Self (*atman*) as found in Vedanta and other forms of non-theistic Hinduism, which the Buddha clearly did not teach. Such notions of essentialism—as opposed to the radical ungroundedness of "emptiness" (Skt. *shunyata* 空 *ku*) enable the speculation of an essential source of origination and power and the subsequent creation of tiered or graded emanations from that source[75], such as in the Vedic caste system and other forms of sanctified hierarchy under which the common person is easily oppressed.

The teachings of *hongaku*, *tathagata-garbha*, and buddha-nature as found in the *Treatise on the Awakening of Mahayana Faith* exhibit many of the key East Asian cultural themes of awakening to True Mind either through a complete cessation of discursive thought or a faith beyond all reason while re-affirming this world.[76] In the end, rather than becoming a teaching accessible to all persons who categorically all possess buddha-nature, enlightenment once again becomes the provenance of the elite ascetic (i.e., Zen master, Theravadin forest ascetic, Upanishadic yogi) or of the obedient and unquestioning faithful (i.e., Vajrayana devotee, Theravadin merit-making lay follower, *bhakti yoga* caste Hindu). These issues will be explored more deeply in chapters to follow, especially in terms of how the revolutionary Kamakura era teachers understood *hongaku* and how Japanese Buddhism adapted to the demands of the state and society in the Meiji and prewar periods.

---

72 Sueki, Fumihiko. "A Reexamination of the *Kenmitsu Taisei* Theory". In *Japanese Journal of Religious Studies*. 1996. Vol. 23, No. 3-4. p. 458.

73 Stone, Jacqueline I. "Placing Nichiren in the 'Big Picture': Some Ongoing Issues in Scholarship". In *Japanese Journal of Religious Studies*. 1999. Vol. 26, No. 3-4. p. 397.

74 Hakamaya. "Thoughts on the Ideological Background of Social Discrimination". p. 344.

75 Macy, Joanna. *Mutual Causality in Buddhism and General Systems Theory*. (Albany, NY: State University of New York Press, 1991), pp. 29–30.

76 Williams. *Mahayana Buddhism*. pp. 111-12.

The *ken-mitsu* ideology, as quintessentially expressed by *hongaku*, further extended the Japanese de-emphasis on the transcendental and potentially axial aspects of Buddhism. While demythologizing the Indian and Theravada ideal of the Buddhist monk as either the ascetic hermit in the jungle or the puritanical practitioner of the monastic *vinaya* living aloof from society, the *ken-mitsu* ideology with *hongaku* at its center seemed to go too far the other way. It allowed any behavior by monastics to be rationalized by the lack of distinction in this "empty" (*shunyata*) world where enlightenment was already present and could be realized in a sudden flash or where the distinctions between good and evil were the deluded fixations of a dualistic mind.[77]

From the heavily immanentalist or world-affirming view of the *ken-mitsu* ideology, we can begin to understand Japanese Buddhism's very unorthodox approach to the monastic *vinaya*, seen as one of the non-negotiable pillars of the entire Buddhist monastic tradition. The classical Four-Part monastic *vinaya* (四分律 *shibun-ritsu*) imported into China from the Indian Dharmagupta lineage was formally introduced to Japan through the Japanese Ritsu school established by the Chinese monk Jianzhen (鑑眞 Ganjin) in 755, some two hundred years after Buddhism's introduction. The six schools of Nara were based on the thirteen early schools 十三宗 of China. However, whereas the *vinaya* was integrated into all schools in China, it stood apart as a separate school of study and practice in Japan.[78] As the Nara imperial government strictly controlled the ordination of monastics and the right to establish ordination platforms (戒壇 *kaidan*), the Ritsu school was able to prosper as part of the official national curriculum. However, with the growth of esoteric Buddhism around the new authorities in Heian-kyo, the school became increasingly marginalized as the Tendai and Shingon established their own ordination platforms.

Saicho, in his wish to emphasize the full development of Mahayana Buddhism and establish his teachings apart from the Nara schools, rejected the full 250 precepts of the Four-Part Vinaya as transmitted through the Ritsu school. In their place, he prescribed, along with twelve years of ascetic practice on Mt. Hiei, ordination and training in the 10 major and 48 minor "perfect and immediate precepts" (円頓戒 *endon-kai*), based on the Chinese version of the *Brahma Net Sutra*

---

77 Bodiford, William M. *Soto Zen in Medieval Japan*. (Honolulu: University of Hawaii Press, 1993), p. 167.

78 *Risshu* 律宗 in the *Digital Dictionary of Buddhism*. http://www.buddhism-dict.net/ddb/

(梵網經 *Bonmo-kyo*).⁷⁹ Whereas the Chinese had harmonized the Four-Part Vinaya and these bodhisattva precepts by making the former as a basis for the latter, Saicho rejected the former in a somewhat unprecedented step in Buddhist history, which until this day in Japan has blurred the typically very strong distinction between monastic and lay in the rest of the Buddhist world. As much as this was part of his spiritual vision, this redefinition of precepts and Buddhist identity was also a statement of organizational independence that would serve as a model for the emergence of new Buddhist sects in Japan's history.⁸⁰ This endeavor to create the first ordination platform outside of Nara was finally granted by the imperial government in 818.

For the Shingon, the Chinese esoteric tradition from which Kukai had received transmission had been "purified" of the unorthodox practices developed in India, and, initially, the Shingon maintained a strict observance of the *vinaya*. However, the monk Ninkan 仁寛 (1057–1123) attempted to re-introduce the more unorthodox forms of Indian tantra, such as ritualized sex, through the Tachikawa lineage 立川流 that experienced periods of popularity and censure until its purported dissolution sometime before the beginning of the Edo period in 1603.

It is unclear exactly when clerical marriage becomes practiced in Japanese Buddhism, although it is certainly before Shinran institutionalizes it in his new True Pure Land sect (浄土真宗 *Jodo Shin-shu*) in the early 1200s. There are references to clerical marriage among important Heian Buddhist figures, such as Kakunin, an estate manager for the grand Todai-ji temple at Nara. Himself born from the powerful Taira clan, he is reported to have sired a son with the nun Shinmyo who became Taira no Chikatori, the governor of Omi province.⁸¹ Indeed, the diversification of types of Japanese monastics during the Heian period seems amazing compared to the relatively simple designations of forest monks and village monks in the traditional Theravada tradition. There was a wide variety of classes from noble monks to scholar monks (学生 *gakusho*) to monastic workers (堂衆 *doshu*) and low level clerics (下僧 *geso*) who had duties outside the monasteries, kept wives, and had secular names.⁸² There was also yet another

---

79   Kasahara. *A History of Japanese Religion*. p. 79.
80   Bodiford. *Soto Zen in Medieval Japan*. p. 168.
81   Adolphson, Mikael S. *The Teeth and Claws of the Buddha: Monastic Warriors and Sohei in Japanese History*. (Honolulu: University of Hawaii Press, 2007), pp. 100-103.
82   Ibid., p. 60.

category called *hoshi* 法師, which denoted people who had taken unofficial Buddhist vows and wandered the countryside dressed as monks. This term along with "mountain" *hoshi* as *yama-hoshi* 山法師 also referred to warriors who had taken Buddhist vows but still lived secular lives.[83] In this way, maintaining the monastic *vinaya* and the traditionally strict separation between ordained and lay found in most of the Buddhist world were not important aspects of this new world of Heian Mahayana Buddhism. This culture continues in contemporary Japan with the strength of lay Buddhist denominations and the way a fully ordained priest from the traditional denominations might change from robes to a business suit for work just as his forbearers might have changed from robes to battle gear.

Indeed, the most egregious breach of monastic *vinaya* that emerges in the Heian period is the variety of armed persons of various levels of ordination, collectively known as *sohei* 僧兵—a Buddhist oxymoron of the highest order combining the characters for monk (僧 *so*) and warrior (兵 *hei*). While the *endon-kai* precepts that Saicho took from the *Brahma Net Sutra* specifically prohibit monks from carrying arms[84], there were already signs in early Chinese Buddhism that temples did maintain arms. The Shaolin monastery, famous for developing Chinese martial arts, was known to be militarily active in the early 7th century.[85] There are also records of monastic warriors in Korean Buddhism from the 11th century as well as monks who led the resistance against the invasion of Japanese warlord Toyotomi Hideyoshi in the 1590s. In fact, it is thought that the Japanese learned the term for warrior-monk (*sohei*) from the Korean tradition of *sungbyong* during the 14th–16th centuries.[86] In this way, the tradition of monks engaging in violent conflict is not solely confined to Japan.

Living with, and often controlling, the powerful new centers of Heian Buddhism (the Enryaku-ji and Onjo-ji temples of Tendai, the Kofuku-ji and Todai-ji in Nara, and Mt. Koya and the Negoro-ji of Shingon), these militarized Buddhists[87] serve as a symbol of the

---

83 Ibid., pp. 70, 75.

84 The Mahayana *Mahaparinirvana Sutra* 大般涅槃經 allows for lay people to keep weapons and to resort to violence to protect the dharma as well as recounting how the Buddha in a previous life killed several Brahmins to prevent them from slandering the dharma. Williams. *Mahayana Buddhism*. p. 161.

85 Adolphson. *The Teeth and Claws of the Buddha*. pp. 21-23.

86 Ibid., pp. 55, 146.

87 I use the term "militarized Buddhists" instead of the blanket term "warrior-monks" (僧兵 *sohei*), which was not in use at this time and is the creation of

decline of the imperial government in the late Heian from the beginning of 10th century into 12th century as well as the shift into the warrior-dominated culture of the Kamakura and Muromachi periods.[88] While we might lay the blame for this development on the *ken-mitsu* ideology, it is vital to also look at the structural causes, principally the influx of warrior-retainers accompanying the Heian nobles who were ordaining at these great monastic centers and bringing their political rivalries with them.[89] Violence within the monasteries also came from class conflicts between these noble monks, scholar monks, and lower rank commoner monks, who all claimed the right to take leadership of the temples.

One of the first and most conspicuous examples of this occurs in 993 with the division of the Tendai sect into two rival factions: the Sanmon at the great Enryaku-ji temple on the top of Mt. Hiei and the Jimon at the Onjo-ji temple in the valley below on Lake Biwa. By 1039, relations had deteriorated to such an extent that some 3,000 Sanmon monks descended from Mt. Hiei to engage in a violent confrontation with the Jimon.[90] Isolated incidents such as these gave way to more distinct militarized campaigns by the late 11th century, when any political campaign needed the support of these big monasteries. The Hogen Rebellion against the Fujiwara regency in 1156 marks the first time political forces enlisted monastic forces in a major battle. As Mikael Adolphson, author of a lengthy volume on the history of monastic warriors, notes, "We find no evidence anywhere that these [monk] commanders either considered it somehow unethical or inappropriate to head such forces, nor did they seem to use religious rhetoric in their efforts to rally the support of the clergy."[91]

Benkei 弁慶 (1155–1189) is considered the epitome and perhaps most exaggerated form of the so-called "warrior-monk", a giant of a man who practiced the acetic life of a monk before dying heroically protecting his lord, Minamoto no Yoshitsune, the half-brother of the founder of the Kamakura military government that ended the Heian

---

scholars in the Edo period. Adolphson. *The Teeth and Claws of the Buddha.* p. 13.

88 Kuroda, Toshio. *Temple and Shrine Forces: Another Medieval Society* (寺社勢力もう一つ中世の社会 *Jisha sei-ryoku: Mo-hitotsu chusei-no shakai*). (Tokyo: Iwanami Shoten, 1980), pp. 32, 34. Kuroda, Toshio. "Buddhism and Society in the Medieval Estate System". Trans. Suzanne Gay. In *Japanese Journal of Religious Studies*. 1996. Vol. 23, No. 3-4. p. 319.

89 Adolphson. *The Teeth and Claws of the Buddha.* p. 8.

90 Ibid., p. 35.

91 Ibid., p. 114.

period. However exaggerated his story is, one is struck by his elevation in popular culture as a Buddhist monk who did not forsake violence and adhere to the axial values of the dharma but rather embodied the primordial Japanese values of loyalty to authority and clan. Here again, we see this complex tension between the civilizational culture of Buddhism and the clannish culture of Japan, and again Hajime Nakamura provides important insight in conclusion:

> This hardly means, however, that Japanese Buddhism was *immoral* or *amoral*. Monks and faithful alike observed assiduously the requirements of their limited human nexus; they were highly moral in this respect. They were devoted to their parents and loyal to their sovereign. They were in every respect quite different from the monks and novices of India and China. Moreover, Japanese monks were devoted workers loyal to the interests of the order to which they belonged. If the followers of one sect founder are divided into a number of different orders, monks in one of the orders become devoted to his particular order to the point of boycotting the other orders. To them the welfare of their small separate orders are their main concern and the doctrine to which they all adhere is reduced to a secondary concern. Here again they are moral in the limited sense that they are devoted to their limited human nexus. The precepts to be kept by an individual as an individual in relation to the Absolute, by an individual in relation to another individual *qua* individual tend thus to become neglected. The interests of their own small limited nexus become the factors determining their actions.[92]

The Pure Land *Hijiri* as Messengers of an Axial Age

As in the Nara Period, the figure of the *hijiri*—the itinerant wandering practitioner who broke from the established enclaves and systems of power—played a critical role in the latter days of the Heian period, breaking away from the rampant political and monastic corruption at the three great centers of Japanese Buddhism at Mt. Hiei, Mt. Koya, and Nara. What is fascinating about this movement is that it centered around a group of itinerant Pure Land practitioners, who would eventually take the world-affirming character of Japanese

---

92   Nakamura. *Ways of Thinking of Eastern Peoples.* p. 416.

Buddhism to its logical extreme while also acting as a source of axial values to transcend the *ken-mitsu* ideology that fused Buddhism to the state. As noted at the end of the previous section on the Nara era, there emerged various classes of itinerants who were displaced as the ancient community structure dissolved during the shift into the Heian period as Buddhism became less regulated. These figures were commonly called *shami* 沙弥 (novice monk, i.e., *shramanera*) or *hijiri* 聖. In this period, they were quite an assortment of random figures known especially for their thaumaturgic powers who were not necessarily Buddhist.[93] As Buddhism continued to grow and develop during the Heian, the character of the *hijiri* changed to a distinctive lifestyle reflected in clothing, behavior, and dwelling places.[94] Generally, there were those who lived in detached hermitages (別所 *bessho*) on the outskirts of major temples or those who lived as wandering itinerants and practiced the earlier tradition of thaumaturgy. As society plunged more deeply into violence in the latter part of the Heian, such self-ordained monks and their anti-establishment character became increasingly appealing to the common people.[95]

The development of a distinctive *hijiri* movement in the Heian comes from the rise of Pure Land Buddhism as a secondary stage in the flowering of the *ken-mitsu* esoteric system. Whereas the core of esoteric Buddhist practice focuses on the recitation of Sanskrit mantras, Pure Land practice, specifically as it developed in China, emphasized the recitation of the Buddha Amitabha's name (南無阿弥陀仏 *namu-amida-butsu*). Known as the *nenbutsu* (Skt. *buddhasmrti* 念仏), the interpretation in China of *nen* as recitation was an innovation from the earlier, more esoteric-like tradition of *nen* as visualization of Amida Buddha. Kuroda notes that, "From this time on in the Tendai school, there was an apparent shift from a doctrinal (教相 *kyoso*) orientation to a meditative (観心 *kanjin*) one, and from an orientation toward written works (文献 *bunken*) to one toward oral transmissions (口伝 *kuden*).... In the wake of this achievement, *hijiri* eventually appeared in Nara Buddhism and the Shingon school as well, and each heralded a *nenbutsu* invested with the characteristics of their own school."[96]

---

93 Kuroda. "The Development of the *Kenmitsu* System as Japan's Medieval Orthodoxy". p. 246.

94 Ibid., p. 259.

95 Kasahara. *A History of Japanese Religion*. p. 97.

96 Kuroda. "The Development of the *Kenmitsu* System as Japan's Medieval Orthodoxy". p. 260.

The iconic figure of Kuya 空也 (903–972), known as the "market place *hijiri*", marks an important point in this emergence of Pure Land Buddhism wedded with the *hijiri* phenomenon. While still known for his thaumaturgic powers, he is hailed as a figure who brought "the true nature of the *nenbutsu* as a Mahayana Bodhisattva practice" to the common people.[97] In this way, an important aspect of the *hijiri* movement is that it "encouraged self-assertion and a critical spirit among self-reliant individuals". The groups of people living at detached hermitages (*bessho*) and forming local *nenbutsu* associations "were fundamentally different from natural communities in that they were composed of self-aware individuals…united by shared religious regulations and a strong sense of common bond." They were distancing themselves from the increasingly corrupt and violent secular and monastic settings of daily life and "in so doing developed the potential to become critical of both the secular and the monastic."[98]

Indeed, as Japanese society further plunged into anarchic warfare amongst rival clans, there was a sense among the people of more than political decline but of the dawning of an age of spiritual decline and potential Armageddon. The Buddhist concept of the Age of the Final Dharma (末法 *mappo*), in which there are no more enlightened masters and the traditional practices of *sila-samadhi-prajna* of are no use, spoke directly to their fears. Pure Land Buddhism with such sayings as "abandoning the tainted world" (厭離穢土 *on-ri-edo*) and "longing for the Pure Land" (欣求浄土 *gongu-jodo*) met these fears directly and offered a spiritual, if not political, solution to them. The *nenbutsu hijiri* became the messengers of this sentiment. In the wake of Kuya's ministry, there was a dramatic increase in the number of *nenbutsu hijiri* and an "explosive development among the populace of the *nenbutsu* known as the 'hometown *nenbutsu*' (郷里念仏 *kyori nenbutsu*)."[99] As Kuroda concludes, "Their emergence presented a historic opportunity for the establishment of a non-authoritarian, non-institutional discourse."[100]

As we close this section on the Heian period and step into the revolutionary times of the Kamakura period, it would serve well to reflect on the *hijiri* in terms of Eisenstadt's original definition of axialization and its leaders. In the Introduction, we noted that the activators of this axial reconstruction emerged from among "autonomous, relatively

---

97 Ibid., p. 257.
98 Ibid., pp. 260-61.
99 Ibid., p. 257.
100 Ibid., p. 314.

unattached 'intellectuals', such as prophets or visionaries". Their visions or teachings ultimately transformed into the basic "hegemonic" premises of their respective civilizations, becoming institutionalized as the dominant orientations of both the ruling and many secondary elites, fully embodied in their respective centers or sub-centers. This indeed came to fore with the Pure Land, Zen, and Nichiren movements, who brought their new spiritual visions to Kamakura era Japan and whose legacies are institutionalized today in Japan's most formative Buddhism denominations. The question left to answer in the following sections is: "Was this truly an axial revolution that transformed the clannish confines of Japanese culture into a 'civilization' steeped in universal values and ethics?"

3

Buddhist Axialization in the Kamakura Period (1185–1333)

The Heian period dawned with a sense of optimism in a new capital and the breakdown of the "ancient autocratic state". Buddhism, as well, saw its potentials in Japanese society grow as *hijiri* began to spread the dharma into the countryside and two new important sects, the Tendai and Shingon, were established. They sought to realize the full potential of a Mahayana Buddhist world in which all sentient beings have buddha-nature and aim for enlightenment in this very body and life. The dawn of the Kamakura period, however, was met with no such optimism. As the Heian period progressed, the decentralization of power led to a growing state of anarchy with a wide variety of groups vying for power across the Japanese countryside, including the major temple complexes based on Mt. Hiei and Mt. Koya as well as in Nara, and their bands of militarized monks. Competition for resources amongst these centers coupled with a growing population and a decline in food production led to increasing numbers of military confrontations in the mid-10th and 11th centuries. By the mid-12th century, the provincial upper class had transformed into a new militarized elite called samurai. In the aftermath of the Hogen Rebellion in 1156, Japan experienced a protracted civil war until the establishment of the Kamakura military government (幕府 *bakufu*) in 1192, creating the form of military rule under a generalissimo (*shogun*), which endured until the return of imperial based rule some seven centuries later in the Meiji Restoration of 1868. Drawing parallels with the time of the Buddha in India again, this development has its similarities to the rise of lower caste warriors in the states of Kosala and Magadha that swallowed up the tribal republics and consolidated power over Northeast India, ultimately leading to Ashoka's conquest of the entire sub-continent.[101]

---

101 Kosambi. *Ancient India*. p. 127.

Mappo: The Ontological Shift that Opened the Way to a Spiritual and Social Revolution

It was amidst this descent into political and social chaos and warfare that the optimism of the early Heian gave way to a new spiritual attitude towards the world, summed up in the Buddhist concept of *mappo* 末法, the Age of the Final Dharma or Latter Dharma. This concept is, as we have seen on numerous occasions, an innovation of Chinese culture and East Asian Buddhism. While Indian culture contains a similar sentiment in the Kali Yuga, the fourth in a series of declining spiritual epochs, Indian Buddhists did not develop a coherent theory of *mappo* and the other two ages (of True Dharma 正法 *shobo* and Semblance Dharma 像法 *zoho*). There are seeds of this concept found in the Pali Canon and later in the Mahayana concepts of the Five Defilements (五濁 *go-joku*) and the Five Periods (五五百歳 *go-gohyaku-sai*) as found in sutras like the *Great Collection Sutra* (大方等大集經 *Daihodo daijikkyo*). However, the concept of the Three Ages of the Dharma (三時 *sanji* or 正像末 *sho-zo-matsu*), and specifically *mappo*, does not become an important part of Chinese Buddhism until the persecutions of it during the rules of the Emperor Wu 大武帝 (424–451) of the Northern Wei 北魏 (386-534) and the Emperor Wu 周武帝 (561–577) of the Northern Chou 北周 (557–581) dynasties.[102]

The Chinese Pure Land Master Daochuo 道綽 (562–645), a critical figure in Japanese Pure Land Buddhism, is one of the first to write about *mappo*. He extolled the Pure Land way as offering the only means available to escape this degenerate world, where enlightened masters no longer exist, by attaining Birth (往生 *ojo*) in the Pure Land, where the conditions for gaining enlightenment are ideal. One of the key points of his *Collection of Passages on the Blissful Land* (安楽集 *Anraku-shu*) is that any dharma, no matter how profound, has no meaning if it does not fit to the age and hence social conditions of the people. This would become a key soteriological point for the new Kamakura masters in convincing the people about the efficacy of their teaching against the established forms of *ken-mitsu* Buddhism.

The teaching of the Three Ages had already been brought to Japan at an early period through Prince Shotoku's examination of it in his aforementioned *Commentary on Three Sutras*. However, Prince Shotoku and other early Japanese Buddhists were focused on using

---

[102] Marra, Michele. "The Development of *Mappo* Thought in Japan (I)". In *Japanese Journal of Religious Studies*. 1988. Vol. 15, No. 1. pp. 27-29.

Buddhism to build a new system for sacralizing and legitimizing the state. They rejected any calculations by the Chinese of the Buddha's death being in the 10th century BCE and thus marking the beginning of *mappo* some 1,500 years later in the 6th century BCE; rather choosing 552 BCE as the Buddha's demise and *mappo* being yet upon them in the coming 10th century. The success of the Ritsuryo political system which harmonized Buddhist law (*buppo*) and imperial law (*obo*) enabled them to believe Buddhism was still not in decline.[103] It was the famous Tendai Pure Land master Genshin 源信 (942–1017) who marked a major shift in this discourse. Having personally suffered the ruin of the Ritsuryo system and the corruption of his own sect through power politics, he wrote the *Essentials for Birth in the Pure Land* (往生要集 *Ojoyo-shu*) as an elaborate warning of karmic retribution for those living amidst the corruption of this age. "From the second half of the eleventh century then, the expression 'final age' (末世 *mas-se*) occurs in many diaries, novels, and works of history, often bringing with it a connotation of fear and inevitability."[104]

The other critical text is *The Candle of the Latter Dharma* (末法燈明記 *Mappo tomyo-ki*), which although attributed to Saicho (767–822) around the date 801 is only first discussed by the first of the great Kamakura masters Honen 法然 (1133–1212). It too becomes a great influence on the other revolutionaries of the Kamakura period: Honen's disciple Shinran 親鸞 (1173–1263), Zen master Dogen 道元 (1200–1253), and Nichiren 日蓮 (1222–1282).[105] In short, the *Mappo tomyo-ki* is a defense of the already perceived decline of the monastic community in the beginning of the Heian period under Emperor Kanmu 桓武 (r. 781–806). It argues that the government in its criticism of the monastic Sangha should recognize that as *mappo* has dawned, monks and nuns cannot be expected to live up to the standards set by the Buddha in the Age of the True Dharma. The implication of the text is that monks and nuns who strive to keep the precepts and the ancient way are overly tied to the formal rules of

---

103 Ibid., p. 40.

104 Ibid., p. 21

105 Eisai 栄西 (1141-1215) is sometimes considered one of the key Kamakura Buddhist masters as the nominal founder of the first independent Zen sect in Japan, the Rinzai 臨済宗, based on the Linji School of Chinese Chan Buddhism. However, he is generally not considered part of the Kamakura Buddhist revolution for his allegiance to Tendai and the fusion of Zen with esoteric teachings, as well as his close ties to the Kamakura military government and promotion of Buddhism as a protector of the state.

Buddhism while losing the deeper human spirit of the dharma.[106] It appears, then, that the Kamakura Buddhist revolutionaries were trying to recapture the critical spirit Saicho had towards Nara Buddhism and the government's control of the monastic Sangha and ordination platforms as well as his deeper dedication to the bodhisattva way of the true Mahayana.

In looking back on Eisenstadt's definition of axialization, he describes how the development of "new types of ontological visions, [and] conceptions of a basic tension between the transcendental and mundane orders, emerged and were institutionalized".[107] Further, the mundane order is perceived as incomplete, inferior, unsatisfactory, or polluted and in need of being reconstructed according to the principles of a higher ontological or ethical order that bridges the chasm between the transcendental and the mundane orders. The *mappo* discourse provided just such a new ontological vision that indeed saw the mundane order as incomplete. In turn, these new visions coming from the Kamakura Buddhist revolutionaries would be able to reconstruct society and bridge the vast chasm between the military anarchy of the end of the Heian Era and the vision of Amitabha's Pure Land in the West. In this way, *mappo* marks a significant shift in Japanese outlook from one that always affirmed this world to one that, like Indian culture, saw it as defiled and in need of escape.

However, there is an important caveat here as well as parallel to the Buddha's response to the Indian discourse about *samsara* and the Kamakura Buddhist masters' responses to *mappo*. The Buddha, of course, taught the Middle Way of an integrated sangha of monastic and lay, while rejecting the worldly escapism of the Upanishadic ascetics and the worldly corruption of the Brahmin ritualists. The Kamakura masters were clearly rejecting the worldly corruption of the Tendai, Shingon, and Nara Buddhist centers. Yet their embrace of the *mappo* discourse was not to create a new elitist form of ascetic, world-renouncing monastics, but rather to create what I believe is a truly axial solution that "bridged the chasm between the transcendental and the mundane orders". This led to a full flowering of the Buddha dharma in Japan in "intentional ethical action" (i.e., Buddhist karma) through bodhisattva ethics (*sila*), an empowering form of "single practice" available to the common person (*samadhi*), and a spiritual vision that did not posit an essentialized source of

---

106 Marra, Michele. "The Development of *Mappo* Thought in Japan (II)". In *Japanese Journal of Religious Studies*. 1988. Vol. 15, No. 4. p. 288.

107 Eisenstadt. *Japanese Civilization*. p. 13.

power and its graded emanations but a completely integrated view of the cosmos that provided a democratic social vision (*prajna*). The challenge of realizing such a delicate balance in an age of anarchic violence would, as we will see, prove to fraught with stumbling blocks.

The Kamakura Axial Revolution:
From Pure Land's Elevation of the Common Person to Zen's Actualized Enlightenment to Nichiren's Liberation of the World

A first important aspect of the Kamakura Buddhist masters was their response to the core ideology of the *ken-mitsu* Buddhist system, the teaching of innate enlightenment (*hongaku*). There is a delicate and difficult tension brought out in this teaching, which we see throughout the Buddhist tradition including in the Theravada. That is: there obviously needs to be an injunction to practice. This is the transcendental element in which we must strive to "transcend", or perhaps better put, "transform" our neurotic mental and emotional habits as well as the suffering of the world. However, when this mentality becomes over-emphasized, a false duality emerges between an ever-present state of brokenness or "lack" and the promise of an enlightened state to be achieved. Such an over-emphasis is also the foundation for the championing of the great meditative ascetic as being closer to enlightenment than the unrefined lay person because of practicing and meditating *more*. The *hongaku* ideology was the Mahayana way of dispelling this duality, emphasizing the quality of intention (*cetana*)[108] and practice as well as championing the potentials of the common layperson. However, when this view (as with all views that are clung to) is over-emphasized, a state of inertia ensues and the status quo with all of its entrenched inequalities and sufferings is accepted as is. As such, the way the Kamakura masters engaged with this issue was of critical importance to the future of Japanese Buddhism.

Honen, having lived most of his life in the Heian era, is considered the first of these revolutionaries not just by chronology but also for the audacity of his teachings. Ordained as a young boy in the Tendai tradition, he spent his formative years attempting to penetrate the core of the Mahayana teachings as a cloistered *hijiri* (別所聖 *bessho hijiri*) amidst the growing anarchy of life on Mt. Hiei. Ironically, as Saicho had rejected the Nara establishment, Honen rejected the

---

[108] For more detail on the key role of intention (*cetana*) in defining the Buddha's articulation of karma vis-à-vis other schools of Indian thought see: Watts. "Karma for Everyone".

Mt. Hiei establishment and its teachings, leaving the mountain to set up a ministry on the edges of Kyoto focused on the "single-minded" recitation of Amitabha Buddha's name, known as the *senju-nenbutsu* 専修念仏.

The *senju-nenbutsu* was revolutionary in several ways. It clearly rejected the complex fusion of Buddhist teachings in the Tendai *ken-mitsu* system, the mastery of which was only possible for an elite class of ascetic monastics cloistered on holy mountains. Standing firmly in a belief in *mappo*, Honen proclaimed that the simple recitation of Amitabha's name, even just ten times, could erase eons of bad karma and gain one entry into Amitabha's Pure Land at the moment of death. This teaching, however, was not designed as a simplified, inferior version of dharma practice, often given by monks to lay people whom they feel are unable to realize the highest forms of Buddhist practice. Rather, in this era of *mappo*, the *senju-nenbutsu* was the best and indeed only way of realizing the highest goal of Buddhism, eventual enlightenment after Birth in the Pure Land (*ojo*).

The proclamation of such an audacious teaching by Honen, who was a highly respected practitioner-scholar among the general monastic world[109], was the proclamation of a spiritual revolution in which all were empowered to practice and realize. As Pure Land Buddhism developed under the Chinese, especially Shandao 善導 (613–681), the idea that only bodhisattvas far advanced in practice could enter the Pure Land was flipped on its head so that under Amitabha's radical vow of deep compassion the most defiled and mired in bad karma, known as *bonbu* 凡夫, became the first subject of salvation. Honen's isolation of this teaching into a single, exclusively focused school of practice marked a spiritual revolution that in many ways was a call to social revolution—a kind of liberation theology for the masses to throw off the domination of the Heian aristocracy and the clan warlords and seek for their own independence.[110] As a social movement, this was not initiated in Honen's lifetime but came

---

[109] Most of the information we have on Honen and his life are in rather idealized hagiographies. However, it is clear that his achievements as both a scholar and practitioner were widely respected among both the powerful at the Heian court and at the three centers of Buddhist power. *Senchakushu* English Translation Project. *Honen's* Senchakushu: *Passages on the Selection of the Nembutsu in the Original Vow (Senchaku hongan nembutsu-shu)*. (Honolulu: University of Hawaii Press; Tokyo: Taisho University Sogo Bukkyo Kenkyujo, 1998), p. 37.

[110] Machida, Soho. *Renegade Monk: Honen and Japanese Pure Land Buddhism.* Ed. & Trans. Ioannis Mentzas. (Berkeley: University of California Press, 1999).

to fore in the Pure Land rebellions (一向一揆 *ikko-ikki*) of the 15th and 16th centuries.

The key notion of Honen's *senju-nenbutsu* as a single, "exclusive" practice, simple enough for all to achieve, was subsequently adopted by Dogen in his simple practice of "just sitting meditation" (只管打坐 *shikan-taza*) and Nichiren's simple and singular recitation of taking refuge in the *Lotus Sutra* (題目 *daimoku*). In terms of the tension between practice and realization, Honen is most conspicuous among the Kamakura masters for never addressing *hongaku* in his teaching, what must be considered a most conscious omission if not rejection as a highly accomplished Tendai scholar.[111] Compared to Shinran, Dogen, and Nichiren, Honen is considered to have more deeply emphasized the schism between the mundane and the transcendental in his strong admonition to chant the *nenbutsu* as much as possible to attain liberation from this world of suffering through Birth in the Pure Land. While gently reassuring lay people from all classes that, however much they practice, a "sincere mind" (至誠心 *shijo-shin*) was also an essential component to such Birth, he drove himself and his monastic disciples in a rigorous life of more than 50,000 recitations per day.[112]

Looking more deeply into his teachings, however, we can see the resolution of the core duality of constancy of practice and quality of intention that the *hongaku* teaching sought to address, since Honen always paired the constant recitation of the *nenbutsu* with the cultivation of the Three Minds (三心 *sanjin*) necessary for guiding practice and the approach to Amitabha. While the omission of the doctrine of buddha-nature in Honen's teachings also shows his focus on the transcendental goal of Birth in the Pure Land, he achieves this with the counter-intuitive idea that the embrace of oneself as a deluded person (*bonbu*) filled with afflictions (*klesha/bonno*) and bad karma was the best means to attain such transcendence. All the common means of achieving the transcendence of Buddhist enlightenment through monastic or lay precepts, meditation, and wisdom were categorically dismissed, and the Japanese world-affirming way of the lay Buddhist was taken to its logical conclusion. The complexity of Honen's Middle

---

111 *Honen's* Senchakushu. pp. 14-15.

112 Honen. "Question 4: Repeat at least Ten Thousand Times" in "One Hundred Forty-five Questions and Answers" (一百四十五箇条問答 *Ippyaku-shijugo-kajo mondo*) in *Honen the Buddhist Saint: His Life and Teaching*. Trans. Harper Havelock Coates & Ryugaku Ishizuka. (Kyoto: Chion-in Temple, 1925), p. 423. Now being re-edited and re-published by the Jodo Shu Research Institute in Tokyo.

Way, a transcendence of the suffering of this world through the total embrace of one's neurotic self in this world, is an aspect of his teaching that is still undervalued in the scholarly world that sees Shinran, his disciple, as the full maturation of this vision.

If Honen's emphasis on *mappo* and the injunction to recite the name of Amitabha as much as possible could be seen as a more transcendentalist notion of the need for more practice to escape this world of suffering, then Shinran's even greater emphasis on one's nature as *bonbu* seemed to lead to a new conclusion that returned to the more immanentalist view of *hongaku*. Shinran felt that the depth of this deluded human nature in fact made it impossible to practice even the *nenbutsu* as a means to reaching Amitabha. Such an attainment could never be the cause of practice or through human agency but only by the cause or vow of Amitabha. One could quickly conclude that this idea seems to lead to the sort of devotional theism as found in the *bhakti* movements of Hinduism or even the abstract monism of Tendai *hongaku*—both prone to a system of graded levels of spiritual power and agency prone to abuse. The Shin Buddhist, however, would de-emphasize the focus on the ontological positions of an eternal being or essential nature and emphasize the existential situation of the *bonbu* living amidst suffering—more of "the absolute based upon the relative".[113] This standpoint returns to Honen's total indifference and neglect to addressing the ontological issues found in the *hongaku* and buddha-nature teachings and re-affirms the aforementioned Chinese Pure Land master Daochuo's emphasis on how the teaching must fit the people and the time they live in. Shinran's teaching seems to flip *hongaku* on its head as not a rationalization of the status quo of those in power but as an empowerment of those with no power, the *bonbu*, and their blessedness and agency to attain salvation "just as they are". Instead of being innately enlightened, Pure Land Buddhists are innately deluded and that means they are more fit to realize salvation due to their groundedness in the realities of the suffering world.

In this way, Honen and Shinran's ministries were a radical rejection of the giant edifice of spiritual materialism in the Buddhist tradition with its highly elaborate philosophies, practices, and rituals that had become the private domain of the monastic elite and social elites, such as those of the Heian era, who patronized and had access to them. Honen's rejection of the foundational core of Buddhism in the

---

113 Stone, Jacqueline I. *Original Enlightenment and the Transformation of Medieval Japanese Buddhism*. (Honolulu: University of Hawaii Press, 2003), pp. 87-88.

Three Trainings of *sila-samadhi-prajna* and Shinran's total embrace of this rejection by openly taking a wife and not shaving his head, becoming "neither monk nor layman", was a message to the common person that not only Buddhist conventions did not need to be followed but also social conventions and entrenched forms of authority. As mentioned, while this did not take actual political form until three centuries later, the anti-authoritarian nature of the movement and the liberties that certain new devotees took with the teachings led to numerous movements by the forces on Mt. Hiei against Honen, and eventually to his, Shinran's, and other leading disciples' exile into the Japanese hinterland.

While Honen and Shinran literally turned Buddhism upside down in their development of a teaching that fit the time and age of *mappo*, Dogen could be said to have turned Buddhism inside out in his resolution to the tension between the transcendental drive to transform mind through practice and the engagement in suffering through acceptance of the world. His ability to recapture the practical essence of Nagarjuna's Madhyamaka thought makes him "generally considered to have been the greatest Japanese philosophical thinker".[114] Dogen's revolutionary spirit is first expressed in his rejection of the mainstream Linji Chan school during his study in China from 1223–1227. The Chan tradition, in general, was against the intellectual study of the sutras, emphasizing realization through the study and practice of *koans* 公案 to short circuit the discursive mind so as to access the True Mind. It is easy to see here the foundations of Chan/Zen in the Cittamatra or Yogacara school of Mind Only and the influence of the teachings of "the womb of the Tathagata" (*tathagata-garbha*) and buddha-nature from the *Treatise on the Awakening of Mahayana Faith*.

Dogen, however, was critical to this approach, which creates a transcendental dualism between the True Mind and the "lower mind" of language and conceptualization. In the *Sansui-kyo* fascicle of his most prominent writing, *The Treasury of the True Dharma Eye* (正法眼蔵 *Shobogen zo*), Dogen criticizes the approach of using *koans* as simply nonsensical ways to cut off thought: "How pitiable are they who are unaware that discriminating thought is words and phrases, and that words and phrases liberate discriminating thought."[115] This quote encapsulates Dogen's mastery of Nagarjuna's dialectic in which, as the *Heart Sutra* says, "form is empty, yet emptiness is form" 色即是

---

114 Williams. *Mahayana Buddhism*. pp. 113.

115 Loy, David R. "Language Against Its Own Mystifications: Deconstruction in Nagarjuna and Dogen". In *Philosophy East & West*. 1999. Vol. 49, No. 3. p. 256.

空空即是色 (*shiki soku ze ku, ku soku ze shiki*). In this way, Dogen did not reject the use of *koans* in training but used them in a different way, not to reject thought but to liberate it.[116] Already possessed of such a critical awareness, Dogen sought out a Chinese master named Rujing 如淨 of the lesser known Caodong (曹洞 *Soto*) lineage of Chan.

The second revolutionary aspect of Dogen's mastery in applying radical emptiness (*shunyata*) was to resolve the *koan* of *hongaku* and the question of how much practice is appropriate. In the Buddha-Nature fascicle of the *Shobogen-zo*, he did not read the *Mahaparinirvana Sutra* as saying, "All sentient being have buddha-nature"—as Saicho and most Mahayana masters did. Rather, he reads it as, "All sentient beings are buddha-nature", thereby rejecting buddha-nature as a sort of essential dharma or ontological form. This in turn led him to deny the usual duality between practice and realization. "To think that practice and realization are not identical is a non-Buddhist view…practice must be considered to point directly to intrinsic realization."[117]

In collapsing the distinctions between having and not having, practicing and not practicing, and actualizing and not actualizing, Dogen is not embracing *hongaku* as either an excuse for non-practice or the reification of more practice as the means to access True Mind. Rather, practice, in this case *zazen*, itself is the manifestation of buddha-nature. This means that it is available to all persons to manifest as sentient beings and not the privileged domain of highly accomplished masters. Although *mappo* did not form an important basis of Dogen's teaching, he maintains the same liberative thrust of Honen and Shinran by collapsing the distinctions between monastic and lay practice and achieving the harmony of realizing the transcendental through a thorough engagement in the world, in this case, the world of the common discursive mind.

Nichiren, the final of the Kamakura Buddhist revolutionaries, would take the soteriological implications of Honen, Shinran, and Dogen to their logical conclusion by outrightly proclaiming a theology based on the transformation of society and not just the individual.[118] As a young boy, Nichiren ordained in the Tendai tradition and was clearly "influenced by the absolute monism of Tendai *hongaku* thought, in which all things just as they are viewed as expressions of

---

116 Bodiford. *Soto Zen in Medieval Japan*. p. 144.
117 Williams. *Mahayana Buddhism*. pp. 114-15.
118 Stone. *Original Enlightenment and the Transformation of Medieval Japanese Buddhism*. p. 88.

original enlightenment".[119] In fact, in this early stage, he even put the Shingon teachings above those of the *Lotus Sutra* for their emphasis on "attaining enlightenment in this very body" (*sokushin jobutsu*). This formed one of the foundations for his strident criticism of the Pure Land movement and their emphasis on "abandoning the tainted world" (*onri-edo*) and "longing for the Pure Land" (*gongu-jodo*).

It was after a period of study on Mt. Hiei that he shifted his view to elevating the *Lotus Sutra* as the culmination of all Buddhist teachings for its promotion of the bodhisattva path. Nichiren saw himself as the person to revive the Tendai sect after centuries of decay and revive Saicho's original vision of the Mahayana path under the engaged bodhisattva. This vision led him to leave Mt. Hiei and begin his career preaching and converting people to faith in the *Lotus Sutra* through the recitation of "taking refuge in the *Lotus Sutra*" (南無妙法蓮華經 *namu-myo-horenge-kyo* or, in short, *daimoku*). This vision also included a strident form of teaching called *shaku-buku* 折伏 (lit. "to break and subdue")[120] that involved rebuking attachment to all provisional teachings.

This path led him to settle down in the new capital of Kamakura in eastern Japan, which was filled with temples of the Pure Land and Zen sects sanctifying the regime of the new military government (*bakufu*) detached from imperial power in Kyoto. Nichiren's ministry there included offering unsolicited warnings to the Kamakura military government about the need to make the *Lotus Sutra* the sole Buddhist teaching of the nation to avoid the calamities befalling it, including the imminent invasion of the Mongols. In this environment, Nichiren's sharp denunciation of other sects, especially Pure Land and the *bakufu's* first choice of Rinzai Zen, created major disturbances and led to his exile on Sado Island off the wind-blown coast of the Japan Sea. Amidst these dark days of individual persecution and the social crises facing the Kamakura government, Nichiren began to shift his thought to the aforementioned theme of the capacity of the individual in a specific historical context or age. In this age, the expression of enlightenment through everyday actions as legitimized by the *hongaku* teaching, or even in Zen practice, was not possible.

---

119 Stone. "Placing Nichiren in the 'Big Picture'". p. 398.

120 This concept is found in the aforementioned *Srimala Sutra* (勝鬘經 *Shoman-gyo*) chosen by Shotoku as one of the key Buddhist texts for the founding of the Japanese nation and also a key text in the *tathagata-garbha* and buddha-nature tradition, which forms the basis for the teaching of innate enlightenment (*hongaku*). It appears often in the works of the founders of the Chinese Tiantai (Tendai) tradition, Zhiyi and Zhanran.

As one of the foremost experts on medieval Japanese Buddhism, Jacqueline Stone, writes, "In Nichiren's view, while this world may in principle be the Buddha's original land, in reality it is filled with strife and disaster; the Buddha land had to be actualized through the practice of *shaku-buku* and the spread of faith in the *Lotus Sutra*, even at the cost of one's life."[121] Thus, by the age of forty, Nichiren appears to have abandoned the Tendai innate enlightenment doctrine's absolute monism and affirmation of reality.[122]

In this way, Nichiren fully embraced the doctrine of *mappo*, and his teaching of the recitation of the *daimoku* begins to look more like the Pure Land *nenbutsu*, "as a practice for ignorant persons of the Final Dharma age that will save them from karmic rebirth in the lower realms of transmigration."[123] Indeed, both the Pure Land and Nichiren orders became beacons to the lower classes, women, and social outcastes living in the dark of the violent rivalries of the ruling classes.[124] Nichiren's teaching also seems to resemble Honen's—the master he had studied deeply as a novice monk yet had come to thoroughly revile—in a stronger thrust towards the need for practice as a means to realize a greater goal. For Honen, it was the realization of the Pure Land in the next world, while for Nichiren, it was the realization of the Pure Land in this world.

Honen was unique, even in comparison to his disciple Shinran, in never speaking of his teachings as offering protection for the state or welfare for society. Nichiren, on the other hand, always had strong tendencies towards seeing the role of Buddhism in establishing the

---

121 Stone. "Placing Nichiren in the 'Big Picture'". p. 400.

122 Ibid., p. 398.

123 Ibid., p. 400.

124 Honen: "In terms of one's capacity, there is no excluding those who have committed the five grievous acts (五逆罪 *go-gyaku-zai*) or any serious crimes; there is no abandoning women or total non-believers (*icchantika*). In terms of one's practice, we accept a single *nenbutsu* or multiple *nenbutsu*. Therefore, there is no need to obsess over the restrictions of the five obstacles and three obediences [put on women] (五障三従 *gosho-sanju*). One should rely on the Vow and be diligent in practice". In *Traversing the Pure Land Path: A Lifetime of Encounters with Honen Shonin*. Eds. Jonathan S. Watts & Yoshiharu Tomatsu. (Tokyo: Jodo Shu Press, 2005), p. 55; Nichiren: "Rather than be great rulers during the two thousand years of the True and Semblance Dharma ages, those concerned for their salvation should rather be common people now in the Final Dharma age…. It is better to be a leper who chants *Namu-myoho-renge-kyo* than to be chief abbot of the Tendai school." … "A woman who embraces this [*Lotus*] *Sutra* not only excels all other women but also surpasses all men." In Stone. "Placing Nichiren in the 'Big Picture'". p. 394.

wellbeing of all of Japan. He took these cues from his Tendai roots and the emphasis on the "identity of this world of suffering with the Buddha's Land of Tranquil Light" (娑婆即寂光土 shaba soku jakko-do). For him, embrace of the *Lotus Sutra* would actually transform the present world both materially and spiritually.[125] In this way, Nichiren, perhaps more than any of the other Kamakura Buddhist masters, fits the definition of axialization by creating a new ontological vision that would resolve the tension of the social and spiritual collapse of the Heian-Kamakura period as the Age of the Final Dharma with the higher enlightened order of the Buddha's Pure Land as realized in the path of the bodhisattva found in the *Lotus Sutra*. In many ways, it is a complete Buddhist path with a critique of suffering and its causes as per the First and Second Noble Truths, a vision of the Buddha's Pure Land as in the Third Noble Truth, and finally the practical path of the bodhisattva as per the Fourth Noble Truth.

Nichiren's final shift is away from Honen's and the Pure Land tradition's apparent retreat from this world of suffering and more towards a non-dual view of "the *daimoku* as enabling the realization or buddhahood in this very body,"[126] and hence the realization of the Pure Land in the world. It also appears closer to Dogen's harmonization of practice as essential but also as not a means to an end but rather the realization of the end, dispelling the means-end dichotomy. Indeed, the challenge of a Middle Way approach is to dispel the dualism between practice and realization. As Stone notes in her analysis of Nichiren and the other Kamakura Buddhist masters, "The simultaneity of practice and realization is not a denial of the necessity of continued practice but a reconceiving of it: practice is seen, not in instrumental, linear terms as a means leading to an end, but instead, as the expression, confirmation, and deepening of a liberation or salvation that in some sense is already present."[127] In this way, there need not be a complete rejection of *hongaku* but a re-balancing of it using the *mappo* discourse to reassert "the importance of practice and engaging the real sufferings and contradictions of this world."[128]

As such, the great contemporary Japanese Buddhist scholar,

---

125 Stone, Jacqueline I. "Nichiren's Activist Heirs: Soka Gakkai, Rissho Koseikai, Nipponzan Myohoji". In *Action Dharma: New Studies in Engaged Buddhism*. Eds. Christopher Queen, Charles Prebish, & Damien Keown. (London: RoutledgeCurzon, 2003), p. 65.

126 Stone. "Placing Nichiren in the 'Big Picture'". p. 400.

127 Ibid., p. 408.

128 Ibid., p. 401.

Tamura Yoshiro 田村芳朗 (1921-89) felt that Shinran, Dogen, and Nichiren achieved "a synthesis between the 'absolute nonduality' of *hongaku* and a 'relative duality', most strongly asserted by Honen, between the Buddha and deluded beings, this world and the Pure Land."[129] Indeed, while the *hongaku* ideology of *ken-mitsu* Buddhism and the *mappo* ideology of Kamakura Buddhism are usually set against each other, the Kamakura Buddhist masters actually seem to have captured a delicate balance of the two. This is the brilliance of the Kamakura Buddhist revolution for positing a higher truth based on the ethics, practice, and wisdom of Buddhism that could be realized in this world by the common person through an engagement in the suffering of the world.

The Legacy of Kamakura Buddhism I: The Ethics of Death and Karma

From the standpoint of the basic re-envisioning of the Buddhist path by the Kamakura masters, there is consequentially a whole series of shifts in the way other key parts of the Japanese Buddhist tradition could be and were understood. In the teaching of *mappo*, the very this-worldly emphasis of Japanese Buddhism is tempered with an injunction towards a higher truth to transcend this world of suffering. As we noted in the opening section on the early formation of Buddhism in Japan, as a mountainous, island culture, the Japanese have exhibited strong tendencies to emphasize the more localized or clannish ethics of taboo and taint (*kega-re*) over the more universal or transcendental notions of sin and karma. This tension, between Buddhism as it evolved in Japan and traditional Japanese moral and spiritual values, mirrors the tension that was created when the Buddha introduced his teachings in opposition to those of the *Vedas*. The early Vedic view of karma was as "ritual action". One's fate in the afterlife was contingent not on one's moral actions in this life but rather the maintenance of caste roles and taboos as well as Brahmanic rituals at the time of death.[130] This is not to say that the people of these early Vedic communities were not moral and ethical, but rather that they had not universalized their ethical culture.

The Buddha's spiritual, and consequently social revolution, was

---

129 Ibid., p. 399.

130 Obeyesekere, Gananath. *Imagining Karma: Ethical Transformation in Amerindian, Buddhist, and Greek Rebirth*. (Berkeley, CA: University of California Press, 2002), p. 100.

opening a direct door to liberation to people of lower castes as well as women, freeing them from the dictates of the Brahmanic hierarchy and their sanctification of social hierarchy. In short, when a culture is fully ethicized, the good life in the present or in the afterlife is based on "ethical action" (i.e., Buddhist karma), that is, the quality of the way we interact with and treat others. Ethical action, as opposed to ritual action, is something not only available to everyone but inherent in the social nature of human beings.[131]

In looking at Japan, Nakamura Hajime notes that the early Japanese saw the value of life in this world via primitive Shinto and did not reflect deeply on the soul or death. They worried little about death or what came after, believing that one's soul (魂 *tama*) continues on in this world after death.[132] As noted, the individual Japanese would understand themselves in terms of their family, clan, village, and language or national group. The dead were also seen as an ongoing part of the community, either as a potentially malevolent spirit or a protective one.[133] With a weak or vague sense of the afterlife—literally referred to as simply "the other world" (あの世 *ano-yo*)—there was little reflection on the transcendent possibility of the soul or spirit or on death or the afterlife, which seemed to not worry or cause fear in traditional Japanese.

Other scholars, however, have noted that the Japanese also referred to the afterlife as "the realm below" (黄泉の国 *yomi-no-kuni*), understood as "the land of darkness" from which no one returns.[134] In this way, Mark Blum, a leading expert in medieval Japanese Buddhism, notes that, "Native Shinto cults had a deep-seated antipathy toward death because of its association with pollution." When important social leaders died—such as kings, ministers, and village chiefs—a ritual purification through an extended period of embalmment was necessary to transform their spirit into a protector deity.[135] This notion of ritual purification through funerary rite to transform the spirit of the deceased into a protecting rather than malevolent one is still central to Japanese beliefs today.

Buddhism's arrival in Japan presented a vast new way of understanding the meaning of death and the meaning of life. Its emphasis on karma and the quality of mental purity rather than physical purity

---

131 Ibid., p. 174.
132 Nakamura. *Ways of Thinking of Eastern Peoples*. p. 361.
133 Blum, Mark L. "Never Die Alone: *Shonen* as Intersubjective Experience". In *Never Die Alone*. p. 2.
134 Matsumoto. "Buddhism and the Kami". p. 373.
135 Blum. "Never Die Alone". p. 2.

meant it had few taboos or notions of pollution in dealing with the dead.¹³⁶ Perhaps more importantly, Buddhism's notion of a personal, private identity that might transcend one's family and social group had, and still has, significant ramifications for how the individual Japanese sees their place in society and the world beyond Japan. In the Heian Period, the great Tendai Pure Land master Genshin helped to popularize the classical six realms of Buddhist reincarnation as well as karma as a metaphysical system of cause and effect and rewards and punishments, through his famous work, the *Essentials for Birth in the Pure Land* (*Ojoyo-shu*). Genshin is also a critical figure for the detailed deathbed instructions with accompanied *nenbutsu* practice found in the *Ojoyo-shu* as well as his creation of the 25 Samadhi Group (二十五三昧会 *Nijugo zanmai-e*), a fraternity of monks supporting each other in spiritual preparation for death and Birth in the Pure Land (*ojo*). This group considered themselves "spiritual friends" (Skt. *kalyanamitra* 善知識 *zenchishiki*) and popularized a tradition of *zenchishiki* as Buddhist masters who came to support the dying on their deathbed in medieval Japan.¹³⁷

In these early stages, however, we can still see that a good death was the right of a highly trained ascetic, like Genshin and his comrades on Mt. Hiei. As such, the normative model of Buddhist death—in which Right Mindfulness (Skt. *samyak-smriti* 正念 *sho-nen*, the seventh practice of the Buddha's Noble Eightfold Path) is essential at the time of death—was still prevalent. This model believes that one's state of mind at death is as much as one hundred times more significant as any other mental activity in life in determining what one's postmortem fate will be. As we have seen, however, Honen's teaching of Pure Land practice flipped notions of spiritual practice and attainment on their heads. While he taught *nenbutsu* practice as essential, he also emphasized the grace or "other power" (他力 *tariki*) of Amitabha's vow to liberate all sentient beings. As an ordinary, deluded fool (*bonbu*) in this Age of the Final Dharma, traditional forms of Buddhist enlightenment were considered virtually impossible. The best path to Birth in Amitabha's Pure Land was not gained through either ritual purification or the realization of a meditative mindfulness at the moment of death, or

---

136 Ibid., pp. 4, 8.

137 There are antecedents to this tradition in China with the famous Master Huiyuan 慧遠 of Lu-shan (Mt. Lu 廬山) (334–416) who in 402 gathered a group of 123 monastics and lay people to make a vow to support each other towards Birth in the Pure Land, albeit through the more traditional form of visualized *nenbutsu* rather than the recited one. Williams. *Mahayana Buddhism*. p. 222.

even the recitation of the *nenbutsu* as a mantra creating positive karmic results.[138] *Ojo* was the gift of Amitabha, and so Honen instructed his followers to die "just as they are", simply reciting the *nenbutsu* a mere ten times at the moment of death. One of the most outstanding examples of this is found in Honen's warrior student, Taro Tadatsuna, who attained *ojo* through chanting the *nenbutsu* after being felled by a fatal blow, rather ironically, while being sent by the government to put down a violent rebellion of warrior-monks on Mt. Hiei in 1192.[139] Shinran's even greater emphasis on pure faith further disconnected the link between practice, and specifically the maintenance of Buddhist precepts (*sila*), as a causal link to a better rebirth.

While we have seen how this shift was an attempt to democratize spirituality, like the Buddha did against the domination of Vedic ritualists and ascetics, there is a delicate balance in maintaining the Middle Way. The logical extreme of the Pure Land approach appears to bring us back to the problems inherent in the innate enlightenment (*hongaku*) doctrine, in which practice becomes irrelevant and people with no ethical standards may be offered liberation, just as they are through commandeering purification rites at the time of death. This connects us to the other important problem found throughout the Buddhist tradition, which is how karma is understood as either a method of ethical action or an excuse for social discrimination based on the karmic determinism of transgressions from previous lives. This is the concern of the contemporary Critical Buddhism scholars of the Soto Zen school.

According to Hakamaya Noriaki, Dogen was very critical of the ritualized forms of confession found in East Asian *hongaku* texts, which teach that evil karma can be eradicated through purification ceremonies (懺悔滅罪 *san-ge metsuzai*).[140] At the end of his life, Dogen was invited by Hojo Tokiyori, the fifth regent of the Kamakura military government, to teach in Kamakura where Rinzai Zen had established its first great stronghold. Not surprisingly, he was quickly disillusioned by the predominance of an esotericized Zen that was being used to sacralize the Kamakura military government.[141]

---

138 Blum. "Never Die Alone". pp. 10-11.

139 Watts and Tomatsu. *Traversing the Pure Land Path*. pp. 34-36.

140 Heine, Steven. "Critical Buddhism and Dogen's *Shobogenzo*: The Debate over the 75-Fascicle and 12-Fascicle Texts". In *Pruning the Bodhi Tree*. p. 259.

141 Collcutt, Martin. *Five Mountains: The Rinzai Zen Monastic Institution in Medieval Japan*. (Cambridge: Harvard University Press, 1981), p. 36. Bodiford. *Soto Zen in Medieval Japan*. p. 154.

The Critical Buddhists argue that, from this point onward, Dogen attempted to clarify his teachings against interpretations leaning towards notions of *hongaku* and the mystical realization of enlightenment beyond the scriptures, which might rationalize the breaking of Buddhist precepts and the rejection of karmic cause and effect.[142] Honen also took such steps, such as in his *Seven Article Pledge* (七箇条起請文 *Shichi-ka-jo kisho-mon*) signed with 163 of his monastic disciples repudiating the use of his Pure Land teachings as an excuse for amoral behavior or religious intolerance.

In conclusion, it is essential to understand that Japanese Buddhism differs from classical Indian and Theravada Buddhism in that the monastic *sila* is not important in making monastics "fields of merit" for lay people to make karmic merit to gain a favorable rebirth in the six realms from which to gain enlightenment. As we will explore later, Buddhism was incorporated into Japanese culture as a means to deal with the polluting aspects of dealing with the dead and to perpetuate the practice of ancestor veneration and the safe repose of dead spirits through funeral ritual. In this way, the ethical logic and psychological focus on meditation in early Indian Buddhism gave way to the more faith-oriented and mystical practices of East Asian Mahayana Buddhism. Japanese Buddhist thought is similarly "mystical" (e.g., the unspeakable truth of Zen, the mantra of the *Lotus Sutra*, the other power of Amitabha Buddha) with a strong emphasis on the purity of faith. Nakamura Hajime notes that faith for Indians and Chinese is a portal to a more contemplative form of practice focused on a vision of truth, while Japanese Buddhism's great contributions are in the area of faith rather than speculative or practical aspects of religion.[143] This emphasis on faith, Nakamura notes, is also commensurate with the Japanese value of security or the feeling of safety (安心 *anshin*) as found in a small-scale or closed social nexus.[144] "This endeavor for mutual relationship serves to create a sense of unity and sympathy among Japanese", but, he critically notes, "It sometimes leads them to accept blindly the principle of authority at the expense of individuality".[145]

---

142 Heine. "Critical Buddhism and Dogen's *Shobogenzo*". p. 277.
143 Nakamura. *Ways of Thinking of Eastern Peoples*. p. 460.
144 Ibid., p. 488.
145 Ibid., p. 466.

The Legacy of Kamakura Buddhism II: The Effect of the New Spiritual Movement on Socio-Political Structure

While the new Kamakura Buddhist movements offered a kind of liberation theology, older as well as newer forms of esoteric Buddhism continued to serve the state in the Kamakura period. Within the old *ken-mitsu* system, the *Gukan-sho* (*Selected Foolish Opinions* 愚管抄), written in 1219 by the Tendai monk Jien 慈圓 (1155–1225), became a critically important text seeking to legitimize and preserve the Kyoto court amidst the Age of the Final Dharma. Kuroda Toshio notes that the *Gukan-sho* marks the emergence of the *shinkoku* 神国 ideology, a reactionary movement within the *ken-mitsu* system to revive imperial rule based on the idea of Japan "as a land uniquely under the guidance and protection of its gods (*kami*)".[146] However, as a Tendai monk, Jien still emphasized the then-mainstream Buddhist teaching of *mappo*, which posits Japan as being at the edge of the (Buddhist) world centered on the mythic Mt. Sumeru in India. As such, by harmonizing Buddhist teachings with the will of the Japanese gods, imperial rule and greater Japan could be restored and prosper.[147] As we will see later, this *shinkoku* ideology would shift away from Buddhist influences towards a more purely indigenous discourse.

From the other *ken-mitsu* centers of Nara and Mt. Koya, we also see a response to the spiritual crisis of the day in the activities of the Shingon monk Eison 叡尊 (1201–1290) and his disciple Ninsho 忍性 (1217–1303). These two sought to revive the practice of the monastic *vinaya* and the Ritsu school of the Nara period amidst what they perceived was the horrific decline of monastic standards in the warrior-monk phenomenon and the Pure Land exclusive *nenbutsu* movement. Today, these two masters are seen as exemplars in the Socially Engaged Buddhist movement for their work amongst the masses founding charity hospitals to care for invalids and lepers. However, both masters also became close with the new Kamakura military government. Ninsho, in particular, went to Kamakura in 1261 and accepted the patronage of the Hojo regents while providing esoteric prayers for the safeguarding of the nation.[148] As such, he became one

---

146 Stone. "Placing Nichiren in the 'Big Picture'". p. 409.

147 Habito, Ruben L.F. "Tendai *Hongaku* Doctrine and Japan's Ethnocentric Turn". In *Pruning the Bodhi Tree*. pp. 377-79.

148 Matsunaga, Alicia and Daigan. *Foundation of Japanese Buddhism: Vol. II The Mass Movement.* (Los Angeles: Buddhist Books International, 1976), pp.

of the principal targets of Nichiren's attacks on the pernicious effects of esoteric ritual, which he felt had brought ruin to the imperial court in Kyoto and was the cause of decline for the nation in general.[149]

The new Kamakura military government was also not free from the desire to sacralize their rule with esoteric ritual and thaumaturgic rites. In the early days of the era in 1199, Eisai 栄西 (1141–1215)—the nominal founder of the Japanese Rinzai sect—was invited by Hojo Masako—the widow of the founder of the Kamakura *bakufu* Yoritomo—to become the founder of the first Zen temple in the city called Jufuku-ji 寿福寺. Although harassed by the monks of Mt. Hiei after his return from China, Eisai never renounced his Tendai identity and saw his teaching of "esoteric Zen" and emphasis on the monastic *vinaya* as a way to reform Tendai.[150]

As the Hojo regents came to control the Kamakura government, their interest in the high culture of Song dynasty China, epitomized in the erudite Chan (Zen) monk, developed as an alternative form of sacralization to the Tang dynasty Buddhism of esoteric Tiantai (Tendai) that sacralized the *ken-mitsu* system. Tokiyori, the fifth regent, and some of the other regents developed a keen appreciation for Zen practice, inviting actual Chan monks from China to form the first great Rinzai monasteries of Kamakura. Zen, with its emphasis on physical self-discipline and practical rather than intellectual wisdom, certainly appealed to the spirit of the new warrior class. However, few samurai had the intellectual curiosity or capability to study the sophisticated forms of Song era Chan through the medium of Chinese, which was the typical way these imported Chinese masters instructed.[151] In this way, the Kamakura *bakufu* also indulged in the esoteric rites performed by other Buddhist schools as well as Shinto to create a rival form of *zen-mitsu* 禅密 ideology to counter the *ken-mitsu* ideology that sacralized the Kyoto imperial government.[152]

We may also consider this time as the beginning of the fusion of Zen Buddhism and the Japanese Way of the Warrior (武士道 *bushido*), which has received so much attention for its promotion during Japan's militarization in the early 20th century. Nakamura Hajime reflects on this situation by noting that:

281-82.

149 Stone. "Placing Nichiren in the 'Big Picture'". p. 389.

150 Collcutt. *Five Mountains*. p. 36. Bodiford. *Soto Zen in Medieval Japan*. p. 168.

151 Collcutt. *Five Mountains*. pp. 59-61.

152 Stone. "Placing Nichiren in the 'Big Picture'". p. 386.

Japanese society has never firmly established a class comparable to the literati in China or to the caste of Brahmin priests in India. It cannot be said that the socio-economic situation in Japan prevented such a class from emerging. It was rather the Japanese inclination to emphasize the order of human nexus that enabled the soldiers, whose essential function was the use of force, to rise to high positions as the rulers of the society.[153]

This cultural value placed on the defense of one's own clan deeply influenced the development of Buddhism in Japan. Whereas laypeople in other Buddhist societies have engaged in direct violence, the abandonment of the first precept of non-harming among various ordained communities in Japan is a unique characteristic, further illustrating the strong sense of this-worldliness and lack of distinction between the sacred and profane.

These developments highlight the ongoing negotiation of imperial law (*obo*) and Buddhist law or dharma (*buppo*) as the spiritual foundation for Japan. In the *ken-mitsu* system of the Heian period, we saw how the three major Buddhist centers of Mt. Hiei, Mt. Koya, and Nara created allegiances to uphold the fusion of these two laws, with, at times, *buppo* holding the greater value. The early forms of the *hijiri* movement were critical of this fusion, if not explicitly. The later Kamakura *hijiri*, Honen and Shinran, clearly rejected such a fusion in their "exclusive" doctrine of the *senju-nenbutsu* and their establishment of communities without reliance or approval of the authorities. Dogen, though not challenging the system as directly as Honen or Nichiren, did create a new *hijiri* movement by establishing his main temple of Eihei-ji and his own ordination system in the remote mountains of Fukui, from where the Soto school spread Zen amongst the remote, rural regions of the Japan Sea coast. In contrast, Eisai and the Chinese Rinzai masters laid the foundation for a three-hundred-year period of Zen-styled warrior rule over Japan that actively fused Buddhist and imperial law. Eisai not only wrote *Promulgation of Zen for the Protection of the Nation* (興禅護国論 *Kozen gokoku-ron*) but also *Vow to Restore the Buddha-Dharma of Japan* (日本仏法中興願文 *Nihon buppo-chukko gan-mon*), in which he explains, "The *obo* is the lord of the *buppo*, and the *buppo* is the treasure of the *obo*."[154]

---

153 Nakamura. *Ways of Thinking of Eastern Peoples*. p. 493.

154 Kuroda. "The Imperial Law and the Buddhist Law". p. 282.

Nichiren is perhaps the most complex of the Kamakura masters in his relationship to the *obo-buppo* tension. In his early writings, Nichiren saw the emperor as Japan's actual ruler and the Kamakura military government as subordinate, the ruler merely in name or form. While in exile on Sado Island, however, his thinking began to change, and in his final years on Mt. Minobu, he came to the conclusion that the emperor is the ruler of Japan in name only.[155] With a vision of a transcendent "world of the *Lotus Sutra*" (法華經の世界 *Hokke-kyo-no sekai*), all legitimacy of rule was to be judged solely by the standard of whether or not the *Lotus Sutra* was upheld.[156] This investment in the ultimate authority of the *Lotus Sutra* undercut and even inverted "all hierarchies constructed on other bases", including loyalty to husband, parent, or lord.[157] Nichiren saw that Buddhism is not in the service of the ruler but, rather, the ruler is obligated to protect the Buddha Dharma—which recalls the model Ashoka developed during his rule in India. While Nichiren was also known to uphold common forms of social hierarchy as long as they did not interfere with faith in the *Lotus Sutra*,[158] he provides perhaps the clearest and strongest articulation of dharma as an axial force that overrides or transcends the traditional allegiances to family, clan, and, most conspicuously, nation and emperor.

In this way, the new Kamakura movements fostered the creation of new temples and meeting halls separate not only from the *ken-mitsu* ideology but just as importantly the *ken-mitsu* social system based on the oppressive rule of manorial estates (莊園 *shoen*). By embracing these new Kamakura Buddhist sects, the lower orders of society, including warriors, rejected the tradition of thaumaturgic rites for good fortune that had become the dominant form of religious practice and faith, and developed new vibrant forms of village communal activity,[159] specifically in what are known as confraternities (講 *ko*). The confraternities acted as a way to teach and spread the new visions of the Kamakura Buddhist masters and, especially among the Pure Land and *Lotus Sutra* groups, did not depend on or fixate around ordained monastic leaders.

The earliest forms of these groups go back to the time of Prince

---

155 Stone. "Placing Nichiren in the 'Big Picture'". p. 388.

156 Ibid., p. 389.

157 Ibid., pp. 394-95.

158 Ibid., pp. 394-95.

159 Kuroda. "Buddhism and Society in the Medieval Estate System". pp. 304-05. Bodiford. *Soto Zen in Medieval Japan.* pp. 112-13.

Shotoku and also the spread of lay sponsored temples (知識寺 *chishiki-ji*) in the provinces during the Nara period. However, it is not until the Kamakura Buddhist revolution that these groups are provided with an axial ideology that had the intentions and motivation to transcend kinship and local community bonds. Based on such universal and inclusive ideologies, they connected to a national network of such associations that eventually connected to the centers of these major new sects and their monastic leaders.[160] In the countryside, the *nenbutsu-ko* of the Pure Land schools and the new Soto Zen communities based around local warriors would emerge as major social forces along with the rapid rise of Nichiren based groups in Kyoto tied to the merchant class. All represented a clear break with the *ken-mitsu* system and supported religion by self-governing communities from the lower strata of society.[161]

The Rise of Shinto Nationalism and Ideologies at War at the End of the Kamakura Era

While all forms of Kamakura Buddhism to some extent tried to resist popular, local forms of thaumaturgy, the problem became that the more their teachings appealed to high abstract ideals and norms—especially those of monastic Zen—the more easily such popular practices for health and good fortune emerged to fill in the gap.[162] Even amongst the confraternities, there developed tendencies towards the practice introduced by Prince Shotoku of "repaying benefits" (*ho-on*), in the conspicuous form of worshipping their charismatic founders or the general practice of family ancestor worship.[163] By the 14th century, the Buddhist monk, often coming from one of the new Kamakura sects, had become totally incorporated into village life, so much so that we might begin to refer to them as "priests" for their laicized lifestyles that included having their own families and working the land as farmers. Their general literacy and learning made them community leaders, especially cultural ones, who served as windows to outside world. They were also known to take advantage of these local self-governing organizations for proselytization, sometimes converting

---

160 Davis. *Japanese Religion and Society*. pp. 28-34.
161 Kuroda. "Buddhism and Society in the Medieval Estate System". p. 312. Bodiford. *Soto Zen in Medieval Japan*. pp. 112-13.
162 Kuroda. "Buddhism and Society in the Medieval Estate System". pp. 291-92.
163 Kuroda. "Buddhism and Society in the Medieval Estate System". p. 296. Davis. *Japanese Religion and Society*. p. 29.

entire villages to one sect.¹⁶⁴

At the higher ends of society, we see the samurai as an emerging ruling class mimicking the Heian aristocracy in the building of temples exclusively to service their clan, known as *ujidera* 氏寺. These *ujidera* were often built by warriors who sought to repent for their sins, and in some cases, take ordination. However, many never really abandoned home, creating yet another class of practitioner in the complicated world of Japanese Buddhist class divisions. These retired samurai were known by the general term *nyudo* 入道 meaning novice-priest or literally "enterer of the way". They built memorial halls in their family homes that promoted clan prosperity, this-worldly benefits including thaumaturgic deity veneration, and ancestor worship over authentic Buddhist doctrine. These halls became the basis for *ujidera* with its resident priest, often a clan member, who owed allegiance to the clan and its prosperity over that of the local people. These types of temples can still be found in contemporary rural Japan and in many ways were institutionalized in the Tokugawa period with local member temples, called *bodai-ji* 菩提寺. These above patterns were especially conspicuous in the spread of Soto Zen into the rural hinterlands of the Japan Sea coast.¹⁶⁵ Kuroda Toshio summarizes this development as, "The original spirit of New (Kamakura) Buddhism, which emphasized renunciation of the world and the search for truth in austerity, regressed as the movement's dependence on the *shoen* (estate) authorities grew."¹⁶⁶

Another disturbing trend at the center of Japanese society that emerged in response to the Kamakura Buddhist movement was the growing development of the *shinkoku* ideology.¹⁶⁷ As noted earlier, this was a reactionary ideology of the failing *ken-mitsu* and manorial estate (*shoen*) system in the face of the rising power of the samurai.¹⁶⁸ It was reactionary in pointing back to a mythical origin of Japan and the sanctified status of the emperor as a manifestation of the Japanese gods (*kami*) in an attempt to prevent the widespread social change

---

164 Kuroda. "Buddhism and Society in the Medieval Estate System". pp. 293-96.

165 Bodiford. *Soto Zen in Medieval Japan*. pp. 123-26.

166 Kuroda. "Buddhism and Society in the Medieval Estate System". pp. 299-301.

167 Habito. "Tendai *Hongaku* Doctrine and Japan's Ethnocentric Turn". p. 382.

168 Kuroda, Toshio. "The Discourse on the 'Land of the Kami' (*Shinkoku*) in Medieval Japan". Trans. Fabio Rambelli. In *Japanese Journal of Religious Studies*. 1996. Vol. 23, No.3-4. p. 383. Rambelli. "Religion, Ideology of Domination, and Nationalism: Kuroda Toshio on the Discourse of Shinkoku". p. 399.

Japan was experiencing.[169] In this ideology, the *kami* are considered to possess an "ethical" or "spiritual" power (神徳 *shin-toku*) and impart this-worldly benefits and protection upon righteous persons. This was felt to contrast with Buddhism, especially Pure Land Buddhism, which was seen to be overly focused on the next life.[170]

As a reactionary doctrine, the *shinkoku* ideology marks the continued development of the way *kami* had come to be understood since the introduction of Buddhism to Japan. During the Heian period, the concept of "origin and manifestation" (*honji-suijaku*) was developed as a way to harmonize Buddhism and Japanese indigenous beliefs by positing that a local Japanese *kami* is the manifestation (*suijaku*) of the deeper essence (*honji*) of a Mahayana buddha or bodhisattva. This served as a powerful tool for political sacralization, in which the local (as expressed in the *kami*) was connected and subservient to central authority (as expressed in the buddhas) through a national system of temple-shrine complexes (寺社 *ji-sha*) centered around the three great *ken-mitsu* Buddhist centers.[171] The influence of Buddhism is further seen as Shinto becomes more systematized in the late Heian and early Kamakura. The doctrine of *hongaku* becomes fused with the Shinto emphasis on purity (清浄 *shojo*) to re-present purity as not only the fundamental characteristic of the *kami* but also as the essence of innate enlightenment (*hongaku*).[172]

A key text in the development of the *shinkoku* ideology is the *Chronicles of the Authentic Lineages of the Divine Emperors* (神皇正統記 *Jinno shoto-ki*) written by Kitabatake Chikafusa 北畠親房 (1293–1354) in 1339 to support the return of imperial rule under the new Southern Court in Nara, which had overthrown the Kamakura military regime in 1333. As opposed to Jien's *Gukan-sho*, which posits Japan at the periphery of the world in the age of *mappo*, it emphasizes Japan's inherent holy essence as the center of the cosmic universe with India and China on the periphery. This optimistic view of the world and Japan is explained by the eternal, unbroken line of Japanese emperors as the descendants of the great sun goddess, Amaterasu. Chikafusa, who also appears to have been influenced by *hongaku* teachings, writes that Japan is the "land of the *kami*", because "it was created by the heavenly ancestor, and that it will forever be ruled by the descendants

---

169 Rambelli. "Religion, Ideology of Domination, and Nationalism". p. 391.

170 Ibid., p. 416.

171 Kuroda. "The Imperial Law and the Buddhist Law". p. 275.

172 Kuroda. "The Discourse on the 'Land of the Kami' (*Shinkoku*) in Medieval Japan". p. 363.

of the *kami* of the sun".[173]

Whereas the Buddhist norm is the "moral king" (*dharma-raja*) who is human and rules through dharma, the particular character of the emperor is his "breed" (種姓 *shusei*) underscoring his existence as a descendent of the gods[174]—a shift to the "divine king" (*deva-raja*) concept seen in Hindu mythology and certain iterations of Theravada Buddhist kingdoms in Southeast Asia. This text became important later on for contemporary Japanese nationalists in building an ideology of cultural and racial exceptionalism to legitimize the grounds for holy war, much like the Buddhist-based *Mahavamsa* has been used in Sri Lanka.

The development of both the Kamakura Buddhist movement and the *shinkoku* ideology marks perhaps the most intense ideological battle in Japanese history between the universal ethics of Kamakura Buddhism and the clannish ethics of the *shinkoku* ideology—a battle that closely resembles the one in India between the Buddha's civilizational ethics and Vedic Brahmanism's ethics of caste. Kuroda Toshio's biting analysis of the *shinkoku* ideology highlights these parallels in noting that:

> *Shinkoku* thought enabled a systemization and religious justification of the secular order and ethical code. The concept of the *kami* nature was used to explain the virtues of purity and sincerity…and to organize accepted secular morality into a system of ethics. The power to confer ultimate religious status on those ethical practices was attributed to prayer (祈願 *kigan*) and magic ritual (祈祷 *kito*).[175]
>
> The religious precepts, ritual taboos, and secular ethical norms [of the *shinkoku* ideology were] the result of the ambiguous notion of the 'protection' extended by the *kami* to their sacred territory and to the righteous people living there—a notion that implied a principle of domination by the *kami*. Such domination was justified doctrinally through everyday rituals, which had to be properly performed in order not to jeopardize the cosmological order of the kingdom. Thus, the *shinkoku* discourse attempted to ground the feudal power system in the 'invisible realm' from which the *kami* rule their lands, giving

---

173 Ibid., p. 373.
174 Ibid., p. 375.
175 Ibid., p. 375.

everyone responsibility in maintaining the sacred order of the medieval state.[176]

In the *shinkoku* doctrines are always present incomprehensible facts and insoluble contradictions.... The *shinkoku* discourse was a form of blind mysticism without foundation; its poor conceptual strength cannot be compared with the rigorous logic of the *ikko-senju* doctrines [of the new Kamakura Buddhist sects].[177]

In looking at the Kamakura Buddhist movement, Kuroda felt that the Rinzai sect and the early thought of Nichiren were explicitly influenced by early forms of the *shinkoku* ideology in claiming to represent new and more powerful systems for the protection of the state. However, Honen's *senju nenbutsu* was different in totally rejecting it, the concepts in *honji-suijaku*, and the related systems of domination, thus allowing the Pure Land movement to form a voice for peasant rebellions articulating a different model of power.[178] Nichiren too, in his later thought, is seen to thoroughly reject the *honji-suijaku* concepts and deem the *kami* significant only insofar as they protect the "world of the *Lotus Sutra*." While he accepted the *mappo*-influenced view of Japan being situated on the edge of a horizontal Buddhist cosmos, he also developed his own vertical Buddhist cosmos at the top of which stands Shakyamuni Buddha, the principal buddha of the *Lotus Sutra*. From this standpoint, he concluded that, "The ruler of Japan is not even equal to a vassal of the wheel-turning monarchs of the four continents. He is just an island chief."[179]

Nichiren's socio-cosmological thought is complicated, however. While raising the Buddha and his dharma above the emperor and the *kami*, his identification of Japan as the birthplace of a new Buddhism where the *Lotus Sutra* and Mahayana Buddhism would reach their apex provided the grounds for Buddhist nationalism and Japanese exceptionalism during the Pacific War period and the aggressive conversion strategies outside of Japan by some Nichiren-based groups since then.[180] Further, the employment of his teachings of non-cooperation with other sects (不受布施 *fuju-fu-se* "to neither receive, nor offer") and *shaku-buku* as conversion by any means necessary—as

---

176 Rambelli. "Religion, Ideology of Domination, and Nationalism". p. 419.
177 Ibid., p. 420.
178 Ibid., p. 405.
179 Stone. "Placing Nichiren in the 'Big Picture'". p. 411.
180 Ibid., p. 417.

found in his most famous writing the *Establishing the Right Teaching and Bringing Peace to the Country* (立正安国論 *Rissho Ankoku-ron*)—led to government oppression of certain sub-sects in the Tokugawa period and the denigration of the largest modern sect derived from Nichiren teachings, Soka Gakkai, in the postwar period.[181]

The Kamakura Buddhist movements would continue to develop as part of the wider overturning of class and power hierarchies during the even more unstable Muromachi and Warring States periods—much like the spiritual revolutions and political strife of the time of the Buddha. As we will now see, the ideological and political battles continued to build with the emergence of theological fiefdoms created by the True Pure Land sect of Shinran through the mobilization of their peasant base in revolts called *ikko-ikki*. Meanwhile, Chikafusa's ideas were utilized by the new Muromachi military government, and *shinkoku* became firmly established as the reactionary ideology of feudal domination against the decaying *ken-mitsu* ideology of the fusion of *obo-buppo* and the rise of rebellious communities built around the Kamakura Buddhist movements. From this point onward, the *shinkoku* ideology becomes an important basis in the legitimization of the Japanese nation-state against the foreign threat of the West and Christianity in the early colonial era and, eventually, in the Meiji Restoration of 1868 and Japan's imperialist wars.[182]

---

181 Stone, Jacqueline I. "Rebuking the Enemies of the *Lotus*: Nichirenist Exclusivism in Historical Perspective". In *Japanese Journal of Religious Studies*. 1994. Vol. 21, No.2-3. pp. 231-59.

182 Kuroda. "The Discourse on the 'Land of the Kami' (*Shinkoku*) in Medieval Japan". pp. 382-83.

4

Religio-Ideological Conflict and the Rising of the Masses in the Muromachi Period (1333–1558)

The Muromachi period, roughly defined as lasting from 1333–1558, is a complex time of multiple shifts through: the brief restoration of imperial rule in the Northern and Southern Court period; the century-long domination of the Ashikaga military government into the late 15th century; the roughly century-long Warring States period; and the final succession of the great warlords Nobunaga, Hideyoshi, and Tokugawa Ieyasu—the last of whom finally consolidated Japan under a single rule for the next two and a half centuries. As noted, the late Heian and Kamakura periods marked the rise of the samurai class to rival the power of the aristocratic clans based in Nara and Kyoto. In the Muromachi, this rise was confirmed and consolidated with the increasing emergence of regional lords called *daimyo* with their own military forces. While the three main centers of *ken-mitsu* Buddhism still maintained military forces and connections to political elites until the end of the 16th century, their *ken-mitsu* rhetoric based around the fusion of *obo-buppo* waned in importance as the new *zen-mitsu* ideology based in the Kamakura-Kyoto Five Mountains (五山 *gozan*) system of Rinzai temples became central under samurai rule.

Further, advances in agricultural technology increased the standard of living during this time and stimulated production and trade, giving rise in importance to the merchant class. The improvement in the lives of the common people along with the affirmation of their spiritual and social agency by the Kamakura Buddhist movement led, in the words of Tamura Yoshiro, "to the rise of a popular, life-affirming culture with humanistic values" that seemed to sow the seeds for revolt from below,[183] referred to as "the lower overturning those above" (下克上 *ge-koku-jo*).[184] In this way, Kuroda Toshio marks the

---

183 Tamura, Yoshiro. *Japanese Buddhism: A Cultural History.* (Tokyo: Kosei Publishing, 2000), p.113.

184 Adolphson. *The Teeth and Claws of the Buddha.* pp. 52, 65.

rise in the 15th century of peasant rebellions based on the new Jodo Shin and Nichiren sects, known as *shukyo-ikki* 宗教一揆, as the final end of the *ken-mitsu* system.[185]

The Shadow Side of the Single Practice Buddhist Revolution

The immanentalism that affirmed the agency of the common people predictably had its shadow side. It tended to re-affirm the this-worldly, secular tendencies of Japanese culture that erode the universal ethics used to transcend clannish interests. This is perhaps most clearly seen in the rapid rise of the Jodo Shin sect among the agricultural classes in this period. One of the core theological problems for Shin is that in abandoning almost all the traditional practices of Buddhism, including the ordained and lay precepts of daily life, Jodo Shin quickly became prone to adopting more traditional or indigenous forms of Japanese secular life and morality. Kakunyo 覺如 (1270–1351)—Shinran's great-grandson and the first principal leader of the Jodo Shin sect—explained in *Correcting False Faith* (改邪抄 *Kaija-sho*) that since the five base precepts of all Buddhists (Skt. *panca-sila* 五戒 *go-kai*) of neither killing, stealing, lying, engaging in harmful sexual relations, or taking intoxicants were equal to the more common Japanese morals of benevolence, righteousness, courtesy, wisdom, and faith, Shin followers should simply cultivate the latter.[186] His oldest son, and the next head of the sect, Zonkaku 存覺 (1290–1373), became a central figure in developing the sect's theology. In a similarly themed treatise called *On Refuting Heresy and Clarifying Truth* (破邪顯正抄 *Haja kensho-sho*), he reasserted the ideas of *honji-suijaku* in promoting the worship of clan deities as manifestations of the buddhas and the fusion of *obo* and *buppo*. He even explicitly connected this fusion with support for local authorities:

> The *buppo* and the *obo* are a single law with two aspects, like the two wings of a bird or the two wheels of a cart.... All the more so with practitioners of the exclusive *nenbutsu*, who, wherever they may live, when they drink even a single drop or receive even a single meal, believe that in general it is thanks to the favor of the nobles [of

---

185 Kuroda. "The Development of the *Kenmitsu* System as Japan's Medieval Orthodoxy". p. 235.

186 Tamura. *Japanese Buddhism: A Cultural History*. pp. 122-23.

the capital] and the warrior leaders [of the Kanto], and know that specifically it is due to the kindness of their local lords and estate stewards.[187]

The other complication of rejecting monastic celibacy was that the Shin sect from the very beginning fell into power struggles from the tendency of succession to go through familial and blood ties. This eventually created a clannish system of governance and the worship of Shin head priests as clan deities in spite of Shinran's admonishment that "I, Shinran, have no disciples to be called mine."[188] These sectarian tendencies are also found in the other Kamakura Buddhist sects: in the Nichiren sect, which quickly factionalized around the six appointed successors of Nichiren, and in the Soto Zen sect with its complicated system of revolving abbots.[189] The factionalization in Soto Zen led to the hoarding of sacred texts and the development of secret initiation documents (*kirigami*) to enhance the prestige of a particular temple or faction. By the late medieval period, even the teachings of Dogen himself and his seminal *Shobogen-zo* became only accessible to senior monks.[190]

These trends mirror the aforementioned shift in Tendai in the late Heian from doctrinal study to meditative practice and from written texts to oral transmission of teachings (*kuden*) through an intimate relationship with a single master. Nakamura Hajime, in explaining this point, notes, "It is not the difference in the religious faith or doctrine but merely such specific factors of human relationship as the inheritance of the master's 'endowments' that account for the split of the religious school into multitudinous sects and factions."[191]

This was, and remains today, one of the shadow aspects of the emphasis on the single practice of the Kamakura Buddhist movements. In simplifying Buddhist thought and practice for the benefit of the common person, some of the integrated richness of the tradition was lost along with a greater tendency towards sectarianism or factionalism—a common trait in the clannish mentality of Japanese culture. Buddhism in general is united around the Three Trainings that integrate ethics/virtue (*sila*), meditation (*samadhi*), and learning/wisdom (*prajna*), and in the wider East Asian Mahayana world, the Zen, Pure

---

187 Kuroda. "The Imperial Law and the Buddhist Law". p. 283.
188 Nakamura. *Ways of Thinking of Eastern Peoples*. p. 482.
189 Bodiford. *Soto Zen in Medieval Japan*. p. 128.
190 Ibid., p. 134.
191 Nakamura. *Ways of Thinking of Eastern Peoples*. p. 484.

Land, and *Lotus Sutra* teachings are studied and practiced together. However, Japanese Buddhism eventually carved the Mahayana teachings and practices into mutually exclusive traditions. While the Zen practitioner is assiduously perfecting their practice of *samadhi*, the Pure Land practitioner has completed rejected meditation, while the Nichiren follower cannot shift their gaze beyond the *Lotus Sutra*.

As we have also noted, there is the tendency to fill in the more sparse architecture of the single practice theologies with indigenous or non-Buddhist forms of thought that do not fit or run contrary to them, such as: the replacement of the Buddhist precepts, both lay and monastic, with Confucian and military forms of obedience to authority; the replacement of rigorous Buddhist logic with forms of mystical faith; and the replacement of meditation with the chanting of mantric like spiritual formulae and ritual minutiae. The essential point here is not to condemn the Japanese as somehow more confused and heterodox than other Buddhist cultures, who also have their own unskillful syncretic styles. Rather, it is to clarify these syncretic styles so that we can continue to make sense of historical trends and understand the potentials and pitfalls of Japanese Buddhism as a source of axialization and the development of a civilizational ethic for contemporary Japan.

Ideological Struggle based on a Greater Spiritual Vision: The Shin State and the *Lotus Sutra*

In the Introduction, we noted that in axialized civilizations, universal ideologies created loyalties and communities that superseded or transcended national and ethnic ones; for example, the role of Buddhism as "dharma" under Ashoka and its spread into Central Asia during its first 500 years, or the role of the Christian Church in medieval Europe, as well as its fall to the secular ideologies of human rights, democracy, and socialism. In this vein, Nakamura Hajime makes a critical point about Japanese culture in that:

> We find only a few cases in which sacrifices of life were made by the Japanese for the sake of something universal, something that transcends a particular human nexus, such as academic truth or the arts. And if we exclude the persecutions of the True Pure Land [Jodo Shin] sect, the Hokke [Nichiren] sect, and Christianity, cases of dying for religious faith are exceptional phenomena. Sacrifice

of all for the sake of truth, when it went contrary to the intentions of the ruler, was even regarded as evil.¹⁹²

He further explains that the Japanese emphasis on a limited social nexus and intuitive rather than logical thinking makes them less critical and hence less confrontational. This translates to a type of social change in which the form is altered but not the internal logic, and thus we notice the lack of ideologically-driven revolutions based on universal forms of thought in Japanese history.¹⁹³

The possible exceptions to this point that Nakamura highlights are all movements that occurred during the Muromachi period: the peasant rebellions of the Jodo Shin sect; the rise of merchant class together with the Nichiren sect; and the brief flowering of Christianity in southern Japan.

The first and most prominent of these movements in terms of an actual social revolution was the peasant rebellion movement of the Jodo Shin sect called *ikko-ikki*. In many ways, it was the logical conclusion to the revolutionary theology of Honen established in the late Heian and based around not only the total rejection of previous Buddhist norms but, as importantly, the *ken-mitsu* social system that had laid claim to those norms. As we have noted, Jodo Shin made great inroads among the common people, because it was propagated not from above by a clerical elite but by lay believers, and had an organizational structure that resembled those of the self-governing peasant communities. However, as also noted, Shin eventually established a cult of veneration of clerical leaders based on the blood lineage of Shinran.

This reaches its culmination in the figure of Rennyo 蓮如 (1415-99), who became the eighth patriarch of the Jodo Shin sect in 1458. Shortly afterwards in 1465, the still active militarized personnel of the Tendai center on Mt. Hiei stormed Kyoto and destroyed the increasingly powerful Shin base at the Higashiyama Hongan-ji Temple. This pushed Rennyo to move up the coast of the Japan Sea to an area called Yoshizaki in present-day Ishikawa, where a small city of Jodo Shin followers had been established. This is where the beginnings of the *ikko-ikki* movement emerged. In 1488, they led a peasant rebellion in nearby Kaga overthrowing the local lord and taking control of this region for the next hundred years.¹⁹⁴

---

192 Ibid., p. 414.
193 Ibid., p. 401.
194 Tamura. *Japanese Buddhism: A Cultural History.* p.124.

Under the leadership of Rennyo, this era was marked by the collapse of the Ashikaga military government and the spread of peasant rebellions against the *daimyo* and samurai who had been exploiting them and their lands. Their singular faith in Amida emboldened them to reject the esoteric sanctification of power that the *ken-mitsu* and *zen-mitsu* ideologies had built through thaumaturgy, especially the local Shinto gods that the *daimyo* and samurai used as protector deities.[195] Numerous Soto Zen temples also met their fate at the hands of these rebellions.[196]

As these rebellions spread and gained momentum, Rennyo found himself in a difficult situation of trying to balance relations with the still formidable military establishment. Amongst these Shin communities, he tried to re-emphasize the Buddhist precepts and the prohibition against violence in general. He also re-affirmed the teaching of *honji-suijaku*, teaching that the *kami* were manifestations of the true body of Amitabha Buddha and that the imperial law (*obo*) and the Buddha dharma (*buppo*) were one. In his frequent and popular encyclicals, he once wrote, "One should outwardly place emphasis upon the *obo* but cultivate the *buppo* deeply in one's heart".[197]

Yet the general rejection by the devout lay Shin communities of local military power and their ideologies led to a huge expansion of Shin at this time across Japan from Tohoku in the north to Kyushu in the South. This included the mass conversions of peasants connected to another Pure Land school called the Ji sect 時宗, which had become allied with military officials because of their founder Ippen's family background as samurai. Such developments as these only further inflamed resentment towards the immense new power of the once heterodox Pure Land movement. By 1559, Kennyo 顯如, the eleventh Shin patriarch, had gained the full recognition of the imperial house, and the Jodo Shin sect began making its own formal alliances with warlords, becoming a major political and military force on par with the old established temples of the *ken-mitsu* system.[198]

Paralleling the rise of the Shin sect, the Nichiren sect came to prominence in Kyoto among the newly emerging merchant class under Nichizo 日像 (1269–1342), the disciple of Nichiro 日朗 (1245–1320), one of Nichiren's six appointed successors. With continual growth and the establishment of sub-lineages in the capital, Nichiren

---

195 Matsunaga. *Foundation of Japanese Buddhism: Vol. II.* p. 119.
196 Bodiford. *Soto Zen in Medieval Japan.* p. 110.
197 Kuroda. "The Imperial Law and the Buddhist Law". p. 283.
198 Matsunaga. *Foundation of Japanese Buddhism: Vol. II.* pp. 120-23.

followers became the target of the dreaded *sohei* on Mt. Hiei. As such, they became increasingly embroiled in politics, and by the 1390s, the Kenpon Hokke sub-sect 顕本法華宗 began issuing official "rebukes" known as *kokka-kangyo* 国家諫暁 of the Ashikaga military government in the style of Nichiren during his days in Kamakura.[199] By 1460, twenty-one different sub-sects had created a form of de-facto rule over Kyoto. Further drawing on the militant precedents set by Nichiren, such as the use of armed guards to protect himself against assassins, Nichiren-based merchants in Kyoto developed merchant militias (法華一揆 *hokke-ikki*) to defend themselves against attacks by both the *sohei* and the *ikko-ikki* as it spread into the capital.[200] Eventually, many of the 21 Kyoto based temples were built up as armed fortresses to serve as headquarters for *daimyo*. The first important *hokke-ikki* was a campaign in alliance with *daimyo* and forces from Mt. Hiei against the presence of the Jodo Shin in Kyoto. They led 30-40,000 troops against the Yamashina Hongan-ji in 1532, completely destroying it. However, in 1536 the Mt. Hiei forces turned against them and burned southern Kyoto where the merchant classes lived, expelling the 21 Nichiren sects from Kyoto, of which only fifteen had returned by 1545.[201]

The third ideological force of this period was Christianity, introduced to Japan by the Jesuit Francis Xavier in 1549. Within forty years, it is estimated that two percent of Japan (roughly 150,000 people) had become Christian with many *daimyo* converting in hopes of gaining favor with the increasing number of Western traders. Like Jodo Shin, its teachings connected with lives of the peasant classes and their struggles against the *ken-mitsu* and *zen-mitsu* systems. Like the Nichiren sects, they held a strident and singular obedience to an authority that transcended traditional Japanese loyalties to lord, clan, nation, and emperor. As formidable competitors, the new foreign missionaries, unsurprisingly, found the Nichiren groups the most to their disliking.[202] The Christian movement also found an ally in the

---

199 Stone, Jacqueline I. "When Disobedience Is Filial and Resistance Is Loyal: The *Lotus Sutra* and Social Obligations in the Medieval Nichiren Tradition". In *A Buddhist Kaleidoscope: Essays on the* Lotus Sutra. Ed. Gene Reeves. (Tokyo, Kosei Publishing Co., 2002), p. 277.

200 Tamura. *Japanese Buddhism: A Cultural History.* pp. 125-26.

201 Matsunaga. *Foundation of Japanese Buddhism: Vol. II.* p. 178.

202 Tamura. *Japanese Buddhism: A Cultural History.* p.141. In this way, one wonders that the very low percentage in modern Japan of Christians, especially evangelicals, as in South Korea, may be due to the incredible popularity of lay-based Nichiren movements.

rising figure of the great warlord Oda Nobunaga (1534–82) who saw it as a way to overcome to persistent menace of the various militarized Buddhist sects and their communities.

Nobunaga, however, was no Christian. Perhaps, most closely aligned with Confucian sentiments, he felt no fear or awe of the *kami* and buddhas, developing his own personal cult of divinity and proclaiming himself the ruler of the world.[203] This fearlessness was manifested in his total destruction of the sacred precincts of the Enryaku-ji Temple and Mt. Hiei in 1571, followed by the submission of the other *ken-mitsu* powers of Mt. Koya and Kofuku-ji at Nara. The Shin movement proved to be the most difficult of campaigns, with a number of failed attacks beginning in 1576 on their new center in Sakai, modern-day Osaka. A blockade finally brought the Shin fortress to its knees in 1580 and the end of the *ikko-ikki* movement.[204] Nobunaga would not be able to realize his own vision as a divine ruler (*deva-raja*), taking his own life through *seppuku* after being surrounded in an assassination plot. However, his successors, the powerful warlords Hideyoshi Toyotomi (1536–98) and Tokugawa Ieyasu (1543–1616), would finish the work of tearing down the *ken-mitsu*, *zen-mitsu*, and *ikki* systems and ushering in a period of peaceful and severely regulated state Buddhism.[205]

The lasting and ongoing question, then, is what is the legacy of the Kamakura Buddhist movement? Was it a true axial one that empowered the common people of Japan to find not only spiritual liberation in this life and the next but also a socio-political liberation in the throwing off of clannish forms of sacralized power and injustice? Or was it merely a flash of insight that quickly became overwhelmed by the deeper cultural systems of esoteric rites for this-worldly benefit (a.k.a. thaumaturgy), veneration of ancestors and other forms of hierarchized authority, and clannish ethics that honor the defense, usually in violent ways, of limited forms of community? From the vantage point of the Meiji Restoration and the descent into Japanese imperialism and world war, the answer seems surely the latter. Kuroda Toshio notes that from this point onward, *buppo* became always subordinate to *obo* in Japanese society:

> What is common to the Buddhist stance in both periods [the subsequent Tokugawa and Meiji periods] was nei-

---

203 Ibid., p. 120.
204 Matsunaga. *Foundation of Japanese Buddhism: Vol. II.* pp. 122-23.
205 Tamura. *Japanese Buddhism: A Cultural History.* pp. 128-29.

ther outright defeat nor spiritual autonomy, but, in fact, Buddhism's surrender, a submission to a relationship of mutual dependence in which Buddhism held the subordinate position.... I believe we must acknowledge how oppressive this matter has been in the history of Japanese Buddhism—a central problem from which there has been no liberation.[206]

Japanese Buddhism's recent embrace of various forms of Socially Engaged Buddhism, however, may offer a dissenting opinion and the hope that the legacy of the Kamakura Buddhist revolution still offers a roadmap for social change based on egalitarian ethics that encourage tolerance and non-violent conflict resolution. In the spirit of Dogen, the understanding that language, conceptual thought, and ideologies can be vehicles for the constant creation of buddha enlightenment gives us hope that such a movement is possible.

---

206 Kuroda. "The Imperial Law and the Buddhist Law". p. 284.

5

The Brahmanistic and Confucian Turns of Buddhism in the Tokugawa Era (1603–1868)

As noted by Kuroda Toshio, the Tokugawa era begins an extended period of the marginalization of Buddhism in Japanese society, which we could say has continued up to the present day. With Nobunaga's military, political, and ultimately spiritual conquest of the *ken-mitsu* and *zen-mitsu* systems of previous establishments as well as the Shin- and Nichiren-based social movements of the masses, Buddhism was no longer sought out as an important source for sacralizing authority and political power in Japan. Countervailing cultural movements had already begun in the Muromachi period, which Yoshiro Tamura characterized as a "triumph of the secular" in which "a life-affirming culture"—as opposed to the Kamakura era ethos of *mappo*—"with humanistic values" was popularized among the common people. This "secular" culture is seen in the shedding of overt Buddhist colorings to popular art and culture, and the increase in Confucian and Shinto ideological themes, such as "harmony" and "sincerity", as found in Kitabatake's *Chronicles of the Authentic Lineages of the Divine Emperors*.[207]

In certain ways, this historical shift mirrors a similar 200-year period following the death of Shakyamuni Buddha and before the rise of Ashoka's "conquest by dharma" (*dharma-vijaya*). During that time, the Machiavellian text, the *Arthasastra* ("the science of material gain") became the dominant state ideology that served the consolidation of power under the Mauryan dynasty after a period of ruthless warfare—paralleling the anarchy of the Warring States period leading to consolidation under the Tokugawa. Recalling the prominent role of the *ikki* movements, the rise of Christianity, and the flowering of Zen culture as part of the Song Chinese cultural movement, it might actually be a stretch to call the Muromachi period a "triumph of the secular". In fact, with the eventual suppression and destruction of all the above religious-backed political forces by the end of the 16th century,

---

207 Tamura. *Japanese Buddhism: A Cultural History*. pp. 113-26.

we could more truly characterize the Tokugawa Era as the triumph of the secular.

The Reigning in of Buddhist Power

The Tokugawa's first step to reign in the still formidable loyalties of the various Buddhist centers was the ending of various special privileges they had accrued over the centuries, especially through the seizing of vast tracts of land over which they had ruled. Such work was most conspicuous in the Tokugawa's division of the now massive Jodo Shin sect in 1602 into two separate sects: the West or Hongan-ji order 本願寺派 and the East or Otani order 大谷派. This not only diluted their power but engendered further factional rivalries throughout Japan amongst its followers. At the same time, the Jodo sect—which had not enjoyed the Shin sect's popularity amongst the masses due to its affiliations to Muromachi period aristocrats and samurai—seized on these old alliances and became the family temple of the Tokugawa, experiencing lasting power and privilege during this era.[208] In general, however, the Tokugawa created a multiple head temple system with branch temples for all Buddhist sects, as a way to dilute and control their power. Doctrinal study was also strongly emphasized to turn the focus of the priests inward towards sectarian minutiae and away from social and political engagement. Most of these new regulations were issued in the first years of the Tokugawa regime under Ieyasu himself between 1601–15, with total uniformity applied to all sects by 1665.[209]

These regulations were not only used to reign in the power of the massive Buddhist orders but also to quell the rise of Christianity and the influence of the West during this time. In 1613, Ieyasu issued the Order to Expel Christian Priests (伴天連追放令 *Ba-te-ren Tsui-ho-rei*).[210] This was followed by the execution of 120 missionaries and converts in 1622, and the final comprehensive ban on Christianity in 1638. Three years earlier in 1635, the Tokugawa government issued the *Closed Country Edict* prohibiting Japanese from leaving the country and preventing foreigners from entering, thus ushering in more than two hundred years of cultural isolation during the height of Asia's encounter with colonial Europe.

---

208 Matsunaga. *Foundation of Japanese Buddhism: Vol. II.* pp. 84, 125.
209 Kasahara. *A History of Japanese Religion.* p. 337.
210 Tamamuro, Fumio. "Local Society and the Temple-Parishioner Relationship within the Bakufu's Governance Structure". In *Japanese Journal of Religious Studies.* 2001. Vol. 28, No. 3-4. p. 266.

The year 1638 is a critical watershed, less for the banning of Christianity and more for the enforced system of temple registration that made every Japanese register at a local Buddhist temple. This system, called the *tera-uke seido* 寺請制度 or *danka seido* 檀家制度, enabled the Tokugawa to restrict movement throughout the country by making residence change almost impossible and to police citizens through using temples and monks as government officials. The *tera-uke seido* was made into a nationwide system through an explosion in the construction of Buddhist temples, estimated at some 13,000 in the Kamakura period to some 470,000 in the Tokugawa.[211] The system not only helped to weed out Christians by forcing them to pledge allegiance to a local Buddhist temple but also helped stamp out the remaining Buddhist sects that refused to submit to controls over their doctrine and institutional set-up, such us underground Pure Land groups, and the Fuju-fu-se 不受不施派 and Hiden 悲田派 sub-sects of the Nichiren movement.[212]

Through these developments, the role and attitude of the Buddhist priest shifted greatly during the Tokugawa period. From the earliest days of the *hijiri* phenomena in the Nara and Heian periods through the grassroots spiritual revolution of the Kamakura and political revolution of the Muromachi, many Buddhist priests had come to support the people in life and death, living among them and leading them. In the Tokugawa, the other historical thread of monks acting as heads of feudal domains that oppressed the common citizen, as seen in the *ken-mitsu* and *zen-mitsu* systems, was updated to the confines of the Tokugawa military state. Buddhist sects and temples became fused to their pre-existing class alliances (e.g. Zen for the samurai, Pure Land for the farmers, Nichiren for the merchants, Tendai and Shingon for the aristocracy) in the institutionalization of a rigid class society based on Confucian teachings called the *shi-no-ko-sho* 士農工商.[213] This feudalization of Buddhism and the monastic Sangha has also been noted in other countries, such as Sri Lanka during the latter

---

211 Kitagawa, Joseph M. *On Understanding Japanese Religion*. (Princeton, NJ: Princeton University Press, 1987), p. 164.

212 Kasahara. *A History of Japanese Religion*. p. 334. Tamamuro. "Local Society and the Temple-Parishioner Relationship within the Bakufu's Governance Structure". p. 265.

213 Kasahara. *A History of Japanese Religion*. p. 334. The *shi-no-ko-sho* 士農工商 refers to samurai (士 *shi*), farmers (農 *no*), artisans (工 *ko*), and merchants (商 *sho*). Tokugawa society was actually more diverse, with an aristocracy that was nominally at the top of the system, an outcaste class engaged in "polluting" professions, and a sizeable clergy class of both Buddhist and Shinto priests.

part of the Anuradhapura period (377 BCE–1017) in which monks were given ranks with stipends and landholdings in return for their work for the state.[214]

The Birth of Funeral Buddhism and the New State Theology

In tandem with these institutional changes, a critical shift in the culture of Japanese Buddhism took place in the Tokugawa era, away from the liberation theologies of the Kamakura to a systemization of ancestor veneration as state ideology that sacralized the new institutionalized class system and top-down authority of the Tokugawa. As noted at the very beginning of this historical survey, the early Japanese adapted various Chinese Buddhist concepts around the veneration of elders and ancestors to their own forms of clan worship—such as the teaching of repaying benefits to parents, all sentient beings, rulers, and the Three Treasures (*shi-on*). In tandem with the growth of the Kamakura Buddhist movements, all Buddhist sects began to develop funerary rituals for common citizens during the Kamakura-Muromachi periods through a combination of local, indigenous traditions and Buddhist ideas and practices.[215] Still, until the 16th century, temple priests had little to do with graves and funerals for common people. These were more usually handled by a specific kind of *hijiri* called *kanjin hijiri*, for the "pledge books" (勧進 *kanjin*) they carried with them to record their activities.

During the Tokugawa period, temple priests took over this role as a means of income and expanded the system greatly by the middle of the period.[216] This expansion included taking the Chinese practice of holding memorial services for the dead on the 49th day, 100th day, first anniversary, and third anniversary and extending it to the seventh, thirteenth, seventeenth, twenty-fifth, thirty-third, and fiftieth anniversaries[217]—a system that is still observed today and keeps Buddhist priests and their families economically viable. This system was codified in the new *tera-uke* regulations for sects and their parishioners as found in the following typical regulations:

---

214 Watts. "The 'Positive Disintegration' of Buddhism". p. 109.

215 Nara, Yasuaki. "The Soto Zen School in Modern Japan". https://www.thezensite.com/ZenEssays/DogenStudies/Soto_Zen_in_Japan.html

216 Kasahara. *A History of Japanese Religion*. p. 335.

217 Nakamura. *Ways of Thinking of Eastern Peoples*. p. 425.

A parishioner (*danka*), even the head parishioner, who fails to attend services for the death anniversary of the sect's founder, for the death anniversary of the Buddha, for Obon, during equinoctial week, or for the death anniversary of his ancestors, will have his name removed from the registry; the office for religious affairs will be notified; and the *danka* shall certainly be investigated.[218]

A heterodox sect is one in which people do not receive the teachings of the family temple, do not give money for the priests and central projects of the temple, or do not accept and give money to people of other religions. People ought to give money to the world in order to gain the blessing of heaven, and to priests in order to gain the blessing of the Buddha. This is the true Dharma; therefore, [these parishioners] should be investigated.[219]

The Zen sects in particular were important for developing the foundations of this system and what is now referred to in a pejorative way as Funeral Buddhism (*Soshiki Bukkyo*). In their wholesale importation of Song era Chan, the Japanese Zen sects performed funerals for their monastics based on Song monastic regulations that involved the recitation of the monastic precepts as a way to link the power of the *vinaya* with future salvation after death. The Chinese always kept a clear distinction between funerals for monastics and for lay with the latter always being referred to by their secular name even if they had taken lay ordination. However, as the Japanese from the period of Saicho rejected the core Dharmagupta *vinaya* (*shibun-ritsu*) in favor of the *Brahma Net Sutra* bodhisattva precepts (*endon-kai*), the division between ordained and lay had always been nebulous. The strong influence of Tendai on the development of early Rinzai Zen further eroded any insistence on the traditional *vinaya* by the numerous Chinese masters who came to Japan. As such, Hojo Tokimune, who built the great Rinzai temple Engaku-ji in Kamakura, received ordination on his death bed in 1284 by Chinese master Wuxue Zuyuan (無学祖元 Mugaku Sogen) and subsequently received a full monastic Zen funeral. This created a precedent so that by the 14th century some regional lords who had received lay ordination before

---

218 Tamamuro. "Local Society and the Temple-Parishioner Relationship within the Bakufu's Governance Structure". p. 266.

219 Ibid., p. 268.

death were given monastic funerals.[220]

These trends were further developed by the Soto Zen sect as it sought to spread amongst the masses, especially under the impetus of the disciples of Gasan 峨山 (1276–1366), the abbot of Soji-ji 総持寺 on the Noto peninsula and the major center of Soto Zen in the medieval period.[221] Faced with the challenges of adopting the stricter and more monastic style of Dogen's vision of liberation through seated meditation to the common people as the Pure Land and Nichiren sects had successfully done with their single invocation mantras, the Soto sect began to develop more popularized forms of worship, principally based on lay ordination and funeral services. Dogen, in his rejection of the political powers of the day, established his own eclectic ordination system at Eihei-ji in which he also rejected the Dharmagupta *vinaya* while relying on the bodhisattva precepts and traditional Chan/Zen monastic codes.[222] He also performed lay ordination, which his successors further developed to strengthen the bonds between temples, their patrons, and the general lay community.

By the 15th century, Soto Zen was conducting mass ordinations to introduce Zen teachings, promote new temples, and popularize funerals for lay people, including the ordination of the dead. Whereas the Pure Land schools had the *nenbutsu* and the Nichiren schools had the *daimoku* to link the common person with the spiritual power of the dharma, Soto Zen used lay ordination. This ritual connected lay people to the spiritual power of the ascetic, meditating Zen monk and further to the Buddha himself, whose enlightened mind the Zen tradition had preserved through its ancient monastic lineage.[223] In the end, however, ordination became more of establishing a "karmic link" (結縁 *kechi-en*) to Buddhism rather than a way for people to commit themselves to the non-violent (*ahimsa*) ethics that form the foundation of all the precepts. In this way, people could become devout Buddhists and take lay ordination but remain as warriors and not follow the precepts[224]—a situation that is not uncommon in any Buddhist nation in the world.

This development then fed into the practice of full ordination at death for lay people to receive a monastic-style Zen funeral, further enhancing their karmic link with the Buddha and posthumous

---

220 Bodiford. *Soto Zen in Medieval Japan.* pp. 185-94.

221 Ibid., p. 108.

222 Ibid., p. 170.

223 Ibid., p. 182.

224 Ibid., p. 184.

salvation. While the barrier between monastic and lay had already been broken down, the barrier between the conscious and intentional taking of the precepts by the living (a fundamental condition in the *Brahma Net Sutra*) and the static, unconscious reception of the precepts by the dead needed to be surmounted. Here, the third major part of Soto popularization, the ritualized use of *koan*, played an important role in offering mystical rationalizations for these practices, such as the "noble silence" of the dead as the intention to ordain.[225]

The "logic" of this fusion of ancestor worship and Buddhism, which still exists as the mainstream practice of Japanese Buddhists today, works as follows: When a family member dies, a series of Buddhist funeral ceremonies including a wake service (通夜 *tsuya*) are held. During these, the deceased is traditionally given tonsure with the shaving of their head and being dressed in Buddhist pilgrim robes for the journey onward, though this practice is increasingly skipped today. They are also given an ordination name (戒名 *kaimyo*), which in the Tokugawa period became connected with class as well as outcaste, the length and complexity becoming in the modern era open to price ranking and a major source of temple profit. Like the Catholic Church's practice of indulgence, the ordination name and the complete set of funerary rites with connected memorial dates spanning over fifty years guarantees the so-called "attainment of Buddhahood" (成仏 *jobutsu*) of the deceased and their enshrinement as a "buddha" (仏 *hotoke*). Examining the way a typical Japanese Buddhist would use and understand these terms, the "attainment of Buddhahood" is more understood as the attainment of Amitabha's Pure Land or the more vague sense of an "ancestral land" (高天原 *takamaga-hara*), the abode of the heavenly gods (天津神 *amatsu-kami*). Often depicted as located up in the sky, this land is believed to be connected to the Earth by the "Floating Bridge of Heaven" (天の浮橋 *ama-no uki-hashi*). The status of a *hotoke* refers more to a term of ancient Japanese origin that is better translated as "ancestral spirit" rather than a buddha.

It is striking at how the logic of this system closely resembles the Brahmanic one of ancestral rites performed by Indian Brahmin priests to secure the "salvation" or gaining of heaven for the deceased—a system the Buddha most thoroughly rejected for linking a good afterlife with karmic ritual rather than the karmic merit of one's ethical actions.[226] Dogen's aforementioned repudiation of the esotericization of Rinzai Zen in Kamakura to create the *zen-mitsu* ideology also seems

---

225 Ibid., pp. 195-96.
226 Watts. "Karma for Everyone". pp. 17-19.

to be at odds with this development. Indeed, Nara Yasuaki 奈良康明 (1929–2017)—another prominent contemporary Japanese Buddhist scholar and Soto Zen priest—described these developments: "Making clear doctrinal explanations of funerals and its relationship to Buddhist [and Zen] soteriology is not particularly easy.... These doctrinal reflections simply make facile associations between a selected number of Soto Zen concepts and funeral practices, rather than provide logical explanations on the meaning of funerals for laypeople."[227] Kuroda Toshio summarizes the development of this system for all Buddhist sects in the Tokugawa:

> Buddhism, bereft of its original logic and depth of belief, became a hollow, popularized version of itself that proposed a generally easy realization of Buddhahood after death, leaving it little alternative than to turn into "funeral Buddhism"; this, however, amounted to the subordination of religion to politics.... The soul that attains Buddhahood (成仏 *jobutsu*) after death must be seen, however, as in a far lower spiritual state than that of a person who achieves *jobutsu* in its original sense of becoming an awakened being and realizing the dharma.... [This] was not a manifestation of respect towards the dead; it was, rather, nothing but a false consciousness created by the political exploitation of religion.[228]

Indeed, by the end of the Warring States period, the practice of the veneration of ancestors, and in turn hierarchical power, was being manipulated to also venerate secular rulers after their deaths as *kami* or buddhas. After his death in 1616, Tokugawa Ieyasu was deified with the name "Great Gongen, Light of the East" (東照大権現, Tosho Daigongen, a *gongen* being a buddha who manifests as a *kami* in this world), and the famous temple-shrine at Nikko was built for the installation of his remains. A fascinating historical thread to further investigate is the chain of causes from:

1. the veneration of the Buddha's relics and the building of memorial stupas after his death in ancient India to

---

227 Nara, Yasuaki. "The Soto Zen School in Modern Japan".
228 Kuroda, Toshio. "The World of Spirit Pacification: Issues of State and Religion". Trans. Allan Grapard. In *Japanese Journal of Religious Studies*. 1996. Vol. 23, No. 3-4. p. 343.

2. the co-optation of this practice by Buddhist monarchs as "dharmic rulers" (*dharma-raja*), if not "divine rulers" (*deva-raja*), in Southeast Asia to
3. the adoption of such practices by clan leaders and aristocrats in early Japan to
4. finally reaching the common people in the Tokugawa period.

As much as it could be seen as a democratization of the form by allowing the common people to honor their ancestors and loved ones as "buddhas" and venerate their ashes as "buddha relics", this system also tied the common people of Japan to a vertical system of veneration of authority and power: from ancestors and elders to local rulers and priests to regional lords and sectarian founders and, finally, to the military leaders and the emperor himself.

We could see this systemization of veneration as the Tokugawa military government using Buddhism to sacralize its rule as had been done in the *ken-mitsu* and *zen-mitsu* systems. However, as Kuroda points out, this new form of Funeral Buddhism was a hollowed-out version of Buddhism. In its place, a more Confucian system of ancestor veneration was inserted with the Buddhist priest acting more as a Brahmanical ritualist. Buddhist temples and denominations remained intact, giving the appearance that Buddhism was still forming a basis for the social order, but its previous forms that had been used to sacralize rule became increasingly unimportant in Tokugawa society. Within this shell of Buddhism emerged an increasing emphasis on the principles and ethics of Confucianism, or rather Neo-Confucianism. In China, Neo-Confucianism had developed as a more sophisticated system of traditional Confucian teachings in response to the arrival and flourishing of Indian Buddhism's highly developed system of metaphysical outlooks coupled with practical ethics.

While Confucian influences in Japan are evident as early as Prince Shotoku's *Seventeen Article Constitution* and even before, Neo-Confucianism did not emerge as an important cultural force until the end of the Muromachi period. Its teachings were, ironically, spread by Zen Buddhist monks who had brought them back from their studies in China and found them useful in teaching their samurai class devotees.[229] During this period, the infamous "Way of the Warrior" (*bushido*), which was first conceptualized under the influence of Zen Buddhism in the late Kamakura period, became

---

229 Tucker, John. "Japanese Confucian Philosophy". In *The Stanford Encyclopedia of Philosophy*. Spring 2018 Edition.

increasingly imbued with the core Confucian ethical norms of the five social virtues (五常 *go-jo*) and the five hierarchical relationships (五倫 *go-rin*). The former—consisting of benevolence (*jin*), righteousness (*gi*), propriety (*ri* a.k.a. filial piety), wisdom (*chi*) and loyalty/trustworthiness (*shin*)—defined the moral and ethical comportment towards the people in one's life. These people were compartmentalized in the *go-rin* as a series of relationships between ruler and subject, father and son, elder brother and younger brother, husband and wife, friend and friend. This system of ethics was much more suited to the needs of the military class, and in turn the military government, for maintaining loyalty and a hierarchical social order. It clearly contrasted the ethical thrust of the Kamakura Buddhist movements, which had instructed the common people to discover their own salvation through loyalty only to such transcendental powers as Amida Buddha or the *Lotus Sutra*.

Neo-Confucianism also found important resonances with the ancient form of Japanese ancestor worship, which would become the predominant form of practice in Buddhist temples in the Tokugawa era on up to the present day. The aforementioned veneration of military rulers, like Ieyasu, evolved from the practice of worshipping tutelary deities (*ujigami*) by the various large and small clans of ancient Japan. Related by blood with common ancestors and occupations, the tutelary deity would ground their collectivity. Nakamura Hajime notes that, "It was not the actual ancestors who were deified for worship; it was that the deities worshipped were regarded as their common ancestors."[230] As noted earlier, this culture ultimately affected even the universal and liberational Kamakura Buddhist movements insofar as that, by the Muromachi period, they began to devolve into insular, clannish fiefdoms based around a veneration of their sect founders. The Tokugawa military government was ultimately able to consolidate these groups into a national feudal class system with the Neo-Confucian ethics of the five relationship and five social virtues systematizing the ancient Shinto customs of clan deities while operating through the national system of Buddhist temples.

For the city commoners of the Tokugawa era along with the rural farmers and fisherfolk, the more secular concepts and values of Neo-Confucianism were less obvious and operative. The faith-based practices of Buddhism and local Shinto customs had stronger influence on family customs and human relationships. The highly patriarchal Confucian family system and its ethics were a more conscious

---

230 Nakamura. *Ways of Thinking of Eastern Peoples*. p. 417.

element of not only the Tokugawa military class but also great landowners and merchants along with the nobility.[231] As we will explore later, this sort of basic two-class system has endured into the modern era comprising the urban elite as compared with rural and/or working-classes. Ultimately, the fundamental tenets of the five relationships and five social virtues continued to serve as important tools for social cohesion and control for not only the Tokugawa military government but onward to the new Meiji nation-state, the post-Meiji military state, and the postwar bureaucratic state. In this way, Confucianism, or rather Neo-Confucianism, has not so much created the ethical outlook of modern Japanese as much as "articulate the values by which Japanese society works".[232]

Karmic Taint, Veneration of Authority, and the Japanese Caste System

In the opening section on the early formation of Buddhism in Japan, we noted that the Japanese have tended to value more localized or clannish ethics based on taboo and taint (*kega-re*) over more universal or transcendental ethics based on sin and karma. This distinction parallels Buddhism's own differentiation from Vedic Brahmanism, which developed a four-fold caste system plus an additional outcaste level based on notions of cosmic and ritual purity. As we have seen above, the Tokugawa were able to legitimize an institutionalized class system through solidifying pre-existing class alliances with certain Buddhist sects and tying it to a vertical structure of power based on the veneration of ancestors and Neo-Confucian respect for authority. While there is a long history in Japan of social discrimination against slaves, lepers, criminals, strangers, residents of undesirable areas, and so forth,[233] Tokugawa Buddhism took ancient Japanese notions of *kega-re* to a new level by fusing them with so-called Buddhist teachings of karma. Although Japan's class system of military leaders, farmers, artisans, and merchants was not based on ritual taboos as with the Indian caste system, more clearly articulated notions of *kega-re*

---

231 Smith, Robert J. "The Japanese (Confucian) Family: The Tradition from the Bottom Up". In *Confucian Traditions in East Asian Modernity*. Ed. Tu Wei-Ming. (Cambridge: Harvard University Press, 1996), p. 169.

232 Smith. "The Japanese (Confucian) Family". p. 171.

233 Bodiford, William. "Zen and the Art of Religious Prejudice: Efforts to Reform a Tradition of Social Discrimination". In *Japanese Journal of Religious Studies*. 1996. Vol. 23, No. 1-2. p. 14.

developed under Buddhist auspices to support patriarchy and create a clearly defined outcaste population called *burakumin* 部落民—literally "people of the village", but sometimes also referred to as *eta* (穢多 "those full of defilement") or *hi-nin* (非人 "non-humans").

One of the core distortions was not only the adoption of Vedic notions of ritual karma, in which the proper performance of rites affects one fate in this life and the next, but also other Indian interpretations of karma as retributive and rigidly deterministic.[234] This latter interpretation, which has also been common to Buddhists in other countries, has been used to sanctify the status quo by rationalizing social status, rank, and differentiation on purported acts performed in a previous life, the fruit of which are being reaped in this life, and the endurance or penance of which form the basis of a good rebirth in the next life. These distortions crept into the Theravada tradition through critical commentaries like Buddhaghosa's *Path of Purity* (*Visuddhimagga*) and also into the Mahayana tradition through Buddhism's ongoing adaptation and negotiation with Indian culture. The *Lotus Sutra*, one of the earliest Mahayana texts, warns in its conclusion that whoever slanders the scripture will be stricken with leprosy, or will be reborn blind or with harelips, flat noses, deformed limbs, body odor, impurities, and so forth, for many lives. The *Mahaprajnaparamita Shastra* (大智度論 *Daichido-ron*)—a commentary on the *Great Perfection of Wisdom Sutra* which is an essential text to all of the Mahayana tradition and especially Zen—states that karmic retribution for previous sins prevents victims of leprosy from ever being cured.[235]

The Soto Zen sect provides another very salient example of the distortions of the Tokugawa period. It can be found that even before the implementation of the temple registration system, Soto Zen teachers already had developed special funeral rituals for people of outcaste status as well as for victims of mental illness, leprosy, and other socially unaccepted diseases. These people were referred to as "non-human" (*hinin*), and Soto Zen created a special form of the aforementioned *kirigami* ritual texts for them, which instead of supporting the salvation of the deceased rather described rites to sever all karmic connections between them and local people.[236]

Earlier on in this section, we noted how Shinto, with its traditional taboos against blood and impurity, allowed Buddhism to take over the work of dealing with the dead in Japan, because in theory

---

234 Watts. "Karma for Everyone". pp. 20-21.
235 Bodiford. "Zen and the Art of Religious Prejudice". p. 14.
236 Ibid., p. 14.

Buddhists have only concern for mental purity not physical. Japanese Buddhism, however, has longstanding practices of discriminating against women for their supposed physical impurity in menstruation and childbirth. The great Buddhist mountains of Japan, such as Mt. Hiei and Mt. Koya, forbade the entry into the mountain by any woman up until modern times. Soto Zen developed a variety of misogynistic rituals in which women were taught that menstrual blood pollutes the earth and offends the spirits, dooming them to a karmic destiny in the special hell containing a "blood pool lake" (血盆池 *ketsubon i-ke*). Soto Zen monks were, of course, the only ones who could save them from such a fate through the bequeathing of a special talisman and a specially consecrated copy of the *Blood Pool Sutra* (血盆經 *Ketsubon-kyo*), another creation of the Chinese Buddhist tradition.[237]

As mentioned, Zen monks, especially Rinzai ones, also began importing Neo-Confucian ethical norms that promoted respect for authority. The Neo-Confucian teachings of Zhu Xi 朱熹 (1130–1200) became particularly favorable to the Tokugawa establishment for their emphasis on the eternality of social hierarchy. The strong emphasis on the five relationships and the five social virtues created a hermetic container for human relationships that the individual was not to go beyond. In these teachings, one's "inherent dignity" is acquired not by their personal relationship with a transcendent God, as in the Abrahamic faiths, or with some enlightened and compassionate figure, like the Buddha, but rather "by occupying a social position given to them and fulfilling the duty attached to it".[238]

Like the Hindu caste system, carrying out one's social duties and role in relation to one's immediate horizontal and vertical relationships serves as the meaning of life itself. As we will explore later, postwar social critics, like Maruyama Masao 丸山眞男 (1914–1996), felt this period in Japanese history and the influence of Neo-Confucianism have had long-term damaging effects on the ability of Japanese to develop a level of personal autonomy (主体性 *shutaisei*) to overcome authoritarianism and a "universal morality applicable to humankind"[239]—a point echoed by Nakamura Hajime at the beginning of this volume.

With the development of such theologies, Tokugawa Buddhism had the cultural means to further institutionalize the structure of a rigid class system, which formed the longest period of unbroken rule

---

237 Ibid., p. 15.

238 Sasaki, Fumiko. *Nationalism, Political Realism and Democracy in Japan: The Thought of Masao Maruyama*. (London: Routledge, 2012), pp. 55-56.

239 Ibid.

in Japanese history. One of the most insidious systems for keeping track of and keeping in place class distinctions was the creation of death registries or necrologies (過去帳 *kako-cho*), which recorded the posthumous names (*kaimyo*) given to individuals after death and the dates for the necessary memorial services to be performed in their name. The length and sophistication of these names would denote social status and could be determined by a variety of ambiguous criteria including family lineage, wealth, social position, and donations made to the temple or sect.[240] While the first records of such practices date to the 16th and 17th centuries, this system of social ranking using *kaimyo* became prominent around 1735.[241]

These death registries were used not only to denote high status but also low status, such as regulations that former Christians and their descendants down to the fifth generation could not be registered in the standard temple registries but had to be recorded separately in a book known as "off the registry" (帳外れ *cho-hazu-re*).[242] This practice was also applied to the families of outcastes, criminals, homeless people, lepers, and the disabled. William Bodiford, in his revealing study of these practices, notes, "Because of the complexities of the titles and the use of obscure Buddhist terminology, the exact correlation between occupations, social status, and the entries in any given temple's necrology usually is clear only to the resident priests at that particular temple. Thus, the Buddhist titles in necrologies often function almost as a secret social code, incomprehensible to the average Japanese."[243] However, sometimes necrology entries were more explicitly discriminatory with outcastes being labeled as *sendara* 旃陀羅, the Japanese transliteration of the Sanskrit word *candala*, who are none other than the Untouchable class of the Vedic caste system. In other cases, the Chinese character for "beast" (畜 *chiku*) was used. These terms have also been found carved on family tombstones, leaving a permanent public record of the social status of those families. While the Soto denomination was the most prominent practitioner of this system, even the Jodo Shin denomination, with their affiliation with the peasant farmer classes and *burakumin*, engaged in such nefarious customs. Their separation of them into *burakumin*-only temples called *eta-ji* 穢多寺 only re-enforced the

---

240 Tamamuro. "Local Society and the Temple-Parishioner Relationship within the Bakufu's Governance Structure". p. 273.

241 Ibid., p. 276.

242 Bodiford. "Zen and the Art of Religious Prejudice". p. 8.

243 Ibid., p. 9.

acceptance of their class status and the fulfillment of their karmic destiny while waiting for salvation in the Pure Land at death.[244]

These practices were thought be left in the dustbin of the Tokugawa period, yet the records and sometimes still secret practices remained intact until the latter part of the 20th century. As we will examine in detail in a later chapter, the exposure of these practices to the modern public further tainted their perception of Buddhism as an archaic and useless remnant of the past. In this way, the effect of the descent of Japanese Buddhism in the Tokugawa into the kind of Vedic Brahmanism that the Buddha spent his life denouncing, demystifying, and ethicizing to create a teaching that has been a civilizational force throughout Asia and now increasingly in the Western world cannot be underestimated. The deep corruption of the monastic Sangha—who developed so much power that egregious forms of breaking the monastic *sila*, like the molestation of women, could be swept under the rug[245]—and the institutional rot from the financial wealth it gained by offering a structure for the Tokugawa to disseminate its own state ideology led the common people to drift away from Buddhism for their spiritual needs. Meanwhile, the new intellectual leaders of the Tokugawa increasingly turned to Neo-Confucianism and Shinto to develop social ideologies. The Meiji Restoration was the first major strike against this corruption. The post-World War II boom of new lay Buddhist orders was yet another. Yet the persistent inability of the traditional sects to pro-actively reform the *tera-uke* system, which persists despite being delinked from state legal norms, is the legacy of the Tokugawa period that still haunts Japanese Buddhism today.

Alternatives to State Buddhism that Turned Inward Instead of Towards Axialization

As we have seen throughout this survey, for better and worse, Japanese have always de-transcendentalized Buddhism to fit their culture, emphasizing the way of the laicized bodhisattva (Tendai) and the attainment of salvation in this life (Shingon, Zen, Nichiren, Jodo Shin) as much as in the next (Jodo). While Tokugawa Buddhism's support for state ideology is not so different from previous Buddhist alliances with the ruling class, the creation of a *transcendental* theology based

---

244 Tamura. *Japanese Buddhism: A Cultural History.* p.151.

245 Tamamuro. "Local Society and the Temple-Parishioner Relationship within the Bakufu's Governance Structure". p. 282.

on salvation only taking place through the endurance of one's class roles in this life while requiring a down payment in elaborate funeral and memorial rites for the next life appears to be out of character. The anti-Buddhism movement of the 17th century that rose among Confucian, Shinto, and National Learning scholars hit at this transcendental dualism by emphasizing feudalistic and secular moral concepts, often tinged with "a simplistic, emotionalistic nationalism."[246] The Neo-Confucian scholar Ito Jinsai 伊藤仁斎 (1627–1705) made pointed criticisms of Buddhist monastics, writing that while monks might seem like awe-inspiring men when meditating in isolated retreats, they appeared confused and wild and of less value than normal people when they returned to society. They forgot the lessons of society while off in meditation, so when they returned, they were more easily tempted by them.[247]

In this way, Neo-Confucianism continued to develop as an important way to envision a more systematized, high feudal system under the Tokugawa. Zhu Xi's ideas continued to be formative but not without reservation. Importantly, his couching of the five hierarchical relationships and five social virtues within the universal concept of the Mandate of Heaven means that one's morality is tied to a universal concept of Truth or Principle (理 *ri*) rather than the arbitrary dictates of one's senior. In this way, Zhu Xi built on the ideas first articulated by Mencius in the 4th century BCE about the moral responsibility of rulers and emperors under the Mandate of Heaven to ensure the well-being of the people[248]—a concept akin to the Buddhist notion of the *dharma-raja*. Ito rejected this critical aspect of Zhu Xi's thought, feeling that ethics were not a matter of religion or a universal truth but of individual determination and conscience[249]—a value that is still very prevalent in Japan today.

In this way, Neo-Confucian socio-political thought went through a process of Japanization in the Tokugawa period. Thinkers, like Ogyu Sorai 荻生徂徠 (1666–1728), held more liberal views on the cultivation of human character through more emotive forms of study and cultivation in literary, linguistic, and ritualistic techniques. Other thinkers, like Koga Seiri 古賀精里 (1750–1817) and Shibano Ritsuzan

---

246 Tamura. *Japanese Buddhism: A Cultural History*. p.131.

247 Ibid., p.132.

248 Adler, Joseph A. "Chance and Necessity in Zhu Xi's Conceptions of Heaven and Tradition". *European Journal for Philosophy of Religion*. Spring 2016. Vol. 8, No. 1, p. 159.

249 Tamura. *Japanese Buddhism: A Cultural History*. p.145.

柴野栗山 (1736–1807), followed the more samurai-influenced line of disciplined moral cultivation through the practice of the martial arts and practical learning.[250] This intellectual ferment eventually led to a more direct integration of Confucianism into the bureaucratic apparatus of government and a Confucian-based examination system in bureaucratic appointments, but not until well into the later stages of the Tokugawa rule in the 1790s.[251]

The other important strain of intellectual and social thought developing in the Tokugawa came from Nativist and Shinto thinkers. One of the notable Shinto intellectuals of this period was Yamazaki Ansai 山崎闇斎 (1618–82), originally a Rinzai Zen monk who renounced his monastic status and founded the Suika Shinto movement 垂加神道. He used Confucian influences to arrive at a faith that exalted the Way of the Emperor and emphasized feeling over intellect, writing, "Speaking with an almost childlike innocence while respecting the old theories is the way to interpret Shinto works."[252] Yoshikawa 吉川神道 was another developing strand of Shinto, which began to spread more widely among the people in the early Tokugawa. Yoshikawa Koretari 吉川惟足 (1616–94) taught that the values of true love, justice, and harmony had been best realized in Japan and that the act of praying for the eternal prosperity of the sacred nation expressed the true national "spirit of Japan" (大和魂 *yamato-damashii*).

The National Learning movement (国学 *koku-gaku*), as systematized by Motoori Norinaga 本居宣長 (1730–1801), also taught similar themes in relation to Shinto, emphasizing the abandonment of narrow knowledge and the return to childlike purity while relying on the will of the *kami* in everything. Both Motoori and Hirata Atsutane 平田篤胤 (1776–1843), the founder of Restoration Shinto (復古神道 *Fukko Shinto*) developed teachings on the afterlife based on Shinto teachings. Motoori believed that good and evil exist in the world because of the actions of the gods Naobi and Magatsubi-no-kami and that no matter the quality of one's life, all go to the realm of darkness, "a dirty and evil land", after death. Atsutane had a more positive view of the afterlife based on a moral view of the next world through reverence of the emperor that emphasized the delegation of governance to local people as subjects of the emperor and a criticism of the

---

250 Paramore, Kiri. "The Nationalization of Confucianism: Academism, Examinations, and Bureaucratic Governance in the Late Tokugawa State". *The Journal of Japanese Studies*. Winter 2012. Vol. 38, No. 1, p. 39.

251 Ibid., p. 26.

252 Kasahara. *A History of Japanese Religion*. pp. 348–49.

Tokugawa system. It also sought to unite Shinto ritual and national politics.[253]

As we move into the latter parts of the Tokugawa era, we see a merchant culture flowering in the early 19th century. However, unlike European capitalist culture that gave way to working class revolts and communism's overturning of the old feudal systems, the Japanese masses continued to be educated and influenced from above by these Tokugawa forms of Neo-Confucianism, Neo-Shinto, and Buddhism.[254] Nakamura Hajime notes that the general lack of individual self-agency retarded the growth of urban areas in Japan, especially in a European style of city-states with an independent consciousness full of autonomous beings. "This situation formed an obstacle to the growth of a general public morality as well as to an ethics for the individual."[255] In this way, the this-worldliness and anti-religious tendencies became even stronger among the merchant class as they poured their energies into conspicuous consumption rather than social change[256]—another enduring trend in Japanese society today. Here we see more clearly how Tamura's "triumph of the secular" was much more the calling card of the Tokugawa than the Muromachi periods.

Such socio-political inertia, however, could not last under a system of such graded inequality and exploitation. With the great famine of 1836, peasant rebellions against exploitation by the military government started to grow into something larger. Perennial forms that we have seen throughout this survey, such as local confraternities (*ko*) and the mobilization of peasants (*ikki*), led to a new form of movement for "world renewal" (世直し *yo-naoshi*). Many of these groups had religious influences, such as the *myoko-nin* 妙好人 movement originating out of grassroots communities of the Jodo Shin sect. This movement, however, was ultimately seen as reactionary in viewing the solution to the people's problems in an individualistic withdraw into a religious faith of leaving all solutions to the power of Amitabha. When the peasants rose in rebellion, these *myoko-nin* leaders refused to join while attempting to quell the uprisings. One of the most famous *yo-naoshi* movements in the very last days of the Tokugawa was a nationwide movement called *ii-janai-ka*, meaning "Why not?" or "It's OK!". A Bohemian-like movement, it consisted mostly of mass groups of people assembling in outrageous costumes, cross dressing, and breaking

---

253 Ibid., pp. 353-55.
254 Tamura. *Japanese Buddhism: A Cultural History*. p.147.
255 Nakamura. *Ways of Thinking of Eastern Peoples*. p. 431.
256 Tamura. *Japanese Buddhism: A Cultural History*. p. 147.

into wealthy persons' homes to take things in the spirit of *ii-janai-ka*. The problem of such bohemian movements was that it only created the illusion of liberation but never really engaged in social reform.

In general, the problem with these movements and of the more prohibitive Meiji Restoration movement was the attempt to create a new age by modeling themselves on an ancient past.[257] This is yet another enduring legacy of the Tokugawa period that remains relevant today and brings us back to the core theme of this survey, which is: Japan struggles to axialize, that is, to embrace the plurality and diversity of views inherent in civilizational movements that form the core element in cultural health and vitality, further engendering a creativity to develop truly contemporary solutions based in perennial and essential human values.

---

257 Ibid., p.155.

Part II

Archaic Modernity and the Foundations of Socially Engaged Buddhism in Prewar Japan

6

Archaic Continuity across the Tokugawa and Meiji Periods

Although there is a perennial aspect to it dating back to the historical Buddha, Socially Engaged Buddhism has been defined, and can be properly circumscribed, as a movement that began in response to the influences and dislocations of Western colonialization and modernization in the late 19th and early 20th centuries.[1] A number of seminal figures emerged during this period with creative new approaches to Buddhist thought and practice for the modern era: the lay-Buddhist reformer and internationalist Anagarika Dharmapala (1864–1933) in Sri Lanka; the anti-colonial activist monks U Ottama (1879–1939) and U Wisara (1889–1929) in Myanmar; social reformer and visionary of Humanistic Buddhism Master Taixu 太虛大師 (1890–1947) in China; anti-caste activist and social visionary B.R. Ambedkar (1891–1956) in India; and a socially radical, forest monk named Buddhadasa (1906–1993) in Thailand. Although there were important Japanese Buddhists who had global profiles during this period, none are mentioned in the same breath as the figures mentioned above, nor held up as exemplars of progressively-minded Socially Engaged Buddhism.

This is perhaps due to the mass reversion of most Japanese progressives, including Buddhists, to a wholesale embrace of the cult of the emperor and Japanese imperialism by the 1930s. Not only from an international perspective but also from a postwar indigenous Japanese one, this loss of moral standing retards their legacies and stands in contrast to the above figures, who continue to inspire younger generations in the struggle for democracy and social justice in their own nations. While the eventual capitulation of Japanese Buddhism to the Confucian-Shinto-centric, modern imperial state indeed leaves a complicated and disturbing legacy, it also obscures some of the most dynamic and complex social thought by Buddhists of any nation in

---

1 Queen, Christopher S. "Introduction: The Shapes and Sources of Engaged Buddhism". In *Engaged Buddhism: Buddhist Liberation Movements in Asia*. Eds. Christopher S. Queen & Sallie B. King. (Albany, NY: State University of New York Press, 1996), p. 20.

Asia during this late colonial era. This section will attempt to highlight some of the most important figures and movements that contributed to Socially Engaged Buddhism's development in Japan today. These movements only further embellish the complex development of Buddhism in Japan, especially in terms of the struggle to axialize the archaic thinking and ways of the Japanese people.

The Confucian-Shinto Sacralization of State in the Late Tokugawa and Meiji Periods

By the mid 19th century, the combined forces of socio-political schisms within Japan and economic political forces from the colonial West brought down Japan's longest single ruling regime, the Tokugawa military government (1603–1868), thus ushering in a radical *restructuring* of Japanese society. My emphasis placed on the *restructuring* of Japanese society during the Meiji period (1868–1912) is an attempt to highlight the less than radical *re-culturing* in the transition from the medieval Tokugawa military government to the modern Meiji nation-state. In the opening section of this volume, we identified certain key aspects of the axialization of a society from archaic and clannish forms of social organization into universal and civilizational social systems, such as: *an emerging view of the mundane order as incomplete, inferior, unsatisfactory, or polluted and in need of being reconstructed*; and *a principled discontinuity between different regimes or "stages" of institutional change*. While it is clear that the Meiji Restoration marked a new style of government—the shift from a feudal system led by a military chieftain (*shogun*) with lords, vassals or samurai, and peasantry to a modern bureaucratic state run by a group of urbanized oligarchs and bureaucrats—we need to look at the ideological currents of the late Tokugawa to reconsider if there was, as Eisenstadt describes, such a "principled discontinuity" between these two regimes and whether this drive for change saw the mundane order as "unsatisfactory or polluted".

As we have seen in the previous chapter, Tokugawa policy quickly crushed the nascent spread of Christianity in the early 1600s and completely co-opted Buddhism. A vast national temple system was built to create a sanctified class society based on the reification of authority in a circumscribed version of Neo-Confucianism coupled with ancient beliefs in ancestral veneration. The intent was clearly to curtail the transcendental and universal aspects of these three foreign theologies.[2]

---

2   Eisenstadt. *Japanese Civilization*. p. 195.

Christianity and Buddhism, especially evidenced in their role in the 16th century Warring States period, had already proved to be a threat to the feudal loyalty towards military rulers and lords during the successive military regimes of medieval Japan. While this domestication of Buddhism during the Tokugawa embedded it in the culture of the local village, it also robbed it of its wider, national vitality.

By the latter half of the era, more dynamic Neo-Confucian and Nativist or Shinto schools of thought began to emerge among the growing population of educated classes in urban as well as rural Japan. Neo-Confucianism was increasingly used to establish social ideology³ through the far-reaching expansion of Confucian education for samurai, merchants, and some peasants in the late 1700s and early 1800s in schools and academies called *hanko* ("clan school" 藩校). These *hanko* contrasted the more localized, village Buddhist temple schools called *tera-koya* 寺子屋. Together, they transformed Japan into one of the most literate pre-modern societies and created the ideological-political ferment for the Meiji Restoration.⁴

Confucianism, however, also had its axial, if not transcendental, components that, like Buddhism, needed to be pruned to fit the needs of the Tokugawa military government. As Eisenstadt notes, "The logocentric tendency of Confucianism and especially of neo-Confucianism went in many ways against the grain of the more mythocentric, nondiscursive orientations, seemingly rooted in the 'archaic' Japanese culture, that were prevalent among many Japanese intellectuals and throughout much of Japanese society."⁵ Nakamura Hajime further comments that, "Most of the Japanese Confucianist scholars, even when they followed the metaphysical doctrines of Zhu Xi 朱熹, never chose the dualism of 'principle' (理 Ch. *li*) and 'material force' (気 Ch. *qi*). All of the characteristically Japanese scholars believed in phenomena as the fundamental mode of existence."⁶ This was a critical move in the eyes of renowned postwar social critic Maruyama Masao, because it tore apart the creative dialectic of the system and the critical connection between human behavior and universal ethical principles.⁷ This tendency—as noted in the previous chapter by Neo-Confucian scholar Ito Jinsai 伊藤仁斎 (1627–1705)—corresponds

---

3   Ibid., p. 194.

4   Ibid., pp. 194, 200-01.

5   Ibid., p. 243.

6   Nakamura. *Ways of Thinking of Eastern Peoples.* p. 355.

7   Kersten, Rikki. *Democracy in Postwar Japan: Maruyama Masao and the Search for Autonomy.* (London: Routledge 1996), pp. 54-55.

to points made throughout this volume of the Japanese emphasis on the more archaic or tribal notion of purity or impurity of form over the more axial or universal notion of sin as in the Abrahamic faiths or transgression of principle as in Buddhism and Confucianism.

This collapsing of the Principle into the material or "phenomenal" (事 *ji*) served to prune another key axial aspect of Confucianism in the moral and ethical claims on a ruler—ones that could have exposed the Shogun to revolt and his legitimate removal from power under the Mandate of Heaven. In China, the emperor was considered to embody the source of moral authority or legitimacy in the Mandate of Heaven while also holding the highest power to make decisions for the state. In Japan, however, these roles were split so that the emperor served only as a moral symbol of the authority and legitimacy of the state, while the real power to make governing decisions was held by those who existed in his shadow. Maruyama traces this separation back to the earliest days of the Yamato court in the 7th century when the Japanese imported the Chinese system of centralized bureaucracy, yet created a new institution called the Council of State (太政官 *dajo-kan*) that actually ran the government.

This system has been perpetuated from this earliest period to the Fujiwara regency of the Heian period, the entire medieval period of military rule from the Kamakura to the Tokugawa shogunates, the restoration of imperial rule from the Meiji to the war, and the postwar era with an unending series of short-term prime ministers controlled by the insular faction heads of the Liberal Democratic Party as well as the deeper level of power held by elite bureaucrats. Maruyama notes that, "In all of these cases, the relationship between power and legitimacy is the same, always separate and distinct."[8] In all these eras, even the one of military rule when the shogun appeared as a singular ruler, the emperor was never fully deposed or renounced. Yet the style was so persistent that in different periods the shogun himself became a symbol of authority and legitimacy while a tertiary level of power developed in a shogunal regent (執権 *shikken*) during the Kamakura period or a Council of Elders (老中 *roju*) in the Tokugawa period.

By instilling authority in the emperor and drawing upon it through court rituals to legitimize the state, successive shoguns could use him as a shield or veil for the perpetuation of the actual political power they wielded.[9] The emperor served as the ultimate means of authority. Acting as a manifestation

---

8   Eisenstadt. *Japanese Civilization*. p. 287.

9   Ibid., p. 207.

of the original ancestor of the people and of the "body-politic" (国体 *kokutai*), his divinity was inscrutable and thus implicitly always moral—in the same way a monotheist would regard God as implicitly moral or perhaps in the vein of Indian and Southeast Asian notions of the *deva-raja* ("god-king"). In this way, the shogun could avoid all moral and ethical challenges to his sovereignty through appeals to serving the eternal sovereign of the emperor. This system of sacralizing power through the authority of the emperor became more pronounced in the Tokugawa as Buddhism lost its vitality and role in sacralizing the state.

As such, the Meiji Restoration does not truly represent a principled discontinuity but rather an amplification of this system as the ruling oligarchs, who had replaced the shogunate, receded further from public view, while the emperor was thrust more into the forefront. In both the Tokugawa and Meiji, a circumscribed or Japanized version of Neo-Confucianism emphasizing the five social virtues (*go-jo*) and the five hierarchical relationships (*go-rin*) was used to provide a system of public morals consisting of discipline, loyalty, harmony, filial piety, perseverance[10], and subordination of individual rights to the collective. This was combined with the archaic and mythic legitimization of authority in the emperor through Shinto cosmology and rituals to form a complete socio-political ideology. In this process, Buddhism and Christianity were labeled as foreign and impure as a way to mask their more axial presentations of a universal authority that transcended the national and of a social ethics that might empower the individual to exercise a principled form of resistance to the collective and the hierarchization of power.

Archaic Restoration Ideology in the Meiji Period

In further reflecting on the potentials of axialization, the late Tokugawa period does show a growing awareness of the mundane order as unsatisfactory or polluted. While increasing dissatisfaction with Tokugawa rule seemed to have little effect on Buddhism, Neo-Confucian and Nativist Shinto thought became increasingly dynamic in this ferment. An important contribution to the further development of this Confucian-Shinto system of rule that emerged in the latter half of the Tokugawa era and paved the way for the Meiji Restoration was the Mito School (水戸学 *Mito-gaku*). The Mito School was established in the earlier half of the Tokugawa period as a Neo-Confucian project to

---

10   Ibid., p. 65.

historically ground the continuous rule of the emperor dating back to the primordial Emperor Jinmu 神武天皇 (r. 660–585 BCE), who is said to have been the direct descendent of the great sun goddess Amaterasu 天照大神. The school collected its scholarship in the *History of Great Japan* (大日本史 *Dai nihon-shi*) and offered it to the Tokugawa military government for use in the legitimization of its rule.

The second stage of the school, however, consisted of a more activist, regional socio-political reform movement among the followers of the feudal lord Tokugawa Nariaki 徳川斉昭 (1800–1860) of Mito, in present day Ibaraki. During the 1830–50s, this movement grew to meet the growing internal problems of the Tokugawa system and the increasing external threat of the West. Their ideology was expressed in the slogan, "Revere the Emperor, expel the barbarians" (尊王攘夷 *sonno-joi*), which became a national rallying cry in the latter days of the Tokugawa.

The Mito School developed concepts that had formative influences into the Meiji period and beyond, such as *kokutai* 国体, which can be translated as "national-body", "body-politic", "national structure", or even "citizens of the state and subjects of the emperor"; as well as *saisei-icchi* (祭政一致) translated as the "unity of religion and government", "unity of rite and rule", or "theocracy". These concepts were developed and popularized in the *New Theses* (新論 *Shin-ron*) written in 1825 by Aizawa Seishisai 会沢正志斎 (1782–1863), an authority on Neo-Confucianism and leader of the Mito School at that time, who supported the direct restoration of the Imperial House of Japan. Aizawa developed these concepts as well as *sonno-joi* using the scholarly arguments of Motoori Norinaga 本居宣長 (1730–1801), who we noted in the previous chapter as the founder of the National Learning movement.

Like the Mito School's early endeavors, Aizawa sought to use Neo-Confucianism to make an argument that the national myths found in the historical chronicles of Japan, the *Koji-ki* 古事記 and the *Nihon sho-ki* 日本書紀, were historical facts and proved that the emperor was directly descended from Amaterasu. Aizawa's concept of *saisei-icchi* emphasized this combination of Neo-Confucian morality for social ethics and Shinto mythology for existentialist meaning and social rituals.[11] Combined with a modernized bureaucracy that had been developing through the expansion of Neo-Confucian

---

11 Ketelaar, James E. *Of Heretics and Martyrs in Meiji Japan: Buddhism and Its Persecution.* (Princeton, NJ: Princeton University Press, 1990), p. 95.

education[12], it was felt Japan could develop a resilient response to the threats of the West.

While such ideological movements could certainly be said to represent *an emerging view of the mundane order as incomplete, inferior, unsatisfactory, or polluted and in need of being reconstructed*, Eisenstadt expresses doubt that such efforts represent a truly modern method of developing an historical basis to *transform the basic hegemonic premises* of Japanese society through imperial restoration. He sees the Mito School in light of other millennial movements of this time that, as noted at the end of the previous chapter, could not translate their transcendental views of social decline and the possibility of human liberation into more pluralistic and universal (or even national) movements for social reform rooted in a *principled discontinuity* from the status quo. He notes, "The Mito vision was informed by a strong millenarian stance, couched in terms of an 'inverted utopianism' of imperial restoration [which] could perhaps best be seen in their vision of the ideal community and government.... The qualities of imperial 'government', the behavior of the court in Kyoto, made it a perfect concrete image of government by rites and music."[13]

Such a system refers to the major influence of Neo-Confucian Ogyu Sorai 荻生徂徠 (1666–1728) who broadly divided the Confucian teachings into those of rites (礼 *rei*), which gave the basis of social order, and of music (楽 *gaku*), which provided an emotional basis for human development. As such, rather than being a truly historical discourse of "progress involving a break with the past and justified by universalistic-transcendental orientations"[14] as in the social revolutions of Europe, China, and Russia, the Japanese nation as *kokutai* was envisioned "as a unique type of collectivity, defined in primordial sacral-natural terms."[15]

Buddhism, with its own universalistic-transcendental orientations, was critiqued by influential ideologues of the period—such as the aforementioned Hirata Atsutane, the founder of Restoration Shinto—in numerous and predictable ways, such as being foreign, polluted (*kega-re*), and both antithetical to family values as well as economically unproductive for its emphasis on monasticism—these latter claims common to earlier persecutions of Buddhism in China. Hirata singled out the Pure Land and Nichiren schools as particularly

---

12   Eisenstadt. *Japanese Civilization*. p. 222.

13   Ibid., p. 209.

14   Ibid., p. 216.

15   Ibid., p. 32.

pernicious for their sublimation of Japanese gods to buddhas and hence their lack of true loyalty to the emperor and the nation.[16] Hirata, reflecting the historical project of the Mito School, further attempted to discredit Buddhism, as Western colonialists had done, on the basis that its sacred texts lacked any historical accuracy and were often the fabrications of later writers.[17] He felt that Buddhism, in fact, had created a gap or fissure in Japanese history between the present and an unadulterated antiquity. The medieval period during which Buddhism held sacral supremacy over the state and the people was seen as "decadent, distortive, and destructive."[18]

In contrast, many Japanese historians, especially Buddhist ones, would view the Kamakura period as the richest period of Buddhist ferment in Japan, akin to the later Christian Reformation in Europe that ultimately gave birth to liberal society and, hence, one in which axialization seemed most possible. The central concept of *mappo* (the Age of the Final Dharma), which flourished during this period, also shares with these later Nativist-Shinto schools the view of an ancient golden period—that of the *shobo*, the Age of the True Dharma, when the historical Buddha was alive. In general, the *mappo* discourse is unusual for the typical, immanental Japanese cosmological view, which also pervaded Heian Buddhism through the concept of innate enlightenment (*hongaku*). *Mappo* is part of a Buddhist view of history based on transcendental Indian concepts of time, and as such does not so much seek a return to the conditions of the Buddha's time but rather *a new creative response* to the present based on the essential concepts of the Buddha's teachings. With such an understanding, the new Kamakura Buddhist reformers—who fit Eisenstadt's definition of axial "activators" as "autonomous, relatively unattached 'intellectuals', such as prophets or visionaries"—re-interpreted Buddhist thought and practice in distinctive new ways to meet the specific historical tumult and widespread social and political crisis at the end of the Heian Court. They made practical the universal, perennial, and essential human ethics of Buddhism to transform both the individual and society towards a new social vision, very much expressed in Nichiren's view of realizing the Pure Land in this world.

The imperial restoration discourse of the late Tokugawa also held visions of realizing an ideal world but rather through the return to an archaic past that romanticized the exceptional and divine character of

---

16 Ketelaar. *Of Heretics and Martyrs in Meiji Japan*. pp. 34-35.

17 Ibid., p. 30.

18 Ibid., p. 64.

the Japanese *kokutai* under the divinity of the emperor. While both visions have their mythic sensibilities, the Buddhist vision is based in axial ethics promoting the universality of the human condition and elevating each individual with personal and social agency. This universal agency transcends ethnic or national lines while also deconstructing a collectivist obedience to authority and a graded system of power built on access to an inscrutable source of power, be it God, the Emperor, or some mystic Absolute. Based in the view and practice of radical emptiness (*shunyata*) and dependent co-origination (*pratitya-samutpada*), Buddhism undercuts any appeals to an inscrutable source of power, yet, as we will see, is also prone to distortions that reify such power.

As noted at the end of the previous chapter, there were a variety of millennial themes to the frequent occurrence of peasant revolts that numbered over one thousand between the 1830s and 1870s.[19] They emphasized communal equality, autonomy, and direct relations to nature, but these did not translate into or become adopted values by the new Meiji order. Further, unlike the ideological contributions of religious groups like the Puritans in the English and American Revolutions, or of ideologues and intelligentsia in the French and Russian revolts, there was an "almost total absence of distinct, autonomous religious or secular intellectual groups among the *active* participants in the political process" of the Meiji Restoration.[20] The Restoration was led by a group of secondary samurai, while different class groups such as merchants and peasants remained relatively isolated in their own protest movements and played little role in the final shift. These groups provided a backdrop of discontent leading to the end of the Tokugawa but played no role in the Meiji Restoration.[21] The Restoration was essentially a revolution from above with the toppling of one samurai group by another, particularly from the regions of Choshu and Satsuma, with no real ideological shift.

It seems important to also consider the effect of the two hundred and fifty years of cultural isolation that Japan endured during the Tokugawa lockdown from the early 1600s to mid-1800s. The Kamakura Buddhist Reformation of the 12th and 13th centuries predates the European Protestant Reformation by some three hundred years, and, like the latter, had far reaching socio-political influences for centuries to come. It grew out of a five-hundred-year period of intellectual ferment and interchange with China's Tang and Song

---

19 Ibid., p. 52.
20 Eisenstadt. *Japanese Civilization*. p. 268.
21 Ibid., p. 267.

dynastic cultures. Similarly, the Western social revolutions of the 18th and 19th centuries evolved out of the formative cultural movements that spread across numerous nations in Europe. The Renaissance, the Protestant Reformation, and the Scientific Revolution created brand new articulations, both secular and religious, which transcended national and ethnic sentiments. However, in Tokugawa Japan, Christianity was banned, Buddhism co-opted, and Confucianism pruned amidst a barricade on interaction with international currents during this highly dynamic international period. While European social thought came of age at this time through the contributions of such thinkers as Hobbes, Locke, Rousseau, Hegel, and finally Marx, Japanese social thought, as we have seen, retreated from the radical and progressive thought of the Kamakura Buddhist masters into an archaic one of imperial restoration—as seen in the educational and public ritualist movements towards Shinto nationalism based on Hirata Atsutane's extremely immanental concept of the "unity of rite and rule" (*saisei-icchi*).[22]

This was perhaps an understandable response driven out of fear of the colonial West rather than what might have developed in a new, forward-looking vision to build bridges with international currents, especially those previously imbedded in Japanese culture from the Asian continent. Indeed, by the dawn of the Meiji in 1868, Europe itself was retreating from classical liberal humanism and its themes of rationalism, positivism, bourgeois society, and liberal democracy towards the emotionalism, irrationalism, subjectivism, and vitalism of what became the early 20th century fascist movement. As we will soon see, however, within one generation of extended international exposure, Japan and Japanese Buddhism developed rich new currents of thought unparalleled since the Kamakura period.

Meat, Marriage, and Military:
The Final Immanentalization of the Japanese Buddhist Monk

The Mito School did not simply initiate an intellectual movement against Buddhism. It provided a template for a nationwide campaign called to "abolish Buddhism and destroy Shakyamuni" (廃仏毀釈 *haibutsu kishaku*) at the dawn of the Meiji era. Following the new regulations on Buddhism implemented in the early decades of the Tokugawa period, the Mito realm enacted a particularly strict

---

22 Ketelaar. *Of Heretics and Martyrs in Meiji Japan*. p. 64.

interpretation on not only Buddhism but all forms of religion.[23] As early as the 1840s, a much more active stripping away of vestiges of Buddhist culture took place in Mito, beginning with the forced laicization of priests and their "return to farming" (帰農 *ki-no*) and other forms of productive work, eventually extending to the destruction and closing of almost half of the 2,400 temples in the domain. Especially notable amongst these closures was the shutting down of halls and hermitages used for seasonal festivals by wandering Buddhist itinerants, who were seen as particularly subversive for their unregulated status. Another critical shift was the change in the annual festival calendar of communities, which banned many important Buddhist seasonal events based around ancestor worship, like Obon, and replaced them with Shinto rites.[24] In this way, the Mito domain offered a complete blueprint for the ideological implementation of imperial restoration.

The nationalization of this movement in the *haibutsu kishaku* began in the early days of the new Meiji regime with the official mandate, in April 1868, to sever all ties between Shinto shrines and Buddhist temples, called *shin-butsu bunri* 神仏分離. In Japan, as in basically all Buddhist communities and nations in Asia, there has been a mixing of local, indigenous religious beliefs and customs with Buddhist ones. This was developed strongly during the Heian period with the concept of "origin and manifestation" (*honji-suijaku*), in which Japanese gods (*kami*) came to be regarded as manifestations of buddhas and bodhisattvas. Restoration ideologues like Hirata Atsutane roundly denounced this concept,[25] and the *shin-butsu bunri* policy brought about its eradication. This policy followed many of the precedents carried out in Mito with a nationwide movement of forced laicization of Buddhist monks, conversion of public Buddhist rituals including funerals into Shinto ones, and widespread destruction of Buddhist images, texts, and temples, which by the end of the persecution in 1874 numbered over 40,000 temples.[26]

This policy could be carried out with such success, despite the protests of the large and powerful Buddhist denominations, due to the Office of Rites in the new Meiji government. Occupied by Nativist Shinto ideologues, it was responsible for the implementation of the ideology of the "unity of rite and rule" (*saisei-icchi*) and played a critical

---

23 Ibid., p. 47.
24 Ibid., pp. 49, 54.
25 Ibid., p. 36.
26 Ibid., p. 7.

role in the formulation of the Charter Oath that established the Meiji Emperor as the new head of state.[27] While this policy was successfully implemented in regions that strongly supported the Restoration, such as Mito, Buddhist strongholds in various parts of the country began a resistance movement with sometimes violent protests against these policies. Counter revolts in Toyama in late 1870, Mikawa in present day Aichi in 1872, and Fukui in 1873 created such a general level of disturbance around these policies that secular factions within the new Meiji regime brought an end to the more forceful aspects of the *shin-butsu bunri* policy by 1874.[28]

A perhaps more critical set of reforms were instituted in 1872 with the law deregulating state control over, and enforcement of, the Buddhist monastic *vinaya*, known as the "meat eating and marriage" (肉食妻帯 *nikujiki saitai*) policy. In short, it ended all penalties for Buddhist monks who violated state and denominational standards by eating meat, marrying, letting their hair grow, or abandoning monastic robes at any time.[29] This regulation and its aftermath represents the logical conclusion of the immanentalization of the Buddhist monk in Japan: beginning with the lay bodhisattva values espoused by Prince Shotoku at the opening of the 7th century; which were brought to fruition by Saicho's abandonment of the classical Dharmagupta *vinaya* in favor of the exclusive practice of the *Brahma Net Sutra* bodhisattva precepts at the opening of the 9th century; which eventually gave birth to the Pure Land movement's guarantee of salvation without any of the classical monastic trainings of *sila-samadhi-prajna* and the Jodo Shin sect's complete abandonment of the monastic *vinaya* in the 12th and 13th centuries. It is more than ironic that the Pure Land movement, which had been considered a wildly heretical cult and endured numerous persecutions in the Kamakura period, became the standard bearer of meat eating married priests that has become the present-day norm in almost all Buddhist sects.

As with the localized resistance to the separation of shrines and temples policy, the meat eating and marriage policy received considerable push-back, from not only leaders in the more monastic denominations like Zen but also, rather ironically, from Pure Land leaders like Fukuda Gyokai 福田行誡 (1809–1888) of the Jodo sect. Fukuda argued, very prophetically as it turns out, that it would be impossible

---

27 Ibid., p. 88.

28 Ibid., p. 7.

29 Jaffe, Richard. "Meiji Religious Policy, Soto Zen, and the Clerical Marriage Problem". *Japanese Journal of Religious Studies*. 1998. Vol. 25, No. 1-2. p. 46.

to re-instill discipline in the monastic Sangha if this regulation were allowed to take effect.[30] The rapid increase in married priests after the 1872 policy indicates this was already a common practice that was not done openly due to general disapproval from parishioners. It has been estimated that by the middle of the Meiji period, some forty to fifty percent of all Buddhist priests were married.[31] Further, in a survey from 1936 by the Soto Zen sect—which doctrinally has strong, traditional regulations on celibacy—families lived in more than eighty-one percent of temples.[32]

The new policy led to creative developments in the more conservative monastic-centric schools, such as the Shingon denomination, which created a two-tier system of ordination with "pure" (青衆 *shoshu*) and "impure" (雑衆 *zasshu*) priests, as well as the Tendai denomination, which divided their ordained priests into unmarried ones (解脱僧 *gedatsu-so*) and married ones (近事僧 *gonji-so*).[33] These attempts were part of a wider movement during this period—as we saw under the Shingon Ritsu master Eison in the Kamakura period—to revive the practice of the precepts in an age of perceived social and religious decay by Buddhists.

The *nikuji-saitai* policy was followed by others, such as those that classified priests as common citizens (国民 *kokumin*), who had to register as belonging to a household, even as a "temple family" (寺族 *ji-zoku*). They were also pushed to take a common surname, as opposed to the Mahayana monastic convention of taking *shaku* 釈, the Buddha's name, as a surname. In contrast to the precept revival movement, the much stronger Japanese inclination to the lay bodhisattva path led to a modern Lay Buddhist (在家仏教 *Zai-ke Bukkyo*) movement, which continues to be a distinctive feature of Japanese Buddhism today. Not surprisingly, it was led by Jodo Shin reformers, like Inoue Enryo 井上円了 (1858–1919) and Shimaji Mokurai 島地黙雷 (1838–1911), who were proponents of the marriage of priests based on the already existing hypocrisy of monks having children clandestinely. Because of the hidden nature of these relationships, Inoue and Shimaji argued that the ordained Sangha was becoming genetically tainted by the kinds of marginal women who would get involved in such affairs, such as those past the age considered optimal

---

30   Ibid., p. 60.
31   Ibid., p. 63.
32   Ibid., p. 76.
33   Ibid., p. 64.

for marriage, destitute widows, and former prostitutes.[34] The Jodo Shin sect, on the other hand, had for centuries been practicing clerical marriage, and the wives and mothers of the denomination, they claimed, came from the finest women in their communities. In tune with emerging trends in Meiji modernist discourse, they argued that monastic celibacy was anti-modern, anti-scientific, and unpatriotic.[35]

While the support for such modern policies might appear as a violation of traditional Buddhist norms, there is once again a continuity to be found from the Tokugawa era in the Buddhist support for class and gender discrimination based on the notion of pollution or taint (*kega-re*). These attitudes found new ways to express themselves through the eugenics movement brought from the United States and Germany. The marriage of ancient concepts of *kega-re* and modern eugenics were critical in the prewar period in controlling the reproductive rights of women to bolster the population for war while also purifying the gene pool through forced sterilizations—the latter of which continued until 1996.[36] As we will explore in Volume II, these attitudes have also led to the ostracization of the radiation victims (被爆者 *hibakusha*) of Hiroshima and Nagasaki as well as Fukushima for fear of giving birth to a generation of genetically inferior citizens.

As we will now examine, what began as an anti-Buddhist, Nativist-Shinto program for the creation of a theocratic state under the "unity of rite and rule" (*saisei-icchi*) ended up becoming something much more complex as international currents began to sweep over Japan and introduce competing ideological norms, specifically in secular liberalism and scientific modernism. While the celibate Buddhist monk in Japan was finally and thoroughly immanentalized and has now become an endangered species, the new laicized Buddhist priest was freed of the shackles of Tokugawa state regulation and could engage in a civilizational movement and its axial potentialities.

---

34   Ibid., p. 71.

35   Ibid., p. 70.

36   Hovhannisyan, Astghik. "The Testimony of a Victim of Forced Sterilization in Japan: Kita Saburo". *The Asia-Pacific Journal*. Japan Focus. Apr 1, 2020. Vol. 18:7, No. 2.

7

The Meiji Buddhist Enlightenment

Buddhist Liberalism and the Opening of Japan to the Challenge of Civilization

As noted, the *haibutsu kishaku* persecution of Buddhism only lasted a few years until 1874, and this reflected the reservations of certain key Meiji reformers like Iwakura Tomomi 岩倉具視 (1825–1883) and Okubo Toshimichi 大久保利通 (1830–1878), who did not fully identify with a theocratic state based on the unity of rite and rule (*saisei-icchi*). The important Shinto leaders in the Ministry of Rites, such as Hirata Atsutane's adopted son Kanatane, were marginalized,[37] and by 1872 a new Ministry of Doctrine was established. This ministry sought to incorporate Buddhist teachers together with Shinto ones in a more balanced and non-partisan system of national pedagogy for educating the masses on the ideology of the Restoration.[38] For the Buddhists, this system was still an affront to their independence, since they were not allowed to work as Buddhist priests but had to don Shinto robes. The Great Teaching Academy (大教院 *Daikyo-in*), which served as the center of this system, was located at the grand, main temple of the Jodo sect, Zojo-ji 増上寺, which had been the family temple of the Tokugawa during its rule. During the days of the Academy, however, it was refurbished to look like a Shinto shrine, including the replacement of the main image of Amida Buddha with Shinto deities.[39]

Such affronts to their independence resulted in the withdrawal from the Academy by Buddhist denominations in 1875, led by Jodo Shin Buddhists like the aforementioned Shimaji Mokurai. Shimaji, who had been involved in local militias in Choshu in southern Japan to forcefully oppose the *haibutsu kishaku*, wrote a thirteen-article appeal to the government bemoaning Japan's backward creation of a new state religion based on the "blind foolishness" of the worship of animist gods. Linking Buddhism with the axial qualities of the Greek and Indian traditions, Shimaji promoted Buddhism as an indigenous

---

37   Ketelaar. *Of Heretics and Martyrs in Meiji Japan*. pp. 66-67.
38   Ibid., p. 70.
39   Ibid., p. 122.

resource for Japan based in a "unified and rational articulation of mind, principle, and spiritual training."[40] He made a further appeal to "the great road of civilization" (文明の大道 bunmei-no dai-do) that can be attained when useful scientific and legal systems are learned from abroad and "not interpreted as the fulfillment of mysterious and divine orders, as the brilliance and munificence of a divine rule, or as the glorious manifestation of a religion of the hidden."[41]—an obvious direct attack on the common tendencies towards cultural exceptionalism at the time.

Shimaji's efforts were central to what became a growing movement against the policy of *saisei-icchi*. Instead, for perhaps the first time in Japanese history,[42] the "separation of religion and rule" (政教分離 *sei-kyo bunri*) was advanced, culminating in the 1889 Meiji Constitution's Freedom of Religion Clause: "Japanese subjects shall, within the limits not prejudicial to peace and order, and not antagonistic to their duties as subjects, enjoy freedom of religious belief." Shimaji's work was part of a wider strand of thought in the first two decades of the Meiji Restoration that was looking beyond the narrow confines of the Neo-Confucian-Shinto Restoration ideology to international sources of "civilization and enlightenment" (文明開化 *bunmei kaika*).[43]

The term *bunmei kaika* has various translations depending on how one fully interprets it. The latter term *kaika* actually has a Buddhist origin and means to teach the dharma and guide sentient beings to enlightenment. However, the term is often translated in the context of the Meiji era as simply "Westernization", since the *bunmei kaika* movement signaled the mass adoption of Western ideas and technology. The term was brought to prominence by Japan's foremost early liberal thinker, Fukuzawa Yukichi 福澤諭吉 (1835–1901) in the early days of the Meiji and signaled a dynamic period in the spread of liberal thought until the end of the century. During this time, the works of European liberals like John Stuart Mill, John Locke, Herbert Spencer, Jeremy Bentham, and Jean-Jacques Rousseau spread amongst the new urban classes of lawyers, teachers, doctors, nurses etc., who wished to distinguish themselves from the "decadent" aristocracy and "backward" masses. They were drawn to a new conception of society and the citizens who occupied it.[44]

---

40   Ibid., p. 127.

41   Ibid., p. 129.

42   Ibid., p. 216.

43   Eisenstadt. *Japanese Civilization*. pp. 25, 35.

44   Garon, Sheldon. "From Meiji to Heisei: The State and Civil Society in Japan".

Western liberalism offered a completely new understanding of the individual, as, in the words of John Locke (1632–1704), existing naturally in "a State of perfect Freedom to order their Actions...as they think fit...without asking leave, or depending on the Will of any other Man." In Western liberalism, individual freedom is normative, and restrictions on liberty must be justified.[45] Furthermore, an economic system based on private property is necessary for such individual liberty and, in turn, becomes the embodiment of freedom.[46] With this fundamental basis that humans in their original natural state are atomistic, self-defined individuals, society—and the state in particular—is viewed an artificial construction necessary to guarantee the negative liberty of the minimization of obstacles to freedom. From this basic orientation, the modern, social contract theories of Thomas Hobbes (1588–1679), Jean-Jacques Rousseau (1712–1778), Immanuel Kant (1724–1804), and Locke developed with the notion that, "The state is an artifact, a human contrivance...a functionalist and contractualist conception."[47]

As Germaine A. Hoston notes in his powerful analysis of liberalism in prewar Japan, "In both these respects—in its contractualism and in its differentiation of state and society—Western liberalism differs fundamentally from the organic conception of the polity embodied in *kokutai* thought and from the conceptions of the polity in its Shinto and Confucian antecedents in Japan."[48] Based in the collectivist, circumscribed interpretation of Neo-Confucianism, individual rights in Japan have never been allowed to stand above the collective well-being, and this is reflected in the Meiji's importation of Italian and French civil codes that provided maximum bureaucratic control over citizens groups[49] rather than German ones.

As one of the key leaders in the *bunmei kaika* movement, Fukuzawa emphasized the need for a new public sphere based on private institutions—such as Japan's first private university, Keio

---

In *The State of Civil Society in Japan*. Eds. Frank J. Schwartz & Susan J. Pharr. (Cambridge University Press, 2003), pp. 46-47.

45 Gaus, Gerald; Courtland, Shane D.; and Schmidtz, David. "Liberalism". In *The Stanford Encyclopedia of Philosophy* (Fall 2020 Edition), Ed. Edward N. Zalta. https://plato.stanford.edu/archives/fall2020/entries/liberalism/. p. 1.

46 Gaus et al. "Liberalism". p. 4.

47 Hoston, Germaine A. "The State, Modernity, and the Fate of Liberalism in Prewar Japan". In *The Journal of Asian Studies*. May, 1992. Vol. 51, No. 2, p. 293.

48 Ibid., p. 293.

49 Pharr, Susan. "Targeting by an Activist State: Japan as a Civil Society Model". In *The State of Civil Society in Japan*. p. 333.

University, which he founded in the early 1870s—based on his maxim, "Independent individuals make for an independent country." Such concepts also found their way into the rural populace, which had already developed high levels of literacy through the old Tokugawa era clan schools (*hanko*). Most notably, the Sanshi-sha 三師社 (Society of Mihara District Teachers) in Fukushima promoted the values of the *bunmei kaika* movement and called for the establishment of a national assembly on the basis of Locke's natural rights doctrine. While its appeal may have been "cloaked in terms consonant with Confucian orthodoxy" from which the clan schools evolved, their activities led beyond even liberal trends to more socialistic ones in the Freedom and Popular Rights Movement (自由民権運動 *Jiyu Minken-undo*).[50]

While it is clear that Shimaji Mokurai became deeply influenced by this Western liberal conception of the individual and society during his tour of Europe in 1872, he and other important Meiji Buddhist leaders like Anesaki Masaharu 姉崎正治 (1873–1949) also developed ideas on civilization through important Buddhist sources that preceded those of Europe. The essential source for Meiji era Japanese Buddhists was the *Record of the Transmission of the Buddha Dharma through the Three Nations* (三國佛法傳通緣起 *Sangoku buppo denzu engi*) written in 1311 by Japanese Buddhism's most important, early pan-sectarian historian Gyonen 凝然 (1240–1322). Gyonen created a comprehensive history of the sects and teachings of Japanese Buddhism by first tracing its transmission across the great civilizations of India and China and finally into Japan.[51]

In this way, Meiji Buddhists were not only responding to the chauvinism of archaic Nativist-Shinto state ideology but also the implicit chauvinism that saw the apex of human civilization as evolving from the Greek-Christian-secular liberal lineage of the West. In the work of re-articulating Buddhism as a firmly historical movement that reflected an international and civilizational ethic, they sought a third way for modern Japan. Such a universal and international Buddhist articulation of civilization, as referenced throughout this volume, is a lesser-known contribution to the earliest forms of Socially Engaged Buddhism in Asia, specifically Anagarika Dharmapala's (1864–1933) Maha Bodhi movement.

Shimaji's work also laid the foundations for what is called the Buddhist Enlightenment Movement (仏教啓蒙活動 *Bukkyo Keimo-katsudo*), which began around 1886 in this more open and

---

50   Garon. "From Meiji to Heisei". pp. 46-47.

51   Ketelaar. *Of Heretics and Martyrs in Meiji Japan*. pp. 178, 213.

liberal period before the promulgation of the new Meiji Constitution in 1889. This period is seen as coming to a close in 1910 with the attempted assassination of the emperor in the High Treason Incident at the end of the Meiji.[52] Shimaji's Jodo Shin colleague in the clerical marriage movement, Inoue Enryo (1858-1919), was another seminal figure at this time for combining a rationalistic view of religion based on logic and reason with an anti-Christian bias and an "essentialistic, organic vision of Japan". This vision was promoted through his Philosophy Center (哲学館 *Tetsugakkan*) founded in 1887, which later evolved into present-day Toyo University.[53] Inoue and his Jodo Shin Otani sect colleague Kiyozawa Manshi 清沢満之 (1863-1903), who had become Tetsugakkan's secretary, studied Western philosophy together, specifically Hegelian and Darwinian social theory, at Tokyo University under Ernest Fenellosa (1853-1908), who introduced Japanese Buddhism and fine art to the United States.[54] Inoue's renunciation of his ordination in 1885, his influence on Kiyozawa's search for a more secular and modern Buddhism, and the activities of the Philosophy Center were important in establishing lay Buddhism "as a coherent social force" seeking to go beyond the rigidified Buddhist institutions leftover from the Tokugawa that had been the target of both reactionary Nativist and progressive modern critiques.[55]

Priests from the Jodo Shin schools were not the only important ones of this movement, which came to include those from all core Japanese Buddhist doctrinal standpoints. One especially influential line of reformers was the Rinzai Zen lineage of Imakita Kosen 今北洪川 (1816-92), Shaku Soen 釈宗演 (1859-1919), and Suzuki Daisetsu 鈴木大拙 (1870-1966) based at Engaku-ji 円覚寺, the great Kamakura-era Five Mountain (*gozan*) temple that had been built by Hojo Tokimune. Even as an ordained monk in the rigorous monastic tradition of Rinzai Zen, Imakita helped to lead a new influential lay Zen group based in Tokyo called the Association for the Abandonment of Concepts of Objectivity and Subjectivity (両忘協会 *Ryobo Kyo-kai*). Having strong Confucian leanings, Imakita's goal was to contribute to the lay Buddhist movement by showing the way of personal and communal moral cultivation that would create the basis of a good society. His efforts are important to note as typical of many Meiji

---

52 Shields, James Mark. *Against Harmony: Progressive and Radical Buddhism in Modern Japan*. (New York: Oxford University Press, 2017), pp. 33-34.

53 Ibid., p. 35.

54 Ibid., p. 75.

55 Ibid., p. 10, 36.

Buddhist reformists who carried on the Neo-Confucian emphasis of personal cultivation in morals and culture while disconnecting them from political matters[56]—a tendency that remains strong in Japanese Buddhism today.

His disciple Shaku Soen, whose influence reached far beyond Japan, is one of the most important members of the Meiji Buddhist Enlightenment. His forward-looking and inquisitive nature led him to convince Imakita for permission to study at Fukuzawa's new Keio Private School (慶應義塾 *Keio Gijuku*), which soon became Keio University, and then to spend three years in Sri Lanka practicing the lifestyle of ancient Buddhism as preserved in the Theravada tradition.[57] Soen's internationalism is further exemplified by his participation as one of the five Japanese Buddhists at the epochal World Parliament of Religions in Chicago in 1893 and by his subsequent tours of the United States to teach Zen. Like others of the Meiji Buddhist Enlightenment, he refuted archaic forms of "sentimentalism" that lead to "mysticism" and felt that metaphysical speculation was a preparation for ethics and for practical and spiritual goals. As with his master Imakita, however, he saw suffering in the world as coming from individual, moral failing rather than social systems or culture.[58]

In contrast to Imakita and Soen was Hirai Kinzo 平井金三 (1859–1916), who was not a monastic but a lay practitioner of Rinzai Zen based in Kyoto. Born in the same year as Soen, their lives have numerous parallels. While Soen encountered the famous Sri Lankan Socially Engaged Buddhist reformer Anagarika Dharmapala during his time in Sri Lanka, Hirai supported him and American Colonel Henry Steel Olcott on a tour of Japan in 1888 to spread their Theosophical movement and plans to unify Buddhism globally. Both Soen and Hirai reunited with Dharmapala at the World Parliament of Religions, where Hirai became perhaps the most notable Buddhist figure. In an impassioned speech, he acknowledged Japan's persecution of Christianity in the Tokugawa period but defended its position against the economic, political, and cultural imperialism of the Christian West. Hirai punctured the veneer of brotherhood and facile ecumenism with a hard-driving critique that would later be extended to Japan's own imperial outlook and to religion within Japan itself.[59]

---

56 Ibid., p. 41.

57 Fields, Rick. *How the Swans Came to the Lake: A Narrative History of Buddhism in America*. (Boulder, CO: Shambhala Publications, 1992), pp. 110-13.

58 Shields. *Against Harmony*. pp. 46-47.

59 Ketelaar. *Of Heretics and Martyrs in Meiji Japan*. pp. 169-70.

The Meiji Buddhist Enlightenment

In *Religion and Politics* (宗教と政治 *Shukyo-to seiji*), published five years after the Parliament in 1898, Hirai emphasized that for religion to have the power to transform social injustice, it must be open to self-critique of its own use and misuse of power. Religion "is an integral element of the social order and as such must serve as both a moral and an ethical guide, as well as a tool for expanded social production and the distribution of wealth."[60] Poking at the archaic ideology of the Restoration, he argued that religious thought and morality must be applied "scientifically" rather than "poetically" and that the failure of moral education in this age must be confronted structurally as well as individually through a large-scale social transformation that includes some public ownership of industry.[61] James Shields, in his detailed portrait of Japanese Buddhist reformers during this era, recognizes Hirai's work as a precursor to that of the Critical Buddhism (*Hihan Bukkyo*) movement of the 1980s led by Soto Zen intellectuals. Hirai's calls for religion to self-critique in order to lead a more comprehensive social transformation are also echoed strongly in the career of Thai social critic Sulak Sivaraksa (1932–), the leading founder of the International Network of Engaged Buddhists (INEB).[62]

If Hirai represents a more critical adjustment to the ideas of Imakita and Soen within the Zen community, then the work of Murakami Sensho 村上専精 (1851–1929) marks a similar critique of the limits of the social-political thought of his Jodo Shin Otani sect contemporaries Inoue and Kiyozawa. Building on the historicization project of Buddhism in Gyonen's three-nation theory of Buddhist civilization and fellow Jodo Shin priest Shimaji's critique of archaic Nativist-Shinto thought, Murakami searched for a common platform to unite all Buddhist schools, if not institutionally then, in basic ideals.[63] In his *On the Unification of Buddhism* (仏教統一論 *Bukkyo toitsu-ron*), he criticized the Mahayana's attempts to claim legitimacy over older schools in India by establishing an eternal timelessness to its teachings, for example, the eternal Shakyamuni of the *Lotus Sutra*. Murakami notes, "It is natural for scientific research to conclude that Shakyamuni Buddha was a historical figure. To regard him as a transcendent being is pure foolishness."[64]

---

60   Shields. *Against Harmony*. p. 55.

61   Ibid., p. 56.

62   Swearer, Donald K. "Sulak Sivaraksa's Buddhist Vision for Renewing Society". In *Engaged Buddhism: Buddhist Liberation Movements in Asia*. pp. 215, 219.

63   Shields. *Against Harmony*. p. 67.

64   Ibid., p. 68.

Such chauvinistic interpretations of Mahayana Buddhism became part of the *bunmei kaika* movement and common among Meiji Buddhist Enlightenment figures like Inoue and Soen. The critiques of them by Murakami and a few others resulted in being labeled as proponents of "the theory that the Mahayana teachings are not true Buddhism" (大乗非仏説論 *daijo hibussetsu-ron*), a clear precursor of the Critical Buddhism movement and also a stance that led to Murakami being defrocked by the Otani sect. It is this critical historical stance, however, that allowed Murakami to see beyond the confines of his own Buddhist tradition and his nation to articulate such universal ethics as follows: "It is extremely difficult to criticize war when one's place of enunciation is located within the state. It is only when one takes a position outside the state [for example] in religion… that war can be shown as evil."[65] Murakami's work stands as an important pivot in the internationalist, civilizational discourse of Meiji Buddhism. As we will see, the creation of a kind of firewall between personal development and social transformation led many others in the Buddhist Enlightenment movement to slide into the nationalistic and totalitarian discourses the emerged in Imperial Japan.

Buddhist Nationalism and the Neo-Confucian Mutation of Liberalism

The issue of what type of civilization Japan was going to build for itself as it entered modernity was an ongoing struggle. Would this civilization be an archaic, ethnocentric one built on the fusion Neo-Confucianism and Shintoism? Would it be a pan-Asian and potentially universal one built on a modernized, Socially Engaged Buddhism? Would it be a secular and scientific one built on notions of European enlightenment? This question had in fact begun to be formulated before the Meiji Restoration when the first Christian missionaries introduced the threat of Western colonization to Japan at the beginning of the Tokugawa era. A major concern in confronting the forces of Western civilization was how much Christianity was actually central to the supposedly secular and scientific vision of modernity. If Japan was going to modernize using Western technology and systems of governance, how could it cope with the fundamental basis of the autonomous individual and the contractual vision of society that were in fact rooted in Christian values coming from the Protestant Reformation?

---

65 Ketelaar. *Of Heretics and Martyrs in Meiji Japan.* pp. 172-73.

For English liberals, like J.S. Mill, the nuclear family and social organization in the capitalist state needed to be grounded in Christian ethics. Fukuzawa also emphasized the role of the nuclear family in providing an ethical core for the new society, helping to initiate a trend that, as we have seen, completely transformed the Buddhist Sangha. However, questions regarding the Christian ethics contained in these Anglo-Saxon notions of social organization would not go away. In this way, the Japanese looked beyond Anglo-Saxon conceptions of liberalism towards Germany for "more culturally embedded models of national morality". Yet in the German models as well, "the Christian element was simply too central to be ignored. It had to be dealt with directly, discussed, and either accepted or replaced."[66] While there were indeed people who seriously advocated the wholesale appropriation of Christianity as part of the modernization of Japan, there was a growing concern amongst more conservative camps that the spread of liberal values was becoming a problem. This was especially evidenced in the activism for voting rights and constitutionalism by the Freedom and Popular Rights Movement led by former samurai and others who had lost out in the Meiji power shift.[67]

While the ideas of an archaic Shinto-based imperial restoration promoted by the Mito School and the National Learning movement were central in the Meiji revolution, many of the new rulers of the Meiji government had been raised in domanial Neo-Confucian-based *hanko* schools. As noted in the "separation of religion and rule" (*sei-kyo bunri*) movement against the orthodox Shinto one of the "unity of religion and government" (*saisei-icchi*), important Meiji leaders sought a uniquely East Asian form of modernism by recreating the Western liberal split between private Christian belief and secular public ethics. In this way, intellectual leaders, such as Nishi Amane 西周 (1829–1897), saw the potential for bringing together Neo-Confucian ethics with Western statecraft, thus ridding it of its Christian moral vestiges. Nishi was a colleague of Fukuzawa's in the *bunmei kaika* movement and an important member of the new Meiji bureaucracy. Having gone to study in Europe at the same time as Fukuzawa, he had a seminal influence on translating a variety of European philosophical terms into Japanese that are still in use today. While being heavily influenced by British liberalism, he quickly recognized the Christian values embedded in English liberal texts. Quite critically, he also saw

---

66   Paramore, Kiri. *Japanese Confucianism: A Cultural History* (Cambridge University Press, 2016), p. 148.

67   Sasaki. *Nationalism, Political Realism and Democracy in Japan.* p. 57.

the attempts to bridge Christian morality, based in an ethics of virtue, with utilitarianism based in what can be considered the opposite, an ethics of consequence. Nishi, thus, set about doing likewise in fusing philosophical utilitarianism with the social ethics of Japanese Neo-Confucianism.[68]

As mentioned earlier, Japanese Neo-Confucians had torn apart the dialectic of the Principle (*ri*) and the material or phenomenal (*ji*). In essence, this created an Asian form of Cartesian dualism by relegating the ethical, as expressed in the Principle, to the realm of the private and the individual; thus separating it from the public, the social, and, mostly critically, the act of governance.[69] In Ogyu Sorai's Neo-Confucian thought, an ethics of virtue found in the Principle was replaced by an ethics of consequence, that is, the utility of ends. The legitimacy of government then was not dependent on being consonant with the Mandate of Heaven but on the subjective criteria established by the government itself in realizing its own goals of rule. In short, "the ruler may act against just principles so long as he pursues the political goal of maintaining peace among the people."[70] Nishi saw the implications of Ogyu's thought as facilitating governance to increase its utility and welfare. This discovery of a uniquely East Asian form of modern utilitarianism enabled Nishi and other Meiji bureaucrats to build an entire system of governance.[71]

By 1900, most upper civil servants had university law degrees from Tokyo Imperial University. Through developing a homogenous outlook based on utilitarian principles that sought to weed out as much as to educate, a pyramid structure of authority was built that replaced the feudal one of ascribed status as the new basis for

---

68 Paramore. *Japanese Confucianism*. pp. 126-27.

69 Socially Engaged Buddhist author, David Loy, explains that the Protestant conclusion that faith and salvation is private, and hence humans are isolated individuals is "still our problem with civil society, because that tension between individual freedom and the common good has never been resolved." Loy, David R. *A Buddhist History of the West: Studies in Lack*. (Albany, NY: State University of New York Press, 2002), p. 154. This schism between individual and society, which became the foundation for Cartesian mind-body dualism, haunts modern Western history and its liberal foundations through the rise of racist colonialism, the madness of individual nation states run amok in two world wars, and the ultimate cost of our earth's environment through industrial growth capitalism. See the Afterword for more on this issue.

70 Kersten. *Democracy in Postwar Japan*. p. 55.

71 Paramore. *Japanese Confucianism*. p. 125.

determining leadership eligibility.[72] The authority of such principles was based in the notion that "expertise is synonymous with impartiality" and that "universally applied administrative rules and routines" achieve the highest form of decision making, even above political ones.[73] As long as this system appears fair because it is based on some kind of perceived meritocracy of acquiring expertise through higher education, all social movements can be circumscribed and contained by tweaks to the bureaucratic system. In this way, utilitarian logic was used as a type of dictatorship or monopoly of power to exclude all parties not deemed rational, expert, and utilitarian enough to make decisions, including all politicians.[74]

This is a dialectic from which there is no escape, as Max Weber implies in his reference to bureaucratic formalism as the epitome of the iron cage of capitalism. As the Japanese bureaucratic state emerged into full bloom in the early 20th century, the bureaucracy funneled the growing variety of individual and group interests into a single state system using utilitarian rationale to surpass the concept of individual rights with the collective rights of society,[75] giving birth to the unique East Asian form of modernity in "collective utilitarianism" (集団功利主義 shudan kori-shugi).[76] As we will continue to reference and examine in this volume, this system remains the pervasive form of rule in modern Japan.

In theory, this public-private dualism also freed the individual to be more autonomous and creative, as in the kind of Western liberalism Fukuzawa extolled. However, by the early 1880s, there emerged a backlash to this influx of liberal thought and Western individualism led by even non-Confucian modernists in the government, such as Japan's first modern prime minister Ito Hirobumi 伊藤博文 (1841–1909) and one of the drafters of the new Meiji Constitution Inoue Kowashi 井

---

72 Silberman, Bernard S. "The Bureaucratic State in Japan: The Problem of Authority and Legitimacy". In *Conflict in Modern Japanese History: The Neglected Tradition*. Eds. Tetsuo Najita & J. Victor Koschmann. (Princeton University Press, 1982), pp. 236-7, 248.

73 Ibid., p. 251.

74 Ibid., pp. 251, 255.

75 Ibid., p. 250.

76 In the introduction to the new paperback edition of Robert Bellah's classic *Tokugawa Religion*, Shimazono Susumu 島薗進, the leading scholar on postwar Japanese religion, remarks that he is quoted as calling this system "group utilitarianism" but would like to rephrase it now as "collective utilitarianism". Personal Interview, October 23, 2021. See Bellah, Robert. *Tokugawa Religion: The Cultural Roots of Modern Japan*. (New York: The Free Press, 1985), p. xv.

上毅 (1844–95). In 1881, the Ministry of Education began to ban certain translations of Western books on moral philosophy and ideology, including one of Fukuzawa's works, while promoting those relating to positivism, utilitarianism, the materialism of natural science, and evolutionism—fields of thought clearly in harmony of the emphasis of the phenomenal over the Principle.[77]

These leaders, however, also saw the need for a modern public ethics, a principle, that stressed loyalty to the emperor as the head of state. They allowed the Meiji Emperor's Confucian tutor Motoda Nagazane 元田永孚 (1818–91) to help craft a national education policy "founded upon the Imperial ancestral precepts, benevolence, duty, loyalty, and filial piety".[78] The five social virtues (*go-jo*) and the five hierarchical relationships (*go-rin*) replaced both Christian and secular liberal ethics in this new East Asian collective utilitarianism so as to funnel the creative energy of the private individual into service to authority. This is the shift that liberals like Fukuzawa and, later, Maruyama found most distasteful in their critique of Confucianism.

A further step still needed to be taken in advancing this new form of East Asian collective utilitarianism that was promoting the "separation of religion and rule" (*sei-kyo bunri*) while at the same time fusing Neo-Confucian ethics and a Shintoist veneration of the emperor into public education. These Meiji elite had to take the same step Europe and America had done in designating certain fields as "religion", which would remain "consigned to the individual's free discretion", and other fields as "a public realm called 'morality' being imposed as a national obligation".[79] The separation of Buddhist temples and Shinto shrines (*shin-butsu bunri*) in the early days of the Meiji during the persecution of Buddhism and then the eventual laicization of the Buddhist priest as a family man and common citizen (*kokumin*) were critical steps in this process of relegating Buddhism to the private realm—a realm it is still trying to escape today. During this time, any aspects of Confucianism that existed in quasi-religious form, such as the old state Confucian academy Shohei-ko 昌平黌 and the attached

---

77 Sasaki. *Nationalism, Political Realism and Democracy in Japan*. p. 57.

78 Tsurumi, E. Patricia. "Meiji Primary School Language and Ethics Textbooks: Old Values for a New Society?" *Modern Asian Studies*. 1974. Vol. 8, No. 2, pp. 253-54.

79 Nakajima, Takahiro. "The Restoration of Confucianism in China and Japan: A New Source of Morality and Religion". In *Frontiers of Japanese Philosophy 4: Facing the 21st Century*. Eds. Wing Keung Lam & Ching Yuen Cheung. (Nagoya: Nanzan Institute for Religion & Culture, 2009), p. 42.

Yushima Sacred Hall 湯島聖堂, were shut down or severely curtailed.[80] Like Buddhism, those local practices of the common people related to Shinto were considered part of the private and free realm of individual worship and often practiced in tandem with Buddhism as a syncretic Shinto-Buddhist religion (神仏宗教 shin-butsu shukyo).

State Shinto (国家神道 Kokka Shinto), based around veneration of the emperor, became a new construction labelled as "civil religion". In this way, Neo-Confucian ethics and Shintoist veneration of the emperor as a syncretic Shinto-Confucian religion (神儒教宗教 shin-ju-kyo shukyo) were advanced as an obligatory form of national morality to which the private individual should accede to as a citizen of the state. To view this new public morality as a secular one would seem to stretch logic, yet Japanese leaders felt it to be justifiable in the wider process of bunmei kaika and considering how the West used Christianity as a justification for its colonialization of and civilizing mission in Asia. Ito Hirobumi, in his famous speech opening the Constitutional Convention of the Japanese Empire in 1889, argued this point that Japan too should use religious elements to control and mobilize its citizenry, an argument originally derived from the Mito School's Aizawa Seishisai's *New Theses*.[81]

The culmination of this new public ethics and national ideology was the Imperial Rescript on Education (教育勅語 Kyoiku Chokugo), issued in 1890, the year after the promulgation of the new Meiji Constitution. Although the Rescript was not initially considered an obligatory article of faith for citizens, it became increasingly so as Japan became more militaristic, and eventually all school children were forced to memorize and recite it. Edited and developed by the Meiji Emperor's tutor Motoda Nagazane and his more secular counterpart Inoue Kowashi, the Rescript strongly reflects the line of Japanese Neo-Confucianism coming from Zhu Xi, directly emphasizing the five social virtues (go-jo), particularly filial piety and loyalty. These values were then tied together with veneration of the emperor using the analogy of the state and the kokutai as a family.[82] From this basis, the Rescript further stated that, "Should emergency arise, offer yourselves courageously to the State; and thus, guard and maintain the prosperity of Our Imperial Throne coeval with heaven and earth". In this way, the Emperor replaced the transcendental Principle, and the carrying out of Confucian ethics tied the citizen not to

---

80   Paramore. *Japanese Confucianism*. p. 143.
81   Ibid., p. 142.
82   Sasaki. *Nationalism, Political Realism and Democracy in Japan*. p. 57.

a universal ethical realm but rather to the material maintenance of the nation state.

At the opening of the Meiji in 1868, Fukuzawa had written that, "In spite of the Restoration, the people are spiritless." This was due, he felt, to the still prevalent mentality of Neo-Confucianism towards authority and the institutions built around it that remained intact.[83] Despite his efforts in the opening decades of the era, he too began to buckle under the weight of an ethnocentric *bunmei kaika*. He became increasingly disillusioned by global events that ran counter to a higher level of moral civilization based on the liberal values of individualism and democracy. As such, he began to develop an interest in the increasingly popular trend of Social Darwinism and its views connecting the evolution of world civilization with military prowess. Eventually, he came to embrace not the natural science of humanism but the "imperial house" as the "center of civilization and enlightenment", confirmed in Japan's defeat of China in their first war of 1894–95.[84]

As with Fukuzawa's ideas, Gyonen's three-nation Buddhist civilization narrative could also move in two divergent directions: one towards establishing Buddhism as the foundation for an international discourse and common bond with other Buddhist nations in Asia and other axial nations around the world; the other towards sanctifying Japan as the culmination of the eastward historical development of Buddhism. Such a narrative found resonance in the wider one of Japanese exceptionalism and mirrored such thought that had already developed in the West—for example, the American concept of Manifest Destiny emerging in the 1840s based on Puritan interpretations of the role of Christianity in saving humankind, the roots of which lie in Oliver Cromwell and the dethroning of Charles I in England in the 1640s.[85]

Buddhists during the Meiji period thus began to not only appeal to internationalism, liberalism, and modern science to preserve their role in the secular, enlightenment aspects of the Restoration. They also embraced the more archaic strands of the Restoration by trying to re-establish their role as bastions of Japanese culture and protectors of the state. At the end of the Tokugawa era and through the *haibutsu kishaku*, the Jodo Shin Hongan-ji sect used the slogan "Revere the

---

83   Ibid., p. 58.

84   Hoston. "The State, Modernity, and the Fate of Liberalism in Prewar Japan". pp. 296-98.

85   Loy. *A Buddhist History of the West*. pp. 135, 138, 162-63.

Emperor, preserve the Dharma" (尊王護法 sonno-goho) as a response to the Mito School's slogan of "Revere the Emperor, expel the barbarians" (sonno-joi). It also led a united Buddhist movement to oppose the separation of the ancient fusion of imperial law (obo) and Buddhist law (buppo).[86] By the mid-Meiji, the goho ideology was linked with the other ancient concept of go-koku 護国, "preservation of the nation", with which Japanese Buddhism had long historical linkages.[87]

To back up such slogans and sentiments, Buddhist denominations gained government permission to dispatch Buddhist missionaries to China and Korea, led by the Jodo Shin Otani sect in 1876 and 1877 respectively. The Jodo Shin Hongan-ji sect soon followed, and then the Soto Zen in 1904, the Jodo in 1905, and the Nichiren in 1907.[88] During this time, the major Buddhist denominations also became supportive of the Sino-Japanese War of 1894–95 and, to a lesser extent, the Russo-Japanese War of 1904–05. A telling episode during the latter occurred when Shaku Soen, who was serving as an army chaplain in the war, rejected the famous Russian peace activist Leo Tolstoy's appeal to stop the war. In response to Tolstoy, he wrote, "Even though the Buddha forbade the taking of life, he also taught that until all sentient beings are united together through the exercise of infinite compassion, there will never be peace. Therefore, as a means of bringing into harmony those things which are incompatible, killing and war are necessary."[89]

Still, in their fight for continued relevance and agency, some Japanese Buddhists were able to articulate understandings of society that transcended this archaic fusion of imperial authority, political structure (政体 seitai), and body-politic (kokutai). Shimaji's campaign for the separation of religion and state planted the seeds for Buddhist denominations to establish a variety of new social institutions to prove their usefulness and productivity to modern society, and their cultural ties and loyalty to the imperial restoration. As we will see in a chapter in Volume II, this marked the emergence of the modern Buddhist social welfare movement in Japan with programs to support poor urban laborers, engage in disaster relief both domestically and abroad, and establish kindergartens and other temple-based centers to care for the marginalized[90]—all of which remain forms of

---

86   Ketelaar. *Of Heretics and Martyrs in Meiji Japan*. pp. 72-73.
87   Ibid., p. 85.
88   Victoria. *Zen at War*. p. 63.
89   Ibid., p. 29.
90   Ketelaar. *Of Heretics and Martyrs in Meiji Japan*. pp. 132-33.

social engagement by Japanese Buddhist priests today. In addition, the teaching and training academies of all the major denominations that had been confined to inner sectarian studies under the Tokugawa were now restructured and developed into modern universities where priests were encouraged to develop a wider view of the world through studying non-religious topics.[91]

This created the intellectual ferment that gave birth to the New Buddhist Movement (新仏教運動 *Shin Bukkyo-undo*) of the late Meiji, which began to "develop (and centralize) a modern concept of 'society' that was not equivalent to 'state.'"[92] Their interpretation of the seminal concept of "repaying" or "returning benefits" (*ho-on*), which Prince Shotoku ensconced in the early Buddhist ethos of the nation, is an important illustration of the progressive vs. reactionary tension within Japanese Buddhism at this time. While Restoration ideologues and some reactionary Buddhists emphasized "the repaying of benefits to the ruler of the nation" (國王恩 *kuni-o-on*, i.e., the emperor), some of the New Buddhists, such as the Jodo priest Watanabe Kaikyoku 渡辺海旭 (1872–1933), emphasized the duty to serve society as an expression of "the repayment of debt to all sentient beings" (衆生恩 *shujo-on*).[93]

After spending ten years studying in Germany from 1900–10, Watanabe developed a critical view of the state, specifically the Sensitization & Relief Project (感化救済事業 *Kan-ka Kyusai Jigyo*) created by the Ministry of Home Affairs in 1908. While some who contributed to this project had a genuine concern for the downtrodden, the project adapted modern Western systems of psychiatry, criminology, and eugenics to convert, or in some cases eliminate, juvenile delinquents, orphans, prostitutes, the disabled, and *burakumin* into efficient, hard-working citizens. Watanabe's critique was especially pointed at the many new Buddhist activities to support this policy and to what extent they were actually serving the people or rather the state, and hence their own interests for survival:

> There are signs of a gradual increase in the number of social programs in our country, which are being organized to meet the needs of society. While this is an inevitable trend in view of the development of the nation's destiny, it is a very welcome one from a general point of view. In particular, religious people are

---

91 Ibid., p. 133.
92 Shields. *Against Harmony*. p. 102.
93 Ibid., p. 102.

nowadays very much involved in such projects. From the viewpoint of "religious edification and public morals" (風教 *fukyo*), it is a good thing that the number of institutions for relief and sensitization run by religious people in Tokyo and other prefectures is increasing day by day. However, are the various charities that are now flourishing based on a solid foundation and a certain policy? Or are they just starting out, driven by the demands of the state and society, "without any principles or policies" (無主義無方針 *mu-shugi mu-koshin*)? Perhaps the spirit is truly admirable, but the effort is not worth it because of a lack of regard for "the progress of the times and the appropriate means and methods" (時代の進歩や適当の方法手段 *jidai-no shinpo-ya teki-to-no hoho shudan*). In any case, I would like to ask what kind of principles are at the root of today's Sensitization and Relief Project? What is the policy that is derived from this principle?

In general, the spirit of the Sensitization and Relief Project is not something that should have changed from the past to the present. In essence, it is nothing more than a beautiful act of the only "compassionate and benevolent love" (慈悲仁愛 *ji-hi ni-ai*) that can be expressed. Looking at Empress Komyo's 光明皇后 (701–760) extensive charity in various fields, Bhikkhuni Hokin's 法均尼 (730-799) saving of orphans, and [the Shingon Ritsu monk] Ninsho Bodhisattva's 忍性菩薩 (1217–1303) healing of leprosy, the Buddhist spirit of "benevolence" (*ni-ai*), which is the mainstay of the Buddhist faith, has not changed one iota since the past. Needless to say, the "body-politic" (*kokutai*) of the empire is unchanged from our ancient past. However, it is also true that national policy must be in line with the "progress of civilization" (文明の進歩 *bunmei-no shinpo*) and must progress steadily with the development of the nation's condition.... Therefore, it is no longer possible to continue as in the past.[94]

This powerful writing comes from Watanabe's *Five Policies to Guide Modern Relief Work* (現代感化救済事業の五大方針 *Gendai-kanka Kyu-*

---

94 Watanabe, Kaikyoku. *The Complete Writings of Kogetsu Vol. II.* (壺月全集刊行會 下巻 *Kogetsu-zen-shu kanko-kai, Ge-kan*). (Tokyo: Daito Shuppan-sha 大東出版社, 1933), pp.17-18.

sai-jigyo-no Go-dai-hoshin) written in 1916, in which he laid out the basics of a Buddhist approach to social welfare work. Watanabe's use of terms here is fascinating. He pays lip service to the archaic sentiments of the day concerning the eternal character of the *kokutai*, but then calls for change and progress in line with civilization without using the state slogan of *bunmei kaika*. Instead, he appeals to the timeless Buddhist ethics of "compassionate and benevolent love". The first Chinese character for "benevolent love", *jin* 仁, corresponds to one of the five social virtues (*go-jo*) of Neo-Confucianism that was promoted as part of public morality in the prewar era. By adding the second character *ai* 愛, Watanabe steers the term towards a Buddhist sensibility as *jin-ai* is a synonym for *ji-ai* 慈愛, which is none other than the core Buddhist concept of "loving-kindness" (Skt. *maitri*, Pali. *metta*). Finally, using a guideline emphasized by the great Kamakura era founder of his Jodo denomination, Honen, Watanabe asserted that such principles should be made consistent with "the progress of the times and appropriate means of methods".

In this way, Watanabe went about updating a set of Buddhist principles to guide his social work, such as "interbeing" (共生 *kyo-sei*), "the repayment of debt to all sentient beings" (*shujo-on*), and "the indivisibility of self and other" (自他不二 *ji-ta-funi*). Shields summarizes the impact of Watanabe as, "Of all the New Buddhists, Watanabe was the first to truly cross the 'threshold of modernity', in the sense of not merely recognizing the importance of social reform, but demonstrating an awareness of social and historical contingency, and the resultant conclusion that human beings have the capacity to remake society, which is fundamental to the archetypal 'modern' perspective."[95] This "Buddhist discovery of society" would continue to expand in the later development of Buddhist Socialism and more radical forms of Buddhist social engagement.

For postwar Buddhist social critic Nakamura Hisashi[96], the marginalization of Buddhism from mainstream society pushed it towards a kind of social dynamism and saw the emergence of a variety of public Buddhist intellectuals and even social activists—whom we can consider Socially Engaged Buddhists—that was so lacking in the latter half of the century after World War II. Shields concludes that the participants in the Meiji Buddhist Enlightenment movement of the 1880s and 90s and its successor the New Buddhist movement of

---

95 Shields. *Against Harmony*. pp. 118-19.

96 Personal interview with Prof. Nakamura Hisashi, Professor Emeritus, Ryukoku University. November 13, 2021.

the 1900s and 10s, which included Soen's student Suzuki Daisetsu, sought a Buddhism that was a global, cosmopolitan philosophy fitting for the modern, industrial, and democratic state, yet also able to serve the people and the nation in times of crisis. In this way, however, many of them remained loyal to the emperor and saw the state as the protector of the people against foreign imperialism—sensibilities that mirrored those of the urban, elite liberals of this period. These blind spots led many in the movement to slide into the nationalistic and totalitarian discourses that emerged in Imperial Japan. In this way, Shields summarizes the movements as "an overly intellectual perspective rooted in middle-class and liberal assumptions—aspects that prevented it from emerging as a truly viable alternative for Buddhists in either the pre- or postwar eras."[97]

---

97 Shields. *Against Harmony*. pp. 130-31.

8

Axial Challengers: Buddhist Socialism and the *Lotus Sutra* in the Taisho and Early Showa Periods

Pacifist, Socialist, and Anarchist Buddhists in the Late Meiji Period

On the other end of the Western political spectrum, European socialist theories started to make their impact on Japan within a small circle of Japanese intellectuals in the early 1880s. Despite Japan's long isolation from the West, their high level of pre-existing literacy enabled socialism to take root earlier than anywhere else in Asia, principally amongst disenfranchised ex-samurai who had drifted from Confucianism into Christianity. As domanial Confucian *hanko* schools were increasingly replaced by new state schools focused on Western learning by the late 1880s, those samurai who had remained within the *hanko* system began to convert to Christianity in disproportional amounts. With their new Christian orientation combined with deep seated resentments against the Meiji regime, they became involved in socialist study groups, often sponsored by Unitarians, who grounded their impulses in ethical concerns for social justice of the poor. Within this general leftist movement, two main factions emerged: a more radical one connected to rural movements and the Freedom and Popular Rights Movement; and a more moderate one of humanitarian urban reformers under which concerned Buddhists and Christians unified. While a proper Buddhist Socialism only emerged in the last decade of the Meiji, its roots lie here in the 1880s with such groups as the short lived Eastern Socialist Party (東洋社会党 *Taiyo Shakai-to*), which had a number of Buddhist influences. Like the liberals before them and the many socialist groups to come, they struggled to develop a socialism based on indigenous Asian values that did not devolve into the archaic and naturalist discourse of the Restoration that emphasized harmony and reverence for the emperor as the benevolent protector of the people.[98]

---

98   Ibid., pp. 140-42.

Perhaps the first Buddhist to openly embrace socialism was yet another radical priest from the Jodo Shin Otani order, Takagi Kenmyo 高木顕明 (1864–1914). During the Tokugawa Era, rural Jodo Shin temples had often served the outcaste *burakumin* class, and Takagi had been conscientized to their plight, having been raised in one in rural Wakayama. This background informed his appeal to Shakyamuni as the first socialist in eradicating caste, "I declare Buddhism to be the mother of the common people and the enemy of the nobility."[99] Also departing from traditional interpretations, he proclaimed the Sangha as not the ordained community but all humanity, and the ideal world of the Pure Land as not one in the afterlife but rather "the place in which socialism is truly practiced."[100] These values led him to reject the kind of nationalist views that cropped up in other Meiji Buddhist reformers.

For example, the Jodo Shin sect inverted the classical teaching of the Two Truths (真俗二諦 *shinzoku nitai*) to equate the realization of the absolute truth (真諦 *shintai*) of the Buddha dharma with service to the relative truth (俗諦 *zokutai*) of civil law and the will of the emperor.[101] This concept also served to separate religious ethical claims based on universal Buddhist principles, like non-violence, reserved for the next-life in Amida's Pure Land, from social ethical claims based on service to the state and the imperial law reserved for this-life.[102] As we have seen in the previous section, this inversion had precedents in the rise of Jodo Shin political power during the Muromachi period under the leadership of Rennyo. The Two Truths was also expressed through the Neo-Confucian dialectic of the Principle and the phenomenal,[103] in Tokugawa era thinkers who similarly put the latter in service of the former. The prominent Buddhist liberal, Shimaji Mokurai, used such thought to interpret the non-dual concept of "differentiation is equality" (差別即平等 *sabetsu-soku-byodo*) taken from Chapter 43 of the *Lotus Sutra* to legitimize class differences as karmic retribution.[104]

---

99   Ibid., p. 149.

100 Ibid., p. 150.

101 Davis. *Japanese Religion and Society.* p. 158.

102 Shimazono, Susumu. *Social Ethics in Modern Japanese Buddhism: Living by "True Dharma"* (近代日本仏教の社会倫理: 正法を生きる *Kindai Nihon-bukkyo-no shakai-rinri: Shobo-wo ikiru*). (Tokyo: Iwanami-shoten, 2022). pp. 327-28.

103 See the term 眞諦 (traditional form of 真諦 *shintai*) in the *Digital Dictionary of Buddhism.* http://www.buddhism-dict.net/ddb/

104 Shields. *Against Harmony.* p. 161.

Outwardly critical of these standpoints, Takagi not only proclaimed his opposition to the war with Russia but got caught up in the High Treason Incident of 1910–11 (幸徳事件 *Kotoku-jiken*)—an attempted assassination of the Meiji Emperor by a group of which four of the twenty-five convicted conspirators were Buddhist priests. Defrocked by the Otani sect for his involvement, he died in prison in 1914 allegedly from suicide after his original death sentence was commuted to life imprisonment.

Another important early Buddhist socialist and one of the most radical of the New Buddhists was Inoue Shuten 井上秀天 (1880–1945). Raised as a Soto Zen temple novice, he created a unique blend of Zen and Theravada teachings with socialism, setting the stage for the most well-known socialist radicals of prewar Japanese Buddhism, Seno-o Giro and Uchiyama Gudo. Unlike most of the Meiji Buddhists who travelled in the West, Inoue travelled throughout Asia, meeting the important Chinese Buddhist reformer Master Taixu and, like Shaku Soen, having an important encounter with Sri Lankan Buddhism and Anagarika Dharmapala in the early 1900s. This experience with Theravada instilled in him, unlike Soen, the ethic of absolute non-violence (*ahimsa*), which forms the foundation of the five precepts (*pancasila*) and monastic *vinaya*. His brief time as an army interpreter in the Russo-Japanese war, while Soen served as a chaplain, further instilled his feelings for pacifism, making him one of the few Buddhists to oppose the Russo-Japanese war.[105]

His essay *Ordinary Extreme Pacifism* (平凡極まる平和論 *Heibon kiwamaru heiwa-ron*)—published in the New Buddhist's regular magazine *Shin Bukkyo* 新仏教—is an important and unique contribution. Unlike many of the religious and secular reformers of the age, whom Maruyama Masao bemoaned for calling for change based on emotional arguments for specific policies, Inoue made a *principled* and ethical argument based on the universalist (and axial) human brotherhood between Christianity and Buddhism that was explicitly anti-imperialist and anti-nationalist. Inoue directly criticized Suzuki Daisetsu—who also wrote for *Shin Bukkyo*, but unlike his master Soen or Inoue had no direct experience of the battlefield—for accepting state censorship as necessary and for his scholarly idealism that monks could be good soldiers. These views led Inoue to be sensitive to economic justice issues and to connections with the socialist movement. However, his commitment to non-violence prevented him from becoming close with more radical parts of the movement,

---

105 Ibid., p. 125.

including fellow Soto Zen radical Uchiyama Gudo.[106]

Uchiyama Gudo 内山愚童 (1874–1911) was not only the most radical of the Meiji Buddhists but also, in contrast to most in the movement, an activist more than an intellectual. Raised in the poor farming communities of rural Niigata where Soto Zen had spread some 600 years earlier, he developed a strong sense of solidarity with local peasants. While ordained a Soto Zen monk at age twenty-three, the *Lotus Sutra* and its well-known interpretations for social engagement became a strong influence. Using the Four Noble Truths as a system of analysis and action, he articulated his "anarcho-communist revolution" (無政府共産革命 *mu-seifu kyosan kakumei*) by identifying suffering in social inequality and the exploitation of the rural masses; its causes in the economic and political system; and its elimination through action, such as encouraging the rural poor to resist military conscription and denouncing the emperor system. For Uchiyama, the appeal of anarchism, as opposed to socialism and Marxism, was its focus on direct action over social reform in which the state is transcended and a society is established "where individual freedom is reinforced by communal solidarity and mutual aid".[107] Uchiyama, in turn, saw Zen monasticism and the Sangha as an ideal model for such a communal social system—mirroring similar insights by Takagi Kenmyo and Socially Engaged Buddhists in other parts of Asia during this time. In contrast to immanental interpretations of the teaching of buddha-nature that resulted in a support of the status quo and social passivity, as seen in Shimaji's presentation of "differentiation in equality", Uchiyama interpreted buddha-nature as the active movement to realize socialistic goals and a "secure freedom" (安楽自由 *anraku jiyu*).[108]

The earliest era of Japanese socialist parties (1901–06) gained popularity for their opposition to the Russo-Japanese war, and then became connected with more extreme movements like the anti-religious Kotoku faction, the eventual center of the High Treason Incident. As Uchiyama's radicalism increased, he grew closer to this faction and began producing underground socialist pamphlets in 1908 from his new temple in the mountains of Hakone west of Tokyo. The following year, his temple was raided by authorities, and he was arrested after materials for making explosive devices were also found on temple grounds. In early 1911, he was arrested again with four other Buddhist priests as part of the High Treason Incident. Unlike Takagi whose sentence was

---

106 Ibid., pp. 126-27.

107 Ibid., p. 158.

108 Ibid., p. 158.

commuted, Uchiyama was viewed as a more central member of the purported plot, and he was executed on January 24th.

The Problem of Principled Change amidst Collective Utilitarianism

Although the Emperor was not done in by the Kotoku revolutionaries, he did die from a variety of maladies the following year, and Japan symbolically entered a new era of dynamism and uncertainty, the Taisho (1912–1926). This period is generally regarded to have been a moment of political opening and diversity dubbed the "Taisho Democracy" with activism from university students, especially from the two prestigious imperial universities in Kyoto and Tokyo, increased public participation by women, and the rise of a strong labor and socialist movement through Japan's rapid industrialization. These trends had already been predicted by a variety of public forms of mass protest in the early 1900s, such as the Hibiya Riot against the Russo-Japan peace treaty in 1905. This event is particularly illustrative for the uncontrolled anger against the government from its failure to secure better terms for a war that Japan won.

These movements of diversity and protest, however, actually indicate how the Meiji bureaucratic state was widening its grip on society. From the beginning of the 20th century, the government pursued a more activist state system towards civic life, monitoring, penetrating, and steering it until the end of the war, with a legal framework based on the notion of *kokutai* rather than citizen rights.[109] In this way, while social diversity and interests expanded in the 1920s, "nonbureaucratic participation in formal policy making was limited to the conservative parties, whose senior leadership was composed almost exclusively of former bureaucrats".[110] Through bureaucratic norms and procedures, the bureaucracy limited autonomy and coopted large-scale social movements and voluntary associations through subsidies, legal assistance, and supervision, transforming private interests into public ones and using interest groups to implement state policy.

While these socio-political structures became formative barriers to *principled* social movements, ongoing aspects of Japanese culture also blocked such change. The most conspicuous was the long tradition systematized under the Tokugawa of separating authority and power—the latter of which they held and the former endowed

---

109 Pharr. "Targeting by an Activist State". p. 325.
110 Silberman. "The Bureaucratic State in Japan". p. 240.

in the inscrutable existence of the emperor. In the updated Meiji version, the body-politic (*kokutai*) into which the citizens were enfolded living under the benevolence of the emperor was seen as "absolute, unchanging, eternal."[111] On the other hand, the actual political system (*seitai*) was seen as a place for the common person not to enter and potentially sully the bond between the emperor and the *kokutai*. In tandem with the new public morality based in Neo-Confucian respect for authority, this period marks a critical point in the building of the East Asian paradigm of collective utilitarianism. The construction of the political firewall during this time between citizens and the ruling Iron Triangle of bureaucrats-politicians-corporates has prevented mass movements for democratic change in Japan to this day. As such, Eisenstadt notes, "The Imperial Diet was not a forum where ideal, or ultimate values, were debated or determined; rather it was a political marketplace where policy and interest were negotiated."[112] Any citizen's movement that tried to engage in *principled* change has thus always been contained and rebranded as a specific issue of contention to be handled without challenging the premises of the entire system.

From the citizen's movement standpoint, Maruyama Masao has pointed out problems due to the cultural limitation in which they were birthed. For example, concerning the Freedom and Popular Rights Movement of the 1880s, he wrote from his liberal standpoint,

> In this way, their concept of freedom was confused, and because they could not distinguish between the concept of freedom, whereby it was the spirit which upholds subjectively a certain order, and the concept of freedom, whereby it was an emotional demand for freedom from external constraints, they could do nothing but be receptive to the patriotism and *kokutai* theories of the fief-dominated government.[113]

This is further evidenced in the Hibiya Riot against the unfavorable terms of Russo-Japan peace treaty on September 5, 1905, which resulted in the declaration of martial law in the Tokyo metropolitan area. Unable to see the false face of power in the authority of the emperor, protestors of up to 30,000 collected at Hibiya Park in the downtown to voice their anger against the government. Appealing to the emperor

---

111 Eisenstadt. *Japanese Civilization*. p. 31.
112 Ibid., p. 31.
113 Kersten. *Democracy in Postwar Japan*. p. 70.

through symbolic actions—such as shouting *banzai*, singing the national anthem, *Kimigayo*, and carrying flags of mourning to the imperial palace—they claimed the authorities' suppression of their protest an act of *lese majeste* against the emperor.[114] Thus, while they actually dared to enter the *setai*, they could not awaken to a more fundamental transformation of the vision of *kokutai*, like fish that do not see the water in which they swim.

Such protest movements made appeals for the reform of specific policies but never presented an ideology that would restructure society or the *status quo*.[115] Maruyama concluded that this separation of authority and power meant that at the end of the day, the buck was always passed since those in power could claim a higher authority, leaving final authority in the nebulous hands of the emperor whose real power was dubious at best. In the end, especially by the end of the war, no one felt or took responsibility for what had happened. As such, Maruyama called this a "system of irresponsibility" that kept everyone in a comfortable situation but led Japan into catastrophe.[116]

In contrast, those who joined the growing Marxist movement of the Taisho era actually dared to "point out the means by which the continuing appeal of older cultural forms served to mask new changes in society." In this way, they "found the weight of the Japanese tradition served as a particularly problematic burden."[117] The various interpretations of Marxism that were emerging in Europe became significant to those who sought a new model beyond Shinto or Neo-Confucian systems to analyze the current situation in Japan yet were also disillusioned with the capitalist, liberal paradigm. Eventually, though, they too came to see Marxism as another form of European cultural imperialism that was unable to grasp the particular and unique aspects of Japanese history.[118] Reflecting again on Maruyama's critique of reform movement of this era, Eisenstadt points out how the "strong predisposition of many 'leftist' intellectuals or activists to become reintegrated in the moral consensus of the broader sector of Japanese community [meant] their radicalism was more often based on commitment to a

---

114 Okamoto, Shumpei. "The Emperor and the Crowd: The Historical Significance of the Hibiya Riot". In *Conflict in Modern Japanese History*. pp. 260-61.

115 Eisenstadt. *Japanese Civilization*. pp. 89-90.

116 Sasaki. *Nationalism, Political Realism and Democracy in Japan*. p. 65.

117 Rimer, J. Thomas. "Marxism and Cultural Criticism". In *Culture and Identity: Japanese Intellectuals During the Interwar Years*. Ed. J. Thomas Rimer (Princeton University Press, 1990), p. 132.

118 Ibid., pp. 131-32.

group than to abstract principles."[119] This point echoes ones made earlier by Nakamura Hajime on the allegiance to the particular morality of a community rather than to universal norms that might question it. Under the weight of the archaic Restoration ideology that viewed Western socialism as foreign, individualistic, and materialistic, many Japanese socialists fell into the typical exceptionalist trope of reframing socialism as already present and embodied perfectly in Japan's ancient past.[120]

The Inward Turn of Buddhism in the Taisho Period

The carnage of World War I in Europe gave rise to further doubt among the Japanese of Western modernity, its ideologies, and its institutions. "In Japan, images and writings from Europe depicting the barbarism of the Western Front challenged the association of Western modernity with civilization and order."[121] As such, the inward turn of the Marxist and socialist movements was in fact part of a much wider inward turn that is an important feature of the Taisho era. The young students and intellectuals of this period were the first true post-Tokugawa generation, raised in the Meiji enlightenment culture with strong backgrounds in idealistic German philosophy and the call for the discovery of self.[122] At the same time, they were frustrated by the inability to break through the bureaucratic state firewall that seemed unaffected by civil engagement. These sensibilities gave way to what is called the "inward turn" of the Taisho era and the retreat into the "safe haven" (逃げ場 *ni-ge-ba*) of culture and aesthetics.[123]

This inward turn also manifested itself strongly in the Buddhist world, most especially due to the fallout from the High Treason Incident, which served as a confirmation amongst Nativist-Shinto circles of the foreign and degenerate influence of Buddhism on Japan. Jacqueline Stone, noted scholar of Nichiren movements, has characterized this period as follows:

The religious focus that pervades thought and culture in

---

119 Eisenstadt. *Japanese Civilization*. p. 93.
120 Shields. *Against Harmony*. p. 162.
121 Paramore. *Japanese Confucianism*. p. 153.
122 Rimer, J. Thomas. "The Move Inward". In *Culture and Identity: Japanese Intellectuals During the Interwar Years*. p. 3.
123 Shields. *Against Harmony*. p. 189.

the Taisho period was not the religion of a specific sect, or even necessarily religion in the sense of Buddhism versus Christianity, but a universal truth, in short, religion stripped of its charismatic elements and virtually equated with humanism.... The tendency in the Taisho period to modernize and 'aestheticize' religion has since been criticized as a trend that robbed religion of the true power of faith and made it a tour of literary salons.[124]

While these strands of universalism and humanism did emerge among some creative Buddhists of the Taisho era, they were couched within the confines of a "convergence" of loyalty to the emperor system and a non-political "individualism".[125]

These trends are also evidenced in the rise of numerous experiments in communal and agrarian living inspired by Leo Tolstoy's (1828–1910) writings. Tolstoy's ideas had a wide appeal to modern Japanese for his blend of naturalism and humanism that questioned Western notions of material progress. He was also popular among the New Buddhists for the very modern aspects of his rational view of religion and focus on the individual.[126] His interest in Buddhism and Asian culture, while denouncing Western colonial imperialism, won further supporters. Finally, his open critique of socialism at the end of the Russo-Japanese war confirmed specific Japanese suspicions of it and led progressives with religious leanings to abandon it in search for alternative, utopian communal visions.[127] 1921 marked the peak of this agrarian communalist movement as seen in Buddhist influenced movements, like the Garden of Selflessness (無我苑 *Muga-en*) and the Garden of One Light (一燈園 *Itto-en*) communities.[128]

These movements presented an "intransitive knowledge" through alternative means of self-expression and communal existence, contrasting the utilitarian rationality and authoritarian rhetoric of

---

124 Stone, Jackie. "A Vast and Grave Task: Interwar Buddhist Studies as an Expression of Japan's Envisioned Global Role". In *Culture and Identity: Japanese Intellectuals During the Interwar Years*. pp. 230-31.

125 Moriya, Tomoe. "Social Ethics of 'New Buddhists' at the Turn of the Twentieth Century: A Comparative Study of Suzuki Daisetsu and Inoue Shuten". *Japanese Journal of Religious Studies*. 2005. Vol. 32, No. 2. p. 288.

126 Shields. *Against Harmony*. pp. 169, 170.

127 Ibid., pp. 201-02.

128 Ibid., p. 192.

"objective truth" coming from the Meiji bureaucratic state. This "intransitive knowledge", in which path and goal are one, "hearkens back to the Zen of Dogen."[129] However, it was used in the political climate of this time to collapse differentiation, depoliticize struggle, and assert that suffering was an individual problem or, at best, resolved through self-contained communities. In this way, while the Taisho period is seen as one of liberal awakening and experimentation, it was more of a philosophical, existential, and aesthetic project than one for socio-political transformation.[130]

This confirms Eisenstadt's point of the penchant for Japanese counter-cultural movements to retreat into an archaic naturalism and the "safe haven" (*ni-ge-ba*) of culture and aesthetics—as we also saw in the late Tokugawa period—rather than engage in more economic and political movements to transform the hegemonic foundations of the ruling order. By remaining embedded in the wider Restoration themes still dominant in the modern imperial state, these aesthetic and cultural movements of the Taisho often re-affirmed themes of cultural exceptionalism by embracing archaic naturalism, while "unintentionally becoming patsies and ideological frontmen for others who were playing a harder, deadlier game."[131]

Buddhists of this period also became enmeshed in this search for culture to deal with modernity and the role of the individual within society and nature[132]—exemplified by the aforementioned Kiyozawa Manshi (1863–1903) and the popular cultural figure from this period, Miyazawa Kenji 宮沢賢治 (1896–1933). Kiyozawa was an important young member of the Meiji Enlightenment movement under Inoue Enryo and eventually an important force of reform in his own Jodo Shin Otani denomination. However, his retreat from the world in 1890 to become an itinerant monk was not only an unusual path for a Jodo Shin priest. It also marked his search for a modern universal Buddhism through a more personal existentialist path involving a kind of transformative or pure experience.[133] His explorations and revelations were expressed in the idea of "spiritualism" (精神主義 *seishin-shugi*), which was a return to the perennial, immanentalist

---

129 Ibid., p. 197.

130 Ibid., p. 199.

131 Lafleur, William R. "A Turning in Taisho: Asia and Europe in the Early Writings of Watsuji Tetsuro". In *Culture and Identity: Japanese Intellectuals During the Interwar Years*. p. 234.

132 Shields. *Against Harmony*. p. 199.

133 Ibid., p. 75.

themes of Japanese culture that affirmed the material world as it is. Kiyozawa writes, "We must accept our present life just as it is, whether we are living in large mansions with all comforts around us, or working laboriously in small houses on dirty by-streets…. In other words, we must find our contentment in our own daily living. And in no other way but in *seishin-shugi* can this end be attained." [134]

Sentiments such as this mirror mistakes made by Buddhists throughout history of conflating the Buddha's teaching of karma as intentional action with those of other Indian schools emphasizing karma as fate and as one's social duty, such as found in the *Bhagavad-Gita*.[135] They also show the lingering influence of the Neo-Confucian class ideology of the Tokugawa era. In this way, Kiyozawa's thought often falls in line with the Zen-influenced thought of Suzuki Daisetsu and the Kyoto School, by appealing so strongly to a mysterious Absolute that anything in the world becomes a relative manifestation of it, including acts of violence.[136] Kiyozawa wrote, "When a person has come this far, he may live a moral life…. He may engage in politics or business. He may go fishing or hunting. When his country is endangered, he may march to war with a rifle on his shoulder."[137] One of Kiyozawa's students, Akegarasu Haya 暁烏敏 (1877–1954), who later became the Chief Administrator of the Otani sect, seemed to take these sentiments to heart in encouraging soldiers to "fight courageously" against the Russians and in criticizing the victims of the Ashio copper mine incident of 1902, saying, "Whether they suffer or not is not caused by the copper mine but the mind of the individual."[138] Although Kiyozawa died young before the Meiji era ended, his life and work had a major influence on Taisho utopians, like his student Ito Shoshin 伊藤証信 (1876–1963), founder of the Garden of Selflessness, and Eto Tekirei 江渡狄嶺 (1880–1944), a Tolstoian agrarian utopian who used Buddhism to further develop his work.

Another important exemplar of this period's romantic Buddhist naturalism was Miyazawa Kenji. An enduring figure in modern Japanese consciousness, he is known more as a poet and author of children's literature than as a Buddhist reformer. During his own brief lifetime, he was virtually unknown but started to become a standard bearer for patriotism, love of national culture, and the spirit of

---

134　Ibid., p. 83.
135　Watts. "Karma for Everyone". p. 21.
136　Shields. *Against Harmony*. pp. 80-81.
137　Ibid., p. 80.
138　Ibid., p. 87.

self-sacrifice, with the first three-volume set of his complete works published in 1934–35.[139] Later, in the 1980s, he became popular especially among academics and activists for an alternative, critical form of humanism that rejects progress, consumerism, and individualism.[140] Although raised in a devout Buddhist family of the same Jodo Shin Otani sect of Kiyozawa, he discovered the *Lotus Sutra* in his teens and began devoting his life to its teachings. This led to his involvement in the growing Nichiren-ism movement (日蓮主義 *Nichiren-shugi*) founded by Tanaka Chigaku 田中智學 (1861–1939), another convert to Nichiren teachings from a Jodo Shin household.

With Nichiren and the Bodhisattva Never Disparaging from the *Lotus Sutra* as role models, Miyazawa came to understand that individual happiness cannot be attained unless it is collectively realized. He was attracted to Nichiren's concern with the present suffering of this world and the vision of a Buddha Land (仏国土 *bukkoku-do*) to be realized in the here and now. This translated to a social vision of "radical immanence" that opposed a transcendental one which would offer reward in the afterlife while encouraging patience with one's lot in this life.[141] In this way, Miyazawa's sense of the immanental would seem to result in a different conclusion, a more activist one, than that of Kiyozawa and the Garden of Selflessness movement.[142] While Miyazawa did get involved with some anarcho-syndicalists and supported the Labor Farmer Party 労農党 (*Rono-to*) in the elections of 1928, his vision is a more moderate one of the "gradual evolution" of the individual, society, and the cosmos in harmony with science.

Since he died young, it is hard to develop a clear sense of his political ideology. However, his writings generally highlight themes popular at this time of rural romanticism mixed with cultural exceptionalism and self-sacrifice to the greater collective will.[143] As such, they found resonance with more rank-and-file elements of the Japanese military who hailed from these rural regions. Like their socialistic counterparts, such as Uchiyama Gudo, they sought to uplift their people through violent confrontation with the authorities, such as the 1936 attempted coup d'état known as the February 26 Incident (二・二六事件 *Ni-niroku-jiken*). It is also documented that some of the young

---

139 Sato, Hiroaki. "Miyazawa Kenji: The Poet as Asura?". *The Asia-Pacific Journal*. September 3, 2007. Vol. 5, No. 9.
140 Shields. *Against Harmony*. p. 189.
141 Ibid., p. 193.
142 Ibid., p. 195.
143 Ibid., p. 190.

soldiers involved in the attack on Pearl Harbor had Miyazawa books in their pockets.[144] These conflicting images of Miyazawa, as well as the wide spectrum of ways the *Lotus Sutra* has been used for social activism, brings to point the question that haunts this entire volume as well as the issue of religious-based social action over the history of humankind in general: What teachings can promote social engagement without leading to a violent tribalism that sacrifices the well-being of others for the well-being of one's own community, race, or nation?

A New Collectivist Liberalism and the Neo-Confucian Approach to Capitalism

The failures of Buddhist Liberalism in the Meiji era serve to encapsulate the larger failures of liberalism in Japan with the dawning of the Taisho era. As the foundations of the illiberalism of the state built in the Meiji intensified during the Taisho and early Showa, Japanese liberals were faced with making alliances with either the left or the right to avoid becoming politically isolated, or retreating from political engagement into their own existential and aesthetic salons.[145] New currents of liberalism did indeed emerge, such as an aggressive individualism among literary figures and scholars seeking to free themselves from restraints imposed by the demanding, modernizing state. However, like the Buddhist utopian movements, there was a trend towards a more philosophical, existential, and aesthetic type of liberalism based in German idealism and Tolstoyan utopianism than one for socio-political transformation.[146] These trends are also somewhat mirrored in the early roots of American civil society with the establishment of self-contained Puritan communities that had fled Europe to establish their own utopian societies as well as the later quasi-liberal Communitarian movement.

Another way Japanese liberals addressed the challenges of the utilitarian bureaucratic state was to shift away from the classical liberalism of the 18th century as seen in Locke's ideas advocating the naturally existing individual living freely amidst an artificially contrived social order. They began to discover the new liberalism of the late 19th century and their advocacy of positive liberty as developed by British

---

144 Personal interview with Prof. Nakamura Hisashi.

145 Hoston. "The State, Modernity, and the Fate of Liberalism in Prewar Japan". p. 299.

146 Shields. *Against Harmony*. p. 199.

neo-Hegelians like Thomas Hill Green.¹⁴⁷ Proponents of this new liberalism have been called "collectivists", "communitarians", or "organicists"—labels that indeed seem to better reflect Japanese norms. In the concept of positive liberty, individuals do not use the freedoms of negative liberty to pursue selfish desires that may adversely affect others. Rather, they use such freedoms to liberate themselves from selfish compulsions and invest in long-term ideals that promote personal and collective growth. Such liberals—such as the American John Dewey (1859–1952) who had a strong influence on Indian Buddhist visionary B.R. Ambedkar—advocated that the state play a more active and positive role in supporting the conditions for the material and spiritual development of the individual. In the first half of the twentieth century, such "organic" analyses of society became dominant in liberal theory. Dewey, in fact, visited Japan in 1919 but found disturbing how authoritarian, nationalistic ethics were being indoctrinated into primary education.¹⁴⁸

In line with such trends, we find one of the prominent liberals of this period, Yoshino Sakuzo 吉野作造 (1878–1933), rejecting the notion of popular sovereignty grounded in individual rights on the basis that the Japanese had not fought for their own right to rule as had the English and French in their revolutions. Yoshino harmonized his advocacy of democracy with commonly accepted Neo-Confucian views on government and even drew on more controversial ones such as Mengzi's (Mencius) 孟子 (372–289 BCE) claim that the emperor loses his mandate to rule when he no longer promotes the popular welfare by conducting himself virtuously. His theory of "politics of the people" 民本主義 (*minpon-shugi*) was influenced by Hegel's sense of positive liberty through the "conceptualization of the existing order as the product and facilitator of man's effort to realize his 'true self' (真実の自我 *shinjitsu-no jiga*)".¹⁴⁹ Yoshino's contemporary, Iwano Homei 岩野泡鳴 (1873–1920), took this Hegelian vision of the state serving as the apex of freedom to submerge "individual identity into the identity of the emperor". In contrasting the "relative individualism" of the West with the "absolute individualism" of Japan, he wrote, "In our national polity, the

---

147 Gaus et al. "Liberalism". p. 3.

148 "John Dewey in Japan". In Education in Japan Community Blog. July 6, 2005. https://educationinjapan.wordpress.com/of-methods-philosophies/john-dewey-in-japan/

149 Hoston. "The State, Modernity, and the Fate of Liberalism in Prewar Japan". pp. 301-02.

individual is the state, and the state is the absolute individual."[150]

These interpretations by prominent Japanese liberals indicate the deeper incompatibilities of Western liberalism with Japanese, as well as Buddhist, conceptions of the relation of the individual to society. Hamaguchi Eshun 浜口恵俊 (1931–2008), a prominent postwar sociologist, insightfully described Japanese as "contextuals", noting that, "Their selfness is not a constant like the ego but denotes a fluid concept which changes through time and situations according to interpersonal relations."[151] These remarks echo Nakamura Hajime's observations on the character of the Japanese noted throughout this volume. Hoston, in picking up on this theme, explains:

> A political theory that posits men as atomistic individuals is unlikely to be received in the Japanese context without undergoing transmutations that make it more compatible with an indigenous perspective in which selfhood has meaning only in the context of intersubjectivity within community…. As contextuals, Japanese liberals were disposed to attribute moral value to the community, hence to the state, an organic (as opposed to contractarian) conception of which was closely bound to the idea of the nation in Meiji and pre-Meiji political thought. It is not surprising, then, that virtually no Meiji or Taisho liberals should have subscribed to an individualist variant of classical liberalism in preference to privileging the state as a kind of moral community. The weakness of these Japanese liberals lay not in their collectivism, but in their traditionalist conflation of nation and state. A liberalism founded on an abstract conception of natural rights vested in atomistic egos could no more diminish their pain than the equally alien and traumatic conception of class struggle espoused by Marxists. With the advent of war, their liberalism, as *Japanese* liberalism, had to accommodate disparate notions of self and modernity that ultimately came into such intense conflict that it was either extinguished or transmuted into its opposite.[152]

---

150 Ibid., p. 306.

151 Ibid., p. 310.

152 Ibid., p. 310.

By the end of the Taisho era in 1926, it was becoming impossible to remain consistent to liberal ideals and seek for liberal policies without actually promoting a deeper liberalization of institutions[153]—a paradigm shift, and perhaps even an axialization, that would appear revolutionary and also unpatriotic to the *kokutai*. Any Japanese in this period who sought to define a modern Japan on the kinds of axial ideals that transcended ethnic and national identities—even flawed ones such as liberalism and Marxism—had to contend with the all-powerful Meiji ideology of the emperor and *kokutai*, which "penetrated too close to the essence of individual and group identity for sustained critical confrontation."[154]

From a Socially Engaged Buddhist perspective, the problem lies perhaps not so much in the inability of Japanese culture to embrace any type of liberalism, either classical or new. The fundamental idea of a naturally free and autonomous self, which contrasts the Japanese collective self, also runs counter to the fundamental position of not-self (*anatman*) in Buddhism. Yet, in Buddhism, the self is not extinguished in a mindless collective but rather is transformed into an agent of compassionate change with a strong sense of personal autonomy based in the karmic fulcrum of intention (Skt. *cetana* 思 *shi*) or Right Intention (Skt. *samyak-samkalpa* 正思惟 *sho-shiyu-i*) as found in the Noble Eightfold Path. The emptiness (*shunyata*) of the self as well as the collective enables a dialectical and interdependent process of transformation towards collective awakening or authentic enlightenment (*nirvana*). Such teachings as a foundation for socio-economic development will be explored at the end of the second volume through the modern Japanese definition of Buddhist development called *kaihotsu* 開発.

In this way, neither classical nor new liberalism could ever quite take hold in the prewar era, while the embedded Neo-Confucianism of the Meiji bureaucratic state continued to form the way social relations were viewed. Japanese leaders saw increasing labor unrest as another inherent problem in Western modernity based in the liberal values of individual rights and negative liberty. Again, Neo-Confucian ethics and its view of social relations provided an important resource to not only government bureaucrats but also industrialists, like Shibusawa Eiichi 渋沢栄一 (1840–1931), founder of many of Japan's first modern capitalistic institutions. For Confucian conservatives, like Shibusawa, the problem of capitalism was not the nature

---

153 Ibid., p. 292.
154 Ibid., p. 306.

of its distribution of material wealth amongst individuals but rather social relations amongst a collective.

In this sense, they envisioned a different sort of Asian capitalism based on social relations that rejected the fundamental materialistic standpoints of both Marxist socialism and capitalism which had evolved from Cartesian dualism. Ingrained in the hierarchical ethics of the five relationships (*go-rin*), business leaders worked with the government to mold an economic system through the development of producer groups, as opposed to worker or consumer ones.[155] Yet the *go-rin* and the five social virtues (*go-jo*) still taught a level of collective well-being and benevolence to inferiors. Embracing the classical Confucian ideal of the Kingly Way 王道 (Ch. *Wang-dao*, Jp. *O-do*), Shibusawa believed that, "If Capital deals with Labor according to the *wang dao* and vice versa, believing that their interests are common to each other, there will be no strife." This was one vision towards a solution to the serious social disorder arising from late industrial capitalism, which was realized for a period by Japanese companies in the golden era of the postwar economic boom.[156]

One of the most important aspects of this system was the ability to divide society into a variety of autonomous interest groups that played on Japanese tendencies to form factions or "tribes" (*zoku*), thereby retarding the formation of classes and a class consciousness that would become the basis for a wider Marxist movement.[157] The bureaucracy worked with large scale economic enterprises to declass labor by breaking it into multiple smaller interest groups and offering labor what would become the classic postwar model of "shared growth" in tenure, housing, medical care, and leisure. In this way, labor and smaller interest groups that were unable to create the bureaucratic mechanisms to engage with the state were totally excluded from power. While this led to their radicalization and activism, their effective compartmentalization into splintered interest groups prevented them from ever creating a cohesive social movement.[158] Claims to legitimacy by farmers and small- and medium-sized industries based on appeals to higher truths, like justice and human rights, were easily dismissed as not superseding the utilitarian logic of the well-being of the larger collective, i.e., the greatest good for the greatest number.

---

155 Pharr. "Targeting by an Activist State". p. 333.

156 Paramore. *Japanese Confucianism*. pp. 153-56.

157 Silberman. "The Bureaucratic State in Japan". pp. 242-43.

158 Ibid., pp. 244, 246.

Ultimately, this had a huge effect on the nature of politics. Political parties never needed to establish a broad social foundation since large but segmented parts of the population could not translate electoral power into policy making power.[159] As the power of the military and the goals of the imperial state grew in the 1930s, this system became increasingly centralized and confined, absorbing all private interests in the grand public one of Imperial Japan.

Western Dualism, Asian Naturalism, and the "Empty" Dialectic of Buddhist Socialism

With Western liberal currents well co-opted with the aid of Neo-Confucian ethics, the pressure to de-axialize the growing threat of the socialist and Marxist movements intensified in the 1930s, exemplified in the figure of Sano Manabu 佐野学 (1892–1953). Sano was born into an old elite samurai family and was the nephew of the renowned conservative politician Goto Shinpei 後藤新平 (1857–1929), the head of civilian affairs of Taiwan under Japanese rule (1898), the first director of the South Manchuria Railway (1906–08), and the seventh mayor of Tokyo City (1920–23). Sano graduated from the Faculty of Law at Tokyo Imperial University, where most high level Japanese bureaucrats since the Meiji era have been educated, but began to drift to the left in his twenties, penning an article entitled "Special *Burakumin* Liberation Theory" (特殊部落民解放論 *Tokushu Burakumin kaiho-ron*) in 1921. Less than a year after helping to found the Japan Communist Party (日本共産党 *Nihon Kyosan-to*) in 1922, he defected to the Soviet Union but then returned to Japan in 1925 to rebuild the party. After being arrested in Shanghai and imprisoned for his international communist activities in 1932, he soon engaged in the Japanese penal custom of "recanting and converting" (転向 *tenko*), pledging allegiance to the emperor and state in 1933. This led to a mass of such conversions by other Communist leaders and the collapse of the Japanese Communist Party in 1935.

As noted earlier, Sano like other socialists of this era, struggled between the standpoints of needing a system to objectively critique Japanese society and a system that could fully grasp it and transform it from within.[160] After his conversion, he did not fully renounce

---

159 Ibid., p. 254.

160 Hoston, Germaine A. "*Ikkoku Shakai-shugi*: Sano Manabu and the Limits of Marxism as Cultural Criticism". In *Culture and Identity: Japanese Intellectuals During the Interwar Years*. p. 173.

Marxism but rather came to see the problems of Cartesian dualism inherent in Marxism with its over emphasis on materialism and a mechanical view of history as well as its violent theory of social revolution through class struggle.¹⁶¹

> The basis of the three-thousand-year history of the Japanese Empire is essentially different from Western history. Modern Western materialism is so far different from Japan's tradition. In the West, society is the basic datum, but for the Japanese, the state is the basic datum. Liberalism, communism, and individualism, which are more or less anti-state fundamentally, cannot possibly occupy a basic position in Japan. The national spirit of Japan—which is cheerful, cooperative, and loves symmetry and harmony—could not long endure the lowly people's spirit that moves through individual benefits, struggle/conflict, and hatred and envy....¹⁶² In the Orient, cooperative social characteristics based on natural spontaneous human love are stronger than profit or intellect [as motivations of human behavior].... If we adopt the self-consciousness of the Western European individual and reintegrate into this, then we can show to the world a new social form that Western Europeans must consider.¹⁶³

These words fully encapsulate the traditional Japanese view of society and state and the reason liberalism did not take root in Japan, due to Neo-Confucian values of harmony and loyalty to authority. Such sentiments led Sano, while still in prison after his *tenko*, into a deep exploration of Asian cultural traditions. First, he studied the Japanese classics like the *Koji-ki*, which he found "simple, crude, objective, and artistic as well, but nowhere logical and speculative." Then he engaged in an exploration of the Chinese classics, including Mozi's (Micius) 墨子 (470–391 BCE) "altruistic socialism", which he felt was the key "source of Chinese humanism". He also discovered the axial sources that Tokugawa Neo-Confucians had pruned out of the Japanese tradition, such as the unity of nature and man with heaven as mediator and the concept of "moral empire" by philosophers "based on democracy and regarding making the people's livelihood secure

---

161 Ibid., pp. 174–75.
162 Ibid., p. 183.
163 Ibid., p. 176.

as paramount".[164] While he could not devote himself to a full exploration of Indian classics, he did read about twenty major Buddhist texts and found in Buddhism a religious spiritual basis for resolving social problems: "Buddhism is not content only with a superficial institutional resolution [of the problem of 'exploitation'], as is ordinary socialism, but endeavors to resolve [it] in relation to a revolution in human nature."[165]

Before Sano, other Japanese Buddhists had made efforts to articulate the Middle Way of a Buddhist Socialism between what they felt was the ego-centric individualism of liberalism and the anti-spiritual materialism of Marxism. Inoue Enryo was the first to address this problem head on during the Meiji Buddhist Enlightenment by using the concept of "matter and mind" (物心 *busshin*) to develop a critical Buddhist dialectic. Inoue seemed to be trying to go beyond interpretations of Hegelian idealism that fused thinking and being (subject and object) as well as the teleological or linear progress model of Spencerian and Darwinian evolutionists.[166] Another Jodo Shin Pure Land priest, Takashima Beiho 高嶋米峰 (1875–1949), took this work a step further with his concept of the "union of the material and the spiritual" (物心一如 *busshin ichinyo*), citing the need for practice and realization to prevent Buddhism from falling into a simple idealism. He felt that if Marx had been exposed to Buddhist thought, he would not have been such a strict materialist. A colleague of Takashima's in the New Buddhist movement, Sakaino Koyo 境野黄洋 (1871–1933) developed the concept of "trans-materialism" (超物質主義 *cho-busshitsu-shugi*) to critique the anti-materialist teachings of many religions, especially the various forms of Indian asceticism.[167]

Throughout this entire volume, we have noted East Asian, and specifically Japanese, culture's rejection of the kinds of transcendentalism found in India and Abrahamic religious cultures to locate spiritualism and hence liberation within this world. This outlook is what Shields has termed "transcendental materialism" and helped early Japanese socialists to indigenize socialist thought to Japanese culture through a kind of naturalism. Nakamura Hajime in his massive study of Japanese thought, culture, and religion, remarks in this sense:

164　Ibid., pp. 177-78.
165　Ibid., p. 180.
166　Shields. *Against Harmony*. p. 38.
167　Ibid., pp. 247-8.

> Just as the Japanese are apt to accept external and objective nature as it is, so they are inclined to accept man's natural desires and sentiments as they are, and not to strive to repress or fight against them.... Naturalism in the sense of satisfying man's desires and sentiments, instead, was a predominant trend in Japanese Buddhism.[168]

In this way, many Japanese socialists found in natural and sometimes "amoral" human instincts the "driving power for social revolution and social justice."[169] However, such naturalism in Japan has also often been part of the archaic narrative to "'resolve' contradictions in the name of some greater 'harmony,'"[170] as we have seen in the ideology of Buddhist innate enlightenment (*hongaku*) in medieval Japan and in the Shinto nationalism of intellectuals like Motoori Norinaga and Hirata Atsutane that fed into the Meiji Restoration. While searching for a more progressive formulation of a Japanese modernity than the Meiji utilitarians—who recreated Western liberal dualism by tearing apart the Neo-Confucian dialectic and making religion private—these Buddhist socialists ultimately landed in a very common position of archaic cultural exceptionalism. As Shields notes, "*Busshin Ichinyo* ('the union of the material and the spiritual') becomes a mode of 'merging' with the world or nature, rather than a more nuanced, non-reductive way of addressing the contradictions and problems that arise in modern, material society."[171] Indeed, Sano in his own search for "trans-materialism" ended up critiquing *busshin ichinyo* for its naturalism and individualistic retreat from the world as well as overemphasis on karmic determinism over natural law and science.

Based on such explorations, Sano came to see how Marx overlooked the nonviolent leadership and organizational functions of the state as well as the potential for nonviolent revolution. He concluded that the state was not inherently exploitative and oppressive, "In the countries of other peoples, state and society are in antagonism, and God and the state are not compatible; by contrast, in Japan, God, state, and society form a complete union. To die for one's country is the greatest service to *kami*, the greatest loyalty to emperor, and also the highest way of life as social man. The subjects of His Majesty regard

---

168 Nakamura. *Ways of Thinking of Eastern Peoples*. pp. 372, 376.
169 Shields. *Against Harmony*. pp. 250-51.
170 Ibid., p. 252.
171 Ibid., p. 250.

dying for one's country as the greatest joy."[172] In this way, Sano's *tenko* drifted into Japanese exceptionalism, which led him and others to reject the universalism of communism as treason against the emperor and the *kokutai*. "Mutual love", he felt, was the basis for the nation and a cooperative society that was true socialism. The Japanese state was, in turn, the epitome of such a cooperative community, based in the family-state of the *kokutai* and emperor. Sano's unique kind of socialism mirrored those of Meiji liberals, who saw Japan as the natural leader of "civilization and enlightenment" (*bunmei kaika*) in Asia, and of Buddhists, who felt Japan represented the apex of Buddhism's historical development.

Sano felt Japan had an inherent and superior ability to lead the rest of Asia to national liberation through socialist revolution as the "accumulation of the essence and purity of Oriental culture."[173] The logical incongruity of his revelations—in which Marxist universalism is rejected as cultural imperialism yet Japanese socialism is heralded as a complete model for all of Asia—are highlighted in his sentiment that Korea, Taiwan, Manchuria, and China did not have sufficient cultural differences to warrant their own indigenous national forms of socialism. In the end, Sano's ultimate vision of "socialism-in-one-country" (一国社会主義 *ikkoku shakai-shugi*) came to accommodate the military vision of Japan's Greater East Asia Co-Prosperity Sphere (大東亜共栄圏 *Dai-toa Kyo-ei-ken*) and a resolution to Japan's and Asia's social and economic crisis through military means[174]—the very violent means that he had rejected in Marx's class revolt against the state, as being unfit to Oriental culture.

Sano and almost all these figures eventually were swallowed up by the archaic ideology of this period. Their pitfall always seemed to be this drift into the naturalism of spirit that easily fed into notions of Japanese cultural exceptionalism, a lack of criticality towards social forces and political power, and the neglect of the actual suffering of individuals. Shields concludes this analysis of Japanese Buddhist trans-materialism by noting that, "If materialism as an ontology or ideology is indeed to be 'overcome'—or 'sublated, to employ dialectical terms—the *critical* component with which it is connected in Marx's writings must be retained."[175] While never a devout Buddhist, Sano continued to his explorations after the war into how Buddhism could serve in

---

172 Hoston. "*Ikkoku Shakai-shugi*". p. 183.

173 Ibid., p. 182.

174 Ibid., p. 184.

175 Shields. *Against Harmony*. p. 252.

the process of overcoming egoism in Marxism in his *Communism and Buddhism* (共産主義と仏教 *Kyosan-shugi-to bukkyo*) published in 1953. However, this advanced exploration of Buddhist Socialism did not carry on in Japan after the war, perhaps due to the dismissal of these prewar figures for their conversion to the imperial state.

Other Asian Buddhists, however, did continue such development. The renowned Thai monk Buddhadasa Bhikkhu developed his own approach in Dhammic Socialism and, like the Japanese, found the resolution to material-mind dualism laid in a type of naturalism. However, his naturalism was of a very different source, not grounded in the archaic myths of imperial rule. In defining nature, Buddhadasa equated it with the central Buddhist term of dharma, which he defined as nature itself (Pali. *sabhava-dhamma*), the Law of Nature (*sacca-dhamma*), the Duty of living things according to Natural Law (*patipatti-dhamma*), and the Results that follow from performing duty according to Natural Law (*pativedha-dhamma*).[176] He explained, "Buddhists aim to penetrate deeply to the inner Nature, the spiritual Nature, the Nature which is the Law of Nature, which is the source of everything.... If we realize this Nature, we have no way that selfishness can happen."[177] In this way, Buddhadasa's interpretation of naturalism was quite different than one that would accommodate amoral human instincts and rationalize the use of violence. Finally, his naturalism remained firmly attached to the Buddhist non-theistic view that rejected any appeals to a divine being or divine person as the source of moral authority in society, writing, "If Buddhism has a God, it is in conditionality (*idappaccayata*)", which is none other than the law of Nature.[178] In this way, Buddhadasa never acquiesced to the dictates of the Thai nation state built around a similar veneration as Japan's of its Buddhist king and provided an important civic space for a *principled* articulation and movement towards an alternative modernity.

Lotus in a Sea of War:
Lotus Sutra Socialism vs. Archaic Nationalism

We know turn to a unique figure who held fast to Marx's historical

---

176 Santikaro Bhikkhu. "Buddhadasa Bhikkhu: Life and Society Through the Natural Eyes of Voidness". In *Engaged Buddhism: Buddhist Liberation Movements in Asia*. p. 159.

177 Ibid., 162.

178 Ibid., p. 162.

critique of Hegel and Germany's cultural exceptionalism[179] as well as to his own commitment to a universal Buddhist civilization through the *Lotus Sutra*. If there is any universal, axial ideology that has shown a dogged determination to not be brought down by the immanental tendencies in Japanese culture, it has been the tradition of the *Lotus Sutra* as articulated by Nichiren in the Kamakura era. We have already seen its influence on the most radical of the Buddhist Meiji reformers, Uchiyama Gudo. There is also one specifically Nichiren priest of the Taisho and early Showa who attempted to blend the indigenous axial leanings of the *Lotus Sutra* with the foreign axial thrust of Marxist socialism to create perhaps the most sophisticated form of Socially Engaged Buddhist thought in Japan's modern era.

Seno-o Giro 妹尾義郎 (1889–1961)—living a parallel but historically less renowned life to Miyazawa Kenji—was born into a Jodo Shin family in Hiroshima. In his high school years, he was strongly influenced by Western perspectives on equality and individualism from thinkers like Whitman and Tolstoy through his teacher Nitobe Inazo 新渡戸稲造 (1862–1933). Nitobe was a Quaker and, ironically, the famed promoter of the samurai ideal in the renowned English language best-seller *Bushido: The Soul of Japan*.[180] After the tragic death of his sister and his own debilitating illness, he was exposed to the *Lotus Sutra* and the teachings of both the Nichiren and Tendai traditions, especially the important concept of "one in many, many in one" (*ichinen sanzen*). Eventually, he took ordination in the Nichiren sect in 1915 under a teacher named Shaku Nikken 釈日研 (1854–1927), who had resigned from his post at an important temple to devote himself to helping war orphans. Nikken maintained a strongly critical attitude toward to the Buddhist establishment and the character of common priests.[181]

This orientation led Seno-o to involvement, like Miyazawa, in the Nichirenism movement, which appealed to him as socially engaged and critical of the Buddhist establishment. Indeed, its founder Tanaka Chigaku's efforts to create a modern, lay form of Nichiren Buddhism paved the way for a wide variety of Nichiren lay movements—such as Reiyu-kai 霊友会, Rissho Kosei-kai 立正佼成会, and Soka Gakkai 創価学会—that emerged in the late Taisho and early Showa and then came

---

179 See Marx's *A Contribution to the Critique of Hegel's Philosophy of Right. Introduction*. Trans. Joseph O'Malley. (Oxford University Press, 1970), p. 4.

180 Shields. *Against Harmony*. p. 209.

181 Ibid., p. 212.

to dominate the Japanese Buddhist landscape after the war.[182] However, by the time Seno-o joined, it had already begun its drift into ultranationalism through Tanaka's fusion of Nichiren's ideas on "the true establishment of a secure nation" (*rissho ankoku*) and the imperialist *kokutai* ideology, culminating in Tanaka's creation of the National Pillar Society (国柱会 *Kokuchu-kai*) in 1914.[183] As with the archaization of the socialist movement, the Nichirenism movement used the concept of Japan's divine past to interpret Japan as the culmination of Buddhist civilization, especially embodied in the *Lotus Sutra*. This provided Japan the mandate to bring peace and civilization to the rest of the world, even if by force, through Nichiren's notorious teaching of conversion, known as "breaking and subduing" (*shaku-buku*).[184]

Seno-o, however, would come to represent a very different ideological shift from so many of the Buddhist liberals and modernists who drifted into supporting imperialistic nationalism. In contrast, his concern for economic relations increased as conditions for the working class continued to deteriorate in the 1920s, culminating in the Showa Financial Crisis (昭和金融恐慌 *Showa Kinyu-kyoko*) of 1927 that served as a precursor of the Great Depression. These movements led Seno-o to an interest in socialism as a practical complement to his ideas on social and religious reform. In an essay published in early 1926, he openly criticized an irrational and "selfish nationalism" as being against the spirit of Nichiren's concept of *rissho ankoku*, which raises the teachings of the *Lotus Sutra* above those of any worldly law or authority.[185] *Rissho ankoku* in fact sides with the people, not the government and nationalism, as a promise of relief for the poverty stricken.[186]

Historically, the *Lotus Sutra* is itself an anti-mainstream text written to declare the new lay bodhisattva ethos of the emerging Mahayana movement in India against the monastic establishment at the beginning of the Common Era. In this way, it is ethical (and axial) for promoting the bodhisattva way of life devoted to compassionately serving others. At the same time, it provides more of a statement of intention rather than a series of concrete practices, and as such is often viewed as an empty text through which the reader can develop their own meanings.[187] Seno-o used the emptiness of the *Lotus*

---

182 Ibid., p. 234.
183 Ibid., p. 212.
184 Ibid., pp. 234-35.
185 Ibid., p. 215.
186 Ibid., p. 224.
187 Ibid., pp. 231-32.

Sutra to equate it with socialism as the "single vehicle" (一乗 *ichi-jo*) to realize the Buddha Land in this world for the suffering while also incorporating progressive Christian teachings of the time on social justice.[188]

This growing vision of a Buddhist Socialism centered on the *Lotus Sutra* led to his organization of the Youth League for Revitalizing Buddhism (信仰仏教青年同盟 *Shinko Bukkyo Seinen-domei*) founded in 1931 at an ecumenical, wide-ranging gathering of Buddhists at Tokyo University. At this meeting, they developed a manifesto to revitalize Japanese Buddhism by first engaging in a "critical self-reflection" (自己反省 *jiko hansei*) of their own institutions and teachings and then by developing a Popular Buddhism (大衆的仏教 *Taishu-teki Bukkyo*) for the people. The group applied the Buddhist ethics of the five precepts to critique both capitalism and to express a complete opposition to "imperialist warfare".[189]

Using the Four Noble Truths to create a systematic analysis—as many Socially Engaged Buddhists have since done—Seno-o blended socialistic economic analysis with Buddhist method to reject popular forms of prayer for material and this-worldly benefit (現世利益 *gen-se riyaku*)—a practice prevalent in many schools of Nichiren Buddhism. "According to the words of our Buddha, when you are sick, you should search for an appropriate cure and reflect on the cause of the illness. If you wish to preserve your health, no amount of prayer or devotion can match this."[190] Seno-o further strongly criticized Buddhist liberals, like Shimaji Mokurai, for their use of deterministic karma and "differentiation in equality" to legitimize social inequalities.[191] For the Third Noble Truth, Seno-o presented a social vision through a re-articulation of the core Buddhist teaching of the Three Jewels: Buddha representing the manifestation of human potential, Dharma as the path of selfless love, and Sangha as a communal society rooted in human equality, mutual aid, and freedom from exploitation. Like Uchiyama, Seno-o's emphasis on the importance of society over nation-state shows his anarchist leanings and also his vision of the early monastic community as a model for society and the realization of the Buddha Land in this world.

Seno-o's vision recalls the tension between Tendai's view of innate enlightenment (*hongaku*) that led to the archaic metaphysics

---

188 Ibid., p. 233.

189 Ibid., p. 207.

190 Ibid., p. 217.

191 Ibid., p. 219.

of harmony and support for the status quo versus Kamakura Buddhism's view of the Age of the Final Dharma (*mappo*) as a standpoint for an historical struggle for the transformation of the individual and society. As a Nichiren Buddhist, he showed an unusual ecumenical sense in praising Nichiren's Kamakura rivals Honen and Shinran for creating a "religious revolution focused on actual life."[192] Drawing on Marx's historical critique of Hegel's conservative rationalism, Seno-o saw through and rejected the archaic idealism of the Meiji Restoration while affirming the revolutionary character not only of Japanese history but also Asian Buddhism. He maintained that Buddhism "is nothing other than the truth of development and change" and that it must recapture the revolutionary Kamakura Era spirit of "Buddhism for society".[193] In this way, Seno-o articulated a clearly axial, ecumenical, and universal Buddhism for the economic, social, and political transformation of Japan, in direct repudiation of the archaic ideology of not only the Restoration but of previous historical distortions of Buddhism, such as the *ken-mitsu* ideology of *hongaku*.

Seno-o's life, work, and, in many ways, his legacy eventually got swallowed up in the final crushing of all leftist movements in the late 1930s. Imprisoned in 1936 and surviving under dire conditions, he too was forced to engage in recanting and converting (*tenko*) and to pledge allegiance to the emperor and state. Emerging from prison at the end of the war, he reignited his work for peace and social justice until his death in 1961—which we will examine in the next section.[194] Seno-o's life and writings remain extremely important in showing how both Marxist socialism and Buddhism, especially the Nichiren-*Lotus Sutra* tradition, can answer the questions posed above by the various movements of the Meiji and Taisho on how to avoid the archaization of their ideas to support an ethnocentric nationalism.

---

192 Ibid., p. 224.
193 Ibid., p. 220.
194 Ibid., p. 208.

9

Descent into Holy War and the Conversion (*tenko*) to Imperial Way Buddhism

As we have seen, the High Treason Incident had a formative influence on the modern Japanese Buddhist Enlightenment movement. Not only did it precipitate a more inward turn through the utopian movement but also brought about a more self-preserving nationalist turn by the Buddhist establishment, so that by the early 1930s most Buddhist scholars, leaders, and institutions were backing the archaic imperial status quo of "peace, harmony, and loyalty to the throne."[195] In this way, Imperial Way Buddhism (皇道仏教 *Kodo Bukkyo*) emerged not as a new phenomenon but rather, as we have seen throughout this section, the "codification of previous positions."[196] This trend is evidenced by a wide range of Meiji Buddhist Enlightenment figures' seemingly voluntary *tenko* and adoption of standpoints that appear in direct contradiction to earlier held views on Buddhism's contribution to the rational, universal, and civilizational development of a modern Japan.

One fascinating and complicated example documented by James Shields is Akamatsu Katsumaro 赤松克麿 (1894–1955), whose grandfather Akamatsu Renjo 赤松連城 (1841–1919) was an important priest of the Jodo Shin Hongan-ji sect and a colleague of Shimaji Mokurai in the defense and revitalization of Buddhism during the early Meiji years of persecution. His son and Katsumaro's father, Shodo 赤松照幢 (1862–1921), however, turned his back on the Hongan-ji establishment and joined the popular utopian movement of the Taisho, working specifically for the upliftment of the outcaste *burakumin* population. In 1919, instead of creating his own community, he relocated his entire family to a *burakumin* village, dedicating them to a life of voluntary simplicity in service of the socially oppressed. These efforts, along with those of other radical Shin priests, appear to have had an impact on both the

---

195 Ibid., p. 204.
196 Victoria. *Zen at War*. p. 79.

Hongan-ji and Otani sub-denominations, which formed the Oneness Society (一如会 *Ichinyo-kai*) in 1924 and the True Body Society (信身会 *Shinjin-kai*) in 1926 respectively, to challenge social discrimination.[197]

Katsumaro took his father's work one step further, shifting from the communal to the political as one of the founding members of the Japan Communist Party in 1922. He left the party in 1926 to lead the Social Democratic Party but by 1932 started a rightward drift. After the Manchurian Incident of 1931 that served as the beginning of Japan's full-scale occupation of China, Katsumaro began speaking of a state-centered socialism in the manner of Manabu Sano's post *tenko* writings. From that point forward, he became involved in the formation of a number of increasingly nationalistic organizations, culminating in the League for Carrying through the Holy War (聖戦貫徹議員連盟 *Seisen Kantetsu Gi-in-renmei*) in 1937 and the Imperial Rule Assistance Association (大政翼賛会 *Taisei Yokusan-kai*) in 1940, which became Japan's sole totalitarian party during the war.[198]

While there are numerous other examples of Buddhist leaders of this period who pro-actively supported Japanese imperialism and the war, the Akamatsus offer a fascinating encapsulation of how Buddhism developed during this entire period as well as raising extensive questions about the entire project of articulating and realizing religious based social movements in general and Socially Engaged Buddhism in particular.

The Resurrection of the Warrior-Monk

An historical issue covered earlier in this volume that requires re-examination is the particular fusing of the martial and the spiritual in East Asian Mahayana Buddhism, as expressed most fully in Japan with the so-called "warrior-monks" (*sohei*) of the medieval period. While their true identity was more mercenary warrior hired by temples for a variety of political reasons, there are clear examples of actual Buddhist monks who acted as dharma teachers, factional leaders, and military combatants during this period. By the Warring States period, the most well-known and established bands of *sohei* connected with the great temples of Mt. Koya, Nara, and, especially, Mt. Hiei had gone into decline as the denominations themselves

---

197 Ives, Christopher. *Imperial-Way Zen: Ichikawa Hakugen's Critique and Lingering Questions for Buddhist Ethics*. (Honolulu: University of Hawaii Press, 2009), p. 24.

198 Shields. *Against Harmony*. pp. 28-29.

became marginalized by the growing power of the Kamakura era denominations of Pure Land, Nichiren, and Zen. Ironically, Zen, which sacralized the successive military governments of this period and was renowned for developing a certain martial ethos compatible with the samurai, never developed such bands of *sohei,* nor the violent revolutionary *ikki* movements of the Jodo Shin and Nichiren communities. With Oda Nobunaga's destruction of Mt. Hiei and the total reigning in of Buddhism by the Tokugawa, the *sohei* receded into the mists of medieval history.

However, the dislocations and new challenges of the Meiji brought forth conditions for a new sort of modern *sohei*. One of the formative influences of the Meiji de-regulation of Buddhism that we have noted was the complete secularization of the Buddhist priest as a common citizen (*kokumin*), who openly procreated, took a family name, and lived under a family register like the rest of the national citizenry. With creation of an obligatory national conscription system in the same year as the "meat eating and marriage" (*nikujiki saitai*) policies were passed in 1872, Buddhist priests suddenly became eligible like all citizens for military service, not as specialized religious chaplains but as common foot soldiers. As noted earlier, Buddhists had begun serving as missionaries and military chaplains during the First Sino-Japanese War and other colonial activities. During the Russo-Japanese war, Shaku Soen volunteered to serve as a religious chaplain, and Inoue Shuten served as an army interpreter as well.

The most conspicuous figure of this period, however, was Sawaki Kodo 澤木興道 (1880–1965), a prominent Soto Zen master whose Kyoto temple, Antai-ji 安泰寺, subsequently became popular with Westerners after the war. Unlike Soen and Inoue, Sawaki seems to be one of the first examples of Buddhist priests serving as armed combatants, which then became common after the general mobilization of the population in 1937. Sawaki did not just serve as a soldier but developed renown for his dedication and enthusiasm amongst his fellow soldiers as a true Zen "man with guts". Sawaki in his own writings spoke openly and haughtily of "gorging ourselves on killing people" and of being nominated for a letter of commendation for his ruthlessness in searching out and eliminating the enemy.[199] In contrast, we find the famous Chinese Buddhist reformer Master Taixu and other Chinese Buddhist groups pleading with the Nationalist government in their dire defense of Japanese military invasion in 1936 to change their order to enlist Buddhist monks as foot soldiers

---

199 Victoria. *Zen at War*. pp. 35-36.

"as it is against the Buddhist Commandments to injure life." They requested to be trained in relief work and other "rear guard work, like providing first aid to wounded soldiers, taking care of refugees, burying the dead," etc.[200]

Whether or not Sawaki's reflections are personal words of false praise, he went on to become an important figure in articulating Imperial Way Buddhism and Imperial Way Zen during the 1940s. Recalling the conundrum of the *Lotus Sutra* as an empty text for use in progressive or regressive social reform, Sawaki wrote: "The *Lotus Sutra* states that 'the Three Worlds [of desire, form, and formlessness] are my existence and all sentient beings therein are my children.' From this point of view, everything including friend and foe, are my children." Continuing on, he applied the non-dual logic of total emptiness (*shunyata*), reminiscent of Suzuki Daisetsu's writings on Zen and swordsmanship[201], to say, "Whether one kills or does not kill, the precept forbidding killing [is preserved]. It is the precept forbidding killing that wields the sword. It is the precept that throws the bomb."[202] In his *Advocacy of the Kannon Sutra* (観音経提唱 *Kannon-kyo teisho*) published in early 1944, Sawaki changed the four bodhisattva vows that so many Buddhists in East Asia chant daily as follows:

> Sentient beings are numberless, I vow to liberate them.
> 　　　衆生無辺誓願度 *remains the same*
> Delusions are inexhaustible, I vow to eliminate them.
> 　　　煩悩無尽誓願断 *becomes*
> Enemies of the Court are inexhaustible, I vow to eliminate them.
> 　　　朝敵無尽誓願断
> Dharma doors are infinite, I vow to master them.
> 　　　法門無量誓願学 *remains the same*
> The Buddha Way is unsurpassed, I vow to attain it.
> 　　　仏道無上誓願成 *becomes*
> The Imperial Way is unsurpassed, I vow to attain it.
> 　　　皇道無上誓願成

---

200 Pittman, Don A. *Toward a Modern Chinese Buddhism: Taixu's Reforms* (Honolulu: University of Hawai'i Press, 2001), pp. 136-37.

201 "For it is really not he but the sword itself that does the killing. He has no desire to do harm to anybody, but the enemy appears and makes himself a victim. It is as though the sword performs automatically its function of justice, which is the function of mercy." Suzuki, Daisetz T. *Zen and Japanese Culture*. (Tokyo: Charles E. Tuttle Co., 1959), p. 145.

202 Victoria. *Zen at War*. pp. 35-36.

Sawaki goes on to explain that:

> The Japanese body-politic (*kokutai*), in other words "The Way of the Gods", is absolute, unlimited in heaven and earth, and unlimited in all eight corners of the world. This is, in reality, the very great thing. This great thing that I speak of is something that Japanese understand. There is nothing in this that we do not understand. In this sense, we can say that the vow to attain the Buddha Way is the same as the vow to attain the Imperial Way.[203]

From Emptiness to Nothingness: The Kyoto School's Attempt to Craft a Japanese Buddhist Modernity

Here at the precipice of world war, we find the Japanese having spent over seventy years struggling with and largely failing to resolve the civilizational poles of Western modernity and archaic Japanese naturalism. This is not surprising, as the West itself has had little success in resolving the emergence of modernity, from the failures of the Protestant Reformation and the inherent violence of both liberal capitalism and Marxist socialism. On the other hand, a few of the Buddhists we have encountered, like Inoue Shuten, Uchiyama Gudo, and Seno-o Giro, have shown a way that each of Japan's three dominant traditions—Pure Land, Zen, and *Lotus Sutra*—can be interpreted in a modern context to be socially engaged while holding fast to the core ethical tenets of Buddhism, specifically the first precept of non-violence.

One final experiment in Buddhist modernity in the prewar era deserves our attention, the so-called Kyoto School (京都学派 *Kyoto gaku-ha*) initiated by Nishida Kitaro 西田幾多郎 (1870–1945). While it is a stretch to consider the Kyoto School a form of Socially Engaged Buddhism as they rarely addressed socio-political issues or engaged in social activities, they were and remain important today for the ways they failed in confronting the ideological poles of East and West and, as we will examine later in this volume, for their enduring appeal.

Because of the West's romantic fascination with Zen, Nishida is often viewed as "the first major modern Japanese thinker to

---

203 Shimazono, Susumu 島薗進. "Zen, Imperial Way, and War: How Imperial Way Zen Developed". (禅・皇道・戦争-皇道禅を導き出したもの *Zen-Kodo-Senso: Kodo-zen-wo michibiki-dashita-mono*). In *Samgha Japan: Expanded Edition 5, Zen: Roots, Present, Future, World.* February, 2019. (増補版・禅ルーツ・現在・未来・世界―別冊サンガジャパンVol. 5. 2019年2月)

successfully go beyond learning from the West to construct his own original system of thought."[204] Nishida's first publication, *An Inquiry into the Good* (善の研究 *Zen-no kenkyu*) was published in 1911 in the immediate wake of the High Treason Incident. In this way, Nishida's work emerges out of the context of the variety of Meiji Buddhist Enlightenment thought also seeking to develop a creative fusion of Buddhism and Western modern thought. Nishida's work also exists as part of the existential and inward turn of Buddhism after the High Treason Incident and, as such, had been compared to Kiyozawa Manshi's Jodo Shin styled existentialism.[205]

Further, like Manabu Sano and the Meiji Buddhists who grappled wth the "union of the material and the spiritual" (*busshin ichinyo*) to overcome Western philosophical dualism, Nishida's own dialectic dissolved into a merging of the subjective and objective that resulted in an uncritical naturalism.[206] In this way, Nishida was part of a larger movement, along with anarchist Osugi Sakae 大杉栄 (1885–1923) and novelist Natsume Soseki 夏目漱石 (1867–1916), to develop "a spiritual, largely individual world of consciousness and activity" to counter the materialism of both the Marxist socialist movement and the generation of Social Darwinists at Tokyo Imperial University, who were creating bureaucrats to run the utilitarian capitalist state.[207]

Nishida's efforts also return us to the problems of the Heian era popularization of buddha-nature (*bussho*) and innate enlightenment (*hongaku*), which contemporary scholars like Kuroda Toshio criticized as leading to an "uncritical acceptance of everything"[208] that enabled it to become "an authoritarian discourse that legitimated social hierarchy and the entrenched system of rule at that time."[209] As detailed in the previous section, Chan/Zen was deeply influenced in its formations by the Cittamatra or Yogacara school of "mind-only" and so adopted the teachings of "the womb of the Tathagata" (*tathagata-garbha*) and buddha-nature from the *Treatise on the Awakening of Mahayana Faith*.

---

204 Davis, Bret W. "The Kyoto School". *The Stanford Encyclopedia of Philosophy*. Summer 2019 Edition.

205 Shields. *Against Harmony*. p. 78

206 Ibid., pp. 250.

207 Koschmann, J. Victor. "The Debate on Subjectivity in Postwar Japan: Foundations of Modernism as a Political Critique". *Pacific Affairs*. Winter, 1981-1982. Vol. 54, No.4, p. 614.

208 Sueki. "A Reexamination of the *Kenmitsu Taisei* Theory". p. 258.

209 Stone. "Placing Nichiren in the 'Big Picture'". p. 397.

Postwar scholars of the Critical Buddhism movement, like Hakamaya Noriaki, have examined these later Mahayana teachings and determined them as fundamentally non-Buddhist for their monistic view of reality[210], in which enlightenment is considered as the realization of True Mind that is eternal, permanent, and pure. This sort of "eternalism" (Skt. *sasvata-drsti* 常見 *jo-ken*), which the Buddha clearly rejected, enables the speculation of an essential source of origination and power and the subsequent creation of tiered or graded emanations from that source[211], such as in the Vedic caste system and other forms of sanctified hierarchy under which the common person is easily oppressed. As we have detailed in the previous section, this attitude enabled the establishment of the *zen-mitsu* system sacralizing successive military regimes from the Kamakura era forward, as well as supporting the formation of a rigid class system in the Tokugawa era, which included systematic discrimination towards Japan's *burakumin* outcaste class.

Influenced by this fundamental position of "mind-only" in the Yogacara tradition, Nishida in *An Inquiry into the Good* develops the Zen-like notion of the "pure experience" of "facts just as they are". However, so as not to have this epistemology devolve into what he called "psychologism", he attempted to provide a logic and an ontological ground through his seminal concept of "the place of absolute nothingness" (絶対無の場所 *zettai-mu-no basho*)[212], defined as "the field of consciousness that logically precludes all judgement yet gives rise to all judgements."[213] This type of formulation not only derives from the influence of the Yogacara tradition and its transmission into Japan through the Kegon school in which "the universal principle is seen in the particular thing" (事の中に理を見る *koto-no naka-ni ri-wo miru*). It also exemplifies the tendency of Japanese thought towards extreme immanentalism, as seen earlier, in the collapsing of the Neo-Confucian dialectic of the Principle into the phenomenal by Tokugawa era thinkers.

For the Critical Buddhism scholars as well as many Tibetan Buddhist schools, this is a fatal misstep as developed in the other core

---

210 Hakamaya. "Thoughts on the Ideological Background of Social Discrimination". p. 344.

211 Macy. *Mutual Causality in Buddhism and General Systems Theory*. pp. 29–30.

212 Ives, Christopher. "Ethical Pitfalls in Imperial Zen and Nishida Philosophy: Ichikawa Hakugen's Critique". In *Rude Awakenings: Zen, the Kyoto School, & the Question of Nationalism*. (Honolulu, University of Hawaii Press, 1995), p. 24.

213 Hubbard, Jamie. "Topophobia". In *Pruning the Bodhi Tree*. p. 83.

tradition of the Mahayana, the teaching of *shunyata* by Nagarjuna of the Madhyamaka School. A critical split between the more East Asian-centric Yogacara and the Tibetan-centric Madhyamaka exists in the interpretation and expression of the Five Kinds of Cognition or Wisdom (Skt. *panca-jnanani* 五智 *go-chi*), especially the fourth, known in Sanskrit as *pratyaveksana-jnana* (妙觀察智 *myokan-zacchi*). While this cognition/wisdom is derived from the *manovijnana* (意識 *ishiki*), the "discriminating consciousness" and the sixth of the eight levels of consciousness in the Yogacara system, Yogacaran's ascribe a less critical nature to it. Thich Nhat Hanh, the Vietnamese master trained in the Chinese Linji (Japanese Rinzai) Zen tradition has called it "wonderful observation wisdom". This is similar to the kind of non-critical, abiding wisdom of Japanese Zen that critics of Imperial Way Zen like Ichikawa Hakugen have pointed out as an essential flaw in Zen's easy accommodation with wartime fascism. Ichikawa points out, "In the subject's merging with the object there is true discernment (体認 *tainin*) and contemplation (觀照 *kansho*) but no critical evaluation."

While one could also translate the Chinese characters for this term as the "wisdom of sublime investigation", the Madhyamaka tradition would translate it as the "pristine wisdom of discrimination"[214] or more commonly in contemporary Tibetan texts as "discriminating wisdom". Therefore, rather than an abiding state of awareness that accepts reality just as it is, as common in Zen representations, it acts as a kind of critical awareness that sees all things and realities as illusionary constructs, including of course mythical constructs of an inscrutable, divine emperor. The Madhyamaka dialectic of emptiness thus also exposes the fundamental problem of modern Western dialectics, specifically Hegelian dialectics, in the resolution of subjective-objective dualism through a higher level of integration or synthesis that results in the creation of yet another dualistic object. In Hegel's case, this problem of a new synthesis as yet another object was resolved in its reification as ultimate Truth found in God and manifested in the State.

Nishida's Buddhist influence initially steered him away from a reification of the external towards the more internal "place of absolute nothingness". This *basho*, he contended, enables "both the autonomy and the mutual relativity of individuals" while maintaining a notion of the absolute and hence not slipping into the other extreme of nihilism.[215] However, Hakamaya's partner in the Critical Buddhism movement, Matsumoto Shiro 松本史朗, directly criticizes Nishida's

---

214 https://www.wisdomlib.org/definition/pratyavekshana
215 Davis. "The Kyoto School".

concept of "a place" from which mind and consciousness arise—a kind of transcendental subjectivity of consciousness or mind—as a typical form of monism or *dhatu-vada* found in Indian thought and seeping into Buddhism through the teachings of buddha-nature and innate enlightenment.[216] In the dialectics of "emptiness", all dualities are extinguished or liberated by *shunyata*, not in a "place" or "locus" (*dhatu* 界 *kai*). This emptiness denies the reification of all forms, both of an external God or an internal True Mind, and hence facilitates the letting go of the destructive self into a non-violent and compassionate engagement with the world.

Ichikawa Hakugen 市川白弦 (1902–86)—a Rinzai Zen priest whose important work on Buddhism and war responsibility pre-dates the Critical Buddhism scholars—also spent significant time critiquing Nishida's thought. He felt Nishida's thought ultimately provides no real dialectical resolution to the conflicts of Western dualism but rather a fusion or collapsing of the personal subjective and ethical of "should" into the phenomenal objective and status quo of "is". He explains, "The doubt and negation that constitute the methodology of philosophy were directed completely inwards, toward the self, and because of this, the moment for the maturation of the modern self, which is the subject of the modern critical spirit, was obliterated." In Jungian psychological terms, this is a regressive movement to a pre-conscious wholeness in the darkness of the womb, i.e., ignorance, rather than a progressive wholeness of complete illumination and gnosis, i.e., enlightenment. Ichikawa further locates this problematic fusion in the Zen logic of *soku-hi* 即非 (lit. "identity and difference"), espoused by Nishida's close friend and colleague, Suzuki Daisetsu, and evidenced in Sawaki Kodo's conflation of Buddhist precepts and warfare. For Ichikawa as well, the result is a "monistic view" (一元観 *ichigen-kan*) of seeing society and nature as one and an acquiescent acceptance of the world as is, rather than a place of struggle to realize truth, justice, or enlightenment[217]—ultimately leaving no space for the Buddha's teaching on karma, the ethics of intentional action.

Based on these counter-arguments, Nishida's philosophy thus leads to an uncritical submersion of the self into the world in which the citizen must adjust their attitude or transform their consciousness to meet the demands of the world. In this way, Ichikawa examines the way wartime Zen teachers manipulated the famous saying of

---

216 Swanson, Paul L. "Why They Say Zen Is Not Buddhism: Recent Japanese Critiques of Buddha-Nature". In *Pruning the Bodhi Tree*. pp. 7-9.

217 Ives. *Imperial-Way Zen*. pp. 78-81.

the great 9th century Chinese founder of the Rinzai Zen school, Linji Yixuan 臨濟義玄, "Make yourself master of every situation, and wherever you stand is the true [place]." Nishida appropriated this concept for modern Japan as seen in this passage: "Religiously awakened people can become 'master of every situation' as the self-determination of the absolute present…. For each, 'the place in which one stands is truth'…. From a true religious awakening one can submit to the state."[218] Ichikawa questions such an attitude as: "Is becoming master of one's situation a matter of living as a faithful and pliant organization man who through self-discipline admonishes himself against civil disobedience?"[219] For Ichikawa, the legacy of Zen, especially Rinzai Zen, throughout Japanese history has been as a master of the realm of warriors, the military, the anti-communist right wing, the industrial sector, and the modern state, rather than empowering the common people to be a master of their "everydayness" by developing a critical eye to authority.[220]

For Ichikawa, the way Nishida's dialectic lost track of reality and became an easy victim of the archaic imperial ideology reflects on his upbringing among the old, elite samurai families of the Japan Sea coastal areas, who eventually became disenfranchised during the Meiji era. As such, his diaries reflect a concern for upward mobility and class rather than the suffering of the common people and the critical events of his time, such as the rice riots (米騒動 *kome sodo*) of 1918; the formation of socialist, anarchist, and antiwar movements; and the oppression of them through the Public Order Preservation Law (治安維持法 *Chi-an Iji-ho*) of 1925.[221] Simply, without a grounding in the First Noble Truth of *dukkha* and then an analysis of its causes in social systems and culture in the Second Noble Truth, Nishida's philosophy became a decontextualized form of the Third Noble Truth of nirvana, which turned into the kind of metaphysical speculation the Buddha abhorred and refused to engage in.

Remarkably, Nishida seems to have arrived at the same point as Hegel in reifying the state, and ultimately the emperor as the embodiment of the state, in passages such as: "The state is the power that creates value. The true state must, as the subject of historical formation, be the creator of value…. What is called national value is creative value. For this reason, it is true moral value. In the background

---

218 Ives. "Ethical Pitfalls in Imperial Zen and Nishida Philosophy". p. 23.

219 Ibid., p. 20.

220 Ives. *Imperial-Way Zen*. p. 74.

221 Ives. "Ethical Pitfalls in Imperial Zen and Nishida Philosophy". p. 26.

the state possesses something religious….the national polity in which 'the state, just as it is, is morality' (国家即道徳 *kokka-soku-dotoku*)."[222]

In this way, when the world actually came knocking on his door, Nishida and his colleagues lacked a critically grounded spirit to respond. In a series of essays during the war period—such as *The Problem of Japanese Culture* (日本文化の問題 *Nihon bunka-no mondai* 1938), *The Problem of the Raison d'état* (国家理由の問題 *Kokka riyu-no mondai* 1941), *Principles for a New World Order* (世界新秩序の原理 *Sekai shinchitsujo-no genri* 1943), and *The National Polity* (国体 *Kokutai* 1944)—Nishida showed a disturbing trend of towards archaic cultural exceptionalism rather than a civilized and enlightened modernism, writing: "The zenith of Japanese spirit is in 'actuality just as it is, is the absolute'."[223] Further, "Our national polity is not simply a totalitarianism. The Imperial House is the beginning and the end of our world, as the absolute present that embraces past and future." Further, he claimed that, "In order to build a particular world, a central figure that carries the burden of the project is necessary. In East Asia today there is no other but Japan."[224] For Ichikawa, Nishida's dialectic reflected on the general trend of Japanese to easily submit to the archaic imperial ideology and, in consort with Maruyama Masao's critiques, results in a system of irresponsibility in which personal autonomy (主体性 *shutaisei*) and responsibility is weak.[225]

Nishida's principal successors Tanabe Hajime 田辺元 (1885-1962) and Nishitani Keiji 西谷啓治 (1900-1990) also ended up developing problematic positions that would taint their legacies after the war. Tanabe in the 1920s and later Nishitani in the 1930s studied with the hugely influential German philosopher Martin Heidegger (1889-1976), who also became discredited for his active support of the Nazis. Heidegger's own student Herbert Marcuse (1898-1979) had tried to reconcile Hegelian thought and Heidegger's existentialism to create a progressive social agenda. Tanabe, however, took Hegel's political philosophy in the other direction, reifying the nation-state as an embodiment of ethnic specificity able to raise the people out of their inherent irrationality. This idea led him to propose that the "relative absolute" of the Japanese nation-state could serve as a kind of "supreme archetype" for other nations.[226] Nishitani appears to have

---

222 Ibid., pp. 33-34.
223 Ibid., p. 33.
224 Davis. "The Kyoto School".
225 Ives. "Ethical Pitfalls in Imperial Zen and Nishida Philosophy". p. 27.
226 Davis. "The Kyoto School".

made greater strides in clarifying and adjusting Nishida's concept of *basho* as "an open clearing wherein beings are neither nullified nor reified but rather let be in the mutual freedom of their coming to be and passing away. It is also the place in which a genuine interpersonal encounter can take place."[227]

This more spacious view of *shunyata* rather than Nishida's "absolute nothingness" appeared to help him consider a less naturalistic view of Japanese exceptionalism and a more progressive view of Japan's historical mission to bring about a world that has "no specific center" but rather consists of various "politically and culturally unified spheres". It seems he felt that Japan could only realize this mission if it engaged in this act of "self-negation" and became a "nation of non-ego" rather than a self-centered aggressive empire.[228] However, he too made disturbing claims during the war of Japan becoming the "focal point of world history". Further, in the 1941–43 public roundtable discussions on *The Standpoint of World History and Japan* in which Kyoto School scholars participated, he remarked how people "mistakenly" viewed Japanese actions in China as an imperialist invasion on a par with the imperialism carried out by Europe and the United States.[229]

As with Marcuse to Heidegger, there were some younger members of the school who did break with what they saw as the ethical implications of Nishida's regressive dialectic. Tosaka Jun 戸坂潤 (1900–1945) and Miki Kiyoshi 三木清 (1897–1945) were key figures of what is sometimes called the "left wing of the Kyoto School". After studying philosophy at Kyoto University under Nishida and Tanabe and graduating in 1924, Tosaka began to explore Marxism in the 1920s. In 1935, he published *The Japanese Ideology* (日本イデオロギー論 *Nihon ideorogi-ron*)—inspired by Marx and Engels' *The German Ideology*—in which he directly attacked the Kyoto School, partly through a critique of their use of hermeneutics.[230] Tosaka felt the positions of the Kyoto School resembled those of Heidegger—whose denigration of the "everydayness" (Ger. *alltäglichkeit* 日常性 *nichijosei*) and mediocrity of the common people—and led to an elitist inward existentialist turn "resembling that of the Buddhist monk who retreats from the

---

227 Ibid.

228 Ibid.

229 Ives. "Ethical Pitfalls in Imperial Zen and Nishida Philosophy". p. 38.

230 Prooi, Dennis. "Tosaka Jun's Critique of Hermeneutics". In *Erasmus Student Journal of Philosophy*. 2016. No. 10. p. 40.

hassle of the world in his monastery."[231] He picked up on the elitism of those who exalted Zen *satori* as a mystical state of True Mind captured only by heroic male monks—arguing that any of Zen's universal claims quickly lose value if used as a weapon to exalt Japanese culture over not only Western but also the rest of Asian culture because only the Japanese are sensible enough to experience it and thus have access to the world as it supposedly 'really is'.[232]

For Tosaka, the Kyoto School got lost in the same game of Western cultural imperialism by attempting to show Japanese superiority over other peoples, instead of what should have been the real goal of the Japanese philosophical project in addressing current issues affecting the people, specifically the growing specter of fascism. In the end, "attention to local problems of the here-and-now was sacrificed for an abstract universalism concerned with problems of global proportions".[233] Tosaka's critique stands all the more important because, unlike the subsequent postwar critiques provided above, it was done with foresight and not the hindsight of a nation devastated by war. Further, there was great personal risk to such resistance in which Tosaka and his colleague Miki engaged. Their resistance to the shift in society eventually ended them up in prison where both tragically died on August 9th and September 26th, 1945 respectively as the war was coming to a conclusion.

The works of Nishida, Nishitani, Tanabe, and their colleagues seem ambivalent enough in comparison to the more overt war mongering of certain well know Zen masters of the time or their colleague Heidegger's outspoken support for the Nazis. Some feel a more indepth examination of Nishida's writings and letters show that he was trying to steer Japan away from destructive imperialism and was critical of "invasionism". Further, he was criticized by ultra-nationalists for the Western style of his philosophical approach.[234] Yet, as Tosaka

---

231 Harootunian, Harry D. *Overcome by Modernity: History, Culture, and Community in Interwar Japan.* (Princeton: Princeton University Press. 2002), p. 127. These critiques of Nishida by Ichikawa and Tosaka are quite similar to Marcuse's critiques of Heidegger. Marcuse felt Heidegger's philosophy did not confront those aspects of the contemporary crisis that were social and historical. In becoming pre-occupied with the timeless and ontological, it became ethereal, otherworldly, and, ultimately, elitist. Marcuse, Herbert. *Heideggerian Marxism.* Ed. Richard Wolin & John Abromeit (Lincoln: University of Nebraska Press, 2005), pp. xvii, xxi.

232 Prooi. "Tosaka Jun's Critique of Hermeneutics". p. 36.

233 Ibid., p. 42.

234 Ives. "Ethical Pitfalls in Imperial Zen and Nishida Philosophy". pp. 32-38

and other postwar critics have pointed out, the retreat into metaphysical speculation—like Heidegger's retreat into Being—creates the ground for the loss of critical ethics based on the First Noble Truth of a real encounter with suffering and the first precept of doing no harm. As we will investigate in the next section, Tosaka and Miki's legacies would be important in the postwar period for initially conceptualizing the issue of *shutaisei* as a mean to reconcile the materialism of Marxism and the mystical idealism of the Kyoto School.[235]

In conclusion, a critical question that emerges here at the end of this section as we move forward into the postwar era is the legacy of such "samurai ethics" (a.k.a. *bushido*) for Japanese culture. We have traced an historical line back to the spread of Neo-Confucian ethical norms by Rinzai Zen monks that promoted respect to authority among the warrior class before the Tokugawa era. Then, we noted how such ethics became ingrained in the samurai through Confucian *hanko* schools as they were slowly converted from battle-waging swordsmen into state bureaucrats. In the Meiji, a Shintoistic veneration of the emperor fused with the Japanese Neo-Confucian ethics of authority was presented as not a religion but a common, public morality to which the general public was indoctrinated through the basic education system. With the militaristic turn of society in the 1930s, the stoic Zen discipline of *bushido* was added to create a complete system of political, social, and cultural authoritarianism.

As we examine the rise of state sponsored capitalism in the postwar era and the ongoing domination of society by elite bureaucrats and the Liberal Democratic Party, it is important to look for these unresolved aspects of the mass militarization of society in the prewar era, specifically in the ongoing struggles against violent bullying (*ijime*) in all sectors of society based around a feudalistic system of elder-younger (先輩後輩 *senpai-kohai*) relationship formation. The fact that Buddhism, whose ethical system is built upon the first precept of non-harming, became an important source for the spread of this system is, of course, deeply disturbing. However, as we will explore in the second volume through a variety of case studies of Socially Engaged Buddhism in the new millennium, the potential for Japan to rebuild its social ethics based on this fundamental precept of non-harming as well as the First Noble Truth injunction of solidarity with the suffering is offering real hope for leaving the legacy of the war behind as well as solving the riddle of modernity.

---

235 Koschmann. "The Debate on Subjectivity in Postwar Japan". p. 615.

Part III

Defining Peace and Internationalism
in the Liberal Utilitarian State:
Socially Engaged Buddhism
in Postwar Japan

10

The Sudden Turn Towards Peace in the 1940s and the Question of Principled Social Change

Within the space of six months in 1945, two events threw Japan into spiritual as much as political disorder. The first was the formal surrender of Imperial Japan made by Emperor Hirohito on August 15, which accepted the terms of the Allied Potsdam Declaration, including the tenth clause establishing the freedom of religion. The second was the Emperor's renunciation of his divinity in his annual New Year's Day address to the nation. Ichikawa Hakugen, the renowned Rinzai Zen priest known for his work on Buddhist war responsibility, describes these events in terms used by leftists in their submission to the state during the war: the first in surrender as the emperor's "failure" (挫折 *zasetsu*) and the second in renunciation of divinity as his "recantation and conversion" (転向 *tenko*).[1]

At this time, there was a young Rinzai Zen novice living in a temple in Kyushu, who in the early 1950s would study with Ichikawa at the Rinzai denominational Hanazono University. That novice would grow into a prominent leader in the traditional Buddhist community, serving as not only the Chief Priest (管長 *kancho*) of the Rinzai Myoshin-ji sub-denomination but also the President of the Japan Buddhist Federation (全日本仏教会 *Zen Nihon Bukkyo-kai*). Now, over ninety-years-old, Rev. Kono Taitsu 河野太通 (1930–) recalls those days of confusion:

> From that time, the question arose among us of what is it good to live for now? Amidst everyone's confusion about this, there was rebellion among the school kids with them breaking windows; strikes broke out everywhere; and a rage with no outlet permeated society. Amidst debates with friends who held these same sentiments, we

---

1 Ives. *Imperial-Way Zen*. p. 133.

ourselves came to understand about the militaristic education that we were raised in. We ourselves had been raised according to this kind of "ideology". Then we had to change to a world in which democracy was considered the right thing. During the war, I had a teacher who pushed me very strongly into militarism. After the war, he said, "From now on, this is the age of democracy." He then repeated to me in English Abraham Lincoln's famous words, "Government of the people, [by the people, for the people]." This same teacher during the war had said, "After we win the war, Americans will also come to speak Japanese." In this way, we came to be unable to trust our teachers and other adults.... I thought to myself, 'Will the center of the world change again? Is there a way to live that doesn't fall victim to the vicissitudes of change?'"[2]

Looking for the answer to this second question in Buddhism did not readily lead to any results for Master Kono, because the about-face Japanese Buddhism underwent after the war left him and others with even greater doubts. Yanagida Seizan 柳田聖山 (1922–2006), another prominent postwar Rinzai Zen monk and director of the Institute for Humanistic Studies at Kyoto University, explained that:

> All of Japan's Buddhist sects flipped around as smoothly as one turns one's hand and proceeded to ring the bells of peace. The leaders of Japan's Buddhist sects had been among the leaders of the country who had egged us on by uttering big words about the righteousness [of the war]. Now, however, these same leaders acted shamelessly, thinking nothing of it.[3]

These remarks on not only the state of Buddhism but also of spirituality and existential meaning in Japan at the end of the war recall the important insights of Nakamura Hajime, made in the Introduction to this volume. He wrote:

---

2 Kono, Taitsu. "Nuclear Power is Incompatible with the Way of the Buddha: A Declaration from Critical Self-Reflection on Past Mistakes". In *Lotus in the Nuclear Sea.* pp. 210-12.

3 Victoria. *Zen at War.* p. 159

> Those who observed the moral confusion in Japan immediately after World War II may be led to doubt the proposition that the Japanese in the past were moralistically inclined.... Little difference seems to be discoverable between traditional and recent Japanese morality. The difference seems to lie rather in the fact that what was considered to be morally tenable in Japan's "closed-door" past became untenable under rapidly changing worldwide social and economic conditions to which Japan is adapting itself. The traditional concept of honesty as loyalty to the clan and Emperor is applicable only to the conduct of man as a member of the particular and limited human nexus to which he belongs; it is not applicable to the conduct of man as a member of human society as a whole.[4]

This biting commentary leads us to the significant issue for this section, and indeed, much of this volume, which is: Japan's struggle to develop a *principled* form of social change that would empower it to become, as S.N. Eisenstadt notes, "part of a broader civilization, as sharing basic premises and identity with other societies,"[5] thereby transcending the pitfalls of its archaic cultural exceptionalism and, equally importantly, the confines of dualistic Western modernism. As noted in the Introduction, Eisenstadt does not imply that Japan has not undergone vast changes in its history but, rather, that many new and varied movements were "incorporated without ideological struggle and without principled reconstruction" of the essential "boundaries of the Japanese collectivity" and "its central symbols", such as the emperor.[6]

We have already explored a number of the pitfalls of principled social change in Japan beginning with the core orientation towards the reality of the phenomenal world over the truth of transcendental, universalistic principles. Buddhism in Japan has often suffered due to this orientation, as seen during the war era. However, it has also developed unique forms of liberation, particularly during the Kamakura era Buddhist revolution, freeing its teachings from the pitfalls of overly transcendental interpretations that developed in Indian Buddhism and remain in Theravada Buddhism.

The problem of collapsing the transcendental or ideological into the phenomenal feeds into a second issue: the tendency for social

---

4   Nakamura. *Ways of Thinking of Eastern Peoples*. p. 521.
5   Eisenstadt. *Japanese Civilization*. p. 15.
6   Ibid., p. 421.

movements in Japan to factionalize into insular, hierarchical groups, or what is sometimes even termed as "tribes" (*zoku*), and for ideology to serve more as a group identity marker rather than as a guide for principled action.[7] One classic example of this is the widespread factionalization of Buddhist sects over history, specifically the Nichiren and Jodo Pure Land orders, in which minute changes in doctrine appear to demarcate denominations rather than point to a truly significant change in religious practice—an issue well noted by Nakamura in the historical survey in Section 1, "It is not the difference in the religious faith or doctrine but merely such specific factors of human relationship as the inheritance of the master's 'endowments' that account for the split of the religious school into multitudinous sects and factions."[8]

In the modern era, this is evidenced in the splintering of the Marxist movement, resulting in what Eisenstadt explains as a "radicalism more often based on commitment to a group than to abstract principles." The unfortunate result was the "strong predisposition of many 'leftist' intellectuals or activists to become reintegrated in the moral consensus of the broader sector of Japanese community."[9] As such, while we find movements of protest and rebellion all throughout Japanese history, very few perceived the social order as "in need of being reconstructed according to the principles of a higher ontological or ethical order that bridged the chasm between the transcendental and the mundane orders" and thereby transformed the basic hegemonic premises of society.[10]

These cultural barriers to principled change are accompanied and exacerbated by structural ones, such as the ancient tradition of separating authority from power. This system of governance has its roots in the very founding of the Japanese nation in the 7th century with the use of Chinese bureaucratic models. It continued on throughout history up to the war period with the emperor as head of state while a revolving group of bureaucrats and military men ran the country. This system has been especially well suited in blocking social change from without, because those in power have been able to recede behind the face of authority and make necessary tweaks to the system while the deeper ideological basis for authority remains unchanged and unchallenged.

---

7   Ibid., p. 115.
8   Nakamura. *Ways of Thinking of Eastern Peoples*. p. 484.
9   Ibid., p. 93.
10 Ibid., p. 13.

In the previous section, Maruyama Masao critiqued the Freedom and Popular Rights Movement of the 1880s in this way for having a "confused" concept of freedom that acted as "an emotional demand for freedom" yet remained "receptive to the patriotism and *kokutai* theories" of the state.[11] As such, without a wider, more universal impulse, movements have remained localized to specific issues—such as unfair taxation in the medieval era or environmental pollution in the modern era. Once the issue is resolved, the movement dissolves, enabling the continuity of power and the inherent ideology of it. In the modern era, this inherent ideology has been the Neo-Confucian-Shinto veneration of authority combined with the Western utilitarian logic of the bureaucratic state.

With these tendencies, protest as a fulcrum for social change has been what Eisenstadt calls more "expressive" than "instrumental". Expressive protest aligns social action with personal or group belief, but more for the sake of demonstrating one's sincerity of commitment to the group and the cause rather than for accomplishing a particular end through rational, organized action. In this way, protestors may release frustration and reinforce group solidarity yet fail in attaining meaningful social change.[12] This is well evidenced in the Hibiya Riot against the Russo-Japan peace treaty in 1905 that attacked the government while pledging loyalty to the emperor. In line with the ingrained values of Japanese Neo-Confucianism, it has been important in modern protest movements in Japan to exhibit personal sincerity and total commitment in a spirit of self-sacrifice.[13]

Unfortunately, this sort of social ethics—as seen in the mobilization of society towards war—does not necessarily translate into one that works for non-violent social change and peace, because, as noted by Nakamura, it pertains "only to the conduct of man as a member of the particular and limited human nexus" and not to the wider world of human and even sentient life. The result, as clearly portrayed by Masters Kono and Yanagida, is often seen in sudden shifts of allegiance and moral sentiments—such as from imperial war to international peace—simply because the group in power has changed. In this way, the question that still haunts some Japanese today is: "Has the inner logic of the veneration of authority been truly challenged and transformed in the postwar era?"; or, in the earlier words of Master

---

11 Kersten. *Democracy in Postwar Japan*. p. 70.
12 Eisenstadt. *Japanese Civilization*. p. 116.
13 Pharr, Susan. *Losing Face: Status Politics in Japan*. (Berkeley: University of California Press, 1990), pp. 35-37.

Kono: "Is there a [principled] way to live that doesn't fall victim to the vicissitudes of change?"

Reflecting on the previous chapters of this volume, there have been a few exceptions to these tendencies in Japanese history, and most are found based in religious movements with their devotion to universal principles. The rural farmer's movements (*ikko-ikki*) against the samurai-ruled military state based in the revolutionary teachings of Pure Land teachers Honen and Shinran are one exceptional example. The teaching of principled protest is also found in the writings of Nichiren and has reverberated through the history of denominations evolved from him, such as the banned the Fuju-fu-se and Hiden subsects in the Tokugawa era and, as will be prominently displayed in this section, the postwar lay Buddhist movement. In the previous section, we also found examples in the very sincere efforts of Japanese to harmonize Buddhism with liberalism or Marxist socialism as principled systems by which to develop the foundations for a modern Japan.

The great challenge, as Eisenstadt explains, and major reason for their failures, was "the inability to develop any common ground between their use of universal categories and the particular Japanese reality" and thus "to develop a discourse that would enable them to participate critically, in an autonomous way, in the political arena" to transcend the hegemonic, archaic socio-cultural discourse.[14] In the challenges to alter this discourse, three common paths emerged:

- **retreat** from society in small, self-enclosed communities, such as the utopian movements of the 1920s and the New New Religions (新新宗教 *shin-shin shukyo*) of the last quarter of the 20th century.
- **re-immersion** back into the collectivity through "recanting and converting" (*tenko*) and collapsing their universalist principles into the hegemonic discourse, as seen in the fates of Neo-Confucianism in the Tokugawa era, the Buddhist Meiji Enlightenment movement of the late 19th century, and the Marxist socialist movement of the 1920s and 30s.
- **marginalization**, sometimes in extreme form, as seen the banned religions of the Tokugawa era; the imprisonment of Socially Engaged Buddhists, Marxists, and principled liberals in the lead up to the war; and in the postwar era, the leftover activists from the anti-nuclear, peace, and student movements of the 50s and 60s.[15]

---

14 Eisenstadt. *Japanese Civilization*. p. 118.
15 Ibid., p. 117.

11

The *Lotus Sutra*, Confrontational Buddhism[16] and Social Protest in the 1950s

Admonishing the State and the Problem of Nationalism in the Prewar New *Lotus Sutra* Groups

It is difficult to identify groups associated with the *Lotus Sutra* tradition in the modern era who chose the first path of retreat, defying the very principles of Nichiren's teaching of making a Pure Land of this world. In this section, we will examine the tension between the latter two paths of social accommodation and social marginalization by various *Lotus Sutra* groups that are considered exemplars of Socially Engaged Buddhism in the postwar era. As detailed in the previous section, the modern lay Buddhist movement emerged in the Meiji era spearheaded by the already laicized Jodo Shin Pure Land denominations. Well-known reformers Inoue Enyo and Shimaji Mokurai promoted the new the *nikujiki-saitai* policy that openly allowed clerical marriage. By the Taisho and early Showa eras, a wide variety of *Lotus Sutra* lay groups began to emerge as well—such as Reiyu-kai 霊友会 in 1924, Kodo Kyodan 孝道教団 in 1936, and Rissho Kosei-kai 立正佼成会 in 1938. They formed around the growing needs of the time, specifically, the spiritual and practical needs of the increasing number of migrant workers coming to the cities. These groups were unlike the new, modern styles of Jodo Shin and Zen that appealed to more elitist existentialist themes, like those of Kiyozawa Manshi and Nishida Kitaro.

In keeping with the historical trend of aligning with the merchant class, the new *Lotus Sutra* denominations appealed directly to the economic concerns and needs of the urban working class. They preached about the material, "this-worldly benefits" (*gen-se riyaku*)

---

16 This term, translated from the Japanese (闘う仏教 *Tatakau Bukkyo*), is taken from Kono Taitsu's book *Confrontational Buddhism: Concepts of Modern Religion* (戦う仏教: 現代宗教論 *Tatakau Bukkyo: Gendai Shukyo-ron*). (Tokyo: Shunjunsha Publishers, 2011).

that come through devotion to the *Lotus Sutra,* expressed in chanting homage to it in the *daimoku* formula, *namu-myo-ho-renge-kyo* 南無妙法蓮華經. This lineage of groups emerging out of the Reiyu-kai also added the practice of ancestor veneration as a core part of their doctrine.[17] In this way, these denominations were products of the age and thus often reflected other common social themes—such as the Neo-Confucian five social virtues (*go-jo*), particularly filial piety and loyalty, found in the Imperial Rescript on Education, and the right-wing nationalism of the Nichirenism movement (*Nichiren-shugi*) led by Tanaka Chigaku.

The most well-known of these *Lotus Sutra* groups, which emerged from a different lineage, is the Soka Gakkai 創価学会, founded in 1930 by Makiguchi Tsunesaburo 牧口常三郎 (1871–1944). Before embracing Nichiren Buddhism, Makiguchi was mostly considered a late Meiji and Taisho era intellectual interested in the educational ideas and humanism of the new "communitarian" movement in the West. Raised in the northern frontier of Hokkaido, he came to Tokyo in 1901 to develop his intellectual interests and make a career. While publishing some books of renown, he still struggled economically and spent these first decades teaching in the Tokyo public school system, often clashing with other teachers and the Ministry of Education over the style of education. In 1932, he quit teaching and devoted himself to developing his vision of "value creation" education.

His *Value-Creating Pedagogical System* (創価教育学体系 *Soka Kyo-iku-gaku Taikei*) referenced and paid debt to the work of renowned American new liberal John Dewey. In examining Makiguchi's ideas, one is struck by their advanced and progressive nature in running counter to the standard curricula of prewar and postwar Japan that transmits information to students through rote learning. His advocacy of "discovery and invention" by the student in their "autonomous effort to discover and create value amidst the realities of life"—hence the meaning of the word *soka-gakkai* as "value creation study association"—brings to fore at an early stage the issue of individual "autonomy" (*shutaisei*) that became so important after the war. This new liberal view of making the individual free or autonomous to contribute to society was combined with Buddhist sentiments towards not reifying views as ontological truths. This sense was echoed by Dewey, who wrote, "No longer will views generated in view of special situations be frozen into absolute standards and masquerade as eternal

---

17   Shimazono, Susumu. *From Salvation to Spirituality: Popular Religious Movements in Modern Japan.* (Melbourne: Trans Pacific Press, 2004), p. 78.

truths."¹⁸ This sentiment found resonance with the Buddhist teaching of the law of cause and effect taking precedence over "anything resembling blind faith or dogmatism" as well as one's teachers as an "object of veneration". According to Third Soka Gakkai President Ikeda Daisaku, Makiguchi repeated consistently, "Rely on the law, not the person." ¹⁹

By the time of the writing of the *Value-Creating Pedagogical System*, Makiguchi's vision had also become increasingly influenced by Nichiren Buddhism, of which certain streams seemed to directly contradict his educational philosophies. Around 1916, it is documented that he attended the lectures of Nichirenism founder Tanaka Chigaku. While he never became a member of the movement, the contemporary Western expert on Soka Gakkai, Levi McLaughlin, notes that in the postwar era, Soka Gakkai has employed many of the same institutional practices and technological innovations that were used effectively by Tanaka's right-wing National Pillar Society (*Kokuchu-kai*). These include a corporate hierarchy that divided the organization into a national network of headquarters overseeing regional sub-divisions. McLaughlin writes, "Soka Gakkai's administration is not modeled on that of a temple-based lay Buddhist society but the leadership structure of a modern corporation, civil service, or military."²⁰

In 1928, Makiguchi ended up converting to one of the most fanatical and nationalist forms of Nichiren Buddhism, Nichiren Sho-shu 日蓮正宗, known for its particular emphasis on exclusivity and the supremacy of its religious vision. It seems Makiguchi felt that in order to engage in systemic value creation, one must have an understanding of what is the highest value, which he found in the Nichiren Sho-shu interpretation of the *Lotus Sutra*.²¹ In this way, by the early 1940s, Soka Gakkai began to devote itself to the more religious aims of the denomination, specifically spreading its teachings by Nichiren's controversial method of conversion by any means necessary known as *shaku-buku* (lit. "to break and subdue"). While still enfolded within Nichiren Sho-shu, these activities began to run the association afoul of the

---

18   Dewey, John. *The Public and Its Problems: An Essay in Political Inquiry.* (Chicago: Gateway Books, 1946), pp. 202-03.

19   Ikeda, Daisaku. "John Dewey and Tsunesaburo Makiguchi". Center for Dewey Studies. Accessed March 31, 2022. https://deweycenter.siu.edu/publications-papers/john-dewey-and-tsunesaburo-makiguchi.php

20   McLaughlin, Levi. "Soka Gakkai in Japan". In *Handbook for Contemporary Japanese Religions.* Eds. Inken Prohl & John K. Nelson. (Leiden, Netherlands: Koninklijke Brill, 2012), p. 273.

21   Shimazono. *From Salvation to Spirituality.* p. 79.

new Religious Corporations Law enacted in 1940, which authorized government intervention in the affairs of religious groups.²²

The critical series of events that unfolded from this point revolved around a contentious requirement in this law. All religious organizations, as well as all citizens, had to enshrine in their centers or homes deity tablets known as *kami-fuda* 神札 from the Grand Shinto Shrine at Ise 伊勢神宮 in support of what had become the public morality of State Shinto. Most religious organizations and citizens went along with this policy, simply in order to survive, and Nichiren Sho-shu with its strong nationalist sentiments also agreed to do so. However, through his deep readings of Nichiren, Makiguchi refused and led Soka Gakkai in a revolt against Nichiren Sho-shu, for which they were banned from worshipping at the main temple. On July 6, 1943, Makiguchi, his successor Toda Josei, and twenty other members were arrested. While nineteen of these members would recant and convert (*tenko*) and be released, Makiguchi and Todai remained steadfast in their position. Makiguchi subsequently died of malnutrition in Tokyo's notorious Sugamo Prison on November 18, 1944.

Since the end of the war, Soka Gakkai has maintained that Makiguchi's criticism and rejection of "State Shintoism with full awareness of the ramifications of such actions was…tantamount to rejecting Japanese militarism and imperialism."²³ However, there is evidence that Makiguchi held mainstream nationalist sentiments, writing in 1933 that, "We must make our children thoroughly understand that loyal service to their sovereign is synonymous with love of country." Further, for a period of time, he gained the public support of important economic, political, and military leaders, such as Admiral Nomaguchi Kaneo 野間口兼雄 and Governor General of Taiwan Ota Masahiro 太田政弘. Prime Minister Inukai Tsuyoshi 犬養毅 also provided a handwritten endorsement to the first volume of Makiguchi's *Value-Creating Pedagogical System*.²⁴ Rather than being a pacifist critical of Japanese imperialism, like his fellow Nichirenist Seno-o Giro, it seems that his specific style of nationalism based in Nichiren's teachings rather than in State Shinto is what finally ran him into trouble with the authorities.

---

22 McLaughlin. "Soka Gakkai in Japan". pp. 280-82.

23 Victoria, Brian. "Soka Gakkai Founder, Makiguchi Tsunesaburo, A Man of Peace?". *The Asia-Pacific Journal*. August 4, 2014. Vol. 12, No. 37. p. 16.

24 Victoria. "Soka Gakkai Founder, Makiguchi Tsunesaburo, A Man of Peace?". p. 8.

A deeper examination here of the Nichiren stance towards principled protest and social change is thus essential. While Nichiren had a long and complex history of confronting official authority, there is one particular teaching of his known as "admonishing and enlightening the state" (国家諫暁 *kokka-kangyo*) that informed Makuguchi's disobedience to the authorities and the subsequent postwar social activism of *Lotus Sutra* groups. It is considered that Nichiren engaged in *kokka-kangyo* three times during his life, the first in 1260 when he compiled his most well-known text the *Rissho Ankoku-ron* (*Establishing the Right Teaching and Bringing Peace to the Country*) and submitted it to the head of the Kamakura military government Hojo Tokiyori. In doing so, he remarked, "I did this solely to repay the debt I owe to the country."[25]

This type of protest was subsequently carried out by at least five of Nichiren's six leading disciples, generally in the form of submitting "letters of admonition" (申状 *moshi-jo*) to the shogun or his local representatives but in some cases even to the emperor. The form was most commonly practiced in the Muromachi period (1333–1573) by monks who had broken away from more established Nichiren lineages to found new ones.[26] The content of these admonitions reflects Nichiren's radical approach to authority based in the primacy of the *Lotus Sutra* as the object of highest loyalty. Even before the development and institutionalization of Neo-Confucian ethics in Tokugawa and modern Japan, Nichiren claimed one's obligations to one's parents are subordinate or rather mediated by the higher truths of the *Lotus Sutra*.

In general, as with the radical message of the Kamakura Pure Land masters Honen and Shinran, Nichiren elevates the status of the weaker, inferior person by bonding them with the ultimate truth of the *Lotus Sutra*. Nichiren did not outright reject the position of authority, yet at the same time he empowered the inferior to challenge and ultimately reject it if such authority did not uphold the teachings of the *Lotus Sutra*. This position was advocated by Nichiren for children towards their parents, wives towards their husbands, vassals to their lords, and citizens to the military authority. It was even extended to the emperor in this radical quote, "The ruler of Japan is not even equal to a vassal of the [Buddhist] wheel-turning monarchs of the four continents. He is just an island chief."[27] Nichiren's inversion of authority was not necessarily directed in a liberal manner towards the

---

25 Stone. "When Disobedience Is Filial and Resistance Is Loyal". pp. 274-75.

26 Ibid., p. 277.

27 Stone, Jacqueline I. "Placing Nichiren in the 'Big Picture'". p. 411.

primacy of the autonomous individual nor in a socialistic manner towards the flattening of all social distinctions. Rather, it appears that he wished to infuse the existing social order with the principles of dharma as found in the *Lotus Sutra* so that such relationships as between parents and children were transformed from those of base authoritarianism. *Kokka-kangyo,* thus, formed an important mechanism in correcting the abuses of power.

In this way, it provides a *principled* form of protest in which Nichiren saw society, as noted earlier, "in need of being reconstructed according to the principles of a higher ontological or ethical order that bridged the chasm between the transcendental and the mundane orders." *Kokka-kangyo* provided one of the important means by which the *Lotus Sutra* would transform the world, specifically the Japanese nation, into a buddha-land. Further, the basic hegemonic premises of society would be transformed from the circumscribed Neo-Confucian ethics of authority and the veneration of the emperor into a dharmic society based on the universal and civilizational ethics of non-violence—in theory. The challenge of realizing these two goals at the same time—in which Japan becomes a great nation not because it aggrandizes itself but because it follows a path that manifests universal ethics—is the standpoint by which we will further explore the legacies of the *Lotus Sutra* groups in the postwar era.

In terms of the legacy of Makiguchi, he stated during his police interrogations certain criticisms of the Imperial Rescript on Education, which created the basis for the prewar education system infused with the Neo-Confucian ethics of authority and the veneration of the emperor. Soka Gakkai has claimed his criticisms as proof of his opposition to the emperor system and the war, yet his recorded comments seem to be more rhetoric than a repudiation of veneration for the emperor. Still, at a different point of the interrogation, Makiguchi took the bold step of rejecting the emperor's divinity and referring to him as "an unenlightened being (凡夫 *bonbu*) who as Crown Prince attended Gakushu-in (学習院 the Peers' School) to learn the art of being emperor."[28] The Japanese term *bonbu* has a specific Buddhist bent, especially as used by the Kamakura Pure Land masters, to denote the worst kind of common fool who may still become the first to enter the Pure Land by Amida Buddha's great compassion. To refer to the emperor as a *bonbu* must have enraged his interrogators and, more so, when he suggested that, "Were His Majesty to become a believer

---

28 Victoria. "Soka Gakkai Founder, Makiguchi Tsunesaburo, A Man of Peace?". p. 15.

in the Supra-eternal Buddha (久遠本仏 *Ku-on-honbutsu*) [of the *Lotus Sutra*], then I think he would naturally acquire wisdom and conduct political affairs without error."[29] It is this type of principled conviction that empowered Makiguchi to be one of the few who would not recant and convert (*tenko*) in prison and, in the spirit of many a Nichiren activist, die as a martyr to the cause.

Admonishing the State and the Path of Marginalization in the *Lotus Sutra* based Peace Activism of the 1950s

Makiguchi was not the only Nichirenist to engage in admonishing the state in the turbulent prewar era. Fujii Nichidatsu 藤井日達 (1885–1985) was a young Nichiren denomination priest with a predilection for the asceticism of fasting and self-mortification found in the tradition. In 1916, he began a ritualistic kind of *kokka-kangyo* in front of the imperial palace in Tokyo. Beating a handheld drum with the *daimoku* written on it, he chanted *namu-myo-ho-ren-ge-kyo* for hours a day to remonstrate the Taisho Emperor to take up faith in the *Lotus Sutra*. This type of ritualized and, as noted earlier, expressive protest would become the hallmark of his life and the new school of Nichiren Buddhism he formed called the Nipponzan Myoho-ji 日本山妙法寺. The following year, Fujii took up Nichiren's prophecy—that in this Age of the Final Dharma (*mappo*), Buddhism would spread back from west to east with Japan providing the fulcrum for a world Buddhist renaissance—and spent five years travelling through China spreading the teachings of the *Lotus Sutra*.

His endeavors, however, were also part of Buddhism's attempt to show its worth to the state through missionary work in Japan's colonial territories, and Fujii also served as a type of support chaplain for the military and other Japanese colonial forces. After returning to Japan in 1923 to do relief work in the wake of the Great Kanto Earthquake, he travelled to India in 1930, spending a month at Gandhi's Wardha Ashram in 1933.[30] From this experience and two interviews with Gandhi himself, his views on Buddhism and social change became clearer:

> The people [of India] were trying to reform the government without resorting to violence. If they succeeded in their attempt, theirs would be the ideal form of government. For this reason, I was very interested in what was happening

---

29   Ibid., p. 15.
30   Stone. "Nichiren's Activist Heirs". pp. 78-79.

in India.... Nevertheless Japan...was indifferent to the Indian independence movement. Not only did she [Japan] not cooperate with the movement, she even sided with the British rulers.... I keenly felt that it was not good for Japan, with its proximity to India and her traditional ties through Buddhism, to refrain from helping Indians achieve independence or to suppress their movement. I could not straight-forwardly tell the Japanese government and people, and even if I could, they would not listen. So I decided to cooperate with the independence movement led by Gandhi and pray for its success.[31]

Out of the tradition of Hinduism, there emerged Buddhism, which embodies the idea of non-violence in its most complete form. It was indeed an important development. Buddhism is not only necessary for promoting a peaceful revolution in today's India but also is a tool of spiritual guidance with which to save all the human race who are involved in acts of violence and wars; it encourages abolition of all means of violence.... My wish for "the compassionate return of buddhas and bodhisattva to this world" (還来帰家 *genrai-ki-ke*) and the non-violent revolution which Gandhi advocated came from the same origin, the doctrine of Buddhism.... This concept cannot be fully expressed in the term "revolution", and in Buddhism it is referred to as "attainment of Buddhahood". The ultimate revolutionary aim of Buddhism consists in having both man and the world attain Buddhahood. Completely detached from things like political power, the human race should leap above all such conflicts. This is the true essence of Buddhist revolution.[32]

Despite these words above, it appears Fujii did not yet fully embrace non-violence or discard the hope that a Japan-centric Asia would be the solution to Western colonialization. Visiting Sri Lanka in 1933, he was able to procure a small portion of the historical Buddha's relics on the stipulation that he enshrine them in a stupa to venerate. Later, in 1938, he gave some of these relics to the Japanese army and navy

---

31 Fujii, Nichidatsu. *My Non-Violence: An Autobiography of a Japanese Buddhist.* Trans. T. Yamaori. (Tokyo: Japan Buddha Sangha Press, 1975), pp. 67-68.

32 Ibid., pp. 80-81.

in China hoping their victories would bring peace in Asia, the liberation of Asian peoples, and the reconstruction of Asian culture.[33] It appears that, in Fujii's own recollections, it was not until experiencing the devastation of his own country at the end of the war, specifically with the bombings of Hiroshima and Nagasaki, that he finally made his decisive stance.

> What led me to assert non-resistance, disarmament, and the abolition of war was not my encounter with Mr. Gandhi. When the atom bombs were dropped on Hiroshima and Nagasaki, and I saw hundreds of thousands of innocent women and children die as though burned at the stake and poisoned, victims of a tragedy unprecedented in human history; when I saw Japan forced to accept unconditional surrender, then I understood the madness, folly, and barbarousness of modern war.[34]

In the opening of the section, we noted the sudden about-face of many Japanese Buddhists from promotion of the war to promotion of international peace, and Fujii indeed seems to be one of them. However, unlike those who did so more as a form of posturing with little subsequent action afterwards, Fujii built and developed the Nipponzan Myoho-ji around a complete dedication to ecumenical and non-violent civil protest towards realizing world peace. This commitment to civil protest, even if it tends towards the expressive, makes them "unusual, perhaps even unique among Japanese Buddhist groups"[35] in Japan today.

Myoho-ji is also unique among the new *Lotus Sutra* groups for being centered around monastics, both female and male, and not householder, lay leaders. Their monastic-centric style has translated into a socio-political stance more aligned with the socialist left and the rejection of postwar Japanese consumer culture. This contrasts the lay *Lotus Sutra* groups' general espousal of conservative, middle class social values aimed at attaining wealth and material comforts. Further, unlike the majority of traditional Japanese Buddhist priests who have come to marry, have families, and engage in lay lifestyles since the Meiji period, Fujii and his disciples have maintained unmarried monastic lifestyles supported by the donations of followers

---

33   Stone. "Nichiren's Activist Heirs". pp. 80-81.
34   Ibid., p. 79.
35   Ibid., p. 78.

and not the income gained by doing funerals and memorial services. Yet unlike the few traditional monastics who today remain cloistered in famous temples like Eihei-ji or on holy mountains like Mt. Hiei or Mt. Koya and stay silent on social issues, Fujii's missionary ethos derived from the *Lotus Sutra* has meant a constant engagement by Myoho-ji in difficult socio-political issues that have confronted Japan since the end of the war.

These unique qualities along with their *principled* dedication to peace—which include an admonishing (*kokka-kangyo*) of the postwar Japanese state as well as what could be called an "international admonishing of the state" (国際諫暁 *kokusai-kangyo*) of American global hegemony—has meant the Myoho-ji has occupied the third path of social movements in Japan, the one of marginalization. With one small headquarters temple in Tokyo and just over one hundred monastics worldwide, Myoho-ji again exhibits a very different profile from the mass postwar *Lotus Sutra* groups like Rissho Kosei-kai and Soka Gakkai with some 4.5 million and 8.3 million members respectively.[36]

In terms of national and international peace activism, however, their mark on history is just as significant. Unlike the other two, Myoho-ji was active from the very beginning in the popular postwar peace movement, which many mark from the anti-nuclear movement touched off by the exposure of Japanese fishermen to American nuclear testing on Bikini Atoll in 1954.[37] That year also marks the construction of Myoho-ji's first peace pagoda, which realized the promise Fujii made to the Sri Lankans upon receiving Buddha relics in 1933. In the unique style of Myoho-ji to convert traditional Buddhist spiritual practices into those of socio-political import, they have erected more than eighty such stupas worldwide—less as a veneration of the Buddha or the *Lotus Sutra* and more as a call to world peace.

A second important moment in Myoho-ji's involvement in the Japanese peace movement was working with farmers and local citizens to occupy land earmarked for the new American Sunagawa Airforce Base in Western Tokyo in 1957 during which they endured

---

36 In 2022, Myoho-ji reported an almost equal distribution of 66 monks and 51 nuns. As compared to Soka Gakkai's well-known exaggeration of its number of members, Myoho-ji does not bother to count its number of lay followers, which are certainly nowhere near those of Kosei-kai and Gakkai. (private correspondence with Rev. Takeda Takao 武田隆雄, senior leader of the Myoho-ji Shibuya Practice Center, April 6, 2022). The numbers for Rissho Kosei-kai and Soka Gakkai followers come from circa 2010. McLaughlin. "Soka Gakkai in Japan". p. 269.

37 Stone. "Nichiren's Activist Heirs". p. 77.

police brutality.[38] This movement grew into the popular peace movement against the U.S.-Japan Security Treaty (*Anpo*) and the numerous American military bases being established in new locales after Japan regained its independence in 1951—a movement in which Myoho-ji is still actively involved in 2022.

With the experience of the atomic bombings, Fujii developed a philosophy espousing the power of Buddhism as a civilizational force for peace and non-violence over the scientific materialism of the West, and especially the United States, which would only lead to war and the destruction of the environment.[39] While Fujii was also critical of the violent means used in socialist and communist movements,[40] his views on technology and colonialism naturally led Myoho-ji to an anti-capitalist and anti-American stance that connected to the Japanese labor and student movements of the 1950s and 60s. However, their insistence on non-violence and the power of religious civilization also made them attractive to certain radical youth who identified with the student movement but saw a missing spiritual component to it. Ultimately, Myoho-ji's leftist political ideology and long association with the Communist Party of Japan has kept it as a marginal group within Japan over the years, even as it has grown to some level of fame internationally.

Myoho-ji has complemented its domestic activism with international activism: joining anti-nuclear protests in the United States in the 1980s; leading a peace walk through Central and North America in 1992 to commemorate the 500th anniversary of Columbus' arrival in the New World and the subsequent oppression of indigenous peoples; leading another peace walk from Auschwitz to Hiroshima in 1995 on the 50th anniversary of the end of World War II; participating in numerous peace walks with the renowned peace monk Maha Ghosananda in Cambodia in the 1990s; and attempting to be a peace witness during the civil war in Sri Lanka that led to the murder of one of its monks in 1984. These peace walks are also repeated annually in Japan, such as the three-month walk from Tokyo to Hiroshima culminating on the anniversary of the Hiroshima nuclear bombing

---

38   Fujii. *My Non-Violence*. p. 118.

39   Kisala. Robert. *Prophets of Peace: Pacifism and Cultural Identity in Japan's New Religions*. (Honolulu: University of Hawaii Press, 1999), p. 161.

40   "What is wrong about Marxism is that it allowed one to adopt violence and take the lives of others in the pursuit of his rights. Murder, whether committed by a Capitalist nation or a Communist nation, is the same." Fujii, Nichidatsu. *Buddhism for World Peace*. Trans. Yumiko Miyazaki. (Tokyo: Japan-Bharat Sarvodaya Mitra Sangha, 1980), p. 21.

as well as the more recently established walks to bear witness to the Fukushima nuclear disaster. While the walks are always accompanied by the continual recitation of the *daimoku*, participants from other religions often participate, and there is never any attempt by the monks and nuns to convert others to the *Lotus Sutra*, much less aggressively convert in the tradition of *shaku-buku*.

Like the establishment of peace pagodas, these peace walks transform the missionary zeal of the *Lotus Sutra* tradition into the building of solidarity among peoples of different religions, cultures, and nations into a civilizational ethic of peace and non-violence. While Rissho Kosei-kai and Soka Gakkai have also created a plethora of international peace activities, Myoho-ji stands in contrast with their engagement at the grassroots level with the common people affected by international socio-political currents. In this way, prominent prewar and postwar scholar of religion, Murakami Shigeyoshi 村上重良 (1928–1991), concludes that the peace movement of Myoho-ji and other small new religions in the immediate postwar era was "not proposing an abstract ideal of peace; it faced the realities of Japan and sought concrete means to protect peace."[41]

Along with the early peace activism of the Nipponzan Myoho-ji, the Nichiren priest Seno-o Giro (1889–1961) re-emerged in the postwar era to continue his activism for a Buddhist Socialism based in the teachings of the *Lotus Sutra*. Like Fujii Nichidatsu, Seno-o was attracted to the ascetic side of the Nichiren tradition as it offered a means of overcoming his physical ailments as a young man that he associated with weakness of moral character and a selfish-nature—a comportment typical in the denominations based on the *Lotus Sutra*. In this way, he practiced celibacy and the door-to-door ritual cleaning of toilets (行願 *gyo-gan*)[42] with the motto, "Bear the Buddha into the streets" (仏陀を背負いて街頭へ *Butsuda-wo se-oite gaito-he*).[43] By the 1930s, Seno-o was engaging in far more radical social activism through the Youth League for Revitalizing Buddhism, of which he

---

41 Murakami, Shigeyoshi. *Japanese Religion in the Modern Century*. Trans. H. Byron Earhart. (Tokyo: University of Tokyo Press, 1980), pp. 134-35.

42 The Garden of One Light (一燈園 *Itto-en*) community, representative of the Taisho era utopian movement detailed in the previous section, made this practice a centerpiece of their community. See a full profile of Itto-en and these activities in Davis. *Japanese Religion and Society*. pp. 189-225.

43 Large, Stephen S. "For Self and Society: Seno-o Giro and Buddhist Socialism in the Postwar Japanese Peace Movement". In *The Japanese Trajectory: Modernization and Beyond*. Eds. Gavan McCormack & Yoshio Sugimoto. (Cambridge University Press, 1988), p. 89.

had been a central founder in 1931. The Youth League became active in protests against Japanese militarism and fascism in consort with numerous anti-war labor strikes and those of the Anti-Nazi League to Crush Fascism (反ナチスファッショ同盟 *Han-nachisu-fassho Domei*). For these activities, he was arrested in December 1936 and, under intense pressure in prison, committed *tenko*. Meanwhile, the Youth League was disbanded, and some two hundred of its members were arrested by May 1938. Unlike many others who died in prison, Seno-o was released three years later and spent the war in seclusion. After condemning renowned Marxist Sano Manabu for his *tenko* in 1934, his own *tenko* remained a burning moral self-injury that created great existential suffering and pushed him to continue with his peace activism after the war in part as a means of expiation.[44]

Seno-o came from the mainstream Nichiren denomination (日蓮宗 Nichiren-shu), which was a member of, and had more commonality with, the world of traditional Buddhist denominations rather than the new lay Nichiren and *Lotus Sutra* groups. However, unlike most of the traditional denominations that simply "tolled the bells of peace" after the war, Seno-o quickly joined with other progressive priests to create new social initiatives for building the democratic foundations of postwar Japan. In July 1946, he revived the prewar Youth League with many of the same members under the new title, the Buddhist Socialist Alliance (仏教社会主義同盟 *Bukkyo Shakai-shugi Domei*), which declared its support for the Japan Socialist Party (JSP).

For a brief period under the American occupation, socialists and Marxists who had survived the war in prison became popular and were allowed to promote their political agendas. However, in 1947, the U.S. embarked on what is known as the Reverse Course (逆コース *gyaku-kosu*) upon which socialists and Marxists were purged from governmental, educational, and corporate positions. At the same time, conservative and so-called liberal politicians active in the wartime government were rehabilitated. From this point, Seno-o became increasingly active in political activism, joining the JSP in 1949 and the General Council of Trade Unions (日本労働組合総評議会 *Nihon Rodo-kumiai Sohyo Gikai*), better known as Sohyo, in 1950.[45] This was a time when leading progressives and intellectuals were calling for Japan to distance itself from the U.S., become friendly with Communist countries such as China, and adopt neutralism as an official policy. Such neutralism was part of the growing Non-Aligned Movement

---

44   Ibid., pp. 90-91.

45   Ibid., p. 93.

being promoted by two newly established, important multi-religious Asian nations, Indonesia and India, as well as two prominent traditionally Buddhist nations, Burma and Sri Lanka.

To promote this policy of principled neutrality, Seno-o helped direct two organizations for making friendly relations with Korea and China. He visited China as part of the Japan-China Friendship Association (日中友好協会 *Nicchu Yuko-kyokai*) in 1953 to repatriate the ashes of 560 Chinese who had died in Japan during the war.[46] At the same time, further cooperation among religions increased through meetings such as the Gandhi Peace Alliance in January 1950, the Kyoto Religionists' Consultation Group (京都宗教人懇談会 *Kyoto Shukyo-jin Kondan-kai*) of which Ichikawa Hakugen was a founding member in April 1950, and the Buddhist Peace Roundtable in February 1951. This work culminated in the forming of the Council of Japan Religious Persons for Peace (日本宗教者平和協議会 *Nihon Shukyo-sha Heiwa Kyogi-kai*) in June 1951, which in turn worked with the trade union federation Sohyo to create the larger Japan Peace Promotion Association (日本平和推進会議 *Nihon Heiwa-suishin Kaigi*) in July 1951.[47] Seno-o became a key leader and eventual director of the association due to his close connections to the chairman of the Sohyo, Takano Minoru, as well as with the chairman of the left wing of the JSP, Suzuki Mosaburo. In this way, the Japan Peace Promotion Association took on a prominent role in organizing the large-scale peace rallies in opposition to American military bases.[48] While a minority within their own denominations, progressive Buddhists of this period—both in the traditional world with Seno-o and his colleagues and in the new world with Nipponzan Myoho-ji—"became a major force in the peace movement."[49]

Seno-o, however, could not maintain this level of activism, in part because of persistent health issues that had been exacerbated by the hardships of the war period, especially his three years spent in prison. He also felt discouraged by the growing factionalism of the left and the subsequent collapse of the Japan Peace Promotion Association, due in part to the Communist members' dislike for working with religious activists. His greatest disillusionment, however, lay with Buddhism and the mainstream denominations that remained silent amidst this critical period in Japan's democratic formation. In his personal diary

---

46 Ibid., pp. 95-96.
47 Murakami. *Japanese Religion in the Modern Century*. p. 133.
48 Large. "For Self and Society". p. 95.
49 Murakami. *Japanese Religion in the Modern Century*. p. 133.

of August 1957, he wrote: "I no longer see Buddhism as my ideology. There is no choice but for me to serve my brothers and sisters as a Marxist in the years left to me."[50] Yet still the deepest layer of disillusionment was in his own perceived failures, which he attributed to his *tenko* as a man of weak faith and flawed moral character. He wrote, "All the work to which I have devoted myself has failed." Another journal entry from one month later reads, "I am ashamed of my own *tenko*. I should have not refused to die in prison.... My cowardice and meanness were pitiful. For that, I have lost my eternal soul."[51]

For those, like Seno-o, immersed in a passionate faith of the *Lotus Sutra* that Nichiren and many martyrs after him inspired, such a break in their principled faith is an extremely serious matter. This stands in contrast to those Buddhists who, as Master Yanagida wrote, at the end of the war "flipped around as smoothly as one turns one's hand." History, however, views Seno-o more kindly than he himself did as a symbol of continuity between the prewar and postwar peace movements. Indeed, this continuity gained him the respect and trust of postwar socialists and communists who worked with him and contrasts the postwar ostracization of compromised Buddhist figures, like the members of the Kyoto School. Many—such as Ichikawa Hakugen who often referenced Seno-o in his writings on war responsibility—have since found him compelling for his commitment to a principled form of protest and his campaign for an ecumenical, neutral, and international peace based in a universally applicable form of social ethics.[52]

---

50 Large. "For Self and Society". p. 98.
51 Ibid., p. 99.
52 Ibid., pp. 100-101.

Buddhist Asia and the Modern State

The chart below considers Buddhism in the context of modern nation states in Asia and its role as a progressive or regressive force.

Nation	Date(s)	Ideology: Authoritarian or Democractic Movement
India	1947	independence & Ashokan religious pluralism
	1956	Ambedkar Buddhist renaissance
	2014	resurgence of fundamentalist Hindu rule
Sri Lanka	1890s/1900s	"Protestant" and early Socially Engaged Buddhism
	1948	independence & Ashokan religious pluralism
	1956	Sinhala Buddhist tribalism & authoritarian state
	1958	Sarvodaya movement & Socially Engaged Buddhism
Myanmar	1948-1958	independence & Buddhist Socialism
	1962	authoritarian state & xenophobic Buddhism
	2008-2015	Saffron Revolution & "guided democracy"
	2016	rise of xenophobic Buddhism
	2021	return of military dictatorship
Thailand	1932	Deva-raja Democracy & Socially Engaged Buddhism
	1948	Deva-raja Military State & xenophobic Buddhism
	1970s	Development Monk movement
Cambodia	1953	Deva-raja Democracy
	1975	secular Marxist authoritarianism
	1993	"guided democracy" & authoritarian state
Vietnam	1930s	Humanistic Buddhism
	1960s	Socially Engaged Buddhism & principled neutrality
	1975	communism
China	1920s	Humanistic Buddhism
	1949	communism
Taiwan	1960s	Humanistic Buddhism & Social Welfare Buddhism
	2000	democratic revolt against one-party system of KMT
South Korea	1910-1945	Japanese occupation under Imperial Way Buddhism & Shinto
	1993	democratic revolt ends military state
Japan	1868	Deva-raja (non-Buddhist) Democracy & Neo-Confucian/Shinto ethics
	1930s/40s	Imperial Way Buddhism/Shinto & Fascism
	1955	Secular Democracy under one-party rule of LDP & Neo-Confucian ethics

12

Responsibility and Autonomy in Japanese Social Ethics in the 1950-60s

Where is Socially Engaged Buddhism in the Postwar Era?

Besides the work of the very small and marginal Nipponzan Myoho-ji, the immediate postwar era seems to reveal nothing but skeletons for the role of Buddhism, and institutionalized religion in general, concerning social engagement and social change work, whether it be principled or not. The traditional denominations were in a state of chaos in this time. Firstly, they faced the issue of having to rebuild many of their temples destroyed in the war. Secondly, the new trend of democratization spreading through society also affected them in the form of numerous schisms. New sub-sects emerged in the late 1940s and early 1950s as smaller temples were freed from the long-standing state controls that made Buddhist denominations into rigid centralized hierarchies. Further, lay members sought a greater say over temple management as part of the lay empowerment movement. These disputes only further spoiled the image and trust of Buddhism to the public, feeding the lay movement boom in the new religions.[53] From this point, it became increasingly common for urban Japanese to adopt a new religion as their source of spirituality while maintaining membership in a traditional temple for the continuation of family funerary rites—a trend that pushed traditional Buddhism increasingly towards the postwar malaise of Funeral Buddhism (*Soshiki Bukkyo*).

As Buddhism was co-opted into the imperial war movement, it then became equally co-opted by the postwar movement towards liberal capitalism precipitated by widespread land reform during the American occupation. Land reform hugely affected rural temples whose loss of land and income created the common trend of priests taking a second job, often as a schoolteacher, and the further laicization of the Buddhist priest as a common citizen. These trends and issues and the Socially Engaged Buddhist activities to confront them

---

53　Murakami. *Japanese Religion in the Modern Century.* pp. 124-25.

will be at the forefront of Volume II. The more established, large temples in iconic spots, such as Kamakura and Kyoto, as well as in the large urban centers, were eventually able to take advantage of Japan's economic resurrection. They featured themselves as tourist attractions, more than places of worship, to remain economically viable—a trend that still predominates today.[54]

Indeed, while traditional East Asian Mahayana Buddhism lay in the ruins of the war and the communist revolutions in China and Korea, the immediate postwar era was one of great dynamism in South and Southeast Asia for principled social change, the articulation of a non-aligned Asian modernity, and Socially Engaged Buddhism. For reference and brevity, let us briefly review these Engaged Buddhist movements:

- **India**: Dr. B.R. Ambedkar emerges in the prewar era as an activist for the rights of the untouchable castes and a rival to Gandhi's covert Hindu nationalism. He becomes India's first law minister and is the main drafter of the nation's new independent constitution. As importantly, he converts to Buddhism at the end of his life and begins a mass conversion movement of untouchable and lower caste Indians into a modern form of Buddhism stressing social justice and human rights, which continues to grow today.
- **Sri Lanka**: While Sri Lanka also suffered in the postwar period from the type of racist and violent Buddhist nationalism that Japan experienced in the prewar era, it also gave birth to the largest Socially Engaged Buddhist and grassroots Buddhist development movement in Asia, called the Sarvodaya Shramadana under the leadership of A.T. Ariyaratne. Starting in the 1950s, Sarvodaya developed a style of participatory grassroots development that crossed ethnic and religious divides and has been a key influence in the creation of Buddhist Economics.
- **Myanmar**: Before the collapse of the country into military dictatorship in the early 1960s, Myanmar was the largest experiment in a national Buddhist Socialism under Prime Minister U Nu during the 1950s. Further, some monks continued their democratic activism from the colonial period to a non-violent resistance to the military dictatorship that continues today.
- **Thailand**: Buddhadasa Bhikkhu articulated a critical and engaged style of Buddhism based in Dhammic Socialism. His lay disciple Sulak Sivaraksa began to build a wide national network of Socially

---

54 Ibid., pp. 122-23.

Engaged Buddhist NGOs in the 1960s, giving birth to the Thai Development Monk movement and the International Network of Engaged Buddhists (INEB), which both flourish today.

- **Vietnam**: The non-aligned Buddhist peace movement came to international attention in the self-immolation of Thich Quang Duc in 1964. The renowned international peace activist and meditation master Thich Nhat Hanh was a key member of this Buddhist movement, which showed that Buddhism has the principles to remain true to its fundamental ethics of non-violence during wartime. Thich Nhat Hanh was, and remains, perhaps the most important figure in articulating the way of an ecumenical, civilizational Engaged Buddhism.
- **China & Tibet**: Master Taixu developed the concept of Humanistic Buddhism in the prewar era, which became an important influence on the movement in Vietnam and has deeply informed the Buddhist renaissance in Taiwan. The Tibetan independence movement has been led by the Dalai Lama in exile. As with Thich Nhat Hanh, the Dalai Lama has steadfastly promoted universal ethics and a principled non-violent movement against the Communist oppression of his country.

These are prominent examples of the way Buddhism was used in the early postwar, post-colonial era to develop *principled* alternatives to the violent tendencies of Western modernity in liberal capitalism and Marxist socialism that were spreading through Asia. As such, they mirrored many of the efforts of Japanese Buddhists in the prewar era, detailed in the previous section. In noting the lack of dynamic, principled Socially Engaged Buddhism in Japan in the postwar era, it seems the traumatic effect of the war on Japanese Buddhism cannot be overestimated.

What remains striking is how little influence these alternative visions of Asian modernity have had in Japan compared with liberal and socialist visions as well as archaic Japanese ones that continue to predominate Japanese public discourse. In this way, it is important to examine the place of principled social change work in the immediate postwar era. If Buddhism could not offer a resource to such change, as it so prohibitively did in southern Asia, then what was the source of principled social change in Japan during this time? Further, how did the failure to develop a mature Socially Engaged Buddhism in the postwar period reflect on the state of social ethics? These questions are critical to address in terms of evaluating the development of a thriving new Socially Engaged Buddhist movement in the first two decades of the 21st century and its ability to provide an axial shift to Japanese society.

War Responsibility and Autonomy (*Shutaisei*): The Ideological Battles between Liberals and Marxists in the 1950s

As noted earlier, the U.S. occupation of Japan from the end of the war until the beginning of the Reverse Course offered an unprecedented period of freedom for the Marxist socialist movement. Even after the Reverse Course began, the spirit of democratization continued onward and new spaces for social thought emerged after decades of their erosion at the hands of Japanese fascists from the beginning of the Showa era in 1926. In this dynamic postwar society, new ideological camps soon emerged, competing to articulate a postwar vision of Japan. With the Reverse Course and the rehabilitation of war criminals, there was obviously the perpetuation of the old Neo-Confucian, *bushido*, and tacit Shinto imperialist ethic, which eventually became the somewhat obscured basis of the Liberal Democratic Party after its founding in 1955. A more dynamic and progressive center-left movement also emerged with:

1. the Marxist socialist or materialist camp, which further factionalized *ad nauseum*.
2. a progressive liberal or idealist camp, which espoused a Western style of democracy. It also posited Japan's new peace constitution, specifically Article 9 forbidding war, as a new symbolic, national identity for postwar Japan to replace that of emperor veneration.
3. a more slowly-emerging camp of varied identities, which attempted to reconcile the unique aspects and experiences of Japan, including its now distinctive identity as a victim of nuclear war, with a variety of Western ideologies concerning modernity, such as found in the writings of Jean-Paul Sartre and Herbert Marcuse. This later conglomeration became increasingly important in combination with the growing Western counterculture and international student movement.

The critical contribution of these three new center-left movements in the 50s and 60s was to first wrench apart the fusion of the people as "imperial subjects" (*kokutai*) with the identity of the state that began in earnest in the Meiji era, and then to redefine them as modern "citizens" (*shimin*) with an agency to develop "civil society" (市民社会 *shimin-shakai*, lit. "society of urban people") as an authentic third social force beyond the corporate world and the state. Ironically, it was renowned Marxist and imperial convert Sano Manabu, detailed in the previous section, who first coined the term *shimin-shakai* in 1923 through his translation of Marxist writings into Japanese.[55] The establishment of such an autonomous civil space, however, would entail a much deeper investigation and transformation of the psychological state of the Japanese, that is, the psychology that found itself such an easy victim to collective utilitarianism and the veneration of authority.

This work began quickly after the war, led in many ways by the aforementioned Maruyama Masao, who came into public renown in 1946 with the publishing of his essay on wartime Japanese fascism, "The Logic and Psychology of Ultra-nationalism" (超国家主義の論理と心理 *Cho-kokka-shugi-no ronri-to-shinri*) in the popular and progressive journal *Sekai* (世界 *The World*). Building on the prewar thought of Tosaka Jun and Miki Kiyoshi, Maruyama felt that to redefine the citizen as autonomous from the state in a true civil society, the "agency" or "autonomy" (*shutaisei*) of the individual had to be developed. He explained that the classic separation of authority and power as a "system of irresponsibility" had to be replaced with one of responsibility, which began with a serious and heartfelt examination of "war responsibility" (戦争責任 *senso-sekinin*). In this way, autonomy and war responsibility became touchstones for a new social discourse that evolved among intellectuals and activists in the immediate postwar era. These touchstones were essential, they felt, for quarantining the state from "the realm of value creation", which it dominated and abused in the prewar era, and thus protecting and developing the foundations of postwar democracy.

Within this debate on autonomy, Maruyama became important for speaking about the need to build an "internal spiritual structure".[56] This struck a chord amongst those who had participated in conversion (*tenko*) to the imperial movement from conservatives to liberals

---

55 "Does 'Civil Society' Really Exist in Japan?" (日本に「市民社会」は存在しないのか? *Nihon-ni "shimin-shakai"-wa sonzai-shinai-no-ka?*). An Interview with Uemura Kunihiko 植村邦彦, Author of *What is Civil Society?* (市民社会とは何か *Shimin-shaka-to-wa nani-ka?*) in *Synodos – Academic Journalism On-Line*. January 12, 2018. https://synodos.jp/society/20931.

56 Kersten, Rikki. "Postwar Japanese Political Philosophy: Marxism, Liberalism, and the Quest for Autonomy". In *The Oxford Handbook of Japanese Philosophy*. Ed. Bret W. Davis. (Oxford University Press, 2019), p. 3.

to communists in developing what Maruyama called "the community of repentance."[57] As we will examine later, the question of whether Buddhists were involved in this community is of great debate. As such, "autonomous value judgment and intellectual consistency emerged as key intellectual themes" during this period,[58] and many college students in the 1950s treated Maruyama's most famous book *Thought and Action in Contemporary Politics* (現代政治の思想と行動 *Gendai-seiji-no shiso-to-kodo*) as "a bible" for behavioral guidance.[59]

These various camps were brought together in 1948 by Yoshino Genzaburo 吉野源三郎 (1899–1981), the editor of *Sekai*, which acted as an important bridge between this world of public intellectuals and nascent civil society.[60] Yoshino was also a leader of the pacificist movement and saw the "partial peace" imposed on Japan by international powers as restricting Japanese in making their own decisions.[61] Together with renowned social critic and activist Shimizu Ikutaro 清水幾太郎 (1907–1988), they formed the Discussion Forum on the Problem of Peace (平和問題談話会 *Heiwa-mondai Danwa-kai*) consisting of fifty top public intellectuals to respond to the UNESCO-sponsored *Statement by Eight Distinguished Social Scientists on the Causes of Tensions which Make for War*. Only one Buddhist, the popular yet politically ambivalent Suzuki Daisetsu, is found in this group of fifty, further underscoring the lack of important public Buddhist intellectuals in this period.

At first, the group was united in their feeling of war responsibility, which they concluded as a group was more of a problem of failing to lead public opinion than of individual failure. In this way, the act of taking on war responsibility turned into the duty to take on a kind of postwar responsibility through the articulation of an indigenous and democratic peace.[62] The Forum made two public statements in 1948 and 1950 respectively. While neither mentioned the problem of the emperor system, they did promote a neutralist, non-aligned stance that emphasized including the Soviet Union and China in any treaties. At this point, however, the group started to split along Cold War ideological lines. These splits would later manifest in a lack of unity during the critical 1960 *Anpo* campaign, yet the Forum did leave a leg-

---

57   Sasaki. *Nationalism, Political Realism and Democracy in Japan*. p. 65.
58   Kersten. "Postwar Japanese Political Philosophy". p. 3.
59   Sasaki. *Nationalism, Political Realism and Democracy in Japan*. p. 74.
60   Kersten. *Democracy in Postwar Japan*. p. 178.
61   Ibid., p. 170.
62   Ibid., pp. 180-81.

acy that informed the anti-Vietnam war movement and other social campaigns.[63]

For those in the Marxist camp, Japan's defeat was confirmation that the nation had still been in a semi-feudal stage. Therefore, their failure as a movement was due to the nation not yet being ripe for socialist revolution. The members who did not succumb to *tenko* in prison emerged for a brief period as heroes to the masses for their principled resistance.[64] Among the variety of important figures at this time, Umemoto Katsumi 梅本克己 (1912–1974) remains important to us for his attempts to reconcile the philosophy of the Zen-based Kyoto School—as Sartre and Marcuse had done with renowned German philosopher and Nazi sympathizer Martin Heidegger. For Sartre and Marcuse, one of the key flaws in Marxism was its over-emphasis on materialism and lack of a theory of subjective intentionality. In a similar vein, Umemoto carried on the legacy of Tosaka and Miki of the "left-wing" of the Kyoto School by writing about the "*shutaisei* of historical materialism." He explained that, "If Marxism is simply positivistic social science, then it is unrelated to the people who will change the world."[65] For Umemoto, Nishida's philosophy of "absolute nothingness" (*zettai-mu*) could help to mediate between materialistic determinism and personal freedom.[66] Umemoto felt that if every moment is perfectly "empty" or imbued with such "nothingness", then the potential for agency or autonomy (*shutaisei*) existed for each individual to exercise their creative freedom. In this way, "nothingness" was the essence of life. While rejected by the Marxist establishment and critiqued for his use of such Kyoto School ideas that were felt to easily slide into the archaic discourse of emperor veneration,[67] Umemoto's essays attracted considerable attention not only from Marxists but also from a wide range of intellectuals.[68]

The liberal camp held a predictably different, yet ultimately similar, view to the Marxist socialists of the causes and trajectory of the war, also seeing Japan as occupying an incomplete or inferior stage of social development. For Shimizu Ikutaro, Japan's incomplete

---

63 Ibid., pp. 176-77, 182, 185.

64 Kersten. "Postwar Japanese Political Philosophy". p. 4.

65 Ibid., pp. 8-9.

66 Perhaps, unironically, this mirrors the Buddha's unique articulation of karma based on the intention (*cetana*) of the mind rather than the material karmic determinism of other Indian schools of thought. Watts. "Karma for Everyone".

67 Kersten. "Postwar Japanese Political Philosophy". pp. 8-9.

68 Koschmann. "The Debate on Subjectivity in Postwar Japan". pp. 618-19.

modernity was due to the inability of the common person to be rational and thus to develop *shutaisei*. Similar to Heidegger's critique of the common people and their lives lived in the fog of "everydayness" (Ger. *alltäglichkeit* 日常性 *nichijosei*), Shimizu held little hope for the Japanese people to develop *shutaisei* amidst the "drainage ditch of unreflective, unconscious, custom-driven behavior." While Heidegger and the Kyoto School sought a deeper immersion into the subjective to resolve this problem, Shimizu went in the other direction, feeling that scientific objectivity was critical for Japanese to further develop.[69] Without it, they could once again devolve into the kind of cultural exceptionalism that rejected modernity as Western and inferior to archaic and naturalist Japanese thought.

This kind of discourse reached its apex in the final decade of the war and was known among intellectuals, including Kyoto School ones such as Nishitani Keiji, as "overcoming modernity" (近代の超克 *kindai-no-chokoku*). For Maruyama Masao, as much as institutional change was needed, "a total ethical revolution" was tantamount to Japanese developing real independent thinking and the ability to actually decide something on their own.[70] Striking directly at the tendency found in Neo-Confucianism and Buddhism to collapse the Principle into the phenomenal, Maruyama argued, "From a way of thinking which makes absolute that which is particular, there will never emerge from within oneself the way of thinking which is able totally to transform the self."[71] His response, in turn, was essentially liberal, drawing on Descartes and Max Weber to express the fundamental ontological belief that the individual is always prior to society and stands as an "end in himself."[72] In turn, when people realize that they are the creator of social institutions and that they do not exist in some form of mythic naturalness, a modern age begins.[73]

Finally, Maruyama rejected the classical liberalism of Hobbes' negative liberty in which the individual should be freed from external obstacles. Rather, he espoused the new liberal idea of positive liberty. This means "not the passive withdrawal to internal life"—which we saw so clearly in the utopian spiritualism movements of the Taisho era—but rather "positive action toward the external world…not to escape from

---

69 Kersten. "Postwar Japanese Political Philosophy". pp. 5-6.
70 Sasaki. *Nationalism, Political Realism and Democracy in Japan.* p. 53.
71 Kersten. *Democracy in Postwar Japan.* p. 66.
72 Koschmann. "The Debate on Subjectivity in Postwar Japan". p. 626.
73 Sasaki. *Nationalism, Political Realism and Democracy in Japan.* p. 61.

political order but to constantly challenge it."[74] In the end, Shimizu and Maruyama reached similar conclusions as their Western counterparts, like Marcuse, who saw the key to the transformation of the individual and their subjectivity in the psychological theories developed by Freud and by a generation of Western personality and social psychologists.[75] As we watch Western psychotherapy today in the early 21st century look towards Buddhism for the integrated practice to overcome the deficiencies of Freudian psychology, it is ironic that at this time Buddhism was not a resource to most modern Japanese thinkers.

For all these intellectuals, the transformation of the postwar Japanese consciousness fed into the development of a true alternative politics that transcended this dualistic problem of either embracing the modernity of the West or rejecting it in the archaic and naturalist Japanese social order. For Maruyama, a peace with the West that did not include the USSR and China was yet another form of closed-society mentality founded on the passive acceptance of "nature". Real *shutaisei* was multi-dimensional and creative, not the passive acceptance of natural tendencies.[76] Such creativity meant articulating a specific form of Japanese democracy established by autonomous value creation that rejected both American democracy and Soviet communism. Political resistance, in turn, was proof of this autonomous value creation and the preservation of the individual against the collectivist state. A principled neutralism meant one could not depend on others in alignment and had to engage in autonomous decision-making and a sense of responsibility for those decisions.[77]

In this way, many saw the non-aligned movement as an important means to create a new identity for Japan in the postwar era. Commenting on the Five Peace Principles of the Non-Aligned Movement, Shimizu wrote:

> The five peace principles mark a new stage in the history of the development of democracy. Until now democracy was exclusively a principle related to a country's internal politics, and it was problematic to use it to control relations between states. Especially in the case of Western countries where democracy was developed early, because these countries were at the same time using Asian and

---

74   Ibid., p. 64.
75   Koschmann. "The Debate on Subjectivity in Postwar Japan". pp. 620-24.
76   Kersten. *Democracy in Postwar Japan*. pp. 186-88.
77   Ibid., pp. 193-95.

African regions as colonies, democracy had a false reputation in the context of relations between Asia, Africa, and the West.... If we think about the significance of these five principles, it must be seen as only natural that these principles, differing from the great principles and theories to date, were created not in Washington, Paris, or Moscow, but in a corner in Asia.[78]

The intellectual movement on war responsibility and *shutaisei* along with the popular peace movement that emerged in the 1950s have made a critical and lasting contribution towards an alternative articulation of nationhood for modern Japan. Through the vision of non-alignment and pacifism as ensconced in Article 9 of the postwar constitution, some Japanese have found a common identity to share in solidarity with global citizens' movements while also working to develop their own indigenous ideas on democracy.[79] This is indeed an axial vision and one that continues to inspire Japanese today.

However, its foundations are still rooted in resolving the crippling dualism of social change in modern Western thought—either in the Marxist socialist struggle for subjective intentionality or in the liberal struggle to re-embed the autonomous individual into a meaningful collective. The aforementioned Socially Engaged Buddhist exemplars in other parts of Asia were able to develop a wide range of social activism and development not haunted by this dualism. It seems that the spiritual bankruptcy of Buddhism in Japan during the war as well as the profound secularization of the tradition so spoiled the people to it that they did not bother to notice these dynamic Socially Engaged Buddhist movements as they looked to the non-aligned movement in southern Asia for inspiration.

Anpo and the Emergence of the New Left in the 1960s

This ideological movement together with the civil society peace movement, in which Seno-o Giro and the Nipponzan Myoho-ji were involved, came to a crescendo in the mass protest movement against the Treaty of Mutual Cooperation and Security between the United States and Japan (日本国とアメリカ合衆国との間の相互協力及び安全保障条約 *Nihon-koku-to Amerika-gasshu-koku-to-no-aida-no Sogo-kyo-ryoku-oyobi Anzen-hosho-joyaku*). More commonly known as the

---

78   Ibid., p. 173.
79   Ibid., p. 174.

U.S.-Japan Security Treaty in English and as the *Anpo-joyaku* (安保条約) or just *Anpo* (安保) in Japanese, this treaty permits the presence of U.S. military bases on Japanese soil and commits the two nations to defend each other if one is attacked. It was originally signed in 1951 in conjunction with the San Francisco Peace Treaty that officially terminated World War II in Asia as well as the U.S.-led Occupation of Japan from 1945 to 1952. Protests against this treaty, especially when local lands were appropriated for bases, led to a growing protest movement in the 1950s, such as the aforementioned one in Sunagawa from 1955–57 in which the Myoho-ji was active.[80]

These protests expanded during the tenure of Prime Minister Kishi Nobusuke (1896–1987), who came to power in 1957, concerning policies such as a rating system for teachers and expanding the powers of the police. Besides being the maternal grandfather of recent prime minister Abe Shinzo, Kishi was one of the many notorious war criminals rehabilitated during the Reverse Course. He was known for his brutal economic management of the Japanese puppet state Manchukuo in the 1930s, later earning him the nickname the "Monster of the Showa era" (昭和の妖怪 *Showa-no Yokai*), and also served in the wartime cabinet of Prime Minister Tojo Hideki. While the protest movement encompassed a variety of international issues, such as neutrality and non-nuclear proliferation, the fundamental issue was the domestic crisis of democracy. Of particular concern was the way the LDP and Kishi were going ahead in negotiating the treaty without the full consent of the people.[81]

By March 1959, the movement had further expanded to a wide variety of citizen's groups including women, farmers, and youth, known as "postwar progressives" (戦後革新勢力 *sengo-kakushin seiryoku*).[82] The students, in particular, became active in leading confrontational protests. They blockaded Haneda International Airport in January 1960 to prevent Kishi from going to the U.S. for further negotiation of the treaty. The movement peaked on June 15th with mass protests of some 110,000 people in front of the national Diet building and nationwide labor strikes during which a University of Tokyo female student was killed in a scrum with the police. Although Kishi was pushed to resign in July from these incidents, the movement failed in its ultimate aim, and the treaty was renewed on June 23, 1960.

---

80   Ando, Takemasa. *Japan's New Left Movements: Legacies for Civil Society*. (London: Routledge, 2014), p. 29.

81   Kersten. *Democracy in Postwar Japan*. pp. 202-03.

82   Ando. *Japan's New Left Movements*. pp. 30-31.

During this time, the government urged Buddhist, Christian, and new religious groups to endorse the signing of the *Anpo* while inviting their leaders to welcome Eisenhower's planned, but ultimately cancelled, visit in June. Most of the traditional denominations and some new religions did acquiesce. Soka Gakkai declared its neutrality on the issue, while Myoho-ji, the Shinto-based new religion Omoto-kyo 大本教, and some individual religious activists opposed it by joining in the protests and engaging in hunger strikes. These most radical religious groups were part of the neutrality movement that advocated relations with communist nations. At the same time, a more conservative religious peace movement was promoted by the Union of New Religious Organizations of Japan (新日本宗教団体連合会 *Shin-nihon Shukyo-dantai Rengo-kai*), to which Soka Gakkai did not belong. Spearheaded by Rissho Kosei-kai, it advocated for peace on the basis of anti-communism.[83]

The *Anpo* crisis marked an important shift in the progressive movement away from the ideological battles of the public intellectuals of the 1950s to a movement dominated by more popular activism. As leading postwar religious scholar Shimazono Susumu notes, while most new religions were not so politically active, there was also a fundamental disconnect between the highbrow articulation of issues by the intellectuals and academics of the 50s and the common people from which the large majority of the new religions' members came.[84] In this way, a New Left movement developed during the 1960s led by student radicals. They sought to distance themselves from all forms of authority, including liberal public intellectuals like Maruyama as well as the institutionalized forms of the Marxist socialist movement.

At this time, there emerged an anti-intellectual public intellectual who became their inspiration and *de facto* leader. Yoshimoto Takaaki 吉本隆明 (1924–2012) was born as the third son of a family of boat makers who managed a small boatyard in Tokyo. Unlike most of the public intellectuals of the 50s who graduated from Tokyo University and other elite schools in the liberal and philosophical arts, Yoshimoto graduated university with a degree in electrochemistry. He also developed a love for poetry and literature as a self-proclaimed "militaristic youth" (軍国少年 *gunkoku-shonen*) during the war era.[85] In the months leading up to the June *Anpo* crisis at the Diet, he was invited to speak at meetings of the national university student association Zengakuren

---

83 Murakami. *Japanese Religion in the Modern Century.* p. 135.
84 Personal Interview. October 23, 2021.
85 Kersten. "Postwar Japanese Political Philosophy". p. 12.

全学連 and began to develop a following among radical university students. On the night of June 15, 1960, he was able to force himself inside the Diet fence with Zengakuren students, speaking to them during the early hours of June 16, but was finally arrested by police in the melee following day.[86]

In the aftermath of these protests, Maruyama declared victory for the people despite the ramming through of the *Anpo* legislation by the LDP, because he saw the emergence of a real participatory democracy. Shimizu, however, criticized him for connecting the movement against the treaty with a vague, abstract, and elitist concept of democracy.[87] Yoshimoto's response to Maruyama was to redefine the concept of *shutaisei* using a different yet similar term in meaning, *jiritsusei* 自立性, in order to criticize the implicit liberal concepts in Maruyama's conception of democracy. Further, in contrast to Shimizu's rejection of mass society and the "everydayness" of the common citizen, Yoshimoto felt true autonomy could only be found within the apolitical everyday. To this end, *jiritsu* actually stood for "independence from enlightenment attitudes, vanguardism, and the composite category of modern rationalism."[88] In this way, he shared the view of Herbert Marcuse—who at the same time was becoming an important leader of the student left in Europe and the United States—that rationality was being utilized in the postwar, industrial era to integrate individuals into a self-legitimizing system, in effect suppressing autonomy to create the impression of consensus.[89] Yoshimoto felt that common indigenous ways of thinking as distinguished from those of the elite had never been given due consideration in Japanese intellectual history. Accordingly, *jiritsu* meant a quest for an indigenous pattern of thinking that could be universalized, not only as an instrument of interpretation but also as an instrument of change.[90]

By 1964, Yoshimoto lost whatever interest he had ever had in the organized left-wing political movement. He saw the abstractions and dogmas of international socialism as unable to unite the common people and felt the left's hostility toward the United States after the war was little more than prewar xenophobia in new dress. At the same time, he felt the images of love, folk-experience, instinct, concreteness,

---

86 Olson, Lawrence. "Intellectuals and 'The People': On Yoshimoto Takaaki". *The Journal of Japanese Studies*. Summer, 1978. Vol. 4, No. 2, p. 341.

87 Kersten. *Democracy in Postwar Japan*. pp. 220, 225.

88 Ando. *Japan's New Left Movements*. p. 63.

89 Kersten. "Postwar Japanese Political Philosophy". p. 16.

90 Olson. "Intellectuals and 'The People'". p. 351.

and "ethnic" (民族 *minzoku*) type symbols that came from the right were equally abused and betrayed in the hands of the national leaders. By the late 1960s, this enduring struggle between Western modernity and archaic Japanese thought led him, as so many others profiled in this volume, to an investigation of the religious and ethical.[91]

As a teen, Yoshimoto became attracted to the writings of Miyazawa Kenji, profiled in the previous section, for their emotional rather than intellectual flavor, later recalling, "Kenji Miyazawa by no means creates his work by throwing raw ethical words at them. Nor does he give his work an ethical flavor by interweaving ethical words with logic."[92] In this way, Yoshimoto was drawn to Japanese writers, thinkers, poets, and spiritual leaders who are "all distinguished by their capacity to attract passionate feeling" and had a certain combativeness to their positions.[93] One of the most important of these figures about whom he wrote a number of books was the seminal founder of the Jodo Shin Pure Land school, Shinran. Yoshimoto wanted to make clear that the intellectual history of Japan lacked the concepts of independence and *jiritsusei*, yet in Shinran he found such a person who embodied these qualities. Unlike those intellectuals attracted to the complex psychological existentialism of Zen, Yoshimoto found inspiration in Pure Land Buddhism and its radical solidarity with the unenlightened masses as *bonbu* still capable of realizing salvation through the "other power" (*tariki*) of Amida Buddha.[94] In this way, Yoshimoto built no system nor proposed any special theory, but "persistently exalted the notion of emotional solidarity between intellectuals and 'ordinary' Japanese."[95]

Yoshimoto's works such as *The End of Fiction* (擬制の終焉 *Gisei-no shuen*), *Our Shared Delusions* (共同幻想論 *Kyodo genso-ron*), and *On Maruyama Masao* (丸山真男論 *Maruyama Masao-ron*) became critical texts for radical activist students, particularly during the explosion of youth-led activism in 1968–69.[96] His credo of "wholeheartedness" was manifested by students in the expression of their own form of *shutaisei* through violent confrontation armed with staves and helmets. Perhaps

---

91 Ibid., pp. 346-49.

92 Higaki, Tatsuya. "Kenji Miyazawa and Takaaki Yoshimoto: Schizophrenic Nature in Japanese Thought". In *Deleuze and Buddhism*. Eds. Tony See & Joff Bradley. (New York: Springer, 2016), p. 64.

93 Olson. "Intellectuals and 'The People'". pp. 330-32.

94 Personal interview with Prof. Nakamura Hisashi.

95 Olson. "Intellectuals and 'The People'". p. 329.

96 Kersten. "Postwar Japanese Political Philosophy". pp. 8-9.

in response to the overall failures of the protest movement in the face of the firewall of vested power, *shutaisei* as *jiritsusei* became something more nihilistic in the students' growing individual atomization, self-criticism (自己批判 *jiko-hihan*), and even self-negation (自己否定 *jiko-hitei*).[97]

Ironically, this movement seemed to arrive at similar conclusions from an anti-authoritarian left-wing stance as the right-wing inflected thought of Nishida's "absolutely contradictory self-identity" and his student Nishitani's national "self-negation" in trying to resolve the dualistic contradictions of modernity. The latter negated the self in service of re-immersion back into the collective, while the former did so in service of marginalization from the collective. Since the students rejected anything that they deemed "reformism", such as concrete reform goals, the meaning of activity became the activity itself, to fight "for the battle itself." As such, the student protests did not spawn any reformist political movements, like the Green Party in Germany. By the dawn of the 1970s, the violence had spread to inter-group violence in which students brutalized one another. This shocked and turned off many into leaving the movement. Beyond any illusions of success for the movement, the ethical obligation for self-transformation through self-criticism and self-negation led to a significant level of burnout.

The legacy of this movement today is complex. On one level, direct action and civil disobedience in Japan became deeply discredited for its association with violence, and Japanese students still find the social activism of their peers, not only in the West but in other parts of Asia, unattractive and unmeaningful. In turn, the kind of active, social justice, non-profit movement that is a prominent political force in many other parts of Asia is lacking in Japan. Most social justice NGOs in Japan exist in our third realm of the socially marginalized, while citizen volunteer groups for picking up garbage in parks and beaches and other social order activities continue to thrive, especially amongst the young. Finally, the failure of the 1960 protests at the Diet and the devolution of the peace movement into a violent student one meant that Japanese politics remained unchanged.[98] This failure ushered in the Japanese postwar sense of political apathy and powerlessness towards the Diet and the government, yet another legacy of the war period.

Without the development of a true civil society as the third sector, social protest continued to be confined to specific policy measures in an appeal to the state for incremental change rather than

---

97 Ando. *Japan's New Left Movements*. pp. 50, 62.
98 Ibid., pp. 22-23.

principled change. This situation was exemplified in the environmental and women's movements that emerged in the 1970s and 80s, which were smaller and less political than the citizen's groups of the 50s and 60s. The litany of environmental accidents that began to occur in the 1960s stemming from the policies of "doubling personal incomes" (所得倍増計画 *shotoku-baizo-keikaku*) and rapid industrialization led to a variety of residents' movements (住民運動 *jumin undo*) in the mostly rural areas where these accidents occurred. As these resident groups were mostly created from traditional community organizations, they found little resonance with the New Left movement, which was seen as extreme, urban, and too ideological. This inability or perhaps lack of interest in turning their specific struggles into a universal movement kept them fragmented and small. With their lack of connections to urban activist groups, they tended to isolate themselves from national politics and limit their activism in the long term to lifestyle change. Like the peasant revolts of the late Tokugawa era, such movements were unable to influence the dominant discourse or the decision-making mechanisms in political institutions. As such, the people's unhappiness with rapid industrialization and modernity could not be affirmatively expressed as a political force during the 1970s.[99]

Women's and housewives' associations were central, as in previous eras, in such environmental activism. They also developed some more instrumental forms of activism, such as pressuring manufacturers to produce more easily recyclable packaging or blocking the construction of nuclear power plants in localities, like Makimachi in Niigata in 1996. Some even became political, such as the Seikatsu Club consumer co-operative that won seats in local governments.[100] Yet the feminist movements of this era consciously stayed away from electoral campaigns and the political process. Taking cues from the New Left's rejection of mainstream forms of leftist activism, they rejected all forms of politics based in masculine paradigms of power and traditional gender roles. They also embraced the ideal of self-transformation through "everydayness". As such, they seemed to be developing a deeper type of universal or axial ethos to fundamentally change the way Japanese society was organized. However, the subsequent insularity of the movement recreated common tendencies in previous forms of activism we have surveyed in the prewar era, that is, the inward turn of the first path of retreat. By the end of the century, the move-

---

99   Ibid., p. 168.

100 Igarashi, Akio. *Japanese Contemporary Politics*. Eds. Mark E. Caprio & Miranda Schreurs. (London: Routledge, 2018), pp. 23-24.

ment had, on the one hand, become marginalized into the domain of politically neutral and objective feminist scholars in academia. On the other hand, it had fallen to the second path of re-immersion back into the collectivity through the unending glorification of the charismatic housewife portrayed in advertising and the mass media.[101]

In conclusion, it appears that the key point necessary for all these movements to create a critical axial shift and break down the firewall to civil participation in national politics is the creation of cross-sector alliances, as happens with all great revolutions. However, the Japanese tendency to form closed communities with, as Nakamura described, a "limited human nexus" seems to always defeat this process. As we have seen above, the choices seem to always result in re-immersion into the collective or an insular retreat that evolves into social marginalization. When such critical issues, such as the environment or gender justice, do lead to a more fundamental evaluation and criticism of cultural, economic, and political systems, the common tendency continues to be an inward turn and exhortation for everyone to "think deeply for themselves" about an issue—as evidenced in the Japanese Buddhist Federation's declaration on nuclear energy in 2011.[102] As such, the social landscape is littered with symposiums containing the phrase in their title, "Let's Think About It" (考える会 *kangaeru-kai*).[103] This rather eternal issue of paradigm or axial change in Japan will be examined in earnest in Volume II when looking at the various forms of contemporary Socially Engaged Buddhism that struggle to take the critical next step from "social welfare" to "social transformation".[104]

---

101 Frühstück, Sabine. *Gender and Sexuality in Modern Japan*. (Cambridge University Press, 2022), pp. 92-94.

102 "The Japan Buddhist Federation Appeal for a Lifestyle without Dependence on Nuclear Power". In Watts. *This Precious Life*.

103 A cursory Google search of the term *kangaeru-kai* 考える会, meaning either "conference" or "association" to "consider" or "think about" an issue, yielded 243 million results. May 14, 2022.

104 Socially Engaged Buddhists, such as Sulak Sivaraksa, have delineated between forms of religious based social activism that: 1) address only the First Noble Truth of surface forms of social suffering through charity or "social welfare", thus leaving the systems of structural and cultural violence intact; and 2) address such deeper systems as the next stage of the Second Noble Truth in discovering the causes of social suffering, thus leading to a comprehensive form of "social transformation".

13

Confronting the Past and Defining a New Buddhist Internationalism in the 1970s–80s

Internationalism and the Path of Re-Immersion in the Major *Lotus Sutra* Groups Rissho Kosei-kai and Soka Gakkai

With the traditional Buddhist sects increasingly marginalized in the great migration of citizens out of their ancestral villages to the new secularized cities of postwar Japan, the great urban lay Buddhist boom took place over the 1950s and 60s. As noted, most new Buddhist groups that emerged in this era derived from the Nichiren and *Lotus Sutra* traditions, which have a long history of being aligned with the merchant and business class in Japan. From the foundation of Nichiren's Kamakura-era belief that we are living in the Age of the Final Dharma (*mappo*), these groups elevated the common working-class citizen as the center of this new postwar democratic age. Using Nichiren's interpretation of the *Lotus Sutra*, they grafted a number of other technically non-Buddhist ideas onto their teachings.

Besides the practice of ancestor veneration that was incorporated in the Reiyu-kai stream of new Buddhist groups, a modernized form of vitalistic thought surrounding the "Great Life of the Universe" or "life-force" (生命力 *sei-mei-ryoku*) that derives from ancient Japanese spirituality and folk religion was prominent in many groups, especially Soka Gakkai. A typical presentation of the teaching has been that individuals can find happiness and salvation in this present life through coming into harmony with this great life-force. This harmony is realized through the "transformation of the mind/heart" (心治 し *kokoro-naoshi*) in developing harmonious relations with those in one's community, society, and the environment.[105] This teaching was then commonly fused with a deterministic understanding of karma in which proper faith in the denomination's teachings leads to karmic rewards in this life, i.e., "this-worldly benefit" (*gen-se riyaku*), while

---

105 Shimazono. *From Salvation to Spirituality*. pp. 5, 110-115.

lack of faith leads to a life of punitive karma and suffering. Such an understanding can be found in sections of the *Lotus Sutra* that warn of punitive karma for those who disregard its teachings while assuring karmic reward in this and future lives for faith in its teachings.

These kinds of teachings were especially attractive to the migrant laborers flooding into Japan's metropolises in the postwar era who felt a level of inferiority to the more modern educated urban citizens and wished to experience the upward mobility that the American style of democracy and capitalism promised. As such, many of the groups created a model for a new type of "Market Buddhism" teaching economic gain as a sign of good karma, which has spread throughout Asia in recent decades. This type of teaching has been best exemplified by Soka Gakkai in its modified postwar doctrine. Second President Toda Josei 戸田城聖 (1900–1958), who took over from Makiguchi after his death in prison during the war, is regarded by many as more of an astute businessman who financed Makiguchi's publications than as an educator or spiritual visionary.[106] As noted earlier, Soka Gakkai was built on a bureaucratic corporate model, different from the other smaller *Lotus Sutra* based new religions, such as Reiyu-kai[107], Myochi-kai, and Kodo Kyodan as well as Rissho Kosei-kai. In the postwar era, Toda made important changes to Nichiren Sho-shu's and Makiguchi's teachings by picking up on this trend of vitalistic life-force theory to put further emphasis on the karmic benefit that comes from chanting the *daimoku* in harmony with the Great Life of the Universe. He even once proclaimed, "I recommend that you accumulate good fortune in this life, so that in the next existence of life, you can be born into a family possessing five Cadillacs".[108]

The ramifications of this interpretation of the *Lotus Sutra* through such a vitalistic lens, not to mention through the one of deterministic karma[109], are indeed problematic. As we will continue to examine in the critique of Zen during the war period, this emphasis on achieving harmony with the social and political collective through individual effort returns us once again to archaic themes that have legitimized the veneration of authority and a circumscribed sense of social ethics. In this way, Yasumaru Yoshio 安丸良夫 (1934–2016), one of the leading

---

106 Ibid., p. 79.

107 As the earliest of these groups to form in 1924, Reiyu-kai was actually the model that many of the others studied and replicated. Murakami. *Japanese Religion in the Modern Century.* p. 106.

108 McLaughlin. "Soka Gakkai in Japan". p. 288.

109 Watts. "Karma for Everyone".

postwar scholars on the history of thought in Japan, connects such vitalistic thought to a theme that has been emphasized by other scholars, such as Nakamura Hajime, throughout this volume. He explains that while such thought "may have great validity within the narrow confines of inter-personal relationships, it lacks objective analytical power when applied to society as a whole."[110]

Shimazono connects this point to Maruyama Masao's critique of such closed group morality being related to "Neo-Confucian thought patterns" and resulting in "the dangers of religion being subordinated to political authorities."[111] Various critics see many of these new *Lotus Sutra* groups as promoting the "conventional morality" (通俗道徳 *tsuzoku-dotoku*) built in the Meiji and prewar era based on the fusion of Neo-Confucian ethics and the Shinto-derived veneration of the emperor. As we detailed in the previous section, this veneration of authority along with a simplistic and deterministic understanding of karma creates a politically conservative orientation, because a structural and cultural critique that sees individual and social suffering as co-dependently arising is obscured in a focus on individual effort and industry.[112]

In a way very similar to the classical liberalism of the West, the result can be, in the words of Japanese new religion's scholar Helen Hardacre, "Placing blame and responsibility on the individual also denies the idea that 'society' can be blamed for one's problems; hence concepts of exploitation and discrimination are ruled out of consideration."[113] Renowned international sociologist Robert Bellah also explains that, "Even the new religions, the primary expression of postwar Japanese spirituality, emphasize personal and group prosperity and the morality of group cohesion rather than any more transcendental ethical injunctions."[114] As such, these new Buddhist groups seem to have blended their teachings with the new predominant postwar ethos of liberal capitalism rather than critiquing it as have many leading Socially Engaged Buddhists in other parts of Asia.

---

110 Yasumaru, Yoshio. *Japan's Modernization and Popular Thought*. (日本の近代化と民衆思想 *Nihon-no kindaika-to minshu shiso*). (Tokyo: Aoki Shoten 青木書店, 1974), p. 45.

111 Shimazono. *From Salvation to Spirituality*. pp. 50-51.

112 Stone. "Nichiren's Activist Heirs". pp. 75-76.

113 Hardacre, Helen. *Kurozumikyo and the New Religions of Japan*. (Princeton, New Jersey: Princeton University Press, 1986), p. 23.

114 See Bellah. *Tokugawa Religion*. p. xv.

Shimazono, however, tempers his criticism by noting that while vitalism "is immature as a form of modern social thought," it helped these groups to create a wide sense of human association and connection as modernization "dissolved traditional communal social bonds"[115]—a predominant issue in the Disconnected Society (*mu-en shakai*) of the 21st century. In attending to the mass of rural migrants who flooded into the rapidly industrializing urban areas after the war, the new religions grew at such an amazing rate in the 50s and 60s that each came to encompass a "thriving internal civil society" within the larger urban landscape.[116] Their activities sought to provide and care for not just the spiritual needs of the community but also all the material needs of it. As the largest of these groups, Rissho Kosei-kai and Soka Gakkai could build their own schools, publish their own mass circulation newspapers, and provide other important social services, such as Rissho Kosei-kai's Kosei Hospital built in 1952 and Soka Gakkai's Soka University established in 1971. In terms of the concept of civil society as a third sector, Soka Gakkai, in particular, made an appeal to a different kind of social order, a kind of social reformism, different from both capitalism or communism, and based on the aspiration of the disempowered working classes during the modernization and high economic growth period. By developing a vision of a new social-spiritual order, these new Buddhist groups appeared to be carrying on the work of the Meiji Buddhist Enlightenment.

Further, these groups offered a different kind of *shutaisei* than the one being laboriously articulated by the elite intellectuals of the immediate postwar era. Instead, as Nichiren did during the Kamakura era, they offered an empowering form of social agency not based in the intellectual study of Buddhist texts or the practice of ascetic disciplines, like with the elitist monkhood, but in a simple faith in the *daimoku*. This modern vision not only charted an alternative path to liberal individualism but also offered an alternative collective social vision for the working class to the popular Marxist socialist labor movement of the time. As such, Shimazono remarks that this vision was attractive to many in the vacuum of authority in the immediate postwar era.

By 1964, Soka Gakkai decided to translate this kind of vision and its mass following of urban working class into a political movement in the form of the Komei-to 公明党 party. Originally, Komei-to was a marginal leftist party devoted to social welfare policies supporting its

---

115 Shimazono. *From Salvation to Spirituality*. p. 51.
116 McLaughlin. "Soka Gakkai in Japan". pp. 277-278.

working class membership and also to more controversial religious goals—such as fulfilling the archaic vision of Nichiren in the establishment of a nationally sponsored ordination platform and the uniting of Japan under the *Lotus Sutra* (広宣流布 *kosen-rufu*).[117] Komei-to explicitly portrayed itself as the third way between the corporate capitalism of the LDP and the labor-union centric policies of the Socialist Party of Japan (SPJ).[118]

As Soka Gakkai continued to grow along with Japan's economic miracle, Komei-to began to develop more conservative middle-class values in the 1970s and gradually layered over of their religious platforms with liberal ones, like humanism, education, and world peace. In this way, the promise of a "human revolution" (人間革命 *ningen-kakumei*)—a book by the same name penned in 1965 by Soka Gakkai's Third President Ikeda Daisaku 池田大作 (1928-)—and the ideal of principled social change seemed to fade. In turn, Levi McLaughlin notes that Komei-to did "not frame itself as participating in ideological conflict or targeting structural causes of socioeconomic inequality." Its fundamental religious and social conservatism has meant up to the present a continued focus on the welfare of the patriarchal, urban nuclear family and not the growing number of people who fall outside it, such as the unemployed and homeless, foreign workers and refugees, and members of the LGBTQ+ community.[119] In this way, they have followed the common pattern of alternative social movements in becoming circumscribed by the bureaucratic state and focused on policy adjustment rather than paradigm shift. As such, they again resemble the Meiji Buddhist Enlightenment movement for their eventual re-immersion back into the collectivity. Komei-to's ultimate re-immersion came in 1999 when it became an important junior partner and self-proclaimed "brake"[120] to the conservative policies of the Liberal Democratic Party.

This focus on building their own organizations as manifestations of a new model postwar society for Japan explains why many of these new denominations were not active in the popular peace and civil society movement of the 50s and 60s. For some groups, the nationalistic tendencies of prewar devotees of Nichiren and the *Lotus Sutra* carried

---

117 McLaughlin. "Soka Gakkai in Japan". p. 293.

118 Klein, Axel & McLaughlin, Levi. "Komeito: The Party and Its Place in Japanese Politics". In *The Oxford Handbook of Japanese Politics*. Eds. Robert J. Pekkanen & Saadia M. Pekkanen. (Oxford University Press, 2021), p. 4.

119 Ibid., p. 4.

120 Ibid., p. 11

over in their drive to create this new model society. In Soka Gakkai's case, the fanaticism of the Nichiren Sho-shu manifested itself in the controversial Great March of *Shaku-buku* (折伏大行進 *Shaku-buku Dai-koshin*). This march was led by Second President Toda and his new "army" of more than 10,000 youth converts, whom he addressed at a mass rally in October 1954 while atop a white horse, mimicking the Showa Emperor at military rallies during the war.[121] These evangelical activities have included an emphasis on the *veneration* of Nichiren and the Soka Gakkai presidents through an "indivisible bond of teacher and disciple" (師弟不二 *shitei-funi*)[122] rather than in the *principles* of the *Lotus Sutra*, and thus further indicate a dilution of Makiguchi's founding concepts of "value creation education."

In considering why the Myoho-ji more quickly dispelled the vestiges of its wartime nationalism, perhaps, as noted earlier, their community not as a mass, middle class lay movement but rather as a marginal group of ascetic practitioners provides a critical clue. Their lack of concern with converting the masses certainly allowed them to join as partners in the peace and civil society movements of the 1950s and 60s. While Nipponzan Myoho-ji was organizing "peace marches" (平和行進 *heiwa-koshin*) to help common citizens defend their land from the construction of U.S. military bases, Soka Gakkai spent these two decades trying to convert as many people as possible in the country.

It seems, then, rather ironic that Japan's two largest new Buddhist groups, Rissho Kosei-kai and Soka Gakkai, have been portrayed internationally as the standard bearers of Socially Engaged Buddhism in Japan in the postwar era,[123] since they did not become fully engaged in international peace activities until the popular peace movement was collapsing amidst student violence. Eventually, with the decline of the popular movement and the firm establishment of their denominations, Soka Gakkai and Rissho Kosei-kai did find a new expression for the evangelical tendencies of the Nichiren tradition by developing an internationalism based on advocating for world peace and nuclear disarmament. Their positions towards international peace are clearly built upon the values and concepts of the popular peace movement of the 1950s that Myoho-ji also shares:

---

121 McLaughlin. "Soka Gakkai in Japan". p. 289.

122 Ibid., p. 276.

123 For example, see chapters in: Queen & King. *Engaged Buddhism: Buddhist Liberation Movements in Asia*. and *Buddhist Peacework: Creating Cultures of Peace*. Ed. David W. Chappell. (Boston: Wisdom Publications, 1999).

1. Japan must atone for the suffering inflicted through its imperialism.
2. As the only victim of nuclear war, Japan is in a unique position to work for nuclear disarmament, an especially critical issue during the Cold War.
3. With the Article 9 of their postwar constitution renouncing war and an aggressive military, Japan is in a unique position to lead the rest of the world to similar renunciation.

In outlining his vision for the Komei-to Party in 1967, Ikeda Daisaku summed up these sentiments, "Japan is entirely qualified to be in the vanguard, to mobilize all the peace forces of the world, to assume the leadership, and to rouse world opinion through the United Nations."[124]

Despite these pronouncements, however, Soka Gakkai's work for peace emerged much later than Nipponzan Myoho-ji's activism at the beginning of the popular peace movement in 1954 or even Rissho Kosei-kai's initial efforts in the early 1960s. Their activities began only in 1972 as the second phase of their social and cultural movement. This was initiated after their political movement through Komei-to began to receive widespread national condemnation for mixing religion and politics and engaging in illegal forms of vote garnering.[125] Soka Gakkai's registering as a Non-Governmental Organization (NGO) with the United Nations High Commissioner for Refugees (UNHCR) in 1981 really marks the beginning of its activities and promotion "as a movement for world peace and nuclear disarmament."[126]

This period also marked a shift away from its Buddhist roots in Nichiren towards a revival of the Euro-American liberal humanism of its founder Makiguchi, now portrayed in the Third President Ikeda as a "global humanist icon."[127] While Soka Gakkai advocates for world peace in numerous *international* activities, the Komei-to acts on the domestic front as an important electoral partner of the LDP, which has made numerous attempts to rewrite not only Article 9 but also other parts of the Japanese constitution to raise collective rights over individual ones.[128] The other enigmatic aspect of Soka Gakkai is while they have cultivated a wide variety of international relationships and engaged in non-sectarian peace activities, within Japan they have stayed apart from a wide variety of pan-Buddhist and pan-religious peace

---

124 Stone. "Nichiren's Activist Heirs". p. 86.
125 McLaughlin. "Soka Gakkai in Japan". pp. 294-95.
126 Ibid., p. 300.
127 Ibid., pp. 303-04.
128 Repeta and Jones. "State Power versus Individual Freedom". pp. 304-328.

and civil society initiatives. Apparently reflecting on the influence of Nichiren Sho-shu and Nichiren's most extreme teachings of *fuju-fuse*, that is, not cooperating with other religious groups due to their mistaken teachings, Soka Gakkai has stood largely isolated from the variety of inter-religious social activities in Japan in the postwar era.

A more consistent image of both international and domestic ecumenical work is cast by Rissho Kosei-kai. From the time of its late co-founder Niwano Nikkyo 庭野日敬 (1906–1999) serving as the sub-leader of the Peace Delegation for Religious Leaders for Banning Nuclear Weapons to Europe and the U.S. in 1963, it has been deeply engaged in international ecumenical peace dialogue. It has been a longtime leader in the World Council for Religion and Peace (WCRP-now known as Religions for Peace) founded in 1970 and headquartered at the United Nations in New York. Its Niwano Peace Foundation has brought a wide variety of Socially Engaged Buddhist figures in Asia to the attention of the Japanese public through its annual peace prize, the kind of international alliance with progressive Buddhist leaders in Asia in which Soka Gakkai seems uninterested. Finally, it regularly works with not only other new Buddhist groups from the Nichiren tradition but also develops alliances with traditional Buddhist groups, including serving as integral player in the Buddhist NGO Network that focuses on international aid work.

Shimazono marks the founding of WCRP in 1970, as well as the movement against the establishment of the Yasukuni Shrine as a war memorial, which included the traditional Buddhist denominations, as the beginning of a new kind of grassroots religious-based peace movement. He feels that while some of these groups like Rissho Kosei-kai and Soka Gakkai had developed great wealth and social prestige by this time, their members still mostly came from the working classes that spawned the immediate postwar peace movement. They felt in consort with the peace work of these new Buddhist groups as part of the creation of an alternative national identity for Japan as a global leader of neutrality and peace. In this way, they became known as the Socially Engaged Buddhism of Japan at this time.[129]

Still, such progressive internationalism and peace work has tended to be confined to conferences, publications, declarations, and charity aid with very little, if any, critique of Japan's political and economic complicity with the state of conflict all over the world. As we will document in Volume II, with the exception of Nipponzan Myoho-ji, these groups keep the issue of nuclear disarmament separate from

---

129 Personal Interview. October 23, 2021.

the development of nuclear energy within Japan, which the LDP has pursed with vigor through the active support of the U.S. since the 1950s. This separation of issues has allowed Buddhist groups to put on a critical international face blaming the U.S. and Russia for nuclear proliferation, while completely side-stepping Japan's growing stockpile of plutonium and nuclear facilities that have the potential for military use. In this way, "international peace" becomes a form of rhetoric by which both new and traditional Buddhist denominations try to project a positive image of themselves, while skirting issues of war responsibility and national policy. This line is also the critical one that separates the smaller Buddhist groups and individuals as marginalized actors engaging in more principled forms of protest that challenge the underlying structural and cultural violence from the mainstream denominations that remain immersed in the dominant ideology of collective utilitarianism and veneration of authority.

Perpetuation of the Neo-Confucian Bureaucratic State and the Return of Japanese Exceptionalism

Thus far we have examined a number of progressive responses to problems of war responsibility, the perpetuation of the bureaucratic authoritarian state as collective utilitarianism, and the need to develop the autonomy (*shutaisei*) of citizens to create principled change. As is evident, especially in the Reverse Course, there were considerable regressive tendencies that the Japanese state embraced in the postwar era as it sought to rehabilitate conservative leaders tainted by war. This issue was further complicated by the schizophrenic demands of the United States for democratic reform along with the occupation of Japan's territories for military bases from which to wage war in Asia. These conservative tendencies mark the perpetuation of what Shimazono calls "state authoritarianism" (権威主義国家 *ken-i-shugi kokka*). He explains that while China is considered the epitome of this tendency in East Asia, Japan was the first to achieve success using this model in the modern era through the creation of the bureaucratic nation state in the Meiji era.

All throughout the prewar era and into the postwar one, the bureaucracy in Japan has maintained a high status and the highest power to form public policy. The top civil servants continue to come from the highest echelons of education, such as Tokyo University. From this foundation, they have been able to develop a strong organizational ethos and considerable autonomy from short-term political pressures. As such, they have been able to actively manipulate politicians by leveraging their expertise, mediating among politicians, and favoring certain ones over others to achieve their own policy preferences. [130] Revisiting the perennial theme of the Japanese separation of authority and power, Bernard Silberman writes, "One is forced to conclude that a central characteristic of prewar Japan's political structure was a continued disjunction between legitimacy and authority.... Seen in this light, the central problem for Japan after 1868 was, and perhaps still is, the search for an appropriate structure of authority, a problem seemingly focused on the question of integrating the state bureaucracy into society."[131]

This model of bureaucratic control has been weaker in those areas where LDP politicians have targeted resources to their constituents, particularly visible in the one area that Komei-to has been given power in the alliance with the LDP. In their concern for supporting their middle-class constituency, they have been powerful in enlisting the Ministry of Construction and local government officials to carry out specific public works projects. Still, such measures tend to favor the powerful companies in the construction sector in a policy of "corporatism without labor", meaning that business is systematically incorporated into the heart of the policy process but the interests of the workers are not. In this way, the bureaucracy's power to form the Iron Triangle with the LDP coalition and major corporations has severely "restricted the participation of civic groups and minority interests in the policy process, limited accountability to the broader public, and fostered collusive partnerships with politicians and favored interest groups."[132]

As we will examine later in the growth of the Buddhist NGO movement, certain civic groups have been considered as allies and provided with preferential access to resources and inclusion in the policy process in exchange for passive compliance or active collaboration in policy implementation. For example, among consumer groups, in a tradition developed in the prewar era, the government has mobilized housewives associations to promote household savings and product quality, while shunning and containing other groups that have protested government policies or been allied with opposition parties.[133] Another significant example is how "nonprofit organizations (NPOs)

---

130 Vogel, Steven K. "The Rise and Fall of the Japanese Bureaucracy". In *The Oxford Handbook of Japanese Politics*. pp. 1-3.

131 Silberman. "The Bureaucratic State in Japan". p. 231.

132 Vogel. "The Rise and Fall of the Japanese Bureaucracy". pp. 1-2.

133 Ibid., p. 7.

interested in the energy sector continue to have limited success in shaping energy policy choices in nuclear energy due to the continued links between the utilities, ministries, and the governing party."[134] This type of firewall system in which democratic electoral politics and civil society initiatives are unable to reach the inner sanctums of bureaucratic policy development results in the continual political apathy and fatalism of common Japanese towards social change.

Education, as we saw in the prewar era with the Imperial Rescript on Education, has continued to be an important method for perpetuating the veneration of authority based on the circumscribed principles of Neo-Confucianism found in the five social virtues (*go-jo*) and the five hierarchical relationships (*go-rin*). With the new Fundamental Law of Education, established in March 1947, there was a brief period of shifting towards the kind of new liberalism seen earlier in Dewey and Makiguchi's writings that would promote an individualism with the attitude and skills to participate positively in society in order to build a democratic society.[135] Ironically, the year before, in 1946, the Ministry of Education had tried to lay the deficiency of such attitudes by the people as the cause of the war, issuing a pamphlet stating that the Japanese are "deficient in critical spirit and prone blindly to follow authority.... They lack the spirit of rationality; their scientific level is low." Therefore, "the people as a whole should accept responsibility for the war."[136]

In the 1950s, with the revival of conservative forces within Japanese society, especially under the Kishi administration, the education system was reformed again, shifting to a prioritization on the acquisition of knowledge necessary for economic development and expansion. In 1958, moral education was reintroduced to the school curriculum as an independent subject called "morals" (道徳 *dotoku*). The central aim was described as one of ensuring that the "spirit of human respect should be supported." In the 1980s, yet another shift began the search for a type of education that would enable Japanese students to cope with the more sophisticated global economy and the demands of globalization. This new wave was promoted by Prime Minister Nakasone Yasuhiro (1918–2019) and endorsed by Dewey-

---

134 Hughes, Llewelyn. "Energy Policy in Japan: Revisiting Radical Incrementalism". In *The Oxford Handbook of Japanese Politics*. p. 8.

135 McCullough, David. "Moral and Social Education in Japanese Schools: Conflicting Conceptions of Citizenship". In *Citizenship Teaching and Learning*. July 2008. Vol 4, No. 1. p. 24.

136 Koschmann. "The Debate on Subjectivity in Postwar Japan". p. 630.

influenced educational progressives as well as the business community. Conservatives, like Nakasone, saw internationalism as a way to promote patriotism and traditional Japanese values, which had been weakened with the Americanization of the country since the end of the war. For them, this educational shift was more about "the development of pride in Japanese culture through moral education rather than education for better understanding of other countries." This tension between progressives, traditionalists, and pragmatists continues to shape the kind of citizenship education provided in Japan today.[137]

In looking at how moral education and social ethics are taught to students in the postwar era, one goal that remains important is a sense of respect for life. This emphasis seems to be derived from ancient Shinto sensibilities for the interdependence with nature, Buddhist influences on compassion for all sentient life, and a sincere reflection in much of society on the horrors of the war, regardless of who was responsible for them. A second major emphasis is the importance of the connection between the individual and the group. This is still largely inculcated through the tacit, if not explicit, transmission of "a sense of social order and hierarchy, stemming from Confucian values of respect for elders and for those in positions of authority." This is most strongly manifested in the enduring mentality of the "senior-junior" (*senpai-kohai*) relational system. From the time they first enter school, children are expected to look up to those with more experience, even if it is negligible, and to follow their instructions. At the same time, the elders are expected to take responsibility for the training and welfare of those younger and with less experience than themselves. This system, however, does not end at the grade school or even university level, but continues on into professional life, being an important feature of the corporate world.[138]

Unfortunately, this system is also often infused with the lingering values of *bushido* held by those conservative leaders from the war and their progeny who still populate leadership positions in the government, most conspicuously former Prime Minister Abe Shinzo and his maternal grandfather Kishi Nobusuke. In this way, the reasonable ethical tenets of Confucianism—such as discipline, loyalty, harmony, filial piety, and perseverance—are poisoned with a militaristic ethos in which violence becomes the method of ensuring compliance to them. As such, the problem of "bullying" (*ijime*) has gone beyond being a prevalent issue in Japanese schools in the post-

---

137 McCullough. "Moral and Social Education in Japanese Schools". pp. 24-25.
138 Ibid., pp. 29-30.

war era and has led to the secondary issues of school-dropouts (不登校 *futoko*), social withdrawal (*hikikomori*), and youth suicide. As fundamental forms of developing social relationships, these issues continue on in the adult world with bullying being a common problem in the corporate workplace and even in the training centers of Buddhist monasteries.

For a long time, these issues were seen as incidental rather than endemic to the postwar system. As Shimazono Susumu explains, the economic success of the postwar era swept the nation up in a feeling of succeeding as a group, and this collective utilitarianism and so-called Japanese way of corporate management were seen as inherent advantages to Japanese society. He comments, "This euphoria let us forget the bitter experience of WWII and bask in the glow of this economic miracle. The new religions, such as Soka Gakkai, also resonated with these trends. They helped provide a new object of veneration in their charismatic leaders to replace the void left by the emperor's retreat. This also allowed people to not reflect on the failures of the war."[139] The bureaucratic, corporate, and political elite never really became modern, rational liberals but rather remained loyal to the national morality created in the prewar era, which Shimazono refers to as "a syncretic fusion of Confucian ethics and Shintoist veneration of the emperor" (神儒教宗教 *shin-ju-kyo shukyo*). Most conservative politicians avoided reference to such Neo-Confucian and Shinto values connected to the symbolism of pre-1945 fascism and the emperor system. By identifying themselves with the democracy, liberalism, internationalism, and anti-communism of a pro-American order, they were able to avoid any links to their own dubious wartime pasts.[140]

Ironically, the freedom of religion and separation of religion and state clauses in the American-sponsored postwar constitution have supported the perpetuation of this system. Through the end of the 20th century, religious groups were barred from participation in the public sector, such as serving as chaplains in hospitals. Just as in the prewar era, the religion of the masses has been confined to the private sector while public morality, specifically in the form of moral education in the schools, is still defined by policy makers loyal to this Neo-Confucian-Shinto fusion. This issue serves as a critical starting point for our explorations in Volume II on the denial of death in postmodern Japan and the challenges of Buddhists and other religious professionals to

---

139 Personal Interview. October 23, 2021.

140 Paramore. *Japanese Confucianism*. p. 172.

engage in chaplaincy training, especially in medical institutions.

By the 1970s, the cumulative effect of these attitudes of public euphoria and state sponsored collective utilitarianism gave birth to a new sort of nationalism called Theories of Japanese-ness (日本人論 *Nihonjin-ron*), which might be more aptly translated as Theories of Japanese Exceptionalism. Shimazono comments that at that time, even the academics and intellectuals, much less the common people, did not understand that the postwar political system was in fact a recycling of East Asian authoritarianism with its positive slant on the myth of Japanese uniqueness. In short, *Nihonjin-ron* has taken either the form of denying Japan's deep-rooted traditional connections with its East Asian neighbors or of claiming that Japan has uniquely embodied and perfected "the essence of the East."[141] While on the surface, Japan appeared as a fully developed modern nation based in a rational secularism, "this cultural essentialism provided an important element of real intellectual infrastructure."[142]

The movement became more publicly embraced by Prime Minister Nakasone during his tenure from 1982–87. In speeches extolling the virtues of the "monoracial state", he suggested that the presence of racial minorities in the United States dragged educational standards there down. In 1987, he appropriated twenty million yen to build the International Research Center for Japanese Studies (国際日本文化研究センター *Kokusai Nihon Bunka Kenkyu-senta*) led by Prof. Umehara Takeshi 梅原猛 (1925–2019), a renowned scholar of Japanese culture and a postwar member of the Kyoto School.[143] As such, in this new phase of nationalistic *Nihonjin-ron*, a more overt revival of the ethics of *bushido* occurred, and the thought of Nishida Kitaro and his Kyoto School became re-popularized. Nakasone is also remembered as the first postwar prime minister to visit the Yasukuni Shrine, a precedent then followed by the two longest-standing and most important LDP prime ministers after him, Koizumi Junichiro and Abe Shinzo, to the outrage of the Chinese and Korean governments.

Nakasone also was known as an avid Zen practitioner who frequented a Rinzai Zen temple named Zensho-an 全生庵 during his time in office. The temple and its master, Yamamoto Genpo 山本玄峰 (1866–1961), seem to have been on the side of the Imperial Way Zen movement. Yamamoto was not only a confidant of Suzuki Kantaro 鈴木貫太郎 (1868–1948), an admiral in the Imperial Navy who served

---

141 Davis. "The Kyoto School".

142 Paramore. *Japanese Confucianism*. p. 177.

143 Buruma, Ian. "A New Japanese Nationalism". *New York Times*. April 12, 1987.

as the last prime minister of the war era. He also counted among his disciples the influential political advisor Yotsumoto Yoshitaka 四元義隆 (1908-2004), a leading member of the ultranationalist League of Blood (血盟団 *ketsumei-dan*), which attempted to assassinate important capitalists and liberal politicians in 1932. The League was in fact masterminded by a follower of Nichirenism founder Tanaka Chigaku, a Nichiren Buddhist priest named Inoue Nissho 井上日召 (1887–1967), for whom Master Yamamoto testified in support during his court trial for these plots. In the immediate postwar era, Yotsumoto's influence grew as he forged a reputation as a power broker, serving as adviser to Prime Ministers Yoshida Shigeru (1946–47, 1948–54), Ikeda Hayato (1960–64), Sato Eisaku (1964–72) and eventually Nakasone, whom he introduced to Zensho-an and Master Yamamoto. Nakasone, in turn, introduced Abe Shinzo to the temple, where he supposedly went after his first failed tenure as prime minister to revive his spirit for his second, long running tenure.[144]

Shimazono Susumu feels the revival of Nishida, however, is less about nationalism and Imperial Way Zen and more about Buddhist metaphysics and how it links to social thought, especially environmental issues.[145] The Nishida philosophy is felt by many to offer an antithesis to Anglo-Saxon utilitarianism and to provide Japan with an indigenous form "humanism" (人文主義 *jinbun-shugi*). Shimazono further explains that this humanism or post-metaphysical way of thinking has become widespread in Japan and has led many academics to express opposition to authoritarianism, especially under the Abe regime. Shimazono's points echo the work of high-level Western scholars on Japanese Buddhism, such as James Heisig of the Nanzan Institute for Religion and Culture in Nagoya. In his comprehensive work on Nishida, Heisig states that the ideas of the Kyoto School thinkers should not be completely discarded as they have important nuances in the development of modern Japanese thought.[146]

---

144 Yuzuru, Demachi. "Zen and Politics: The Counsel of Yamamoto Genpo". *Nippon.com*. May 9, 2017. https://www.nippon.com/en/views/b06103/

145 Environmentalism is another facet of *Nihonjin-ron* in which Shinto and Japanese culture are viewed as deeply in harmony with the natural world in contrast to the dualistic, anthropocentric attitude towards nature of the Christian West. From a theoretical standpoint, this may make sense, however, observing the litany of environmental accidents in postwar Japan, including the catastrophic Fukushima nuclear accident, makes one reconsider the saliency of this argument.

146 Heisig, James W. *Philosophers of Nothingness: An Essay on the Kyoto School*.

At the same time, we should recall Shimazono's comments on the disconnect between this kind of elitist Zen discourse and the mass consciousness of average citizens reflected in the new Buddhist groups. Unlike the liberation theologies of the masses made by Nichiren and Pure Land founders Honen and Shinran, the Zen discourse of the Kyoto School has reflected the long historical trend of it as a resource to the elite and powerful. This is a trend that only a few modern Zen figures have tried to counter, such as Ichikawa Hakugen who wrote in the early 1950s: "Zen figures have been passionate in their denunciation of communism. That's fine. But what liberation movement have they developed with equal passion?"[147]

This is the place where a robust Socially Engaged Buddhist movement has great meaning for Japanese society. As noted earlier in the SEB movements in other parts of Asia, their leaders—like Ambedkar, Sivaraksa, Ariyaratne, Nhat Hanh—have been highly educated and critically intelligent yet also able to speak to the masses in a compelling and relatable way. Perhaps not accidentally, they model the Buddha himself, who was a highly educated aristocrat but chose the vernacular of Pali rather than the elitist Sanskrit of the brahmins to teach peoples of all classes. The Kamakura masters of Japan also have similar profiles, except perhaps Nichiren, of well-educated backgrounds who renounced their privilege to work for the masses. The strength of the Socially Engaged Buddhist movement over the last 100-plus years is this blending of a discriminating wisdom into the social causes of suffering with a compassionate voice of empowerment and *shutaisei* for the common people. Further, Engaged Buddhist social ethics help to chart an important middle ground between the elitist discourse of Zen epitomized in the Kyoto School and the rather uncritical populism of some of the new *Lotus Sutra* groups, especially Soka Gakkai. As we will explore in the case studies in Volume II, the discriminating wisdom of the Japanese Socially Engaged Buddhist movement is still lagging behind its compassionate social activities.

War Responsibility, Social Discrimination, and Critical Buddhism amongst the Traditional Buddhist Denominations

As documented in the previous section, the era of modernization beginning in the Meiji introduced secular and modern bureaucratic

---

(Honolulu: University of Hawai'i Press, 2001), p. 6.

147 Ives. *Imperial-Way Zen*. p. 90.

institutions that began to eat away at the traditional civil society roles of the village priest as teacher, doctor, counselor, and ritualist. In response, Buddhists developed a variety of new modern institutions, most notably Buddhist-based universities, temple-based kindergartens, and social welfare activities. These examples suggest how Buddhists attempted to develop social models in line with modern, liberal ideas that fostered, in the words of Fukuzawa Yuichi, "independent individuals" through modern education and with civil society concepts that showed their role in working for the "public good" (公益 ko-eki). In the postwar era, this prewar structure of an activist state that monitors, penetrates, and steers civil society has been preserved in policies like "public benefit corporations" (公益法人 ko-eki hojin). Religious groups have been enfolded into this system in which their legal and financial status is directly monitored and can be revoked by the government.[148]

After the war, the traditional Buddhist orders did not establish themselves as participants or a potential third sector in wider civil society, in part due to the unconfronted shame of their role in promoting imperialism and war. Further, the communal life of traditional rural temples became weakened with the immigration of many of their members to the cities, where they converted to the new Buddhist groups[149] and slowly drifted into the anti-religious secularism of mainstream society. In their own attempts to re-immerse themselves into the postwar social fabric, these traditional sects have generally counseled their believers to accommodate to social circumstances rather than change them and to avoid public protest as not befitting what proper religions should do.[150] As Helen Hardacre has pointed out, the traditional denominations "seldom become involved in public debate, show little activism within Japan and only a low level of international activity."[151]

The other important legacy of the Meiji era was the expansion through all Buddhist denominations of lay lifestyles for priests based on nuclear families. In the postwar era economic boom, the temple nuclear families benefitted from the tide that lifted all boats, and Funeral

---

148 Hardacre, Helen. "Religion and Civil Society in Contemporary Japan". *Japanese Journal of Religious Studies*. 2004. Vol. 31, No. 2. pp. 395-96.

149 Watts, Jonathan S. and Okano, Masazumi. "Reconstructing Priestly Identity and Roles and the Development of Socially Engaged Buddhism in Contemporary Japan". In *Handbook for Contemporary Japanese Religions*. p. 348.

150 Hardacre, Helen. "After Aum: Religion and Civil Society in Japan". In *The State of Civil Society in Japan*. pp. 142-43.

151 Ibid., p. 139.

Buddhism was born as a form of Buddhism deeply compromised with the new capitalist values of society. People began to note how their abbot had a mind more like that of a businessman. As the Meiji era reforms also turned him into a common citizen (*kokumin*) of no special distinction, he joined the other men of society in enjoying the new mainstream pleasures of the consumer society, such as golf, nice cars, and drinking parties. While other Buddhist nations in Asia are rife with scandals of the inappropriate behavior of monks, it is also common to find intellectually or spiritually recognized monks and even nuns active in public discourse. In Japan, one is struck by the almost total lack of prominent public intellectuals coming from the Buddhist world.

As we will see in Volume II, the social welfare movement of Japanese religious and Buddhist groups is one of the few socially engaged legacies from the Meiji and Taisho that continues on today in postwar Japan. While such activities did not outrightly support the state in the postwar era, the general lack of involvement in public debate and increasing irrelevance in mainstream society perpetuated the view held by non-religious Japanese working in civil society organizations that Buddhism was still an appendage of the conservative old guard. This problem was, in fact, foreseen in the prewar era, noted in the discussion in the previous section of one of the founders of the New Buddhist movement as well as the modern social welfare movement, Watanabe Kaikyoku, and his concerns about whether Buddhist social welfare and aid work were driven by the demands of the state and society "without any principles or policies" (*mu-shugi mu-hoshin*)?"[152] Using an expression developed by Shimazono, we might say they lack "an autonomous social ethics" (自律的な社会倫理 *jiritsu-teki-na shakai-rinri*).[153] Thus, for many, it seems that little has changed among traditional, mainstream Buddhism since the end of the Meiji era.

Shimazono uses the term *jiritsu* as "autonomy" with a different Chinese character 自律 rather than the one Yoshimoto Takaaki used for *jiritsu* 自立 as "independence" and still further distinct from the term postwar intellectuals used for "autonomy", *shutaisei*. He explains this choice of 自律 as a clearer articulation of the freedom to "think" and "judge" rather than the more existential and liberal nuance of

---

152 Watanabe. *The Complete Writings of Kogetsu*. p. 17.
153 In the new 2022 edition of Shimazono's *Social Ethics in Modern Japanese Buddhism*. First published in 2013, he provides a new ending chapter that discusses "the challenge of autonomous social participation" (自律的な社会参与という課題 *jiritsu-teki-na shakai-sanyo-to-iu kadai*).

shutaisei as the agency or subjectivity of the "independent individual" (独立した個人 *doku-ritsu-shita ko-jin*).¹⁵⁴ This nuance is important because it reflects on criticisms made of the Kyoto School and the Imperial Way Zen movement for lacking critical, autonomous thought and responsibility. At the beginning of this section, we profiled the Rinzai Zen monk Kono Taitsu's dismay at the moral confusion in Japan's sudden shift from the rhetoric of emperor veneration to that of American democracy after the war ended. Rev. Kono's mentor as a student at the Rinzai Zen affiliated Hanazono University was the well-known Rinzai Zen scholar Ichikawa Hakugen. In 1970, he published his research in *The War Responsibility of Buddhism* (仏教の戦争責任 *Bukkyo-no senso-sekinin*).¹⁵⁵

In this volume, he presents twelve points for how Japanese Buddhism became receptive to the growing authoritarian nationalism of the Taisho and early Showa periods. These critiques echo some of the key points we have examined throughout this volume, especially in the work of Nakamura Hajime, such as:

1. a subservience to the state for protection by focusing on the limited social nexus of nation as one larger family while denying transnationalism.
2. an overvaluing of the archaic over critical creativity.
3. an emphasis on karmic determinism, which is also shared by many other Buddhist cultures.
4. an emphasis on inner peace over social justice.
5. the lack of a transcendental power to which people can dedicate themselves, resulting in the neglect of discursive thought and logic.
6. the immanental logic of *soku* 即, "just as it is", which leads to a static, aesthetic, subjective harmony with things—a pointed criticism of the Kyoto School and Suzuki Daisetsu.¹⁵⁶

The Critical Buddhist movement that subsequently emerged in the 1980s made an even more in-depth examination of the various potholes in the East Asian Mahayana tradition that enable the total loss of a critical logic—the very skill that made Shakyamuni such a transformational figure in the history of human thought and religious development. Hakamaya Noriaki in his numerous critical essays

---

154 Personal correspondence. October 20, 2022.
155 Shields. *Against Harmony*. p. 144.
156 Victoria. *Zen at War*. pp. 173-74.

that began to emerge in 1990, like many other critical postwar Buddhist writers, has looked at the problematic cultural value of "harmony" (和 *wa*) and its role in Buddhism since it was first promoted by Prince Shotoku in his 17-Article Constitution. For Hakamaya, the value of *wa* became a way of encouraging an uncritical acceptance of any teaching or ideology, which during the war period led Japanese citizens to silently sacrifice themselves.

On the contrary, Hakamaya feels Buddhists must rely on critical thinking, the type of which is found in the classical explanation of Buddhist "faith" through the Pali and Sanskrit terms *saddha* or *sraddha* as well as the Madhyamaka emphasis on "discriminating wisdom" over the Yogacara emphasis on "abiding" or "observational wisdom". Like many other modern Japanese Buddhists, he uses the *Lotus Sutra* as a source that teaches how to believe in the words of the Buddha while using intellect or *prajna* to distinguish false views from true ones. Buddhists, he feels, must respond with words and actions against such mistaken views as opposed to the uncritical mentality of *wa* used during the war. For Hakamaya, emperor worship is another example of the murky logic and syncretism found in the teachings of innate enlightenment (*hongaku*) and the Shinto gods as manifestations of enlightened dharma (*honji-suijaku*) that serve to muffle any ideological criticism. He extends this critique to Buddhists like Suzuki Daisetsu, who also embraced ideas of mysticism and the Zen value of wisdom that lies beyond language. In the end, Buddhism for Hakamaya must teach causality, promote altruism and the well-being of the other, and value the use of language to express truth.[157]

For Ichikawa, this lack of criticality, especially in Zen, reflects on the issue raised by postwar intellectuals concerning the problem of *shutaisei*. In fact, Ichikawa as a young radical intellectual in the Taisho era was influenced by Miki Kiyoshi, one of the alternative leftist thinkers of the Kyoto School who articulated the problem *shutaisei* even before the war.[158] After the war, like other leftists and Buddhist Socialists, Ichikawa struggled with how to harmonize the spiritual and material. He focused on "subjectively embodying" (主体化する *shutaika-suru*) Chinese Zen master Linji's famous words "making oneself master of each situation" and Marx's idea of becoming master of oneself,[159] which he eventually crystallized as "*sunya*-anarchism-communism" (空-無政府-共同体論 *ku museifu kyodotai-ron*). In this concept of

---

157 Swanson. "Why They Say Zen is Not Buddhism". pp. 18-20.

158 Ives. *Imperial-Way Zen*. p. 6.

159 Ibid., p. 9.

"s-a-c", he distances himself from the Marxist movement by not using the common term for communism, *kyosan-shugi* 共産主義, but rather the term *kyodotai-ron*, which literally means "theory of community". Like his contemporary Buddhadasa Bhikkhu who was developing the concept of Dhammic Socialism in Thailand, Ichikawa attempted to resolve the limitations of communism by inflecting it with the subjective, ethical tenets of Buddhism and the non-dual dialectic of emptiness (*shunyata*).[160]

Mirroring Maruyama Masao's critique of Japan's prewar social system as one of a "system of irresponsibility", Ichikawa saw the Zen collapsing of critical subjectivity into the logic of "just as it is" (*soku*) as lacking any rigorous sense of responsibility and falling far short of an "ethics of character" (人格倫理 *jinkaku-rinri*).[161] Based in this Japanese Zen "ethics of feeling", Ichikawa argues that, "Insofar as the war started with an imperial decision (聖断 *seidan*) and ended with an imperial decision, no consciousness of responsibility arose. The only responsibility was vis-à-vis the emperor for the defeat." The repentance that many felt was not "toward any acts the Japanese committed in that war" or toward the peoples of Asia but rather toward the emperor for having failed him in military defeat. This shift "absolved the emperor of any responsibility for the war" and "spread responsibility for the defeat equally among the Japanese without any distinctions."[162]

Ichikawa's critique offers a critical insight into the nature of the ease by which not only Japanese Buddhist denominations but the larger Japanese public "flipped around as smoothly as one turns one's hand and proceeded to ring the bells of peace." For Ichikawa and Maruyama,[163] the emperor's call at the end of the war for the collective repentance of the hundred million (一億総懺悔 *ichi-oku so-zan-ge*) was no different than his wartime call for the sacrificial death of the hundred million (一億玉砕 *ichi-oku gyokusai*). Both lacked an ethics of principle and rather reflected the clannish ethics of a limited social nexus that had been built into the Shinto-Confucian-Zen public morality of *bushido*. This is epitomized in the statement made in 1947 by Sugawara Jiho 菅原時保 (1866–1956), then abbot of the great Kamakura era Rinzai Zen temple Kencho-ji, "Without being biased, we should think of ourselves as a boat and proceed without contending against the drift of the times. Religionists and ordinary people ought

---

160 Ibid., pp. 239-40.
161 Ibid., p. 131.
162 Ibid., pp. 131-32.
163 Ibid., pp. 131-32.

to think carefully about this.... If we were to go against the drift we could not move forward, and for this reason we should accommodate and acquiesce (順応 *junno*), or, more bluntly put, we have no other path but to listen and do what America says."[164]

It became natural for many to simply follow the United States as literally the new shogunate (*bakufu*) in a long historical lineage of military rule. This easy shift in allegiance also explains the act of *tenko* as less than a real repudiation of principles and more a subjugation to new authority. It also reflects more deeply on the inability of Buddhist ethics and Buddhist precepts to take root in Japanese society. In the development of Buddhism in Japan, we can chart the historical course of the abandonment of the Buddhist precepts from:

1. Saicho and Tendai's focus on bodhisattva precepts over the classic monastic ones in the 9th century.
2. the Pure Land movements total abandonment of them in the 13th century.
3. Zen's ritualization of them and adoption of Neo-Confucian moral norms in the 14th century.
4. the brahmanization of the precepts as Funeral Buddhism in the conferring of precepts on the deceased for enlightenment in the next world rather than on the living for enlightenment in this world from the Tokugawa era onward.

It can thus be argued that this shift in ethical focus has deprived Japanese culture of the historical Buddha Shakyamuni's core ethic of non-harming that is applied to all sentient beings. As such, social ethics has often devolved into the purification of transgressed communal norms and taboos through the performance of ritualistic repentance—the kind of ritualistic karmic act found in Indian Brahmanism that the Buddha directly repudiated. The karmic act of the intentional ethics of non-harming, which he did teach, means there is a subjective taking of responsibility for transgressions related to harming and the rededication to training in these ethical principles.

Through the articulation of the *shutaisei* issue, many in the intellectual and civil society movement in 1950s grasped this principled taking of responsibility and the training of postwar responsibility through making Japan a non-aligned state renouncing war through its peace constitution. As bastions of the old order, the traditional Buddhist denominations and the bureaucrat and LDP-led

---

164 Ibid., pp. 133-34.

government, however, did their best to avoid such intentional ethical karma by waiting until the 1990s to make any clear statements on war responsibility. For many, the inability of the denominations to truly confront their war responsibility in the way many of the important public intellectuals did in the 1950s has prevented them from serving as respected public intellectuals and moral leaders in society.

Kono Taitsu's confrontation with these issues began even before he encountered Prof. Ichikawa. As a teenage novice at a training temple in Kyushu, he was shocked one day when he heard a layperson address the chief monk as "commander" (隊長 taicho), meaning the monk had not only served as a soldier in the war but acted as a leader at some level in armed combat. He recalls, "I joined the Buddhist community, because I was looking for a way of living that was always right. I was looking for an infallible way of life, but I was shocked to find out that Buddhist monks had gone to the battlefield carrying guns."[165] Concerning war responsibility, Master Kono explains that "I believe that many people felt deeply ashamed, but they lacked courage." As his mentor Ichikawa Hakugen also wrote in 1975,[166] Kono admits himself that, "If I find myself in such a situation, I may keep my mouth shut as well, because the thought of torture is frightening [but] I have the opportunity to speak freely now. That's why I am speaking up."[167]

As with many other Japanese, he feels a sense of pride and national identity with the postwar constitution and Article 9, further reflecting:

> Some people say Article 9 is an obstacle, but we should see it as Japan's pride. We can proudly and confidently recommend this to other countries. They too should have a constitution like ours…but there is a movement now to have this Article 9 removed from the constitution. If we don't speak up now, it will be too late. Then all that is left for us to do is to remain silent and be swept away by the current. That's why I would like to see every monk speak up courageously now. I wish they would say this.[168]

---

165 *Zen and War*. Documentary film directed by Alexander Oey. (Netherlands: Buddhist Broadcasting Foundation (BOS), 2013), 8:30.

166 From Ichikawa's last book *Religion under Japanese Fascism* (日本ファシズム下の宗教 *Nihon fashizumu-ka-no shukyo*). Ives. *Imperial-Way Zen*. p. 10.

167 *Zen and War*. 51:14-52:46.

168 Ibid., 55:33-57:27.

These sentiments led Master Kono to push his Rinzai Zen Myoshin-ji denomination to make an open admission of their actions during the war and a public apology. He explains that in 1994:

> I had made several recommendations about offering apologies about the war to admit that mistakes had been made during the war. We had collaborated with the army and made a significant contribution towards the war. I wanted us to admit that this has been a mistake and make a confession quickly but there was no response from our denomination's headquarters.[169]

Unfortunately, it took a level of international embarrassment about the issue—specifically through Brian Victoria's presentation of Prof. Ichikawa's work in *Zen at War* published in 1997 along with personal appeals by shocked Western devotees—for the denomination to issue such a declaration in 2001. Myoshin-ji's declaration followed a movement that had begun earlier by the Jodo Shin Pure Land denominations, which issued such declarations in 1987 by the Otani sub-sect and in 1991 by the Hongan-ji sub-sect. The Soto Zen denomination also made one in 1992.

These fell in line with the political movement towards apologizing for the war that began to percolate in 1985 when the first reference to the war as one of "aggression" (侵略 *shinryaku*) was made by Prime Minister Nakasone. Such an admission came, however, in defense of his controversial visit on the anniversary to the end of the war to the Yasukuni Shrine where Japanese war criminals started to become enshrined in 1978. The first use of the term "apology" (謝罪 *shazai*) was made in 1993 by Prime Minister Hosokawa Morihiro, and what is considered the first clear and explicit apology was made in August 1995 on the 50th anniversary of the ending of the war by Prime Minister Maruyama Tomi-ichi. These latter two prime ministers were the first ones since 1955 not from the conservative LDP when they took over Japanese politics.[170]

The Rinzai Tenryu-ji sub-sect joined the Myoshin-ji declaration in 2001. Finally, the Jodo Pure Land denomination issued a declaration in 2008. Ironically, the mainstream Nichiren denomination still

---

169 Ibid., 14:26-14:58.

170 Shoji, Jun-ichiro. "Historical Perception in Postwar Japan: Concerning the Pacific War". National Institute for Defense Studies (防衛研究所 *Boei Kenkyu-jo*). *NIDS Security Reports.* March 2003. No.4. p. 123.

has not directly addressed the issue. As with the late arrival to the peace movement of the major lay *Lotus Sutra* groups, the traditional Buddhist world arrived some forty years after the popular confrontation with war responsibility. In this way, one is reminded of the critique made by Maruyama Masao at that time that Japan needed "a total ethical revolution" for Japanese to develop independent thinking and the ability to *pro-actively* decide and act on their own without external pressure. Even the much-maligned Suzuki Daisetsu, who was the only Buddhist to work with Maruyama in the Discussion Forum on the Problem of Peace, wrote in 1946: "Generally speaking, present day Zen priests have no knowledge or learning and therefore are unable to think about things independently or formulate their own independent opinions."[171]

One other controversy that rocked the traditional Buddhist world in the postwar era and became the principal reason for the creation of the Critical Buddhism movement was the so-called Machida Incident of 1979. At this time, Rev. Machida Muneo 町田宗夫 (1916–2009), acting as the Director-General of the Soto Zen denomination in tandem with being President of the Japan Buddhist Federation (JBF) that represents all the traditional denominations, participated at the third World Conference on Religion and Peace, which Rissho Kosei-kai co-founded. Near the end of the conference, a motion was put forward for a group declaration to condemn the legitimization of the practice of untouchability on religious grounds.[172] This was clearly directed at the ancient practice of untouchability in India based on certain teachings in the Hindu tradition sanctifying the caste system. However, it was also directed at a similar practice that developed in Japan and was institutionalized during the Tokugawa era, specifically towards a group of people called *burakumin*—literally "people of the village", but sometimes also referred to as *eta* ("those full of defilement") or *hi-nin* ("non-humans").

As detailed in Section 1, Buddhist temples were highly complicit in the stigmatization of these people by assigning them derogatory posthumous names during funeral and memorial rites, such as "beast" (*chiku*) or *sendara*, which refers to the Untouchable caste (*candala*) of the Indian Vedic caste system. These terms have not only been found in the private records of temples but also carved on family tombstones, leaving a permanent public record of their social status. While the Meiji government abolished these practices in 1871,

---

171 Victoria. *Zen at War*. p. 148.
172 Bodiford. "Zen and the Art of Religious Prejudice". p. 2.

long-held Japanese customs surrounding impurity (*kega-re*) meant some temples continued to use them, especially in the more western regions of Japan. By 1993, the Japanese Government still recognized 4,442 such communities known as *dowa-chiku* 同和地区, under the less pejorative name *dowa*, along with 298,385 *dowa* households, and 892,751 *dowa* people who qualified for government aid. However, as many *dowa* wish to not be identified, the Buraku Liberation League estimated there were actually 6,000 such communities with a population of three million.[173]

The controversy set off by Rev. Machida was his claim that such communities no longer existed and that discrimination towards people of such backgrounds had ended. Rev. Machida's claim appeared all the more outrageous since he came from Shimane prefecture on the southwest coast of Japan where there are *burakumin* communities and an awareness of their situation. Upon returning to Japan, he was met by a hailstorm of accusations by a number of vocal *dowa* organizations, and the Soto Zen sect was forced to endure five public "confess and denounce" or "impeachment" assemblies (糾弾会 *kyudan-kai*) held by the Buraku Liberation League over four years. At the last one in 1983, Machida acknowledged his prejudice, admitted the Soto denomination's practices, and pledged Soto would change. He followed this up with a public apology at the next WCRP conference held in Nairobi in 1984.

Under such public duress and examination, other Buddhist denominations were exposed for similar such practices. A 1983 study revealed the practice of keeping records on discriminatory names in 5,649 Soto Zen temples, 1,771 Jodo Pure Land temples, 254 Tendai temples, and 40 Shingon Koyasan temples, along with discriminatory tombstones found at 1,911 Soto temples, 231 Jodo Pure Land temples, 10 Tendai temples, and 102 Shingon Koyasan temples.[174] Further, it became known that families with engaged children were still hiring private investigators to illegally gain information from temples as to whether the fiancé came from such a *dowa* background or not.

The resolution to the issue was, as with war responsibility, a reactive rather than pro-active response. In 1981 the Solidarity Conference of Religious Groups for the Solution of the Dowa Problem (同和問題にとりくむ宗教教団連帯会議 *Dowa-mondai-ni Torikumu Shu-*

---

[173] Alldritt, Leslie D. "The *Burakumin*: The Complicity of Japanese Buddhism in Oppression and an Opportunity for Liberation". *Journal of Buddhist Ethics*. 2000. No. 7. http://jbe.gold.ac.uk/7/alldritt001.html

[174] Bodiford. "Zen and the Art of Religious Prejudice". p. 11.

kyo-kyodan Rentai-kaigi or simply 同宗連 *Do-shu-ren*) was founded with the participation of fifty-nine religious groups and the Buraku Liberation League. With many denominations having set up specific offices on this issue,[175] the work has expanded to other human rights issues in Japan, especially discrimination towards lepers (in which Buddhist temples also historically engaged) as well as towards Korean immigrants, Ainu, women, and AIDS victims. Unfortunately, Soka Gakkai has not participated in this activity due to its usual style of non-participation with other groups, while Rissho Kosei-kai has been an active participant. In 2001, when the Rinzai Zen Myoshin-ji denomination was preparing its war responsibility declaration, its secretary general Hosokawa Kei-itsu summed up the conflicting nature of Buddhist efforts on war and *burakumin* responsibility: "As in the case of the School's response to the issue of Dowa discrimination, however, it was only as a result of outside pressure that Myoshin-ji was finally able to acknowledge its past errors."[176]

While the voices of the Critical Buddhists, Ichikawa Hakugen, and Kono Taitsu may be unusually forthright and challenging in the Japanese Buddhist world today, they are exceptionally important contributions to resolving not only the problems in Japanese culture but also similar cultural issues in other Buddhist countries that lead to tribalization, ethnic exceptionalism, and violent nationalism. While Socially Engaged Buddhism continues to spread and flourish around the world today, we are still witnessing disturbing trends in the rise of xenophobic nationalism amongst Buddhist leaders, especially in the Theravada Buddhist world. These lesser-known Japanese contributions to such essential conundrums are thus even more important today and should be raised to a higher level of awareness both within in Japan and the rest of the Buddhist world.

---

175 As noted in the previous section, the Jodo Shin Hongan-ji and Otani sub-denominations formed the Oneness Society (一如会 *Ichinyo-kai*) in 1924 and the True Body Society (信身会 *Shinjin-kai*) in 1926 respectively to challenge social discrimination against *burakumin*. Ives. *Imperial-Way Zen.* p. 24.

176 Ibid., p. 180.

14

Towards a Global Buddhist Civil Society in the 1980s–90s

Buddhist NGOs and a New Internationalism from the Traditional Buddhist Denominations

The international face of Japanese Buddhism in the postwar has been for the most part dominated by the new religions, especially Rissho Kosei-kai and Soka Gakkai. The former created the WCRP headquartered at the United Nations while establishing the well-regarded international Niwano Peace Prize. The latter saw the remarkable growth of communities in the United States, India, and South America that included a number of high-profile musicians and artists, while its charismatic leader Ikeda Daisaku created a series of dialogues with international figures from a variety of social fields. The traditional Buddhist denominations' first steps in reviving the internationalism in which they were so involved during the Meiji era came with their involvement in the World Fellowship of Buddhists (WFB). The WFB was inspired by the international work of renowned Chinese Socially Engaged Buddhist, Master Taixu (1890–1947), who created the concept of Humanistic Buddhism that influenced the early stages of the Socially Engaged Buddhist movement in Vietnam. WFB was formed, however, by renowned Buddhist scholar and diplomat G.P. Malalasekera (1899–1973).

In order to host the second General Conference of the WFB in 1952, priests from the traditional Buddhists denominations created a confederation that was formalized in 1957 as the Japan Buddhist Federation (JBF *Zen Nihon Bukkyo-kai*). The Federation has since developed as an important platform for traditional Buddhist groups to coordinate policies towards public issues in Japanese society. However, the WFB has remained a largely passive, friends association of Buddhists. Furthermore, the new religions have been excluded from the JBF and, consequently, the WFB, which only recognizes Buddhist denominations affiliated with the JBF. In contrast, the International

Network of Engaged Buddhists (INEB) has partnered with both the traditional and new Buddhist denominations in a variety of activities, and even members of the Soka Gakkai International community have joined in collaborative INEB work. With JBF's strong ties to the WFB, it has thus not developed much of an international presence beyond charitable programs for disaster aid, befitting the style of social engagement of the central leadership of these traditional denominations.

In the late 1970s, a new generation of priests from the traditional Buddhist orders emerged and began to confront the conservative and outdated modes of engagement by their denominations. They also were looking for solutions to the growing criticism in the postwar era by mainstream media that traditional Buddhism had become irrelevant to modern society and that Buddhist priests had no concern for the general well-being of people. Born and coming of age in the tumultuous period of peace and student activism in the 50s and 60s, these priests developed a new kind of internationalism focused on responding to the humanitarian crisis in Indochina. By the 70s and 80s, however, such a response did not involve the kind of ideological activism of the 60s as the region had already fallen to the communist cause. The work was centered on international relief for the boat people of Vietnam and the mass of Cambodian refugees living on the border of Thailand.

While these priests were seeking a way to express their frustration with the inwardness of their denominations, they also sought to revitalize the identity of priests as contributors to society rather than as funeral specialists. They were outwardly-looking enough to notice the international stature that the new Buddhist groups had gained through their peace activities. They were also becoming aware of not only the remarkable non-violent political protest campaigns of Buddhists in countries like Vietnam and Cambodia but also the new kinds of responses to modernization and economic development by Buddhists in places like Sri Lanka and Thailand. Through establishing their own Buddhist-based NGOs, they attempted to link to these issues and become part of the regional civil society movement in which many of their Socially Engaged Buddhist counterparts in Southeast and South Asia were so active.

With Japan emerging onto the global scene after rebuilding from the war, these priests echoed the sentiments of many Meiji Buddhists who had eye-opening experiences in the first exposure of Japanese to the world after the centuries-long Tokugawa era lock-down. When they first entered the Cambodian refugee camps on the border with

Thailand, many expressed shock and embarrassment at the high level of international aid work by Christian religious-based groups. They were further impressed by the Cambodian monks in the camps creating educational and other sorts of aid and development programs. At the inaugural public symposium of the Buddhist NGO Network (BNN) in 2002, Rev. Ito Yoshimichi 伊藤佳通, Chairman of the Buddhist Aid Center (BAC), recalled those first days: "Here I was, a priest of the Mahayana (Greater Vehicle) tradition which emphasizes the selfless path of the bodhisattva, coming from Japan with nothing much to offer except a suitcase of money. In the camps, I found monks of the Theravada or Hinayana (Lesser Vehicle) tradition, who supposedly are only focused on personal enlightenment, working in the barest conditions, using their heart to pass on whatever wisdom and abilities they could to the common people."

These sorts of experiences spawned a movement of international relief activities by Buddhist NGOs created by rank-and-file priests outside the confines of denominational management or influence. Eventually, such work was adopted by various official organs of most Buddhist denominations, both old and new. These first Buddhist NGOs and their denominational affiliations were: the Renge International Volunteer Association (ARTIC, Shingon, 1979); the Shanti Volunteer Association (SVA, Soto Zen, 1980); the Buddhist Aid Center (BAC, Nichiren, 1982); Relief, Assist, Comfort, Kindness (RACK, Rinzai Zen, 1985); and the AYUS International Buddhist Cooperation Network (predominantly Jodo and Jodo Shin, 1993).[177]

An important caveat to make in terms of the influence of this international work on domestic activities by Buddhists in Japan is that the term "NGO", as it was adopted by Japanese civil society and these Buddhist organizations, has a specific meaning that differs from the common conception. The term "NGO" stands literally for "non-governmental organization". It has been very consciously defined, especially in the post-Cold War global order, as civil society organizations that see themselves as autonomous from state bodies as well as from the corporate world and as typically concerned with some form of social welfare or social justice work. Japanese NGOs would definitely share this social welfare concern. However, in the Japanese context, NGO, as with many imported foreign terms, has been redefined to refer specifically to an organization engaged in "international

---

[177] Watts, Jonathan S. "A Brief Overview of Buddhist NGOs in Japan". *Japanese Journal of Religious Studies*. 2004. Vol. 31, No. 2. pp. 417-18.

cooperation activities" (国際協力活動 *kokusai kyoryoku katsudo*).[178] While international NGOs play a part in the movement to create a global civil society, it is usually felt that a country must develop its own civil society movement *before* it can fully engage in the international one. Because of the relationship between civil society and the state in Japan, the NGO movement as one in line with international standards was extremely late to develop in Japan. In this way, the Buddhist NGOs with their international focus left little mark on the general civil society of Japan during the 1980s and 90s. In turn, Buddhist social engagement through civil society organizations *within* Japan was not significant in the postwar era until the end of the millennium.

A seminal moment in the shift from internationally to domestically focused Buddhist social engagement was the great Hanshin Earthquake of 1995. The paralysis of governmental bodies to respond in a timely manner to the earthquake, which devastated Japan's second largest megalopolis centered around Osaka, led to a huge and spontaneous outpouring of relief work by common Japanese. The Buddhist NGOs, which had developed a certain level of experience and expertise in providing emergency relief in their work overseas, were well placed and ready to respond to the crisis. In this way, Buddhist priests and organizations rekindled their ancient and prewar traditions as civil society actors by taking part in these efforts.

As we will see in Volume II, the Buddhist NGOs have helped Japanese Buddhists to develop a variety of aid activities for disaster victims throughout Japan in the new millennium. Their experiences during the Hanshin disaster combined with the rise of various social problems as the Japanese economy began to falter in the 1990s made Buddhist NGOs more sensitive to domestic issues as they continued their international work. An example of such an increasing domestic focus is the Buddhist NGO AYUS, founded by a group of predominantly Jodo and Jodo Shin Pure Land priests. Unlike most other international cooperation NGOs that engage in direct relief activities in foreign countries, AYUS engages in the critical but usually neglected work of supporting the administrative capacities of other NGOs inside Japan as well as overseas. Thus, instead of retracing or repeating the work of other NGOs, as many groups do, they attempt to increase the integrative efficiency of the NGO movement by supporting its infrastructure.

---

178 Shimizu, Hitoshi 清水均. *Basic Knowledge of Contemporary Terminology* (現代用語の基礎知識 *Gendai-yogo-no kiso-chishiki*). (Tokyo: Jiyu Kokumin-sha, 1999), p. 699.

Another watershed in the domestic development of Japanese civil society was the 1998 Non-Profit Organization (NPO) Law (特定非営利活動法人 *Tokutei Hi-eiri Katsudo-hojin*). Amongst other things, this law enabled NGOs to raise funds by appealing to the tax write-off afforded to donors, a practice common in liberal, capitalist nations, even within Asia, with an already well-established civil society sector. This is yet another example of the different views of the relationship between state and society in the United States and in Japan. In the former, individual entrepreneurs donate large sums of money to social causes and issues that in Japan would be considered the responsibility of the state or contained within the once collective communities of the business world. In relation to the term NGO in Japan, as outlined above, NPO in Japanese has generally a broader meaning encompassing both international and domestic activities but with a certain emphasis on the latter. One of the important effects of this law is that it greatly opened up funding possibilities for Buddhist NGOs. At the start, many of these NGOs had some sort of affiliation or connection with their denomination to maintain basic financial support, yet have become increasingly less dependent through the new diversity of funding sources. For example, the Buddhist NGO now known as the Shanti Volunteer Association (SVA) was established in 1980 by the Soto Zen sect as the Japan Soto-shu Relief Committee (JSRC) for the purpose of aiding Cambodian refugees. As it continued to develop, it took the name Soto-shu Volunteer Association (SVA) and became one of the largest NGOs in Cambodia. In 1999, when it acquired its new legal status as an NPO, it changed its name to the Shanti Volunteer Association (SVA), in part to clearly separate it from any religious or sectarian ties that would interfere with receiving government financial aid or other such non-affiliated financial support.

This development presented the opportunity for an increased integration of Buddhist NGOs into the general civil society movement without the constraints of some of the more conservative influences of traditional Buddhist denominations. However, it also carried with it the danger of a deeper dilution of the already thin Buddhist identity and ideology that these organizations have carried, evidenced in SVA dropping its religious name "Soto-shu" and adopting a secular one "Shanti", meaning "peace". Rather than bringing specific Buddhist ideas and practices to their work, as many of the best Socially Engaged Buddhist groups in the rest of Asia do, these Buddhist NGOs have for the most part mimicked the methods of other secular NGOs, leading some to remark that they are common forms of aid work that just happen to be run by Buddhists.

Since then, other Buddhist NGOs have followed the pattern of SVA but not without an increasing social conservatism from being tied to government financial support and bureaucratic regulation that leads to not speaking out on issues that conflict with government policy—once again echoing the concerns voiced by Watanabe Kaikyoku and Shimazono Susumu of the lack of "an autonomous social ethics" (*jiritsu-teki-na shakai-rinri*) by Buddhist groups.

An example of this has been the ongoing political strife in Myanmar, a fellow predominantly Buddhist country that has been under a crushing military dictatorship for over sixty years. While Buddhist NGOs have created a variety of projects there, such as building monastic schools and supporting local children's education, they have never made any systematic effort to educate the Japanese public on the large amounts of Japanese overseas development aid (ODA) and corporate investment that has propped up the military government for decades. With the brutal military coup d'état there in 2021 setting off another chain of repression, only AYUS has come forward among the Buddhist NGOs to engage in public criticism and join other non-Buddhist NGOs in a divestment campaign.

In conclusion, after the so-called first stage of postwar Socially Engaged Buddhism in the peace work of the new *Lotus Sutra* groups, these Buddhist NGOs represent an important second phase. While they demonstrate another level of engaged, ecumenical internationalism, by 2020 they had become somewhat marginal to the domestic, Socially Engaged Buddhist movement that emerged at the beginning of the millennium. While still offering support and expertise in times of local disaster, like the northeast tsunami disaster of 2011, many of these Buddhist NGOs are now staffed by professional aid and common NGO workers with little interest in or understanding of Buddhism.

The Search for a Japanese Socially Engaged Buddhist Ideology

Through these last two sections, we have taken an in-depth look at Japanese Buddhism's attempts to redefine itself in the modern world since the beginning of the Meiji Restoration in 1868. We examined the Buddhist Liberalism of the Meiji Buddhist Enlightenment and the New Buddhist Movement of the early and late Meiji periods respectively. We then examined the developments of inward-looking, existentialist, and utopian forms Buddhism and, at the other extreme, radical and activist forms of Buddhist Socialism in the Taisho and early Showa periods. Amidst these progressive movements, we also marked their ultimate co-optation into nationalist forms of Buddhism promoting archaic, Japanese cultural exceptionalism and finally Imperial Way Buddhism.

In the postwar era, wide ranging and creative new forms of Socially Engaged Buddhist thought and practice flourished throughout Asia in the dynamic environment of the post-colonial order. In Japan, which was a leader in early modern Buddhist thought, this postwar period has been a relative ideological vacuum as Japanese society became increasingly secularized and Buddhism remained marginal to the public sector. While the work of radical postwar Japanese Buddhist intellectuals like Ichikawa Hakugen and the scholars of the Critical Buddhism movement are important in the postwar landscape, they are largely confined to the academic community and did not engage in creating activities that we might deem as Socially Engaged Buddhism.

The failures of Japanese Buddhism to develop mature forms of Socially Engaged Buddhism from the end of the war to the opening of the new millennium reflect the larger ideological struggles outlined in this section. These struggles might be viewed through the energetic forces of Buddhism's Three Poisons (*tri-visa* 三毒 *san-doku*): a social vision that neither *pulls back* into archaic nationalism (anger, *dosa* 瞋 *shin*); nor loses its moorings in the *aggressive advance* of Western liberalism and capitalism (greed, *raga* 貪 *ton*); nor *remains stuck* as it is today in the collective utilitarianism of the bureaucratic nation state (delusion, *moha* 癡 *chi*). The fundamental thesis of these two volumes is how Buddhism, specifically a Socially Engaged Buddhism, can chart a "middle way" between these extremes—perhaps through Buddhist Socialism and dharmic civil society—and provide Japan an indigenous yet internationalist vision for realizing coexistence among its East Asian neighbors, wider Asian civilization, and the global community.

In this way, we next look at a few important figures who attempted to re-articulate Japanese Buddhism in light of postwar society. As such, they have provided an important foundation for the development of the variety of new forms of Socially Engaged Buddhism in the post-millennium era. These four figures are: Rev. Arima Jitsujo, co-founder of SVA; Rev. Maruyama Teruo, co-founder of INEB Japan; Prof. Nishikawa Jun, Buddhist economist at Waseda University; and Prof. Nakamura Hisashi, Buddhist development expert at Ryukoku University.

Rev. Arima Jitsujo 有馬実成 (1936-2000): Rev. Arima began his work for society at his native temple in Yamaguchi prefecture in central Japan many years before the formation of SVA, where he created special memorial services for the neglected remains of Korean laborers forced to migrate to Japan during the war. He then initiated social welfare projects within the Soto Zen denomination, culminating in the creation of the Japan Soto-shu Relief Committee (JSRC) for aiding Cambodian refugees. Unlike some of the international peace activities profiled above that seem to be more focused on raising the public image of the denomination, Arima's work was clearly more focused on serving wider society. In this way, he gained an unusually high level of respect from the larger secular NGO community. In this era, the NGO community in Japan was quite small and usually populated with leftists who were anti-religious in sentiment and saw Japanese Buddhism as part of Japan's tainted archaic regime. In this sort of environment, most socially minded Buddhists had low self-confidence in their credentials as priests and did not integrally use Buddhist ideas in understanding society and their own work.

In 1990, Arima spent two years in Thailand learning about the NGO movement there, where he was surprised to see the major role Buddhist monks played in the movement, contrary to Japan, especially in Northeast Thailand where rural poverty is most severe. He found striking similarities between this region and his own rural community in Japan, where the traditional economy had been systematically destroyed by modern development and the remaining elderly felt a deep sense of loneliness and isolation (孤独 *kodoku*)—an issue that will be explored in detail in Volume II. He thus developed not only a sense of responsibility for the poverty Northern nations like Japan had wrought on the South. He also created a solidarity with these fellow rural citizens of Thailand, much like the Japanese intellectuals and activists of the 50s and 60s sought to connect to the non-aligned movement. Arima concluded that, "The change that is needed to bring a halt to this ailing local Japanese society is to become part of 'global civil society' (地球市民社会 *chikyu shimin-shakai*) through building solidarity between South and North. I wonder if we can voluntarily create a global society of equality based on new values."[179] As a Buddhist priest, he felt that the local temple has a strong

---

179 Arima, Jitsujo 有馬実成. "Understanding Buddhism through Development Studies" (開発の学としての仏教を学んだ *Kaihatsu-no gaku-to-shite-no bukkyo-wo mananda*). In Wongkul, Pitthaya ピッタやー・ウォンクーン. *Development Monks who Repay Their Debt of Gratitude to the Village People.* (村の衆には借りがある: 報徳の開発僧侶 *Mura-no shu-ni-wa kari-ga aru: Hotoku-no kaihatsu*

responsibility to the people in reviving such civil society.

When Arima met the renowned Thai development monk Luang Pau Nan (1930-2015) during this time, he knew he had met a kindred spirit. Nan also redefined the image that many Japanese Buddhist priests had of self-centered Theravada monks of the "smaller vehicle" (*hinayana* 小乗仏教 *shojo bukkyo*) tradition who stayed aloof from the people in their personal search for enlightenment. Beginning in the 1960s, Nan's work in his native area of Surin in the heart of Northeast Thailand was strongly supported by Sulak Sivaraksa during a sensitive time in Thailand when he was harassed by military authorities as a communist. Sivaraksa sent Nan to Sri Lanka to learn about Buddhist-based development from the Sarvodaya Shramadana movement, creating an important Socially Engaged Buddhist lineage between the two nations.

Arima was struck by Nan's exceptional use of Buddhist teachings in social development. Nan not only used the Four Noble Truths as a process for reflection and action, as many other Socially Engaged Buddhists have done. He also resurrected the original spirit of "reciprocal offering" (*dana* 布施 *fu-se*) between the ordained and lay sanghas, much of which has been lost in the perversion of almsgiving to monks through money in return for the spiritual materialism of gaining merit.[180] In contrast, Nan spoke of the debt he owed the villagers and his duty to serve them. "Only when you help the villagers eliminate all their debts and hunger can you say that you have made a complete 'offering.'"[181] Interpreting Ven. Nan's work from his own Mahayana tradition, Arima saw one of the key principles of his work as the practice of "working together" (Skt. *samanarthata* 同時 *doji*)—one of the four methods that bodhisattvas employ to approach and liberate people (四摂法 *shi-shoho*).[182] Arima writes, "Working together means that you and others must always be equal or co-equal, that generosity and helpfulness must not be accompanied by conceit or superiority over others, and that you must always think and act from the same perspective as the other person."[183]

This understanding again recalls the work of Watanabe Kaikyoku to underpin his social work with Buddhist principles. His similar

---

soryo). (Nontaburi, Thailand: Sangsan Publishing Co. Ltd., 1993). p. 129.

180 Santikaro and Visalo, Pra Paisan. "Goodness and Generosity Perverted: The Karma of Capitalist Buddhism in Thailand". In *Rethinking Karma*. pp. 146-47.

181 Arima. "Understanding Buddhism through Development Studies". p. 141.

182 See the term 四摂法 in the *Digital Dictionary of Buddhism*. http://www.buddhism-dict.net/ddb/

183 Arima. "Understanding Buddhism through Development Studies". p. 140.

principle of "mutual aid" (共済 *kyo-sai*) was "created from the Mahayana Buddhist teaching of equality found in 'the indivisibility of self and other' (*ji-ta-funi*) and of 'repaying benefits to sentient beings' (*shujo-on*), and then interpreted and theorized in a modern way in light of the social solidarity thought of the time."[184] In this way, Arima made important contributions in introducing the work of Socially Engaged Buddhists in Southeast Asia to the Japanese public and especially the Japanese Buddhist world. Unfortunately, this kind of principled thought could not be sustained in SVA as their work has become increasingly secularized over the decades.

Rev. Maruyama Teruo 丸山照雄 (1932–2011): In contrast, we have the figure of Rev. Maruyama, a very outspoken critic of Buddhism's role in society and Japanese political culture—and not surprisingly from the *Lotus Sutra* tradition. Maruyama was born into a mainstream Nichiren denomination temple located at the foot of the denomination's holy mountain, Mt. Minobu. However, the traumas of the war, the early death of his mother, and the ideological flip-flopping of Japanese Buddhism from war promoter to international peace advocate and back to supporter of conservative power made him distrustful of the world and pushed him to seek his own understanding of it. By the early 1950s, he had joined the Communist Party of Japan and became a regional leader whilst still a student at the Nichiren-affiliated Rissho University. These activities naturally ran him afoul of his university, his denomination, and his family.

However, this period formed the basis for creating his livelihood outside the temple as an investigative journalist. While working in other jobs is not unusual for modern Japanese priests, creating a life completely independent and untethered to a home temple is an experience he felt to be essential for the conscientization of Buddhist priests and the reform of Funeral Buddhism in Japan—rather ironically returning to the original roots of the Sangha as a band of "home leavers" (Skt. *pravrajita* 出家者 *shukke-sha*). After working to reform the Nichiren denomination in the 1960s, Maruyama became more active in social issues in the 1970s, such as the campaign to stop the construction of Narita airport in the rural farming areas of Chiba. In the late 1980s, he joined Sulak Sivaraksa in creating the International

---

184 Shimada Hajime 島田肇. "Watanabe Kaikyoku's 'Mutual Aid' Philosophy: Social Work as a Holistic and National Project (渡辺海旭の「共済」思想: 全体的・国民的事業としての社会事業 *Watanabe Kaikyoku-no "kyo-sai"-shiso: zentai-teki kokumin-teki jigyo-toshite-no shakai-jigyo*). In Tokaigakuen University *Journal of Interbeing and Culture Studies* (共生文化研究 *Kyo-sai Bunka Kenkyu*). March 31, 2016. Vol. 1, No. 1 創刊号. p. 107.

Network of Engaged Buddhists (INEB).

From his life as a social critic and iconoclast, he developed a very engaged sense of Buddhism along the lines of the Critical Buddhism movement noting that, "Original Buddhism in my view is conscientization."[185] For Maruyama, this is conscientization to suffering, to one's historical roots, and to the present social structure. He felt from this first step of conscientization, each individual can find their own way of working for the betterment of society. Rather than establishing a single blueprint for social action or a single social ideology, Maruyama felt it was important for each person to come to their own understanding in order to be able to change their own lifestyle and engage in social action on a highly conscious level—perhaps reflecting some influence from the anti-authoritarian movement by university students in the 60s. When everyone is empowered from having created their own standpoint, then it is more possible to create a harmonious, just society. Maruyama's process philosophy, akin to the Four Noble Truths methodology of many INEB activists, came from his understanding that Buddhism does not really teach a single truth or have a single essence. Rather, Buddhism offers a *way* for deeply seeing into the process or methodology of any phenomenon. When we can understand the process of any phenomenon, he felt, then we can act in proper accordance with it rather than imposing our own preconceptions on it.[186]

While Maruyama was at times an important ideological leader, his combative nature as a critic often isolated him and his small circle of associates in the Japan branch of INEB. In this way, INEB Japan remained caught in the small circle of postwar leftist, social activism, which became increasingly marginalized as Japan's economic miracle unfolded. With his death in 2011 and the death of INEB Japan's director Rev. Suzuki Ryowa 鈴木了和, a radical Jodo Shin Otani priest, in 2004, INEB Japan ceased to function and was replaced by a new generation who formed the Japan Network of Engaged Buddhists (JNEB) in 2009.

Prof. Nishikawa Jun 西川潤 (1936–2018): The third important Socially Engaged Buddhist thinker of this period was Prof. Nishikawa. He offers us a different image in that he came from outside the

---

185 Maruyama, Teruo. "The Methodology of Truth: A Nichiren Priest's Struggle for a Socially Valid Buddhism". In *Entering the Realm of Reality: Towards Dhammic Societies*. Eds. Jonathan Watts, Alan Senauke & Santikaro Bhikkhu. (Bangkok: International Network of Engaged Buddhists, 1998), p. 50.

186 Ibid., pp. 39-40.

Buddhist community and illustrated a growing interconnection with the larger civil society movement. Prof. Nishikawa was one of the most prominent development economists in Japan, who in his later years became interested in various models of alternative development. In the 1990s, he translated into Japanese books that had become important in the new anti-globalization movement, such as David Korten's *When Corporations Rule the World* and *The Post-Corporate World*. He also hosted from his position at one of Japan's most prestigious universities, Waseda University, an ongoing series of international conferences with academics and civil society leaders from all over Asia, such as "Civil Society in Asia: Toward New State Governance of the Post-Developmentalist Era." From these interests, Nishikawa began to discover the work of Socially Engaged Buddhists in South and Southeast Asia working on sustainable development. From 1994–1995, he organized his graduate seminar in development economics on the theme of development monks in Thailand, culminating in a comprehensive volume on Buddhist-style alternative development in Thailand that featured Buddhadasa Bhikkhu and Sulak Sivaraksa.[187]

In the opening chapter of the book, Prof. Nishikawa introduces and elaborates on the Thai scholar monk Ven. P.A. Payutto's distinction between development as a solely material process (Th. *patana*) and development as a holistic spiritual process (Pali/Th. *bhavana*). This distinction had actually been made earlier by Buddhadasa, "who took pains to distinguish the Buddhist understanding of *bhavana* from the material and economic 'development' promoted by the Thai government and the World Bank, as well as the competing ideology of communist materialism."[188] The common term for "economic development" in Japan is *kai-hatsu* 開発 (*kai* = to open, begin; *hatsu* = to emit, arise, awaken). Prof. Nishikawa and his colleagues re-read the two Chinese characters for this word in the traditional Buddhist way as *kai-hotsu*. In East Asian Mahayana Buddhism, this character for *hatsu/hotsu* is used to refer to "the resolve to attain enlightenment and develop *bodhi-citta*" (発菩提心 *hotsu-bodai-shin*) or to "the vow to follow the Buddha's way" (発願 *hotsu-gan*). This play on words was

---

187 Nishikawa, Jun 西川潤 and Noda, Masato 野田真里. *Buddhism, Development, NGO: Learning from Thai Development Monks the Wisdom of Interbeing* (仏教・開発・NGO —タイ開発僧に学ぶ共生の智慧 *Bukkyo · Kaihotsu · NGO: Thai kaihotsu-so-ni manabu kyosei-no chie*). (Tokyo: Shinhyoron, 2001).

188 Buddhadasa, Bhikkhu. *Seeing with the Eye of Dhamma*. Trans. Dhammavidu Bhikkhu & Santikaro Upasaka. (Boulder, Colorado: Shamabala Publications, Inc., 2022), p. xxiii.

significant in that it presented a way to develop a new kind of language to express a different orientation towards development. At the same time, it did not present a new kind of religious jargon that is opaque to economists, secular activists, and other groups involved in social change. In elaborating this concept, Prof. Nishikawa focused on how certain key Buddhist concepts like the Middle Way and interdependence can help Asia, with its significant Buddhist population, to develop its own unique understanding of civil society and the civil virtues on which it is based.

While the term has not become part of mainstream Japanese society, it has become a common term in the growing Socially Engaged Buddhist movement to articulate a new vision for social development in Japan. As such, it marks an important shift to an interest in confronting and critiquing government and corporate policy while considering an entirely new social paradigm, and perhaps an axial turn. In the 2000s, Prof. Nishikawa not only became a popular speaker at a wide variety of Buddhist events in Japan, he also became an active member of INEB, frequently attending their international conferences and engaging in discussions on *kai-hotsu* with this larger international community. As we will document in Volume II, he continued to develop this new social vision in response to the Fukushima nuclear disaster and the increasing levels of suffering created by the present development paradigm in Japan.

Prof. Nakamura Hisashi 中村尚司 **(b. 1938)**: Our final profile looks at a contemporary of Nishikawa's in the world of development economics. Prof. Nakamura was born and raised in Kyoto during the war and then took part, as with Maruyama, in the immediate postwar Marxist movement. Despite his radical sentiments, Nakamura graduated from Kyoto University and in 1961 became a researcher at Japan's most prestigious, semi-governmental, social science think tank, the Institute of Developing Economies (アジア経済研究所 *Ajia Keizai Kenkyu-jo*). Shortly after, Nakamura embarked on a long career of fieldwork and activism in South and Southeast Asia, particularly in Sri Lanka, of which he is Japan's leading expert. While in Sri Lanka, he became familiar and then close with A.T. Ariyaratne and his Sarvodaya Shramadana movement. These connections led him to Thailand and into a close relationship with Sulak Sivaraksa, the founder of INEB, the present chairperson of which is Ariyaratne's nephew, Harsha Navaratne.

In this way, Nakamura developed his own interests in Buddhism, its ancient history, and its potential to define a specific kind of Asian modernity beyond the liberal and socialist models offered by the West. Nakamura has contrasted the American and French liberal revolutions' emphasis on freedom and civil society with the Russian and Chinese communist revolutions' emphasis on equality, which he feels is of greater importance to Asians. Yet he outlines a third revolution, one of solidarity, mutual aid, and fraternity.[189] He feels this is the unique contribution of South and Southeast Asia as opposed to the Chinese and Japanese focus on material development and civil engineering.[190] He notes that since Southeast Asia had a slower and later state formation process, they have a great advantage in 21st century development through the organization of people outside the nation state system[191]—what might be considered as dharmic civil society.

Reflecting on both the ancient development principles of the great Buddhist *dharma-raja*, Ashoka,[192] as well as the most recent trends in global civil society, Nakamura highlights the values of circulation and diversity to enable societies to thrive. In this way, the stranger or person from outside is key for social change and revolution in this era as well as a means to resolve the conflicts that occur between localized vested interests. He points out how mixed children and foreign immigrants are making important contributions to Japanese society now and how this will be important as Japan continues to struggle to develop a post-capitalist development paradigm.[193] For Nakamura, this is the type of indigenous Asian civil society that will be a key component in balancing the nation-state and market as Asia moves into the 21st century.

Within Japan, Nakamura, like Arima, has played an important role in guiding the larger NGO movement. With his background based more in Marxism and social development than Buddhism, he became the co-chair of the Pacific Asia Resource Center (PARC), one of Japan's earliest and most important civil society NGOs. Like Nishikawa, he has become a regular speaker at recent Socially Engaged Buddhist events in Japan and a regular participant in INEB activities on Buddhist economics and anti-nuclear environmental activities. Finally, he translated all these activities into helping the Jodo Shin Hongan-ji denomination to create their own international

---

189 Nakamura, Hisashi. In *The Asian Future: Dialogues for Change*. Vol. 2. Eds. Pracha Hutanuwatr & Ramu Manivannan. (London, Zed Books, 2005), p. 184.
190 Ibid., p. 181.
191 Ibid., p. 192.
192 Watts. "The 'Positive Disintegration' of Buddhism". pp. 92-105.
193 Ibid., p. 201.

development NGO, JIPPO, which has also worked for environmental and community rehabilitation in Fukushima.

In conclusion, all four of these figures stand out for their introduction to Japanese society of Buddhist-based indigenous development movements in Asia during a time when Japan was immersed in the postwar American development model. These contributions and nascent social visions have now become important resources in the 21st century for a Japan still trying to define its future path and its own responses to the challenges of our time.

A Critical Evaluation of Japanese Socially Engaged Buddhism at the End of the 20th Century

As the 20th century drew to a close, Japanese Socially Engaged Buddhism seemed limited despite certain accomplishments, especially in comparison to the dynamic range of grassroots Socially Engaged Buddhist movements across Asia and even emerging in the West. In Section 3, we noted a significant coming together in 2002 of the various Japanese Buddhist NGOs that had emerged during the Indochina wars and refugee crisis of the 1970s and 80s to form the Buddhist NGO Network (BNN)—one of the first examples of grassroots, non-sectarian movement building among Socially Engaged Buddhists in Japan in the postwar era. The keynote speakers for the event were Nishikawa Jun, scholar and promoter of "Buddhist development" (*kaihotsu*), and one of the leading practitioners of *kaihotsu* in Thailand, the "development monk" (開発僧侶 *kaihotsu-soryo*) Pra Paisan Visalo.

Paisan has been a leading Socially Engaged Buddhist monk in Thailand since the early 1990s because of an incredible range of talents and activities. Unlike some monks who ordain as children and remain ignorant of the world, Paisan was an activist in the democracy and student movements of the 1970s, coming under the direct tutelage of renowned Socially Engaged Buddhist Sulak Sivaraksa. In this way, his awareness and knowledge of social issues before and after ordaining has always been especially sophisticated for a monk. After taking ordination in his late 20s, he trained under one of Thailand's renowned Northeast meditation masters, thus developing a deep contemplative practice that many urban monks fail to receive. His teacher, Ven. Khamkhian Suvanno, was also known for his community development work, helping Paisan to round out a complete education in grassroots development work. Paisan has since become a leading figure in numerous social activist projects from community development to environmental protection to non-violence training and, finally, end-of-life care. As a highly respected public intellectual, he has written a vast number of important articles and books on the problems with the present Thai monastic system and the role of religion in Thai civil society. In this way, we might regard him as the epitome of what it means to be a Socially Engaged Buddhist. Since the late 1990s, he has been frequently invited to Japan by Thai immigrants, civil society organizations, and Buddhist groups to share his perspectives.

In his talk at this opening of the Buddhist NGO Network, he outlined four areas where he felt Japanese Buddhist activists and NGOs could deepen their cooperation in the development of a more empowered civil society. These four areas will help us to critically conclude this volume and offer a framework for making a final evaluation of Japanese Socially Engaged Buddhism in the postwar era.

- **Humanitarian Relief**: As we have seen, this has been a particular strength of Japanese Buddhist organizations in the wake of Japan's economic boom. Over the last twenty to thirty years of the century, they diverted large amounts of capital from Japan to the developing world in all sorts of humanitarian aid and relief. Some of this aid, especially from individual temples and donors, was not wisely spent and created multiple local problems, especially in Sri Lanka. Buddhist NGOs educated the traditional Japanese Buddhist world to become much more aware of the complexities of such overseas aid while also developing alternative means of aid.
- **Peace Activities**: This has also been a perennial theme of emphasis among Buddhist organizations. However, as detailed in this section, there has needed to be more substance to the rhetoric of "peace", which is so pervasively spoken of among Buddhist groups in Japan. Pra Paisan felt activities such as becoming peace workers, witnesses, and activists in various parts of the world could be an important contribution for Japanese Buddhists. A model of such work is, of course, the Nipponzan Myoho-ji, which has been engaged since the 1950s both inside Japan and globally across Asia, Europe, and the Americas. However small and marginal it remains, it serves as a model of such grassroots peace work.
- **Structural Critique of Present Social and Political Systems**: This has been the most glaring weak point for Japanese Buddhists in the postwar era, mostly adopting the secular critiques and methods

developed by other civil society groups, while lacking firm Buddhist principles or policies, as Watanabe Kaikyoku critiqued in the prewar era. Indeed, Pra Paisan highlighted that one of the essential aspects of such a critique is developing new principles and new paradigms for society based in Buddhist teachings. In the postwar era, it took a non-Buddhist academic, Prof. Nishikawa, to import from another country and introduce to Japanese Buddhists such principles as *kaihotsu*. Normatively, this area marks the full maturation of a Socially Engaged Buddhist movement from common and simplistic kinds of social welfare offered by typical religious institutions to a holistic form of social transformation in which religion plays a central part in a dharmic civil society. As we will see in the second volume, it is an area that is still slowly developing among Japanese Socially Engaged Buddhists.

- **Development of Inner Peace and Spiritual Well-being**: For Pra Paisan, a proper critique of social and political systems requires more than intellectual analysis. It involves a psychological and emotional grounding that a spiritual discipline offers. Buddhist practice provides such psychological, intellectual, and emotional tools that neither Western liberalism nor socialism can offer. As such, it provides a third way, a type of holistic resolution to modernity of which we have seen promoted by Socially Engaged Buddhists from B.R. Ambedkar to Buddhadasa to Nakamura Hisashi. In the modern era, however, this was another of Japanese Buddhism's weaknesses. Its traditions and disciplines were first attacked by the forced secularization of the Meiji state, then completely demolished by the ideology of Imperial Way Buddhism during the war, and finally sold to the highest bidder in the Funeral Buddhism and promotion of "this-worldly benefits" in the postwar liberal state. As we will see in the second volume, the new millennium has shown important shifts towards the reclamation of the spiritual depth of the Buddhist priest. This shift began in the existential angst of young priests growing up in the post-bubble economic downturn. It further developed through their engagement with the suffering of so many who have become "karmically disconnected" (*mu-en*) in the new millennium. The most recent maturation has been in their growing interest to train as compassionate caregivers and develop systems to cultivate Buddhist chaplains.

Conclusion

The Promise of Principled Protest and the Buddhist Resolution to Modernity

This chapter brings Volume I and the historical survey of Socially Engaged Buddhism in Japan to a close and leads us into the numerous contemporary case studies of it in post-millennium Japan. The millennium serves as an appropriate cut-off point between the postwar Japan of economic and social revitalization and this new era marked by economic stagnation, social dis-ease (*dukkha* 苦 *ku*), and human disconnection (無縁 *mu-en*). As we have noted above, the Hanshin earthquake of 1995 and the 1998 Non-Profit Organization (NPO) Law helped shift the focus of Buddhist NGOs and Socially Engaged Buddhist work towards the domestic problems starting to accumulate within Japan. 1997–98 also marked the Asian Economic crisis that led to wide-ranging changes in the Japanese banking system and the beginning of the era of 30,000 annual suicides[194], which lasted into the 2010s.

In terms of reviewing the central theme of this section on the problem of *principled* social change and Buddhist engagement in political issues—such as war responsibility, peace, and social justice—we need to examine some final issues that revolve around the major watershed event thus far of the 21st century, the triple disaster of the Northeast Japan earthquake, tsunami, and nuclear accident of March 11, 2011. One important aspect of this event is that it has acted like a collective, social version of the return of repressed parts of traumatized consciousness in an individual who has not completed

---

194 By 2008, Japan ranked well above the rest of the G7 nations at a rate of 25.2 suicides per 100,000 people, compared to the respective rates of France 18.2, Germany 12.5, and the United States 12.7. Its neighbor South Korea, however, had already passed Japan in 2004 and by 2008 had a rate of 28.6. Data on Japan is from *Summary Data on Suicide for 2008* (平成20年中における自殺の概要資料 *Heisei niju-nen-chu-ni okeru ji-satsu-no gaiyo-shiryo*). National Police Agency Department of Community Safety (警察庁生活安全局 *keisatsu-cho seikatsu anzen kyoku*). Published May 2009. Data on other countries from the World Bank "Suicide Mortality Rate". https://data.worldbank.org/indicator/SH.STA.SUIC.P5

a psycho-spiritual transformation. In short, the Fukushima nuclear accident recalled the trauma of the Hiroshima-Nagasaki nuclear bombings that ended the war and began a new chapter in Japan's struggle with modernity. Like the mass peace movement that began as protests to American nuclear testing in the South Pacific and culminated in the *Anpo* crisis of 1960, the Fukushima incident re-ignited a mass citizens' protest movement. It began as an appeal against nuclear energy and has spread to a larger re-examination of the state of democracy in Japan with the attempts of the second Abe Shinzo administration to revise Japan's peace constitution. Amidst this now decade-long shift towards more social protest, Buddhists have yet again, as in the 1950s, been confronted with the challenge of remaining silent observers to the *status quo* and hence allies of the collectivist state, or joining with the mass of common citizens calling for change.

Bureaucratic Utilitarianism Remains Predominant

While many of these themes will be discussed at length in Volume II, a review of some of the key political developments will help to provide context for further reading. While the rise of *Nihonjin-ron* (Theories of Japanese-ness) in the 1970s continued to be an important theme for some in the continuing decades, Shimazono Susumu remarks that the kind of collective euphoria that emerged with Japan's rapid reconstruction after the war began to wane in the 1980s. There arose doubt about a public morality based on collective utilitarianism, and a more individualistic mentality began to become prevalent. Indeed, the engine behind this collective utilitarianism, the entrenched bureaucracy, began to suffer attacks from the political establishment seeking to curb its power. In 1998, Prime Minister Hashimoto Ryutaro (1996–1998) launched a major administrative reform to strengthen the role of the prime minister and the cabinet by creating a Cabinet Office that combined the Prime Minister's Office with the Economic Planning Agency. Prime Minister Koizumi Junichiro (2001–2006) became the most well-known for such attacks on the old bureaucratic order. Taking advantage of these new powers, he implemented a program of neo-liberal structural reform.

In 2009, when the LDP lost its first major election since rising to power in 1955, the new more liberal Democratic Party of Japan (DPJ) came to power with a specific strategy of marginalizing the bureaucracy from policy creation. While much of the popular media blamed the DPJ and Prime Minister Kan Naoto for the failures to respond properly to Northeast Japan disaster in 2011, "It became apparent that bureaucratic compartmentalization at the national level and the, more often than not, rigid application of legal frameworks by bureaucrats hindered an effective and swift response to the humanitarian disaster in the wake of the triple catastrophe."[195] This is yet another in a long line of historical examples of the way power in Japan is able to obscure itself behind the face of authority.

As we will examine in the last chapter of Volume II, a new development was occurring in regional Japanese politics towards concern with post-industrial social issues, like the environment, public welfare, and human rights. Responding to issues of globalization through building networks and exchanging ideas with other countries was also increasingly being carried out by Japanese at more localized levels away from the central government.[196] Ultimately, the DPJ underestimated how difficult it would be to change this system and culture of bureaucratic utilitarianism, entrenched since the Meiji era. With their inability to formulate and implement coherent policies, especially in economic reform, they crashed out of power in just three short years.[197]

The LDP's return to power, however, was not a ringing endorsement of their policies or leadership, but rather what appears to be a deepening fatalism among the Japanese citizenry about piercing the Iron Triangle of bureaucratic-political-corporate power and creating change through the electoral system. In the 2012 election that returned the LDP to power, 10 million fewer people voted than in 2009, a record low of 52.66 percent of the electorate. This marked the steady decline in voter turnout since the end of the war, which was stemmed only briefly in the DPJ's short rise to power when voter turnout nearly reached 70 percent—a further indication of the people's will for change. In fact, the LDP won 2.3 million fewer votes in 2012 than in their electoral rout in 2009 yet increased their number of seats from 119 to 294.[198] This fundamental loss of faith in one of the most important forms of democratic government has continued up to the writing

---

195 Koellner, Patrick. "The Triumph and Fall of the Democratic Party of Japan". In *Party Politics in Japan: Political Chaos and Stalemate in the 21st Century*. Eds. Ronald J. Hrebenar & Akira Nakamura. (Abingdon: Routledge, 2015), p. 109.

196 Igarashi. *Japanese Contemporary Politics*. p. 4.

197 Vogel. "The Rise and Fall of the Japanese Bureaucracy". pp. 8-9.

198 Hrebenar, Ronald J. and Haraguchi, Koji. "The Fall of the DPJ and Return of the LDP to Power: The December 2012 House Election". In *Party Politics in Japan*. p. 186.

of this book. The Pew Research Centre found in 2018 that 62% of Japanese believe elections do not change things. By 2021, more voters supported no party (41%) than supported the LDP (38%) or the reformed DPJ, the Constitutional Democratic Party of Japan (CDP), the main opposition party (7%). The opposition's fundamental weakness means that, as Sone Yasunori of Keio University in Tokyo puts it, "The LDP presidential election is the real game, not the general election."[199]

The second administration of Abe Shinzo (2012–20), the longest lasting of any postwar prime minister, seemed to further weaken the bureaucracy by further empowering the Prime Minister's Office and the Cabinet Office with a special headquarters and offices to coordinate major policy initiatives, thereby transferring some of the policy initiative from individual ministries to these units. It also created a new class of elite bureaucrat, the cabinet bureaucrat, who has played an increasingly critical role in mediating between the political leadership and the individual ministries. However, this did not in fact curtailed the influence of the elite bureaucrats in general, as many of Abe's top advisors in the Prime Minister's Office and the Cabinet Office came from the ministries. As they have for over one hundred years, these elite bureaucrats mastered their new environment. The most important and powerful ones, like the Ministry of Economy, Trade, and Industry (METI), "now take their ideas straight to the Cabinet Office, and they coordinate there."[200] While bureaucrats in this new era have indeed lost some of their capacity to coordinate policy deliberations with politicians and interest groups, it has only resulted in a shift towards more power for elected politicians and no fundamental change in the firewall that continues to separate citizens from the governing process.

Yet further cracks in the system continue to appear. In the final stages of preparing this volume, it has come to public attention that, finally, even the bureaucrats who have designed this insidious system of collective utilitarianism are beginning to break from its inhuman demands. In late 2021 and early 2022, newspaper reports began appearing on the high number of young bureaucrats leaving their positions due to the excessive work hours so many other Japanese have been suffering from for decades. A report from January 2021 noted the average overtime hours for a worker in the Cabinet Secretariat

---

199 "Going round in circles Japan readies itself for an unpredictable ballot. The ruling party's leadership contest may matter more than the next national election". *The Economist*. September 23, 2021.

200 Vogel. "The Rise and Fall of the Japanese Bureaucracy". pp. 10-11.

department averaged 122 hours a month and reached an amazing 378 hours a month for the busiest staffer. The primary cause for this excessive overtime was the need to prepare speeches on areas of expertise for politicians in the Diet giving talks at a wide variety of gatherings—further highlighting the dominance of the bureaucracy in crafting policies that politicians present to the people and vote into law.[201] If the bureaucrats begin to join the legions of citizens making up the ever-widening Disconnected Society (*mu-en shakai*), one wonders who will be left to govern or be governed.

New Conflict over Japan's Peace Constitution and the Struggle for Principled Protest in Soka Gakkai

As noted earlier in former Prime Minister Abe's connection to Imperial Way Zen followers, a strong cultural conservatism accompanied his political conservatism. In his first administration, he made a concerted effort to reform Japanese education by creating a high-powered Education Rebuilding Council to promote the educational views of conservatives, including the reintroduction of corporal punishment and a strong emphasis on "patriotism" in the classroom. The result was that in 2007 the Fundamental Law of Education was amended for the first time since its creation in 1947. It now directly stipulates that children be taught respect for their national traditions and culture.[202] This conservatism, bordering on what some feel is something even more pernicious, became stronger in his second tenure as prime minister. Abe was emboldened to take on much larger agendas, specifically the reform of Japan's postwar peace constitution and the Article 9 forbidding any military action beyond self-defense. As we recall, for many progressives in Japan, this constitution is the most salient form of national identity in the postwar era, one that serves as a middle path of principled neutrality between the LDP's roots in archaic Japanese exceptionalism and the neo-conservative liberalism of the West.

In this way, a litmus test that has been applied to the traditional Buddhist denominations concerning their true sense of taking responsibility for their actions during the war is, "How much they have confronted these increasing shifts under the LDP towards making the Self

---

201 "Vox Populi: Extreme work hours crushing staff in seat of Japanese power". *Asahi Shimbun*. March 9, 2021. Sakakibara, Ken. "Young officials explain exodus of overworked bureaucrats". *Asahi Shimbun*. March 28, 2022.

202 McCullough. "Moral and Social Education in Japanese Schools". p. 32.

Defense Forces a more pro-active military force?"²⁰³ If the traditional Buddhist sects did indeed feel that state policy was wrong during the war and owe an apology for the suffering of both the people of Asia and the common citizens of Japan, it would make sense that they would oppose the re-militarization of the state and its joining other nations, specifically the United States, in future wars of aggression.

One of the first of these tests was to express opposition to the dispatch of the Self-Defense Forces in 2003 in support of the American invasion of Iraq after the incidents of 9/11. The denominations that were most forthright and timely in their taking of war responsibility had the foundations for responding quickly, and so both the Otani and Hongan-ji subsects of the Jodo Shin Pure Land, Soto Zen, Rinzai Zen Myoshin-ji as well as Rissho Kosei-kai denominations either made public statements against the dispatch or sent direct appeals to the government to reconsider. The Buddhist NGOs, such as SVA and AYUS, along with newer networks of young activist Buddhists, such as those associated with the formerly conservative Zenseikyo Foundation & National Buddhist Council for Youth and Child Welfare (全国青少年教化協議会 *Zenkoku Seishonen Kyoka Kyogi-kai*), actively engaged in appeals and actual public protests to Japan's involvement in the war. Soka Gakkai was in a particularly difficult situation as its party the Komei-to acquiesced to the power of its paternal partner the LDP, stating, "Since there is no option but to leave the coalition, we have no choice but to respect the prime minister's final decision."²⁰⁴ This led to a public movement by rank-and-file Soka Gakkai followers to collect 18,000 signatures against this policy and submit them to Komei-to.²⁰⁵

The next challenge occurred under the two different administrations of Shinzo Abe and his attempts to revise the constitution. The

---

203 Such a test was developed by Fujiyama Midori 藤山みどり of the Center for Information on Religion 宗教情報センター (*Shukyo Joho Senta*) in her analysis of "The Religious Community's Perception of History: War Responsibility Statements and Beyond" (宗教界の歴史認識〜戦争責任表明とその後 *Shukyo-kai-no rekishi ninshiki: Senso-sekinin hyomei-to sono-ato*). June 18, 2015. https://www.circam.jp/reports/02/detail/id=5631

204 "Komei-to to approve deployment of Self-Defense Forces to Iraq as part of ruling coalition party". (公明、自衛隊イラク派遣を容認へ連立与党として判断 *Komei, ji-ei-tai Iraku-haken-wo yonin-he ren-ritsu yo-to-toshite handan*). *Asahi Newspaper*. December 4, 2003. http://www.asahi.com/special/iraqrecovery/TKY200312030393.html

205 "Soka Gakkai Volunteers Submit 'Signatures Against Iraq' to Komei Party". (創価学会有志、「イラク反対署名」を公明に提出 *Sokka Gakkai yushi, 'Iraku-hantai-shomei'-wo komei-ni tei-shutsu*). *Asahi Newspaper*. January 21, 2004. http://www.asahi.com/special/jieitai/TKY200401210318.html

most significant of these came in July 2014 when the Abe Cabinet reinterpreted the 1947 Constitution to allow for the "right of collective self-defense" (集団的自衛権 shudan-teki ji-ei-ken). This would allow Japan's military, known euphemistically as the Self-Defense Forces (SDF 自衛隊 Ji-ei-tai), to come to the aid of the United States and other allies under armed attack, even if Japan itself is not attacked directly. This policy was put into law in September 2015 when the Diet passed "security-related legislation" (安全保障関連法案 Anzen-hogai-kanren ho-an), most commonly called the "national security legislation" (安法法案 anpo ho-an) or the "war legislation" (戦争法案 senso ho-an) by upset opponents. A telephone poll by the *Asahi Shimbun* newspaper carried out in the same month showed that 68% of respondents thought the bills were not necessary for the SDF to defend Japan, while 54% were opposed to it and only 29% were in favor of it. In a similar repeat to the events surrounding the eventual renewal of the Japan-US Security Treaty (*Anpo*) in 1960, huge protests erupted in the months leading up to this vote in the Diet. The largest occurred on August 30 when some 120,000 protestors gathered in front of the National Diet, while tens of thousands demonstrated simultaneously at more than 300 other locations across the country.[206]

A key component in the continuing power of the LDP to ignore public sentiment and remain in office with low voter turnout is the essential partnership of the Komei-to party and the virtually guaranteed electoral delivery of its large block of Soka Gakkai members. Komei-to provides an essential electoral base in urban areas where the LDP is less popular, providing the perfect complement to the LDP's stronghold over rural regions bought off from decades of central government subsidies. While Komei-to portrays itself as an important "brake" (*ha-do-me*) on the more conservative tendencies of the LDP, rank and file Soka Gakkai members have increasingly expressed criticism of the party for deviating from the principles of peace emphasized over decades by Ikeda Daisaku and the center of the organization. The Married Women's Division (婦人部 *fujin-bu*) in particular, has become a vocal force of over the last three decades in promoting peace and calling out Komei-to for its breaches of these principles.[207] In this way, certain voices have emerged in Soka Gakkai to reduce engagement in

---

206 McLaughlin, Levi. "Komeito's Soka Gakkai Protesters and Supporters: Religious Motivations for Political Activism in Contemporary Japan". In *The Asia-Pacific Journal*. October 12, 2015. Vol. 13, No. 41:1. pp. 1-2.

207 Ibid., p. 17.

the political arena and to refocus on religious priorities.[208]

During the summer 2015 protests, numerous images circulated through social media of Soka Gakkai followers engaging in and expressing dissent against the political party their own religion created. These protestors carried Soka Gakkai's tri-color flag and placards with slogans criticizing Komei-to Diet members for abandoning the party's and the denomination's long-held principles of peace. One sign called for Komei-to Diet members to "Re-read *The Human Revolution!*" (「人間革命」を読み直せ "*Ningen kakumei*"-*wo yomi-nao-se*), which is the novelized history of Soka Gakkai that tells of the rebuilding of the organization after the wartime imprisonment of its first and second presidents. Such Gakkai members came together through a Facebook group called "People who are Soka Gakkai members but really hate the LDP, let's unite!" (創価学会員だけど自民党が大嫌いな人、団結しましょう *Soka Gakkai-in dake-do Jimin-to-ga dai-kirai-na hito, danketsu shimasho*) and appeared at a protest organized by the new Students Emergency Action for Liberal Democracy (SEALD) in the Kansai region of western Japan on July 19. Just the calling out of those in power reminds us, as leading Soka Gakkai scholar Levi McLaughlin notes, of the practice of "admonishing the state" (*kokka-kangyo*), in which Nipponzan Myoho-ji has engaged since the 1950s.

In fact, Rev. Takeda Takao 武田隆雄, senior leader of the Myoho-ji Shibuya practice center has expressed that, "The current peace marches and street practices are seen as the practice of *kokka-kangyo*. In particular, the prayer activities in front of the National Assembly with the beating of drums and chanting of the *daimoku* are also considered to be the practice of the *kokka-kangyo*."[209] To see at these rallies members of Soka Gakkai in the crowds of old radicals left over from the period of the New Left and the Cold War peace movement was shocking but welcomed. For quite some time, Soka Gakkai has been derided by the mass media and the general public for their religious intolerance, non-participation with other civic and religious groups, and support for a party that gradually abandoned many of its original platforms in order to be part of the ruling party coalition.

These protesters have not, however, received favorable opinion among many of the older, more conservative members. Soka Gakkai's Office of Public Affairs has stated that while these individual members have the right to express themselves, the organization itself remains "absolutely unconcerned/unconnected" (全く感知がない

---

208 Klein & McLaughlin. "Komeito". p. 15.

209 Private correspondence. October 10, 2022.

mattaku kanchi-ga nai) to them. Further, the protestors should not oppose the democratic processes going on in the Diet and that, "It is deplorable that the three-color flag of our Gakkai is being used in a political manner."[210] One finds this selective use of the term "political" (*seiji-teki*) throughout the Japanese Buddhist world when it decides it does not want to get involved in social issues. A common refrain that emerged during the aftermath of the Fukushima crisis was that the issue of nuclear energy was a political matter in which religions should not be involved. Meanwhile, holding peace vigils and conferences about nuclear warfare and Hiroshima continue to be a popular form of engagement.

Shimazono Susumu notes that the LDP's conservative positions do not actually go against the true nature of the Komei-to and Soka Gakkai itself. Some Western scholars residing outside Japan have mentioned Ikeda Daisaku and the Gakkai in the same breath as renowned Socially Engaged Buddhist figures such as the Dalai Lama, Thich Nhat Hanh, Sulak Sivaraksa, and A.T. Ariyaratne—all of whom have spoken out against nation state tyranny. Shimazono, however, sees the Gakkai as using the same model of East Asian "state authoritarianism" (*ken-in-shugi kokka*) based on leader worship that has blended well with the archaic nationalism of the LDP. In a tongue and cheek manner, he remarks that, "You could almost say that this present government is an alliance between Soka Gakkai and the Association of Shinto Shrines (神社本庁 *Jinja Honcho*) [the institutional successor to prewar State Shinto]. One supports veneration of the emperor and the other veneration of Ikeda Daisaku." In this way, he feels Buddhism should have a more important role to play in articulating not so much a political system but a form of social thought that connects to a progressive and democratic form of society.

Principled Protest and Buddhism's Unique Resolution to the Problem of Modernity

The summer 2015 protests were not the first time that such a mass of citizens had emerged to protest the actions of the government in recent years. These demonstrations developed out of the protests by citizens after the Fukushima incident to shut down Japan's nuclear program in 2011 and then prevent the restart of reactors in 2012. They included rallies of over 60,000 people in September 2011 on the six-month anniversary of the beginning of the tragedy and then again in

---

210 McLaughlin. "Komeito's Soka Gakkai Protesters and Supporters". p. 9.

June 2012 to stop the first restart of reactors. While the large numbers would subside in the face of continual failures to affect policy on the national level, the protests continued on and morphed into a widespread movement against the Abe administration and a variety of his policies. These included the Act on the Protection of Specially Designated Secrets (SDS) (特定秘密の保護に関する法律 *Tokutei Himitsu-no Hogo-ni-kansuru Horitsu*), which can put normal citizens in prison for up to five years for publishing any information deemed important to national security.

At the heart of all the protests, no matter how big or small and no matter the season or the weather, one can find the monks, nuns, and lay people of the Nipponzan Myoho-ji. As with Rissho Kosei-kai and Soka Gakkai, they have had long campaigns against nuclear warfare without much consideration of the problems of nuclear energy. That began to change in 2010 when they participated in a march in Limerik, Pennsylvania in the United States at the site of the Exelon's Limerick Nuclear Generating Station to protest nuclear energy and its perception as an alternative green energy to CO_2-generating fossil fuels. In the wake of the unfolding nuclear crisis at the Fukushima #1 facility, Nipponzan Myoho-ji was the first Japanese Buddhist denomination to issue a declaration against nuclear power on March 20, 2011, and to be at the forefront of the protest movement that began that month—very much as they were almost sixty years earlier after the Bikini Atoll nuclear testing incident.

As we will explore in more depth in Volume II, the issue of declarations against nuclear power became as contentious in the Buddhist world as the earlier one of issuing declarations on war responsibility. Once again, Kono Taitsu was at the center of this movement, pushing his own Rinzai Zen Myoshin-ji denomination to issue a statement, as well as the conservative Japan Buddhist Federation to do likewise, in his capacity as the rotating president at the time of the Fukushima incident. Master Kono became a remarkable public Buddhist figure at this time for being a powerful mainstream monk who made alliances with more marginalized anti-nuclear Buddhist ones. He took an even bolder step in declaring that Buddhist support for nuclear energy and unbridled economic development in the postwar era has been no different than support for the imperial war system.

Outside of Master Kono and these more marginal Buddhist priests and groups, the mainstream Buddhist world was typically reactive rather than proactive in making such declarations. The JBF statement took a full nine months after the beginning of the incident to formulate and announce on December 1, 2011. Soka Gakkai and Rissho Kosei-kai did not issue statements until 2012, belying their commitment to end nuclear proliferation by taking the spurious track that nuclear energy and nuclear arms are separate issues. Myoho-ji, on the other hand, enfolded this issue into not only their *kokka-kangyo* activities in front of the national Diet but also their nationwide peace marches. They created a new march to every nuclear reactor complex in the country to engage in a day of fasting and chanting the *daimoku* while presenting an appeal to end nuclear power to authorities at each reactor.

One is continually struck in looking at these activities of the Nipponzan Myoho-ji. As referenced earlier, they exhibit the classic patterns of Japanese social protest in a high level of sincerity, loyalty, and self-sacrifice while engaging in what appears to be more expressive protest rather than instrumental protest that achieves a particular end through rational, organized action. At times, their marches seem to focus more on chanting the *daimoku* rather than building networks among citizens affected by these issues to unite in a strategic movement. Indeed, in comparison to the incredible size, wealth, and influence of Rissho Kosei-kai and Soka Gakkai, their protests seem rather pathetic with a small circle of mostly aged followers numbering no more than twenty to thirty people at a time. Yet their expressive, if not instrumental, protest also seeks to educate the public on the real structural issues behind Japan's compromised position as an active ally of the United States' global military presence. In this way, they have continued to exhibit a high level of war responsibility since the earliest days of the movement in the 1950s when the denomination made a substantive shift from its wartime support of the Japanese military. By making such substantive change decades before other Buddhist denominations confronted their war responsibility, their peace work today has much greater substance than the numerous peace prayer services and grand memorials that many traditional denominations consider their contribution to global peace. This historical record thus pushes one to investigate further what the meaning of their unique kind of activism might have for the larger Japanese civil society movement.

In March 2021, one of Myoho-ji's younger monks, Ven. Kamoshita Yuichi 鴨下祐一 (1984–), made a presentation at the seventh Global Inter-religious Conference on Article 9 of the Japanese Peace Constitution, hosted by the Niwano Peace Foundation, directly affiliated with Rissho Kosei-kai. Ven. Kamoshita lived as a Myoho-ji monk in

India for seven years and then moved to Okinawa in 2013 to support the movement against American military bases there. The movement in Okinawa has a long history, and the Myoho-ji has a small center near one of the main protest sites in Henoko. There, a general group of activists have had sit-ins three times a day timed with the arrival of construction vehicles during which they are usually forcibly removed by police. Ven. Kamoshita remarked at how the intense, violent confrontations with authorities began to create divisions and burnout among the activists and a gradual dispersal of numbers, especially among young people. As typical of the decline of the New Left, many people quit the movement because of the typical problems of hierarchy, sexism, and the feeling that there are wider methods than a purely political approach.

While young Japanese today are notoriously apolitical in this age of global youth activism, Ven. Kamoshita has noticed a new style of engagement in Okinawa by visiting university students. They have created a more festive environment of cook-outs and sharing connection with the local people affected by these military bases. This experience has reminded him of others in which he has participated overseas that, unlike Japan, have a strong religious aspect, especially Native American protests in the U.S., where a real community is built at protest sites. In this way, he feels there needs to be a shift in the way protests occur in Japan that tend to focus on specific policy changes, such as stopping the construction of a new base, to something wider, more holistic—perhaps even principled in a way that affects the very premises of society. He quotes the Myoho-ji founder, Ven. Fujii Nichidatsu, who once said, "If one does a variety of things in addition to a religious movement, each will fail. That's because there is no mirror to illuminate. Religion establishes something like Buddha or God. That teaching becomes a mirror. Politics wanders here and there. There is no mirror. One will be pulled both ways. This results in things like power acquisition or vote collection." [211] These sentiments seem to echo those of Kono Taitsu in his search for "an infallible way of life," one that "doesn't fall victim to the vicissitudes of change." They also reflect directly on the way Komei-to has floated to the right and lost its principled grounding.

In a very subtle way that is not so apparent, Ven. Fujii's words and the activities of the Myoho-ji push out into a new horizon that

---

211 Conference on "Article 9 of the Japanese Peace Constitution and Peace in Asia-Prayer from Okinawa". The 7th Global Inter-religious Conference on Article 9 of the Japanese Peace Constitution. March 2-3, 2021. pp. 129-32.

might offer a path to the resolution of the struggle of modernity in Japan. In this section and the previous one, we have encountered the countless attempts by Japanese Buddhists, liberals, Marxists, utopians, anarchists, and even archconservatives and nationalists, to provide a way to preserve the essential aspects of Japanese culture while bringing them into the qualitatively new space of industrial and post-industrial modern society. The failures of archaic Japanese exceptionalism are evident in the disaster of imperialism and war. The failures of those who attempted to graft Western modernity in the forms of Marxist socialism and liberal capitalism onto Japanese culture and society are also clear from the violent factionalism of the leftist movement and the stultifying existence of the collective utilitarian state that has given birth the present Disconnected Society (*mu-en shakai*).

Without going into depth, the problem of the importation of Western modernity is that it itself is based on a model of brokenness derived from the failed resolution of the Protestant Reformation. The failure to arrive at a new unified vision of Christian faith resulted in the banishment of faith to the private realm of the individual while an instrumental form of reason became the basis for public morality. From these conclusions arose the belief in the natural state of the atomized individual living in an artificially constructed society regulated by scientific rationalism and utilitarianism as well as the horrid mind-body dualism of modernity. The promise of the resolution to this sublimated fallen-ness is provided by liberal capitalism in the road to unbridled growth and economic development and by Marxist socialism as the completion of historical materialism in the utopian communist state. The strength of such teleology in the energetic devotion to improving the material conditions of humans is counterbalanced by the utilitarian logic in which the human spirit as well as the natural environment are sacrificed for an end that never seems to arrive.[212]

As chronicled throughout this volume, the Japanese spirit is deeply antithetical to such teleology, seeing the world not as a place of broken-ness but one filled with gods (*kami*) and innate enlightenment (*hongaku*). The problem we have seen in this approach, however, is a regressive harkening back to a golden age of the pure manifestation of the eternal Yamato spirit of the Japanese race that should be revived here in the present. This mystical presence is then continually used to remind individuals to not offend or disturb (迷惑 *meiwaku*) the harmony (*wa*) of the collective and to adjust their discomforts and sufferings to the omnipresent existence of this spirit in the collective.

---

212 See Loy. *A Buddhist History of the West*.

In the prewar era, this system of belief was manifested in the emperor and the bond with his national family of subjects (*kokutai*). In the postwar era, this system has continued in a sublimated, modern secular way with the bureaucratic state, familial corporation, and LDP providing the social and cultural standards in which the people shall be immersed.

Buddhism offers something clearly different to these worldviews. There is also a sense of brokenness in Buddhism with its teaching of ignorance as the fundamental human condition that concocts a world of greed, anger, and delusion—the Three Poisons. The resolution in Buddhism is part teleological in a disciplined practice of virtue, meditation, and wisdom (*sila-samadhi-prajna*) towards the goal of nirvana. As we have noted, this has caused many Buddhists into a mistaken path of forgoing compassion to others to commit all personal resources to ascetic practice and meditation in hopes of getting there sooner than later. The fundamental Japanese attitude against such a teleological view gave rise to the other extreme, a grasping to the idea of innate enlightenment (*hongaku*) that became one of the earliest examples of using radical immanentalism to legitimize power in the medieval *ken-mitsu* system of rule. The Kamakura Buddhist masters broke through this problem, like all great Buddhist masters do. Specifically, Dogen's approach to Zen meditation as the way to manifest, as opposed to attain, buddha-nature and enlightenment resolved the duality between practice and realization, means and ends. This non-duality is found clearly in the bodhisattva vows that so many Mahayana Buddhists chant daily:

> Sentient beings are numberless, I vow to liberate them.
> Delusions are inexhaustible, I vow to eliminate them.
> Dharma doors are infinite, I vow to master them.
> The Buddha way is unsurpassed, I vow to attain it.

In these vows, we see the teleological drive to resolve brokenness, yet they are expressed in a way that final realization seems impossible. As such, the utilitarian drive towards ends is collapsed into the present process of action, yet the mystical immanentalism of inherent enlightenment is also shattered by the vow to "liberate", "eliminate", "master", and "attain". In this way, the problem of the Kyoto School and Nishida's thought was, as the Critical Buddhists explain, its subtle replacing of emptiness (*shunyata*) as a dynamic form of experience and action with an ontological "place of absolute nothingness". This encouraged a re-immersion back into the collective spirit of the nation and Japanese ethnicity, as evidenced by the use of Nishida's thought over generations by conservative nationalist leaders. Nakamura Hisashi, the previously-profiled international development expert and Jodo Shin Buddhist, has actually charted a new course for this archaic tendency in Japanese culture by exhorting:

> We have to look back carefully to our relationships with the other ethnic groups of Asia, like the Chinese, Korean, Thai, etc. from the Nara era and before that to the Jomon (縄文時代 14,000–300 BCE) and Yayoi (弥生時代 300 BCE–300 CE) periods. We have some cultural influences from them, especially northern Asian people who lived in the Sakhalin islands and Hokkaido. This legacy must be carefully studied. If we don't reconstruct our relationships with these other Asian peoples, we have no future. In short, Japanese are useless without the intellectual support from Korea and China. Almost all major streams of Japanese Buddhism came from Korea and China. Sometimes we have lost a sense of this background. We have to make an effort to rebuild these original relationships and only then can we find our new horizon.[213]

In conclusion, the Myoho-ji's central practice of chanting the *daimoku* and nothing more at its protest activities appears to manifest this non-dual form of Buddhist practice, specifically as articulated by Nichiren. In turn, it demonstrates a kind of Buddhist social activism that differs from other modern forms based in the unresolved dualism of Western modernity and its continual pitfalls in violence and burnout among activists. This activism is at the same time both expressive *and* instrumental, geared to resolving the present suffering of people (First Noble truth of *dukkha*) while providing a principled questioning of the deeper social system (Second Noble Truth of causes). Based in an ecumenical and non-violent method (Third and Four Noble Truths of nirvana and its path), it also provides the vision of an axial and civilizational resolution to suffering that includes all nations and all sentient life. While the Myoho-ji may not be reaching a mass audience with this message, its resolution in the path of non-dual Buddhist ethics is part of a potential turn in Japanese society that the subsequent volume on Socially Engaged Buddhist activism in the 21st century will

---

213 Personal interview. November 13, 2021.

profile. On this note, Shimazono Susumu concludes this chapter with the following observations.

> As the collective euphoria of the economic boom began to wane in the 1980s and 90s and there arose some doubt about a morality based on collective utilitarianism, a new type of religious morality began to appear. Since the 2000s, an increasing interest in Socially Engaged Buddhism began to emerge not so much among the common citizens but more within the Buddhist world. Temples have come to see that their old-fashioned way of community activities is not enough and have begun to reach out to wider society by engaging in a variety of activities from disaster relief, suicide prevention, and so forth. As the very communalistic non-individualistic society linked to a hierarchical authoritarian state has come to be less and less acceptable to people, they have started to look for a new source of morality and ethics. As such, one based in Buddhism seems to be on the rise. I remain hopeful that this new Buddhist morality will be more expansive and universal and might lead to a kind of "autonomous Buddhist social ethics" (自律的な仏教社会倫理 *jiritsu-teki-na Bukkyo shakai-rinri*).[214]

This is the type of new Buddhist social ethics that, as mentioned earlier, might chart a middle way between the pitfalls of Zen elitism and *Lotus Sutra* populism. In conclusion, many outside and inside Japan have worried about the future of Japanese Buddhism and its renewal due to the almost total loss of celibate monastics devoted to meditation and enlightenment. The fascinating clue here for its revival, then, might not be through the door of *samadhi* but through the door of a Socially Engaged Buddhist *sila* in which the practice of bodhisattva ethics has a transformational effect on not only the Buddhist Sangha but on Japanese society at large. This issue will be a central part of our exploration in the second volume.

---

214 Personal Interview. October 23, 2021.

Afterword

Towards an Autonomous Buddhist Social Ethics and a Dharmic Civil Society

Secular Distortions of Spiritual Motivations: A Buddhist Critique of Western Civil Society

At the end of the last chapter, we noted the failed resolution of the Protestant Reformation that led to the sublimated fallen-ness of liberal capitalism in the atomized individual and of Marxist socialism in the loss of subjective agency in the completion of historical materialism. While these insights have been made by various critics, the prominent Socially Engaged Buddhist writer David Loy, who lived and studied Zen in Japan for two decades, provides a compelling version of it based on the core Buddhist teachings not-self and emptiness in his *A Buddhist History of the West*. His analysis of the development of Western civil society, in particular, helps to understand the struggle of Socially Engaged Buddhism to develop in the latter half of 20th century in Japan.

Loy's analysis begins with one of the core themes of Section 2: the flaws of an archaic mythology of divine power and cultural exceptionalism that creates a governing system violent to its own people and to peoples who lie beyond its shore. This example is not, however, the imperial *kokutai* ideology of Meiji Japan but, rather, that of the Catholic Church, whose inscrutable authority ruled Europe for centuries. The Protestant Reformation was the first push of democracy against this system and was supposed to liberate Christian Europe into a new age of religious egalitarianism. Yet things did not go as planned, and this newfound spiritual freedom led to a spate of contending new doctrines. Within a short period of time, Europe began to tear itself apart in the Wars of Religion, culminating in the Thirty Years War (1618–1648), which wiped out between 25 percent to 40 percent of Germany's entire population. The amazing parallel in Japanese history actually predates these European developments. The Kamakura Buddhist Reformation was inaugurated by the revelations of Honen and Shinran, the great Pure Land Buddhist reformers who have been compared with Martin Luther for their emphases on salvation and justification by faith alone. The ensuing the Warring States period (1467–1615) featured class-based communities of samurai, merchants, and farmers that formed around these new teachings, including Zen and Nichiren ones, engaging in over a century of warfare.

The conclusion of both of these reformations was a deep sense of distrust in religious ideals to offer solutions to the organization of society. From the Japanese side, the Tokugawa military state exterminated Christianity and banned certain Buddhist sects resistant to their consolidation of all Buddhist denominations into a pacified village temple system (*tera-uke seido*), which eventually evolved into the Funeral Buddhism of the modern era. In the West, secular modernity was supposed to solve the problems of contending faiths with the discovery of science and the development of pragmatic, rational, and utilitarian logic. God was banished to the realm of personal faith, and the new citizen of the state, as opposed to subject of a divinely sanctioned ruler, was liberated into a world of individual rights and collective liberty.

Rather than communities held together by a shared and unified religious outlook, the concept of civil society grew out of these new secular values. Civil society was first normatively defined by Adam Smith (1723–1790) in his *The Wealth of Nations* as a sphere of self-interested and self-regulating economic activity, apart from the state but sympathetically supported by it.[1] While this definition has continued to shift and change, this emphasis on a realm of economic activity based in the negative liberty of the naturally free individual is still one interpretation that is strongly promoted today. Reflecting on the problem of how such civil societies co-exist with one another as seen in the legacies of colonialism and world war, Loy sees that the failures of the Reformation have carried on and haunted secular modernity as a kind of repressed collective consciousness. He notes, "The lack of an overtly spiritual grounding to our lives means that this 'secular' preoccupation has become religiously compulsive. Because this compulsion is unconscious, not understood by us, these institutions have taken on lives of their own which subordinate us to them while accepting no subordination to anything else."[2]—a conclusion that sounds not so different to the critique of the individual always being subordinate to the collective in Japan. In the West, Loy feels the individual has ultimately become subordinate to the Three

---

1   Loy. *A Buddhist History of the West.* p. 157.
2   Ibid., p. 122.

Poisons of Buddhism in institutional form: ill-will as the militaristic nation-state, in which we are never secure enough; greed as corporate capitalism, in which we never have enough; and ignorance as science, in which we never know enough.[3]

Replicated Distortions in the Development of Japanese Civil Society

As we explored in Sections 2 and 3, the Meiji state was inspired by this European model of civil society, first evidenced in the "separation of religion and rule" (*sei-kyo bunri*) policy that culminated in the 1889 Meiji Constitution's Freedom of Religion Clause. This policy pushed religion into the private sphere and employed bureaucratic utilitarianism as a basis for public morality. Yet, as noted, this new innovation of an East Asian collective utilitarianism attempted to mask the Neo-Confucian and Shinto values of veneration of authority that were being promoted, principally in the 1890 Imperial Rescript on Education—much in the same way the language of secularism and science mask the implicit Christian attitudes and beliefs in the West. Fukuzawa Yukichi coined the term *shimin* ("citizen") in contradistinction to the then normative *kokutai* ("subject") in 1867 as part of his promotion of Japan's "civilization and enlightenment" (*bunmei kaika*) movement. However, the concept of "civil society" (*shimin-shakai*), first coined by Manabu Sano in 1923, was largely developed in Japan by Marxists in the Taisho and early Showa. As renowned sociologist Uemura Kunihiko 植村邦彦 notes, both liberals and Marxists, while sincere in their motivations, took on the Eurocentric view that Japan was an underdeveloped and backward society.[4] The result of these various attempts to modernize Japanese society was, as with the West, not only a predictable period of imperialism based on implicit, if not explicit, spiritual values. There was also the loss, or perhaps the lack of the emergence, of what Shimazono Susumu has called "an autonomous form of social ethics" (*jiritsu-teki-na rinri*).

From the understanding of the sublimated and distorted religious compulsions in modern society, Loy also examines the American model of civil society. He explains that the secular conclusions of the European Wars of Religion led to similar ones in the U.S. as reason and natural law came to replace religious morality as the foundations

---

3   Ibid., p. 109.

4   All quotes and references henceforth come from the on-line article: "Does 'Civil Society' Really Exist in Japan?" An Interview with Uemura Kunihiko.

for civil society as well as for the political and economic spheres. In this way, Loy concludes that the American model of civil society—which has been imposed on so many nations since World War II including, of course, Japan—actually works against the very concept of a civil society by circumscribing morality to the private sphere and transforming reason into a calculative rationality, the victory of which has been the slow disintegration of civil society itself.[5]

In terms of this influence on Japan in the postwar era, Uemura notes how the earliest definition of civil society in the standard national *Kojien* 広辞苑 dictionary, first published in 1955, surprisingly shows a Hegelian-Marxist orientation that reflects the early postwar embrace of socialist values. There is a distinction made between state and civil society, the latter of which is "a community of law-governed organizations based on a free economy…and on the moral principles of freedom, equality and benevolence." These sentiments are embodied in the efforts of the new center-left movements of the 50s and 60s that worked to change the prewar mentality of the people as imperial subjects (*kokutai*), which strongly identified with the state. They sought to redefine the people as modern citizens (*shimin*) with an agency to develop civil society as an authentic third social force. Efforts on the domestic front to articulate responsibility for the war (*senso-sekinin*), develop personal autonomy (*shutaisei*), and articulate a new national identity as a war-renouncing nation found in Article 9 of the constitution, were combined with international work to connect with the civilizational, non-aligned movement. The Buddhist contribution to these efforts was limited, at best, to a small number of progressive priests, like Seno-o Giro, and one small denomination, the Nipponzan Myoho-ji.

The second edition of the *Kojien* published in 1969 shows the major shift Japan underwent in the tumultuous 14-year period of the depletion of the peace movement into a violent inward-looking student one. Uemura notes the new definition articulated the classical liberal values of Locke, Rousseau, and others as a society that "should consist of free and equal individuals rationally united" but in a "state" or "political order created by landowners to protect their property rights." This view perpetuated the prewar tendency to idealize Western society and to consider thar Japan needed to create a civil society on the level of Western Europe. Uemura speaks of this thinking as the kind of internalized Eurocentrism that created the "civilization and enlightenment" (*bunmei kaika*) movement.

---

5   Loy. *A Buddhist History of the West*. p. 166.

Afterword

The next important shift began in the 1970s with Japan's surpassing of many Western economies, much due to its ability to recover more quickly from the oil shock of 1973. This greater resiliency came from the government's further consolidation and control of labor into a vast pyramid of large corporations and subcontracting companies. The education system was also revamped to push students into after school "cram academies" (塾 *juku*) that trained them to survive the intensive hours of adult work life.[6] Uemura explains that during this time, "The term 'civil society' began to lose its meaning as a philosophy of change for Japanese society." As noted in Section 3, Prime Minister Nakasone held strong nationalist sentiments grounded in the prewar social ethics of Neo-Confucianism and Zen-tinged *bushido*. Rather than speak of civil society, he articulated an ascetic kind of democratic society, which is "purified" of "egoism" and "arrogance" and in which citizens not only claim their rights but also carry out their duties in a self-controlled manner.

The flourishing of the new kinds of Japanese exceptionalism known as *Nihonjin-ron* articulated the development of Japanese society from a clan (*uji*) based one to a household (*ie*) based one, evolving from the model of the Tokugawa era warrior clans. This understanding of society provided Japan with an ideology of national unity called "corporatism" (会社主義 *kaisha-shugi*) in which citizens, or perhaps still subjects, were enfolded in the many large corporations of this period. Uemura explains that for such "corporate people" (会社人間 *kaisha-ningen*), "advancement within the company was a more tangible goal for improving their lives than political participation or social change" as members of a civil society. From a Buddhist standpoint, it is fascinating to note the parallel rise of the new *Lotus Sutra* lay denominations with their promotion of the liberal values of the nuclear family focused on "this-worldly benefits" and their organizational structure, specifically that of Soka Gakkai, built more around a corporate model than a religious one. In this way, members could participate in a similar ethos of belonging to a corporate household with less concern on wider society, becoming, as noted in Section 3, civil societies unto themselves.

---

6   Yoda, Tomiko 依田富子. "The Rise and Fall of Maternal Society: Gender, Labor, and Capital in Contemporary Japan". In *Japan After Japan: Social and Cultural Life from the Recessionary 1990s to the Present*. Eds. Tomiko Yoda & Harry Harootunian. (Durham, NC: Duke University Press, 2006), pp. 258-61.

Towards Autonomous Buddhist Social Ethics and a Dharmic Civil Society

As detailed in Section 2, one of the important trends in the development of liberal civil society that found greater footing in prewar Japan was the late 19th century new liberalism of "collectivists", "communitarians", and "organicists", who believed the state should play an active and positive role in supporting the conditions for the material and spiritual development of the individual. This view stresses positive liberty in which the conditions of society help people maximize their potential. Instead of relegating religion to the private sector, the door is opened to the role of religious community in civil society to nurture individual development and, hence, social ethics and social justice. The Italian Marxist Antonio Gramsci (1891–1937) furthered this notion of civil society, defining it as comprised of cultural institutions, including religious ones, and distinctively separate from economic relations. While Gramsci did not see civil society as necessarily always democratic—such as when the Church or other cultural institutions have imposed their values on people—he did see it as the locus for the battle for human liberation.[7] In this way, the more current definition of civil society emerged as the sphere of relations between family, state, and market, and, even further, beyond the confines of national boundaries.[8]

This notion of civil society served leftist groups in Latin America in the 1970s against dictatorship and central European activists in the 1980s against oppressive communist states. Especially among the central Europeans, the notion of civil society drew closer to the ideas of Alexis de Tocqueville (1805–1859) on civil society as a means of self-organization[9] to develop democratic spaces and demand for more accountability from the state.[10] With these developments, a new concept of "global civil society" emerged in the 1990s that attacked the original conceptions found in classical liberalism as part of the anti-globalization movement against the economic neo-colonialism of the industrialized North.[11] Civil society thus began to be defined by people from non-white, non-Christian, non-liberal backgrounds

---

7   Anheier, Halmut; Glasius, Marlies & Kaldor, Mary. "Introducing Global Civil Society". In *Global Civil Society 2001*. Ed. Halmut Anheier, Marlies Glasius, & Mary Kaldor. (Oxford University Press, 2001), p. 13.

8   Ibid., p. 17.

9   Ibid., p. 14.

10 Ibid., p. 11.

11 Ibid., p. 17.

in the fight for self-determination[12] as an alternative space that allows maximum diversity of views and a balance between individual rights and collective well-being.

The concept of civil society today, however, is still occupied by liberals, both classical and new. Among political leaders and policy makers in states built on industrial capitalism, especially in the West, global civil society is another metaphor for liberalism. This sort of civil society reminds us of Marx's equation of civil society with "bourgeois society", a place to maintain the value of the autonomous individual with the liberty to consume and own private property as well as the right of their governments to ensure this liberty vis-a-vis other states by almost any means necessary. In the hands of "emerging democracies" in the South, the state has exploited civil society, specifically through dependence on social welfare NGOs, to cover its own inadequacies and injustices.

Uemura notes that it took some time for the new civil society theory to reach Japan. Once again, the progressive *Sekai* magazine, which played an important role in the 1950s peace movement, helped introduce this new civil society theory as: "A public space created by social relations based on mutual recognition of human dignity and equal rights. The members of such 'civil society' are citizens who act to create and support human relations and society based on mutual recognition of human dignity and equal rights." Such a civil society is "not limited to domestic or private NGOs, but also includes individuals who act independently and voluntarily in the community, workplace, disaster areas, etc., including urban as well as rural areas."

This new definition, however, was still haunted, as Loy might note, by the problem of the atomistic individual free to make choices and decisions within the framework of the market economy while being personally responsible for the results of their decisions. In this way, the new civil society discourse in Japan fed into the neo-liberal structural reform policies of the LDP to overhaul the flagging economy and to better compete with Western and emerging Asian economies. Umeura notes that civil society became equated with "respect for market principles" (市場原理の尊重 *shijo-genri-no soncho*), democracy as "private sector initiative" (民間企業主導 *minkan-kigyo-shudo*), and structural reform as the relaxation of government regulations to allow private companies to engage in free economic activity. Retreating from the notion of society being a corporate household, LDP leaders like Prime Minister Koizumi Junichiro promoted a neoliberal

---

12   Ibid., p. 15.

competitive society dominated by the "self-responsibility theory" (自己責任論 *jiko-sekinin-ron*)—something that sounds similar but is qualitatively different than the values of *shutaisei* and *jiritsusei* promoted by postwar progressives.

This new ideology of the "self-reliant citizen" (自立した市民 *jiritsu-shita shimin*) has been a central fulcrum for the creation of the Disconnected Society (*mu-en shakai*), which will form the foundational theme of Volume II. In short, it has provided the grounds for the deregulation of labor laws and the resultant spike in irregular or part-time workers. As noted above in the "emerging democracies" in the South, the emergence in Japan of NGOs and NPOs working in social welfare as an outgrowth of the development of civil society has also enabled the government to shed its responsibilities and expenditures towards citizens living in an increasing state of precarity. Uemura further notes that this self-responsibility theory has increased the public "bashing" for those still trying to access government welfare programs—an issue we will examine in detail in Volume II. He explains that, "It is clear that this is not the kind of society that the old school of thought and 'civil society theory' wanted." One of the differences is "the public's political sense that the government cannot be relied upon to effectively regulate the endless commercial activities of corporations, while social welfare on the other hand is in retreat." He admits that, "The realization of a society based on the principles of 'liberalism' and 'individualism' subtly overlaps with what 'civil society theory' has aimed for. Both are societies shaped by 'independent citizens', but they are not the same."

This point returns us to Loy's fundamental thesis that neither the decontextualized atomistic individual of liberalism nor the undifferentiated worker bee of Asian collectivism or Western communism can provide the foundation for a true civil society due to the fundamental reliance on materialistic solutions to the resolution of human "lack"[13] (i.e., angst, neurosis, *dukkha*, sin). As a Buddhist, he embraces the Middle Way perspective that Buddhist Socialists in Japan in the prewar era and in other parts of Asia in the postwar era used to develop a balance between the spiritual and material. Loy envisions a postmodern individual as a self-less bodhisattva acting with a host of personal enlightened qualities, like loving-kindness, compassion, sympathetic

---

13   Loy coined this term "lack" to better express in English the Buddhist teaching of the fundamental ungroundedness or emptiness (*shunyata*) of the individual self. This constant experience of a self that cannot be grounded, i.e., "not-self" (*anatman*), results in "lack"—the feeling that "something is wrong with me." Loy. *A Buddhist History of the West*. p. 29.

joy, and equanimity—akin to Shimazono's "autonomous Buddhist social ethics" (*jiritsu-teki-na Bukkyo shakai-rinri*). As a collection of such individuals, such a Buddhistic, or rather dharmic, civil society is deeply interconnected in a vast (Indra's) web of interdependence—a dynamic flux-balance of enlightening individuals with agency to act with wisdom and compassion yet with no essential self. This is the Buddhist resolution to the "autonomy" of the modern individual. Rather than existing free to pursue their own desires, the individual is liberated through the ethics of intentional (*cetana*) karmic action that serves the self and the other while maintaining the integrity of both.[14]

Japanese Buddhism, unsurprisingly, provides rich personifications of these values and, thus, the potential to create a dharmic civil society. The enlightened states of the bodhisattva are embodied in the four main bodhisattvas of the East Asian Mahayana tradition: Avalokiteshvara (観音菩薩 Kannon) as the embodiment of compassion; Manjushri (文殊菩薩 Monju) as enlightened wisdom; Samantabhadra (普賢菩薩 Fugen) as creative activity; and Kshitigarbha (地蔵菩薩 Jizo) as fearlessness.[15] Understood as forms of human character, they provide Japan an indigenized model of autonomous social ethics that are far more supportive of a healthy society than the pruned and withered forms of Neo-Confucianism, State Shinto, *bushido*, and liberal utilitarianism that have been infusing Japanese social ethics since the late 19th century.

A dharmic vision of civil society would certainly complement this newer form of global civil society as articulated from diverse racial and cultural standpoints. The Buddha himself articulated a wide range of conditions and potentials of a dharmic civil society. He taught a variety of ethical systems for different sectors of society creating the foundations of an autonomous social ethics in which religious institutions, state, and business sectors are integrated yet differentiated into a flux-balance.[16] Loy notes that contrary to "the widespread assumption that civil society is a morally-indifferent sphere of self-interested cooperation," a dharmic view recognizes civil society as "that dimension of our lives where we work together to reform society so that it does not objectify greed, ill-will, and ignorance in institutions."[17] In his more recent work, *Ecodharma: Buddhist Teachings for the Ecological Crisis*,

---

14 Watts. "Karma for Everyone". pp. 23-27.

15 Loy, David R. *Ecodharma: Buddhist Teachings for the Ecological Crisis*. (Somerville, MA: Wisdom Publications, 2019), p. 165.

16 Watts. "The 'Positive Disintegration' of Buddhism". p. 97

17 Loy. *A Buddhist History of the West*. p. 170.

he draws on the great Vietnamese Zen master Thich Nhat Hanh's claim that we need a collective enlightenment to stop the course of environmental destruction.[18] For Loy, "This collective realization will clarify what it means to be human. Being a species that is part of something greater than ourselves, our role is to serve the well-being of that whole—which will also heal us."[19] Again, he draws on the deep expressions of Thich Nhat Hanh who once wrote, "We are here to awaken from the illusion of our separateness."[20] This understanding of our deep interconnection and our collectivity makes a deep resonance with Japanese culture and values, not just in the point of a collective consciousness but in the value of karmic connection (縁 *en*). As much as axialization and civilization have been core themes for this first volume, the loss of such karmic connection (*mu-en*) and the rebuilding of it (有縁 *yu-en*) will form the foundation of the second volume.

To conclude this volume, Loy describes the axialization that we need today as not something Japan or pre-axial clannish societies need to develop to join the world of those who have. For it is clear that in places where axialization has taken place, regressive movements back into ethnocentric nationalism based on a single religious tradition remain a major stumbling block to collective enlightenment. Following the Buddha's teaching to not get caught in "clinging to views" (Pali. *ditthupadana*), Loy describes this axialization as a world with "no common ideology".[21] Thus, the goal is not a Buddhist civil society but one based in the idea of dharma as a form of ethical conduct and the wholesome results of such conduct, as described by Buddhadasa in Section 2. Some 300 years after the time of the Buddha, Ashoka attempted to develop such a society through public works, such as hospitals and free medical care, banning the practice of animal sacrifice, issuing environmental edicts to limit the wanton destruction of the wilderness for commercial use, and using non-Buddhist language in his numerous stone pillars to develop a common language for social ethics.[22]

Such dharmic concepts are perhaps finding new ground in Japan now as well. As detailed in Section 3, four important Socially Engaged Buddhist leaders in the late 20th century articulated important aspects of a dharmic civil society. Rev. Arima Jitsujo, the lead-

---

18   Loy. *Ecodharma*. p. 117.
19   Ibid., p. 107.
20   Ibid., p. 98.
21   Ibid., p. 118.
22   Watts. "The 'Positive Disintegration' of Buddhism". p. 102.

er of the Buddhist NGO movement, spoke of a "global civil society" (*chikyu shimin-shakai*) and encouraged Japanese Buddhists to develop solidarity with the citizens of the South, especially in Asia. INEB Japan founder, Rev. Maruyama Teruo, as an ex-Marxist developed a post-ideological process philosophy, akin to the Four Noble Truths, based on no single truth or essence. Buddhist economist Nishikawa Jun worked tirelessly to build bridges with other Asian nations in developing an indigenous paradigm for Asian civil society based in the Buddhist concept of *kaihotsu*. His fellow Buddhist development expert, Nakamura Hisashi, also created a vision of an Asian dharmic civil society.

From an activist standpoint, the Nipponzan Myoho-ji continues to define such participation in civil society with its unique form of dharmic civil protest. Finally, in his latest writing, Shimazono Susumu, as one of Japan's leading public intellectuals, has considered the role of autonomous social ethics through the concept of True Dharma (正法 *shobo*). As I have used the writings of Nakamura Hajime as a foundation for this volume, Shimazono has also used Nakamura's work on early Buddhist social ethics and Ashoka to argue:

> In a society with a democratic orientation, however, Buddhism would actively recognize the existence of other religions and non-religions, accepting them as one in a pluralistic range of thought and religion, and, as such, embodying Buddhism in society. This means recognizing freedom of religion and separation of church and state (the non-monopolization of authority by a single religion) as well as developing the concept of embodying Buddhist ideals and ideas in the public space while spreading them throughout society.
>
> The idea is that a public religion should have a religious foundation but can only speak out and act in a democratic society where diverse ideas coexist. In this way, the social ethics of religion can be transmitted into the world.... While secularization has caused one aspect of religion's influence to recede, it has also given rise to the possibility that religions that are aware of their role as public religions will increase their influence.[23]

For Shimazono—along with the numerous social activists, public

---

23 Shimazono. *Social Ethics in Modern Japanese Buddhism*. pp. 324-26.

intellectuals, and religious persons we have detailed in this first volume—the key to such a healthy public religion and, hence, healthy or dharmic civil society is the issue of autonomy as either *shutaisei* or *jiritsusei* in Japanese society. As we have detailed, bastardized forms of Neo-Confucianism, Shinto, Zen, and liberal utilitarianism have not provided Japanese with such autonomy of thought in the modern era. Perhaps anachronistically, this lack of autonomy has become attributed to Japanese cultural essence, and, indeed, the modern promoters of archaic Japanese exceptionalism would paint the devotion to collective harmony (*wa*) and respect for elders as the cornerstones of Japanese identity.

As we have also seen, however, Buddhism has contributed to the formation of Japanese character and culture from the beginning in different ways. Prince Shotoku attempted to build the first Japanese nation upon the universal standard of dharma. The Kamakura Buddhist revolutionaries of Honen, Shinran, Dogen, and Nichiren taught a deep form of Buddhist autonomy and social ethics from which to critically evaluate and build society. Even amidst the rise of the imperial nation state, Buddhists articulated critical evaluations of society along with progressive social programs to embody dharmic social ethics in service of the suffering. These legacies are not forgotten among Japanese Buddhists in the 21st century. Volume II will detail how they are attempting to revive such autonomous Buddhist social ethics through reaching out to those who have lost karmic connection (*mu-en*) and working to build dharmic civil society.

List of Works Cited

Adler, Joseph A. "Chance and Necessity in Zhu Xi's Conceptions of Heaven and Tradition". *European Journal for Philosophy of Religion*. Spring 2016. Vol. 8, No. 1.

Adolphson, Mikael S. *The Teeth and Claws of the Buddha: Monastic Warriors and Sohei in Japanese History*. (Honolulu: University of Hawaii Press, 2007).

Alldritt, Leslie D. "The Burakumin: The Complicity of Japanese Buddhism in Oppression and an Opportunity for Liberation". *Journal of Buddhist Ethics*. 2000. No. 7. http://jbe.gold.ac.uk/7/alldritt001.html, Takemasa. *Japan's New Left Movements: Legacies for Civil Society*. (London: Routledge, 2014).

Anheier, Halmut; Glasius, Marlies & Kaldor, Mary. "Introducing Global Civil Society". In *Global Civil Society 2001*. Ed. Halmut Anheier, Marlies Glasius, & Mary Kaldor. (Oxford University Press, 2001).

Arima, Jitsujo 有馬実成. "Understanding Buddhism through Development Studies" (開発の学としての仏教を学んだ *Kaihatsu-no gaku-to-shite-no bukkyo-wo mananda*). In Wongkul, Pitthaya ピッタヤー・ウォンクーン. *Development Monks who Repay Their Debt of Gratitude to the Village People*. (村の衆には借りがある: 報徳の開発僧侶 *Mura-no shu-ni-wa kari-ga aru: Hotoku-no kaihatsu soryo*). (Nontaburi, Thailand: Sangsan Publishing Co. Ltd., 1993).

Becker, Carl. B. "Embracing the Pure Land Vision: Coming to Grips with Dying through Living". In *Never Die Alone: Death as Birth in Pure Land Buddhism*. Eds. Jonathan S. Watts & Yoshiharu Tomatsu. (Tokyo: Jodo Shu Press, 2008).

Bellah, Robert. *Tokugawa Religion: The Cultural Roots of Modern Japan*. (New York: The Free Press, 1985).

Blum, Mark L. "Never Die Alone: *Shonen* as Intersubjective Experience". In *Never Die Alone: Death as Birth in Pure Land Buddhism*. Eds. Jonathan S. Watts & Yoshiharu Tomatsu. (Tokyo: Jodo Shu Press, 2008).

Bodiford, William M. *Soto Zen in Medieval Japan*. (Honolulu: University of Hawaii Press, 1993).

— "Zen and the Art of Religious Prejudice: Efforts to Reform a Tradition of Social Discrimination". *Japanese Journal of Religious Studies*. 1996. Vol. 23, No. 1-2.

Buddhadasa, Bhikkhu. *Seeing with the Eye of Dhamma*. Trans. Dhammavidu Bhikkhu & Santikaro Upasaka. (Boulder, Colorado: Shamabala Publications, Inc., 2022).

Buruma, Ian. "A New Japanese Nationalism". *New York Times*. April 12, 1987.

Chappell, David W. (Ed.) *Buddhist Peacework: Creating Cultures of Peace*. (Boston: Wisdom Publications, 1999).

Collcutt, Martin. *Five Mountains: The Rinzai Zen Monastic Institution in Medieval Japan*. (Cambridge: Harvard University Press, 1981).

Conference on "Article 9 of the Japanese Peace Constitution and Peace in Asia-Prayer from Okinawa". The 7th Global Inter-religious Conference on Article 9 of the Japanese Peace Constitution. March 2-3, 2021.

"The Constitution of Prince Shotoku". *Asia for Educators*. (Columbia University). http://afe.easia.columbia.edu/ps/japan/shotoku.pdf

Covell, Stephen G. *Japanese Temple Buddhism: Worldliness in a Religion of Renunciation*. (Honolulu: University of Hawai'i Press, 2006).

Davis, Bret W. "The Kyoto School". *The Stanford Encyclopedia of Philosophy*. (Summer

2019 Edition). Eds. Edward N. Zalta & Uri Nodelman. https://plato.stanford.edu/archives/win2022/entries/kyoto-school/.

Davis, Winston. *Japanese Religion and Society: Paradigms of Structure and Change.* (Albany: State University of New York Press, 1992).

Dewey, John. *The Public and Its Problems: An Essay in Political Inquiry.* (Chicago: Gateway Books, 1946).

— "John Dewey in Japan". In Education in Japan Community Blog. July 6, 2005. https://educationinjapan.wordpress.com/of-methods-philosophies/johndewey-in-japan/

The *Digital Dictionary of Buddhism.* Ed. Charles Muller. http://www.buddhism-dict.net/ddb/

Eisenstadt, S.N. *Japanese Civilization: A Comparative View.* (London: University of Chicago Press, 1996).

Fairley, Peter. "Can Japan Recapture Its Solar Power?" *MIT Technology Review.* December 18, 2014. https://www.technologyreview.com/s/533451/can-japanrecapture-its-solar-power/

Fields, Rick. *How the Swans Came to the Lake: A Narrative History of Buddhism in America.* (Boulder, CO: Shambhala Publications, 1992).

Frühstück, Sabine. *Gender and Sexuality in Modern Japan.* (Cambridge University Press, 2022).

Fujii, Nichidatsu. *My Non-Violence: An Autobiography of a Japanese Buddhist.* Trans. T. Yamaori. (Tokyo: Japan Buddha Sangha Press, 1975).

— *Buddhism for World Peace.* Trans. Yumiko Miyazaki. (Tokyo: Japan-Bharat Sarvodaya Mitra Sangha, 1980).

Fujiyama Midori 藤山みどり. "The Religious Community's Perception of History: War Responsibility Statements and Beyond" (宗教界の歴史認識〜戦争責任表明とその後 *Shukyokai-no rekishi ninshiki: Senso-sekinin hyomei-to sono-ato*). The Center for Information on Religion 宗教情報センター (*Shukyo Joho Senta*). June 18, 2015. https://www.circam.jp/reports/02/detail/id=5631

Garon, Sheldon. "From Meiji to Heisei: The State and Civil Society in Japan". In *The State of Civil Society in Japan.* Eds. Frank J. Schwartz & Susan J. Pharr. (Cambridge University Press, 2003).

Gaus, Gerald; Courtland, Shane D.; and Schmidtz, David. "Liberalism". In *The Stanford Encyclopedia of Philosophy* (Fall 2020 Edition), Ed. Edward N. Zalta. https://plato.stanford.edu/archives/fall2020/entries/liberalism/.

"Going round in circles Japan readies itself for an unpredictable ballot. The ruling party's leadership contest may matter more than the next national election". *The Economist.* September 23, 2021.

Habito, Ruben L.F. "Tendai *Hongaku* Doctrine and Japan's Ethnocentric Turn". In *Pruning the Bodhi Tree: The Storm over Critical Buddhism.* Eds. Jamie Hubbard & Paul L. Swanson. (Honolulu: University of Hawaii Press, 1997).

Hakamaya Noriaki. "Thoughts on the Ideological Background of Social Discrimination". Trans. Jamie Hubbard. In *Pruning the Bodhi Tree: The Storm over Critical Buddhism.* Eds. Jamie Hubbard & Paul L. Swanson. (Honolulu: University of Hawaii Press, 1997).

Hardacre, Helen. *Kurozumikyo and the New Religions of Japan.* (Princeton, New Jersey: Princeton University Press, 1986).

— "After Aum: Religion and Civil Society in Japan". In *The State of Civil Society in Japan.* Eds. Frank J. Schwartz & Susan J. Pharr. (Cambridge University Press, 2003).

— "Religion and Civil Society in Contemporary Japan". *Japanese Journal of Religious Studies.* 2004. Vol. 31, No. 2.

Harootunian, Harry D. *Overcome by Modernity: History, Culture, and Community in Interwar Japan*. (Princeton: Princeton University Press. 2002).

Heine, Steven. "Critical Buddhism and Dogen's *Shobogenzo*: The Debate over the 75-Fascicle and 12-Fascicle Texts". In *Pruning the Bodhi Tree: The Storm over Critical Buddhism*. Eds. Jamie Hubbard & Paul L. Swanson. (Honolulu: University of Hawaii Press, 1997).

Heisig, James W. *Philosophers of Nothingness: An Essay on the Kyoto School*. (Honolulu: University of Hawai'i Press, 2001).

Higaki, Tatsuya. "Kenji Miyazawa and Takaaki Yoshimoto: Schizophrenic Nature in Japanese Thought". In *Deleuze and Buddhism*. Eds. Tony See & Joff Bradley. (New York: Springer, 2016).

Honen. *Honen the Buddhist Saint: His Life and Teaching*. Trans. Harper Havelock Coates & Ryugaku Ishizuka. (Kyoto: Chion-in Temple, 1925).

— *Honen's Senchakushu: Passages on the Selection of the Nembutsu in the Original Vow* (*Senchaku hongan nembutsu-shu*). (Honolulu: University of Hawaii Press; Tokyo: Taisho University Sogo Bukkyo Kenkyujo, 1998).

— *Traversing the Pure Land Path: A Lifetime of Encounters with Honen Shonin*. Eds. Jonathan S. Watts & Yoshiharu Tomatsu. (Tokyo: Jodo Shu Press, 2005).

Hoston, Germaine A. "Ikkoku Shakai-shugi: Sano Manabu and the Limits of Marxism as Cultural Criticism". In *Culture and Identity: Japanese Intellectuals During the Interwar Years*. Ed. J. Thomas Rimer (Princeton University Press, 1990).

— "The State, Modernity, and the Fate of Liberalism in Prewar Japan". *The Journal of Asian Studies*. May, 1992. Vol. 51, No. 2.

Hovhannisyan, Astghik. "The Testimony of a Victim of Forced Sterilization in Japan: Kita Saburo". *The Asia-Pacific Journal*. Japan Focus. Apr 1, 2020. Vol. 18:7, No. 2.

Hrebenar, Ronald J. and Haraguchi, Koji. "The Fall of the DPJ and Return of the LDP to Power: The December 2012 House Election". In *Party Politics in Japan: Political Chaos and Stalemate in the 21st Century*. Eds. Ronald J. Hrebenar & Akira Nakamura. (Abingdon: Routledge, 2015).

Hughes, Llewelyn. "Energy Policy in Japan: Revisiting Radical Incrementalism". In *The Oxford Handbook of Japanese Politics*. Eds. Robert J. Pekkanen & Saadia M. Pekkanen. (Oxford University Press, 2021).

Ichikawa, Hakugen 市川白弦. *Religion under Japanese Fascism* (日本ファシズム下の宗教 *Nihon fashizumu-ka-no shukyo*). (Tokyo: Enuesu Publishing エヌエス出版会, 1975).

Igarashi, Akio. *Japanese Contemporary Politics*. Eds. Mark E. Caprio & Miranda Schreurs. (London: Routledge, 2018).

Ikeda, Daisaku. "John Dewey and Tsunesaburo Makiguchi". Center for Dewey Studies. Accessed March 31, 2022. https://deweycenter.siu.edu/publicationspapers/john-dewey-and-tsunesaburo-makiguchi.php

Ives, Christopher. "Ethical Pitfalls in Imperial Zen and Nishida Philosophy: Ichikawa Hakugen's Critique". In *Rude Awakenings: Zen, the Kyoto School, & the Question of Nationalism*. (Honolulu, University of Hawaii Press, 1995).

— *Imperial-Way Zen: Ichikawa Hakugen's Critique and Lingering Questions for Buddhist Ethics*. (Honolulu: University of Hawaii Press, 2009).

"The Japan Buddhist Federation Appeal for a Lifestyle without Dependence on Nuclear Power". In *This Precious Life: Buddhist Tsunami Relief and Anti-Nuclear Activism in Post 3/11 Japan*. 2nd Edition. Ed. Jonathan S. Watts. (Yokohama: International Buddhist Exchange Center, 2012/2016).

Japan Ministry of Health, Labor, and Welfare. The Issue and Situation of Irregular

Employment (「非正規雇用」の現状と課題 *"Hiseiki Koyo"-no Jotai-to Kadai*). https://www.mhlw.go.jp/content/000830221.pdf
Jaffe, Richard. "Meiji Religious Policy, Soto Zen, and the Clerical Marriage Problem". *Japanese Journal of Religious Studies*. 1998. Vol. 25, No. 1-2.
Kasahara, Kazuo. *A History of Japanese Religion*. Trans. Paul McCarthy & Gaynor Sekimori. (Tokyo: Kosei Publishing, 2001).
Kersten, Rikki. *Democracy in Postwar Japan: Maruyama Masao and the Search for Autonomy*. (London: Routledge 1996).
— "Postwar Japanese Political Philosophy: Marxism, Liberalism, and the Quest for Autonomy". In *The Oxford Handbook of Japanese Philosophy*. Ed. Bret W. Davis. (Oxford University Press, 2019).
Ketelaar, James E. *Of Heretics and Martyrs in Meiji Japan: Buddhism and Its Persecution*. (Princeton, NJ: Princeton University Press, 1990).
Kisala. Robert. *Prophets of Peace: Pacifism and Cultural Identity in Japan's New Religions*. (Honolulu: University of Hawaii Press, 1999).
Kitagawa, Joseph M. *On Understanding Japanese Religion*. (Princeton, NJ: Princeton University Press, 1987).
Klein, Axel & McLaughlin, Levi. "Komeito: The Party and Its Place in Japanese Politics". In *The Oxford Handbook of Japanese Politics*. Eds. Robert J. Pekkanen & Saadia M. Pekkanen. (Oxford University Press, 2021).
Koellner, Patrick. "The Triumph and Fall of the Democratic Party of Japan". In *Party Politics in Japan: Political Chaos and Stalemate in the 21st Century*. Eds. Ronald J. Hrebenar & Akira Nakamura. (Abingdon: Routledge, 2015).
"Komei-to to approve deployment of Self-Defense Forces to Iraq as part of ruling coalition party". (公明、自衛隊イラク派遣を容認へ連立与党として判断 *Komei, ji-ei-tai Iraku-haken-wo yonin-he ren-ritsu yo-to-toshite handan*). *Asahi Newpaper*. December 4, 2003. http://www.asahi.com/special/iraqrecovery/TKY200312030393.html
Kono, Taitsu 河野太通. *Confrontational Buddhism: Concepts of Modern Religion* (戦う仏教： 現代宗教論 *Tatakau Bukkyo: Gendai Shukyo-ron*). (Tokyo: Shunjunsha Publishers 春秋社, 2011).
— "Nuclear Power is Incompatible with the Way of the Buddha: A Declaration from Critical Self-Reflection on Past Mistakes". In *Lotus in the Nuclear Sea: The Promise of Buddhism in the Nuclear Age*. Ed. Jonathan S. Watts (Yokohama: International Buddhist Exchange Center IBEC, 2013).
Kosambi, D. D. *Ancient India: A History of Its Culture and Civilization*. (Cleveland: Meridian Books, 1969).
Koschmann, J. Victor. "The Debate on Subjectivity in Postwar Japan: Foundations of Modernism as a Political Critique". *Pacific Affairs*. Winter, 1981-1982. Vol. 54, No.4.
Kuroda, Toshio 黒田俊雄. *Temple and Shrine Forces: Another Medieval Society* (寺社勢力もう一つ中世の社会 *Jisha sei-ryoku: Mo-hitotsu chusei-no shakai*). (Tokyo: Iwanami Shoten 岩波書店, 1980).
— "The Development of the *Kenmitsu* System as Japan's Medieval Orthodoxy". Trans. by James C. Dobbins. *Japanese Journal of Religious Studies*. 1996. Vol. 23, No.3-4.
— "The Imperial Law and the Buddhist Law". Trans. Jacqueline I. Stone. *Japanese Journal of Religious Studies*. 1996. Vol. 23, No.3-4.
— "Buddhism and Society in the Medieval Estate System". Trans. Suzanne Gay. *Japanese Journal of Religious Studies*. 1996. Vol. 23, No. 3-4.
— "The Discourse on the 'Land of the Kami' (*Shinkoku*) in Medieval Japan". Trans. Fabio Rambelli. *Japanese Journal of Religious Studies*. 1996. Vol. 23, No.3-4.
— "The World of Spirit Pacification: Issues of State and Religion". Trans. Allan Grapard.

Japanese Journal of Religious Studies. 1996. Vol. 23, No. 3-4.

Lafleur, William R. "A Turning in Taisho: Asia and Europe in the Early Writings of Watsuji Tetsuro". In *Culture and Identity: Japanese Intellectuals During the Interwar Years.* Ed. J. Thomas Rimer (Princeton University Press, 1990).

Large, Stephen S. "For Self and Society: Seno-o Giro and Buddhist Socialism in the Postwar Japanese Peace Movement". In *The Japanese Trajectory: Modernization and Beyond.* Eds. Gavan McCormack & Yoshio Sugimoto. (Cambridge University Press, 1988).

Loy, David R. "Language Against Its Own Mystifications: Deconstruction in Nagarjuna and Dogen". *Philosophy East & West.* 1999. Vol. 49, No. 3.

— *A Buddhist History of the West: Studies in Lack.* (Albany, NY: State University of New York Press, 2002)

— *Ecodharma: Buddhist Teachings for the Ecological Crisis.* (Somerville, MA: Wisdom Publications, 2019).

Machida, Soho. *Renegade Monk: Honen and Japanese Pure Land Buddhism.* Ed. & Trans. Ioannis Mentzas. (Berkeley: University of California Press, 1999).

Macy, Joanna. *Mutual Causality in Buddhism and General Systems Theory.* (Albany, NY: State University of New York Press, 1991).

Marcuse, Herbert. *Heideggerian Marxism.* Eds. Richard Wolin & John Abromeit (Lincoln: University of Nebraska Press, 2005).

Marra, Michele. "The Development of *Mappo* Thought in Japan (I)". *Japanese Journal of Religious Studies.* 1988. Vol. 15, No. 1.

— "The Development of *Mappo* Thought in Japan (II)". *Japanese Journal of Religious Studies.* 1988. Vol. 15, No. 4.

Maruyama, Teruo. "The Methodology of Truth: A Nichiren Priest's Struggle for a Socially Valid Buddhism". In *Entering the Realm of Reality: Towards Dhammic Societies.* Eds. Jonathan Watts, Alan Senauke & Santikaro Bhikkhu. (Bangkok: International Network of Engaged Buddhists, 1998).

Marx, Karl. *A Contribution to the Critique of Hegel's Philosophy of Right. Introduction.* Trans. Joseph O'Malley. (Oxford University Press, 1970)

Matsumoto, Shiro. "Buddhism and the Kami: Against Japanism". Trans. by Jamie Hubbard. In *Pruning the Bodhi Tree: The Storm over Critical Buddhism.* Eds. Jamie Hubbard & Paul L. Swanson. (Honolulu: University of Hawaii Press, 1997).

Matsunaga, Alicia and Daigan. *Foundation of Japanese Buddhism: Vol. II The Mass Movement.* (Los Angeles: Buddhist Books International, 1976).

McCullough, David. "Moral and Social Education in Japanese Schools: Conflicting Conceptions of Citizenship". *Citizenship Teaching and Learning.* July 2008. Vol 4, No. 1.

McLaughlin, Levi. "Soka Gakkai in Japan". In *Handbook for Contemporary Japanese Religions.* Eds. Inken Prohl & John K. Nelson. (Leiden, Netherlands: Koninklijke Brill, 2012).

— "Komeito's Soka Gakkai Protesters and Supporters: Religious Motivations for Political Activism in Contemporary Japan". *The Asia-Pacific Journal.* October 12, 2015. Vol. 13, No. 41:1.

Moriya, Tomoe. "Social Ethics of 'New Buddhists' at the Turn of the Twentieth Century: A Comparative Study of Suzuki Daisetsu and Inoue Shuten". *Japanese Journal of Religious Studies.* 2005. Vol. 32, No. 2.

Murakami, Shigeyoshi. *Japanese Religion in the Modern Century.* Trans. H. Byron Earhart. (Tokyo: University of Tokyo Press, 1980).

Nakajima, Takahiro. "The Restoration of Confucianism in China and Japan: A New Source of Morality and Religion". In *Frontiers of Japanese Philosophy 4: Facing the 21st*

Century. Eds. Wing Keung Lam & Ching Yuen Cheung. (Nagoya: Nanzan Institute for Religion & Culture, 2009).

Nakamura, Hajime. *Ways of Thinking of Eastern Peoples India-China-Tibet-Japan*. Revised English Translation. Ed. Philip P. Wiener. (University of Hawaii Press, 1964).

Nakamura, Hisashi. "Nakamura, Hisashi". In *The Asian Future: Dialogues for Change*. Vol. 2. Eds. Pracha Hutanuwatr & Ramu Manivannan. (London, Zed Books, 2005), p. 184.

— Personal interview. November 13, 2021

Nara, Yasuaki. "The Soto Zen School in Modern Japan". https://www.thezensite.com/ZenEssays/DogenStudies/Soto_Zen_in_Japan.html

"New Komeito's Role as Partner to the Right Leaning LDP Led Government". *Japan Times*. September 24, 2014. https://www.japantimes.co.jp/opinion/2014/09/24/editorials/new-komeitos-raison-detre/#.W9qgdJP7RaR

Nishikawa, Jun 西川潤. "The Choice of Development Paradigms in Japan after the 3/11 Fukushima Nuclear Disaster". In *This Precious Life: Buddhist Tsunami Relief and Anti-Nuclear Activism in Post 3/11 Japan*. 2nd Edition. Ed. Jonathan S. Watts. (Yokohama: International Buddhist Exchange Center, 2012/2016).

— and Noda, Masato 野田真里. *Buddhism, Development, NGO: Learning from Thai Development Monks the Wisdom of Interbeing* (仏教・開発・NGO 一タイ開発僧に学ぶ共生の智慧 *Bukkyo・Kaihotsu・NGO: Thai kaihotsu-so-ni manabu kyosei-no chie*). (Tokyo: Shinhyoron 新評論, 2001).

Obeyesekere, Gananath. *Imagining Karma: Ethical Transformation in Amerindian, Buddhist, and Greek Rebirth*. (Berkeley, CA: University of California Press, 2002).

Okamoto, Shumpei. "The Emperor and the Crowd: The Historical Significance of the Hibiya Riot". In *Conflict in Modern Japanese History: The Neglected Tradition*. Eds. Tetsuo Najita & J. Victor Koschmann. (Princeton University Press, 1982).

Okano, Masazumi. "Afterword". In *Lotus in the Nuclear Sea: The Promise of Buddhism in the Nuclear Age*. Ed. Jonathan S. Watts (Yokohama: International Buddhist Exchange Center IBEC, 2013).

Olson, Lawrence. "Intellectuals and 'The People': On Yoshimoto Takaaki". *The Journal of Japanese Studies*. Summer, 1978. Vol. 4, No. 2, p. 341.

Paramore, Kiri. "The Nationalization of Confucianism: Academism, Examinations, and Bureaucratic Governance in the Late Tokugawa State". *The Journal of Japanese Studies*. Winter 2012. Vol. 38, No. 1.

— *Japanese Confucianism: A Cultural History* (Cambridge University Press, 2016).

Pharr, Susan. *Losing Face: Status Politics in Japan*. (Berkeley: University of California Press, 1990).

— "Targeting by an Activist State: Japan as a Civil Society Model". In *The State of Civil Society in Japan*. Eds. Frank J. Schwartz & Susan J. Pharr. (Cambridge University Press, 2003).

Pittman, Don A. *Toward a Modern Chinese Buddhism: Taixu's Reforms*. (Honolulu: University of Hawai'i Press, 2001).

Prooi, Dennis. "Tosaka Jun's Critique of Hermeneutics". In *Erasmus Student Journal of Philosophy*. 2016. No. 10.

Queen, Christopher S. "Introduction: The Shapes and Sources of Engaged Buddhism". In *Engaged Buddhism: Buddhist Liberation Movements in Asia*. Eds. Christopher S. Queen & Sallie B. King. (Albany, NY: State University of New York Press, 1996).

Rambelli, Fabio. "Religion, Ideology of Domination, and Nationalism: Kuroda Toshio on the Discourse of *Shinkoku*". *Japanese Journal of Religious Studies*. 1996. Vol. 23, No.3-4.

Repeta, Lawrence & Jones, Colin P.A. "State Power versus Individual Freedom: Japan's

Constitutional Past, Present, and Possible Futures". In *Japan: The Precarious Future*. Eds. Frank Baldwin & Anne Allison (New York University Press, 2015).

Rimer, J. Thomas. "Marxism and Cultural Criticism". In *Culture and Identity: Japanese Intellectuals During the Interwar Years*. Ed. J. Thomas Rimer (Princeton University Press, 1990).

Sakakibara, Ken. "Young officials explain exodus of overworked bureaucrats". *Asahi Shimbun*. March 28, 2022.

Santikaro Bhikkhu. "Buddhadasa Bhikkhu: Life and Society Through the Natural Eyes of Voidness". In *Engaged Buddhism: Buddhist Liberation Movements in Asia*. Eds. Christopher S. Queen & Sallie B. King. (Albany, NY: State University of New York Press, 1996).

— and Visalo, Pra Paisan. "Goodness and Generosity Perverted: The Karma of Capitalist Buddhism in Thailand". In *Rethinking Karma: The Dharma of Social Justice*. Ed. Jonathan S. Watts. (Bangkok: International Network of Engaged Buddhists, 2014).

Sasaki, Fumiko. *Nationalism, Political Realism and Democracy in Japan: The Thought of Masao Maruyama*. (London: Routledge, 2012).

Sato, Hiroaki. "Miyazawa Kenji: The Poet as Asura?". *The Asia-Pacific Journal*. September 3, 2007. Vol. 5, No. 9.

Shields, James Mark. *Against Harmony: Progressive and Radical Buddhism in Modern Japan*. (New York: Oxford University Press, 2017).

Shimada Hajime 島田肇. "Watanabe Kaikyoku's 'Mutual Aid' Philosophy: Social Work as a Holistic and National Project (渡辺海旭の「共済」思想： 全体的・国民的事業としての社会事業 *Watanabe Kaikyoku-no "kyo-sai"-shiso: zentai-teki kokumin-teki jigyo-toshite-no shakai-jigyo*). In *Tokaigakuen University Journal of Interbeing and Culture Studies* (東海学園大学共生文化研究 *Tokaigakuen-daigaku Kyo-sai Bunka Kenkyu*). March 31, 2016. Vol. 1, No. 1 創刊号.

Shimazono, Susumu 島薗進. *From Salvation to Spirituality: Popular Religious Movements in Modern Japan*. (Melbourne: Trans Pacific Press, 2004).

— "Zen, Imperial Way, and War: How Imperial Way Zen Developed". (禅・皇道・戦争-皇道禅を導き出したもの *Zen-Kodo-Senso: Kodo-zen-wo michibiki-dashita-mono*). In *Samgha Japan: Expanded Edition 5, Zen: Roots, Present, Future, World*. February, 2019. (増補版・禅ルーツ・現在・未来・世界—別冊サンガジャパンVol. 5. 2019年2月).

— Personal Interview. October 23, 2021.

— *Social Ethics in Modern Japanese Buddhism: Living by "True Dharma"* (近代日本仏教の社会倫理： 正法を生きる *Kindai Nihon Bukkyo-no shakai-rinri: Shobo-wo ikiru*). (Tokyo: Iwanami-shoten 岩波書店, 2022)

Shimizu, Hitoshi 清水均. *Basic Knowledge of Contemporary Terminology* (現代用語の基礎知識 *Gendai-yogo-no kiso-chishiki*). (Tokyo: Jiyu Kokumin-sha 自由国民社, 1999).

Shoji, Jun-ichiro. "Historical Perception in Postwar Japan: Concerning the Pacific War". National Institute for Defense Studies (防衛研究所 *Boei Kenkyujo*). *NIDS Security Reports*. March 2003. No.4.

Silberman, Bernard S. "The Bureaucratic State in Japan: The Problem of Authority and Legitimacy". In *Conflict in Modern Japanese History: The Neglected Tradition*. Eds. Tetsuo Najita & J. Victor Koschmann. (Princeton University Press, 1982).

Smith, Robert J. "The Japanese (Confucian) Family: The Tradition from the Bottom Up". In *Confucian Traditions in East Asian Modernity*. Ed. Tu Wei-Ming. (Cambridge: Harvard University Press, 1996).

"Soka Gakkai Volunteers Submit 'Signatures Against Iraq' to Komei Party". (創価学会有志、「イラク反対署名」を公明に提出 Sokka Gakkai yushi, 'Iraku-hantai-shomei'-wo komei-ni tei-shutsu). *Asahi Newspaper*. January 21, 2004. http://www.asahi.com/special/jieitai/TKY200401210318.html

Stone, Jacqueline I. "A Vast and Grave Task: Interwar Buddhist Studies as an Expression of Japan's Envisioned Global Role". In *Culture and Identity: Japanese Intellectuals During the Interwar Years*. Ed. J. Thomas Rimer (Princeton University Press, 1990).

— "Rebuking the Enemies of the Lotus: Nichirenist Exclusivism in Historical Perspective". *Japanese Journal of Religious Studies*. 1994. Vol. 21, No.2-3.

— "Placing Nichiren in the 'Big Picture': Some Ongoing Issues in Scholarship". *Japanese Journal of Religious Studies*. 1999. Vol. 26, No. 3-4.

— "When Disobedience Is Filial and Resistance Is Loyal: The *Lotus Sutra* and Social Obligations in the Medieval Nichiren Tradition". In *A Buddhist Kaleidoscope: Essays on the Lotus Sutra*. Ed. Gene Reeves. (Tokyo, Kosei Publishing Co., 2002).

— *Original Enlightenment and the Transformation of Medieval Japanese Buddhism*. (Honolulu: University of Hawaii Press, 2003).

— "Nichiren's Activist Heirs: Soka Gakkai, Rissho Koseikai, Nipponzan Myohoji". In *Action Dharma: New Studies in Engaged Buddhism*. Eds. Christopher Queen, Charles Prebish, & Damien Keown. (London: RoutledgeCurzon, 2003).

Sueki, Fumihiko. "A Reexamination of the *Kenmitsu Taisei* Theory". *Japanese Journal of Religious Studies*. 1996. Vol. 23, No. 3-4.

Summary Data on Suicide for 2008 (平成20年中における自殺の概要資料 *Heisei niju-nen-chu-ni okeru ji-satsu-no gaiyo-shiryo*). National Police Agency Department of Community Safety (警察庁生活安全局 *keisatsu-cho seikatsu anzen kyoku*). May 2009.

Suzuki, Daisetz T. *Zen and Japanese Culture*. (Tokyo: Charles E. Tuttle Co., 1959).

Swanson, Paul L. "Why They Say Zen Is Not Buddhism: Recent Japanese Critiques of Buddha-Nature". *Pruning the Bodhi Tree: The Storm over Critical Buddhism*. Eds. Jamie Hubbard & Paul L. Swanson. (Honolulu: University of Hawaii Press, 1997).

Swearer, Donald K. "Sulak Sivaraksa's Buddhist Vision for Renewing Society". In *Engaged Buddhism: Buddhist Liberation Movements in Asia*. Eds. Christopher S. Queen & Sallie B. King. (Albany, NY: State University of New York Press, 1996).

Tamamuro, Fumio. "Local Society and the Temple-Parishioner Relationship within the *Bakufu*'s Governance Structure". *Japanese Journal of Religious Studies*. 2001. Vol. 28, No. 3-4.

Tamura, Yoshiro. *Japanese Buddhism: A Cultural History*. (Tokyo: Kosei Publishing, 2000).

Tsurumi, E. Patricia. "Meiji Primary School Language and Ethics Textbooks: Old Values for a New Society?" *Modern Asian Studies*. 1974. Vol. 8, No. 2.

Tucker, John. "Japanese Confucian Philosophy". In *The Stanford Encyclopedia of Philosophy*. Spring 2018 Edition. Eds. Edward N. Zalta & Uri Nodelman. https://plato.stanford.edu/archives/win2022/entries/japanese-confucian/.

Uemura Kunihiko 植村邦彦. "Does 'Civil Society' Really Exist in Japan?" (日本に「市民社会」は存在しないのか? *Nihon-ni "shimin-shakai"-wa sonzai-shinai-no-ka?*). In *Synodos – Academic Journalism On-Line*. January 12, 2018. https://synodos.jp/society/20931.

Victoria, Brian. *Zen at War*. (New York: Weatherhill, 1997).

— "Soka Gakkai Founder, Makiguchi Tsunesaburo, A Man of Peace?". *The Asia-Pacific Journal*. August 4, 2014. Vol. 12, No. 37.

Vogel, Steven K. "The Rise and Fall of the Japanese Bureaucracy". In *The Oxford Handbook of Japanese Politics*. Eds. Robert J. Pekkanen & Saadia M. Pekkanen.

(Oxford University Press, 2021).

"Vox Populi: Extreme work hours crushing staff in seat of Japanese power". *Asahi Shimbun*. March 9, 2021.

Watanabe, Kaikyoku 渡辺海旭. *The Complete Writings of Kogetsu Vol. II.* (壺月全集刊行會下巻 *Kogetsu-zen-shu kanko-kai, Ge-kan*). (Tokyo: Daito Shuppan-sha 大東出版社, 1933).

Watts, Jonathan S. "A Brief Overview of Buddhist NGOs in Japan". *Japanese Journal of Religious Studies*. 2004. Vol. 31, No. 2.

— "Karma for Everyone: Social Justice and the Problem of Re-ethicizing Karma in Theravada Buddhist Societies". In *Rethinking Karma: The Dharma of Social Justice*. Ed. Jonathan S. Watts. (Bangkok: International Network of Engaged Buddhists, 2014).

— "The 'Positive Disintegration' of Buddhism: Reformation and Deformation in the Sri Lankan Sangha". In *Rethinking Karma: The Dharma of Social Justice*. Ed. Jonathan S. Watts. (Bangkok: International Network of Engaged Buddhists, 2014).

— and Okano, Masazumi. "Reconstructing Priestly Identity and Roles and the Development of Socially Engaged Buddhism in Contemporary Japan". In *Handbook for Contemporary Japanese Religions*. Eds. Inken Prohl & John K. Nelson. (Leiden, Netherlands: Koninklijke Brill, 2012).

Williams, Paul. *Mahayana Buddhism: The Doctrinal Foundations*. (London: Routledge, 1989).

Yasumaru, Yoshio 安丸良夫. *Japan's Modernization and Popular Thought*. (日本の近代化と民衆思想 *Nihon-no kindaika-to minshu shiso*). (Tokyo: Aoki Shoten 青木書店, 1974).

Yoda, Tomiko 依田富子. "The Rise and Fall of Maternal Society: Gender, Labor, and Capital in Contemporary Japan". In *Japan After Japan: Social and Cultural Life from the Recessionary 1990s to the Present*. Eds. Tomiko Yoda & Harry Harootunian. (Durham, NC: Duke University Press, 2006).

Yuzuru, Demachi. "Zen and Politics: The Counsel of Yamamoto Genpo". Nippon.com. May 9, 2017. https://www.nippon.com/en/views/b06103/

Zen and War. Documentary film directed by Alexander Oey. (Netherlands: Buddhist Broadcasting Foundation (BOS), 2013).

Index

A

anarchism 158, 166, 180, 188, 192, 258, 297 see also socialism

ancestor worship/veneration 12-13, 28-29, 37-38, 40, 78, 83-85, 96, 102-09, 125, 131, 206, 239 ancestral spirit/buddha (仏 hotoke) 105, 107

ascetics/itinerants (聖 hijiri) 42-46, 56-57, 61, 65, 81, 101 nenbutsu hijiri 念仏聖 58 kanjin hijiri (勧進 kanjin: pledge book) 102 En-no-Gyoja 役行者 42 Kuya 空也 58

autonomy (主体性 shutaisei) 111, 193, 196, 206, 224-30, 233-35, 242, 247, 254, 256-60, 304, 308, 312 as jiritsusei 自立性 233-35, 303, 3009 as jiritsusei 自律性 256-57, 272, 300, 303, 308-09, 312 as autonomous Buddhist social ethics (自律的な仏教社会倫理 jiritsu-teki-na Bukkyo shakai-rinri) 300, 301, 309, 311 Miki Kiyoshi 三木清 194-96, 225, 227, 258 Tosaka Jun 戸坂潤 194-96, 225, 227

axialization 20-24, 34-35, 38, 42, 45, 56-59, 64, 73, 82-83, 92, 96, 117, 122-25, 128-29, 148, 157, 170, 173, 178, 181, 201, 223-24, 230, 236-37, 279, 299, 310-11 see also social ethics: civilizational ethics

B

Brahmanism/Vedism/Hinduism 28, 32-34, 38, 74, 77, 86 Japanized gods of fortune 32 karma as duty & Bhagavad-Gita 165 karma as ritual 74, 110, 260 Upanishads 32, 45 Vedic caste system 29, 33, 45, 51, 74-75, 81, 86, 109, 111-13, 121, 189, 222, 263 Vedic sacrifice 44

buddha-nature (仏性 bussho) 39 n.35, 44, 50-51, 61, 67-71, 158, 188, 191, 298 womb of the Tathagata (Skt. tathagata-garbha 如来蔵 nyorai-zo) 39, 50-51, 69-70, 188 Treatise on the Awakening of Mahayana Faith (大乗起信論 Daijo kishin-ron) 50-51, 69, 188 Srimala Sutra (勝鬘經 Shoman-gyo) 39 n.35, 71 n.20 see also innate enlightenment

burakumin 部落民 & dowa 同和 35, 109-13, 150, 156, 172, 183, 189, 263-65 see also Japanese political structure: class/caste system

bureaucracy 9, 11, 122, 124, 137, 159, 162, 202, 240, 243, 247-54, 260, 272, 286-89, 298 Confucianism 109, 115, 126, 144, 170-71, 196, 251 Iron Triangle with politicians, corporates 160, 248, 287 utilitarianism 145, 163-64, 167, 180, 203, 286, 303

C

capitalism 19, 116, 143-45, 161, 170-71, 187-88, 196, 223, 271, 273, 280, 297, 301, 303, 307 Buddhism 180, 215, 221, 240-43, 256 Japanese corporate model 9, 207, 240, 250-51, 305, 307

Cambodia 48, 215, 220, 268-69, 270, 274

Chinese Buddhism
development of 62 importation 29-30, 32, 36 memorial services 102 Tang & Song cultural influence 80, 99, 103, 129-30

Christianity 20-21, 34, 88, 92-93, 95-96, 100-01, 112, 122-25, 128-30, 138-148, 155, 157, 179, 232, 253 n.145, 269, 297, 301-03 American Puritans 129, 148, 167 Order to Expel Christian Priests from Japan (伴天連追放令 Ba-te-ren Tsui-horei) 100 Protestant Reformation 128, 129-30, 142, 187, 297, 301-02

civil society (市民社会 shimin-shakai) 144, 167, 225-26, 230, 235, 242-46, 249, 255-56, 260, 267-68, 269-71, 273-275, 278-80, 282-83, 295, 303-12 as consumer movement 236, 248 as NGO/NPO movement 235, 248-49, 269, 270-71, 274, 280, 285, 307-08 public benefit corporations (公益法人

323

ko-eki hojin) 255
Confucianism/Neo-Confucianism 21-22, 28, 38, 41, 107-09, 111, 113-16, 121-27, 137, 139-40, 165, 204, 220, 250 academies for samurai/ "clan school" (藩校 hanko) 123, 138, 143, 155, 196, 203 basis of modern bureaucracy 109, 115, 126, 144, 170-71, 196, 251 capitalism, labor 170-71 Cartesian dualism 144, 171 dialectic of Principle (理 ri) and phenomenal (事 ji) 22, 114, 123-24, 144, 156, 175, 189, 228 five social virtues (五常 go-jo) & five hierarchical relationships (五倫 go-rin) 108, 125, 146, 152, 206, 249-50 fusion with bushido and Zen 111, 196, 260, 305, 309, 312 fusion with State Shinto (神儒教宗教 shin-jukyo shukyo) 121, 125-26, 136, 142, 146-47, 203, 224, 241, 251, 259, 309, 312 fusion with utilitarianism 143-46 Mandate of Heaven 22, 124, 144, 168 Mito School (水戸学 Mito-gaku) & "Revere the Emperor, expel the barbarians" (尊王攘夷 sonno-joi) 125-28, 130-32, 143, 147, 149 respect for authority 92, 101, 109, 111, 148, 160, 173, 196, 210, 241, 303 Aizawa Seishisai 会沢正志斎 126 , 147 Ito Jinsai 伊藤仁斎 114, 123-24 Mengzi (Mencius) 孟子 38, 114, 168 Motoda Nagazane 元田永孚 146 Ogyu Sorai 荻生徂徠 114, 127, 144 Shibusawa Eiichi 渋沢栄一 170-71 Zhu Xi 朱熹 111, 123, 147

Critical Buddhism (批判仏教 Hihan Bukkyo) 32, 41, 50-51, 78, 141-42, 188-91, 257, 263, 265, 273, 277, 298 Hakamaya Noriaki 袴谷憲昭 32, 41, 50-51, 77, 188-90, 257-58 Matsumoto Shiro 松本史朗 41, 190

D

Death 74-78
ancestral spirit/buddha (仏 hotoke) 105, 107 attainment of buddhahood through funerary rites (成 jobutsu) 105-06 death registries/ necrologies (過去帳 kako-cho) 112 Funeral Buddhism (葬式仏教 Soshiki Bukkyo) 12-14, 102-07, 221, 255-56, 260, 263, 268, 276, 283, 302 memorial services (供養 kuyo or 法事 hoji) 13-14, 37, 102, 105, 112-14, 214, 263, 274 the other world (あの世 ano-yo) 75 posthumous name (戒名 kaimyo) 12, 105, 112 Pure Land Buddhism 66 the realm below (黄泉の国 yomi-no-kuni) 75, 115 Right Mindfulness (Skt. samyak-smriti 正念 sho-nen) 76-77 death bed guide/ "spiritual friend" (Skt. kalyanamitra 善知識 zenchishiki) 76

Dharma, Age of the Final (末法 mappo) 58, 62-64, 66, 68-70, 72-74, 76, 79, 85-87, 99, 128, 180, 211, 239 The Candle of the Latter Dharma (末法燈明記 Mappo tomyo-ki) 63

dharma-raja (moral king) 33 n.21, 38, 48, 86, 107, 114, 280 vs. deva-raja (god king) 42, 46, 86, 96, 107, 125, 126

dialectics
Buddhist/Nagarjuna 69, 174, 190-91, 259 bureaucratic 145 Confucian 123, 144, 156, 175, 189 Hegelian 168, 174, 190 monism/naturalism/Zen 188, 192-94

E

education, Buddhist
humanism (人文主義 jinbun-shugi) 163, 206, 243, 245, 253 modern universities 150, 255 monastic education 12-13 NGO projects 269, 272 temple schools (寺子屋 tera-koya) 123

education, Confucian
academies for samurai/ "clan school" (藩校 hanko) 123, 138, 143, 155, 196 Confucian/Shinto/bushido vs. liberal values 126-27, 130, 141, 145-47,196, 249-51, 289, 303, 305 Imperial Rescript on Education (教育勅語 Kyoiku Chokugo) 147, 206, 210, 249, 303

education, humanism and John Dewey 168, 206-07, 249-50

education, for nationalism/militarism 168, 200

education, postwar moral (道徳 dotoku) 249-51, 289, 305

Index

education, value creation (創価教育 *soka kyoiku*) 206-07, 244

Emperor Meiji & the High Treason Incident of 1910–11 (幸徳事件 *Kotoku-jiken*) 139, 157-58, 162, 183, 188

emptiness (Skt. *shunyata* 空 *ku*) 32, 51-52, 69-70, 129, 170, 186, 189-91, 194, 259, 298, 308 n.13 vs. Hegelian dialectics 190, 192, 259 vs. individualism 170 Madhyamaka teachings 31, 51, 69, 189-90, 258 vs. monism 69-70, 191, 298 in service of violence/war 186 vs. Western/ Cartesian dualism 144 n. 69, 190, 301

esoteric (Vajrayana) Buddhism 48-49, 53 attaining buddhahood in this very body (即身成仏 *sokushin jobutsu*) 50, 71, 73 oral transmission of teachings (口伝 *kuden*) 57, 91 thaumaturgy (magic, performing of miracles) 43, 49, 57-58, 96 medieval Japanese esotericism (顕密体制 *kenmitsu taisei*) 27 n.1, 49-52, 55-57, 62, 65-66, 79-85, 88-90, 93-96, 99-101, 107, 181, 298 Nara esotericism (南密 *nan-mitsu*) 47 Shingon esotericism (東密 *to-mitsu*) 47 Tendai esotericism (台密 *tai-mitsu*) 47 Zen esotericism (禅密 *zen-mitsu*) 80, 89, 94-96, 99, 105-07, 189

F

Four Noble Truths 11, 20, 73, 158, 180, 192, 196, 237 n.104, 275, 277, 299, 311 *see also* Socially Engaged Buddhism

Funeral Buddhism (葬式仏教 *Soshiki Bukkyo*) 12-14, 102-07, 221, 255-56, 260, 263, 268, 276, 283, 302

G

Gyonen 凝然 & the *Record of the Transmission of the Buddha Dharma through the Three Nations* (三國佛法傳通縁起 *Sankoku buppo denzu engi*) 138, 141, 148 *see also* liberalism, Buddhist

H

Hosso school 法相宗 31

I

India
Ambedkar, B.R. 33, 121, 168, 220, 222, 254, 283 Ashoka 27, 37-38, 46, 61, 82, 92, 99, 220, 280, 310-11 Buddhism 33, 40, 44-46, 86, 106-07, 110, 141, 179, 191, 201 as a civilization 21, 23, 135, 138 independence & Gandhi 211-12, 220 non-alignment 218 tribal republics 43-44, 61 world view 37, 44, 62, 64, 78, 128, 174 *see also* Brahmanism/ Vedism/ Hinduism

innate enlightenment (本覚 *hongaku*) 39 n.35, 50-52, 65, 67--74, 77-79, 85, 128, 175, 180-81, 188, 258, 297-98 *see also buddha-nature*

internationalism & Buddhism
Buddhist development (開発 *kaihotsu*) 19, 170, 274, 278, 281, 283, 311 Buddhist missionaries 149 Buddhist NGOs & international relief 223, 245, 248, 267-72, 274-75, 280-82, 285, 290, 311 Buddhist NGO Network (BNN) 246, 269, 281-82 Shanti Volunteer Association (SVA)/ Japan Soto-shu Relief Committee (JSRC) 269, 271-76, 290 AYUS International Buddhist Cooperation Network 269-70, 272, 290 International Network of Engaged Buddhists (INEB) 7, 141, 223, 268, 276-77, 279-80, 311 INEB Japan 277, 311 Japan Network of Engaged Buddhists (JNEB) 7, 277 *see also* Socially Engaged Buddhism World Fellowship of Buddhists (WFB) 267-68 World Parliament of Religions 140-41

J

Japanese nationalism/militarism
imperialism 11, 16, 18, 41, 96, 121, 147, 168, 184, 193-96, 200, 208, 217, 225, 245, 250, 255, 297 ancient autocratic state (古代専制国家 *koda-sensei kokka*) 27-28, 43, 47, 61 "Revere the Emperor, expel the barbarians" (尊王攘夷 *sonno-joi*) 126, 149 sacred state (神政国家 *shinsei kokka*) 46 spiritual protection of state

325

(鎮護国家 *chingo kokka*) 46-47, 149 state authoritarianism (権威主義国家 *ken-i-shugi kokka*) 39 n.38, 41, 51, 107, 111, 122, 125, 144-49, 196, 203, 220, 241, 247, 252-53, 257, 293, 300

Japanese political structure
citizens as *shimin* 市民/ *kokumin* 国民 133, 146, 185, 256 citizens as *kokutai* 国体 national-body, body-politic, national structure, citizens of the state and subjects of the emperor 8, 125-126, 129, 137, 147, 149, 151-52, 159-61, 170, 176, 179, 187, 193, 203-04, 298, 301, 303-04 class/caste system 35, 72, 101 n.213, 105, 109-113, 156, 171, 183, 189, 263, 287 *see also burakumin*. constitution: prewar Meiji 139, 145-47 postwar & Article 9: 10-11, 17, 224, 230, 245, 251, 260-61, 286, 289-93, 295-96, 304 Shotoku's *Seventeen Article Constitution* (十七条憲法 *Ju-shichi-jo kenpo*) 38-39, 41-42, 107, 258 Democratic Party of Japan (DPJ) (民主党 *Minshu-to*) 9, 286-88 division of authority and power 9, 43, 47 n.67, 124-25, 159-61, 202, 225, 248 eugenics 134, 150 expulsion of Buddhism (廃仏毀釈 *haibutsu kishaku* "abolish Buddhism and destroy Shakyamuni") 130-32, 135, 148-49 freedom of religion 136, 199, 251, 303, 311 Iron Triangle of bureaucrats, politicians, corporates 160 248, 287 Liberal Democratic Party (LDP) (自由民主党 *Jiyu-minshu-to*) 9-10, 17-19, 124, 196, 220, 224, 231, 233, 243, 245, 247-48, 252, 260-62, 286-93, 298, 307 response to disasters (Hanshin earthquake 1995, Northeast earthquake 2011) 10, 17, 270, 285-87 Reverse Course (逆コース *gyaku-kosu*) 217, 224, 231, 247 sacralization of law as Buddhist law (仏法 *buppo*) & fusion with imperial law (王法 *obo*) 39, 45, 47-49, 63, 81-82, 88, 89-90, 94, 96, 149 sacralization of ruler as Confucian Mandate of Heaven 22, 124, 144, 168 as Buddhist *dharma-raja* (moral king) 33 n.21, 38, 48, 86, 107, 114, 280 as Hindu *deva-raja* (god king) 42,

46, 86, 96, 107, 125, 126 of Japanese emperor 8, 22-23, 28, 32, 38-41, 43, 47 n.63, 48, 82, 84-86, 99, 107, 115, 121, 124-26, 132, 146-47, 156, 160-61, 163, 168, 175-76, 192, 196, 199, 201-03, 210, 227, 241, 251, 258-59, 293, 298 separation of Buddhist temples and Shinto shrines (神仏分離 *shin-butsu bunri*) 131-32, 146 separation of religion and rule/ church and state (政教分離 *sei-kyo bunri*) 136, 143-47, 159, 175, 188, 251, 297, 303-04, 306 unity of religion and government, unity of rite and rule, theocracy (祭政一致 *saisei-icchi*) 126, 130-31, 134, 135-36, 143 U.S.-Japan Security Treaty (安保 *Anpo*) & self-defense 214-15, 226, 230-33, 286, 290-91

Japanese social culture
ancient history in *Koji-ki* 古事記 126, 173 *Nihon Ryoi-ki* 日本霊異記 44, 45 *Nihon sho-ki* 日本書紀 126 archaic naturalism/nationalism 8, 18, 22-23, 35, 121-30, 138, 140-43, 148-49, 152, 155, 162, 164, 175-77, 180-81, 183, 187, 192-93, 201, 204, 223, 227-229, 234, 240, 243, 257, 273-74, 289, 293, 297, 299, 301, 312 bullying (*ijime*) & elder-younger (先輩後輩 *senpai-kohai*) relationship formation 11, 19, 196, 250-51 clan system 27-38, 43, 84, 305 clan temple (氏寺 *ujidera*) 84 tutelary deity (氏神 *ujigami*) 28, 108 clannish mentality and "limited social nexus" 18-19, 24, 27-38, 40, 42, 56, 59, 74, 78, 81-82, 86, 90-93, 96, 102, 107-09, 122, 201-02, 259, 305, 310 & re-immersion of alternative protest 204, 235, 237, 239, 243, 299 & tribe (族 *zoku*) 22, 171, 202, 234 civilization and enlightenment (文明開化 *bunmei kaika*) movement 23, 136-38, 142-43, 147-48, 151-2, 176, 303-04 collective rights vs. individual rights 10, 125, 137, 145, 166, 168, 170-71, 230, 235, 237, 240, 242, 245, 297-99, 302, 307, 310, 312 contextual identity 169 exceptionalism 18-22, 79, 86-87, 136, 148, 164, 166, 175-76, 193-94, 201, 228, 252, 289, 297, 301, 312 as Theories of

Japanese-ness (日本人論 *Nihonjin-ron*) 252, 253 n.45, 286, 305
harmony (和 *wa*) 33-37, 41, 99, 115, 125, 149, 155, 173, 175, 180, 183, 239-40, 250, 253 n.145, 257-58, 297, 312 morality 18, 20, 35-36, 38, 40-41, 56, 74, 86, 90, 108, 114-16, 124-25, 161-62, 169, 175, 192-93, 200-03, 241, 250-51, 257, 300 public morality vs. religion 146-47, 151-52, 160, 196, 208, 251, 259, 286, 303-04 naturalism 155, 163-65, 173-77, 187-88, 194, 228-29 as Buddha dharma 177 purity, as impurity/taint/pollution (汚れ *kega-re*) 34-35, 74-75, 109, 127, 134, 254 vs. sin 32-35, 74, 109, 124 purity (清浄 *shojo*) 36, 77, 85-86 & temple labor (作務 *samu*) 35 recanting and converting (転向 *tenko*) 172-73, 175, 181, 183-84, 199, 204, 208, 211, 217, 219, 225, 227, 260 ritualization of Buddhist practice 13-15, 31-32, 36-37, 49-50, 80, 92, 105, 110, 216 of Buddhist precepts 104 for purification 32, 75-76, 78 in Shinto 34, 75, 86, 116 spirit of Japan (大和魂 *yamato-damashii*) 115 soul (魂 *tama*) 75 suicide 9, 11, 19, 251, 285, 300

K

karma 34, 37, 41, 66-67, 74-78, 109-110, 239-41 as connection/link (結縁 *kechi-en*) 104, 110, 310 as duty 165 as determinism/retribution 33-37, 45, 63, 72, 77, 110-13, 156, 175, 180, 239-41, 257 differentiation is equality (差別即平等 *sabetsu-soku-byodo*) 156 as disconnection (無縁 *mu-en*) 9, 283, 285, 310, 312 the Disconnected Society (無縁社会 *mu-en shakai*) 242, 289, 297, 308 as field of merit (Skt. *punya-ksetra* 福田 *fuku-den*) 37, 78 as intentional ethical action (Skt. *cetana* 思 *shi*) 45, 64-65, 75, 77, 170, 191, 227 n.66, 260-61, 309 as merit/reward/benefit 77-78, 105, 239-40

Korea 7, 27-28, 32, 37, 54, 252, 265, 274, 299

god(s) (神 *kami*) 34, 46, 48, 79, 84-88, 94, 96, 105-06, 115, 131, 175, 208, 297

Kyoto School (京都学派 *Kyoto gaku-ha*) 165, 187-96, 219, 227-28, 252-54, 257-58, 295, 298-99 Hegelian dialectics and the state 192 Madhyamaka vs. Yogacara 188-91 naturalism 188 war complicity 191-94 Nishida Kitaro 西田幾多郎 & the place of absolute nothingness (絶対無の場所 *zettai-mu-no basho*) 187-93, 195, 205, 227, 235, 252-53, 298 Nishitani Keiji 西谷啓治 193-94, 228, 235 Miki Kiyoshi 三木清 194-96, 225, 227, 258 Tanabe Hajime 田辺元 193 Tosaka Jun 戸坂潤 194-96, 225, 227 Umehara Takeshi 梅原猛 252 Martin Heidegger 193-96, 227-28 & everydayness (Ger. *alltäglichkeit* 日常性 *nichijosei*) 192, 194, 228, 233, 236 Herbert Marcuse 193-95, 224, 227, 229, 233 Jean-Paul Sartre 224, 227

L

labor
Buddhist support for 149-50, 166, 217-18, 240-43 General Council of Trade Unions (日本労働組合総評議会 *Nihon Rodo-kumiai Sohyo Gikai*) 217-18 policy favoring producers/companies 9, 170-71, 248, 305, 308 strikes 215, 217, 231

lay Buddhism 16, 40, 93, 133 conventional morality (通俗道徳 *tsuzoku-dotoku*) 241 Kodo Kyodan/Kodosan 孝道教団/孝道山 10 n.5, 17, 205, 240 Neo-Confucianism 206 Reiyu-kai 霊友会 178, 205-06, 239-40 lay-sponsored temples (知識 *chishiki-ji*) 42 vitalism & "life-force" (生命力 *sei-mei-ryoku*) 239-42 *see also monasticism & rules*

liberalism 9, 22, 128, 130, 134, 136-38, 142-46, 148, 160, 164, 167-70, 173, 204, 206, 221, 223, 224-30, 241, 249, 251, 256-57, 280, 283, 286, 289, 297, 301-09 classical liberalism of 18th century & negative liberty 137, 168, 170, 228, 302, 306-07 new liberalism of late 19th century & positive liberty 167-68, 228, 306-07 civilization and enlightenment (文明開化 *bunmei kaika*) movement 23, 136-38, 142-43, 147-48, 151-2, 176, 303-04 nuclear family 143, 243, 255, 305 "self-responsibility theory" (自己責任論 *jiko-sekinin-ron*) 308 Charles Darwin 139, 148, 174, 188 John Dewey 168, 206, 249 Fukuzawa Yukichi 福澤諭吉 136-37, 140, 143, 145-48, 255, 303 G.W.F. Hegel 130, 139, 168, 174, 177, 181, 192, 304 & dialectical apex in the state 168, 190, 192-93 Thomas Hobbes 130, 137, 228 Iwano Homei 岩野泡鳴 168 John Locke & autonomous self 130, 136-38, 167, 170, 228, 304 J.S. Mill 136, 143 Nishi Amane 西周 143-44 J.J. Rousseau 130, 136-37, 304 Yoshino Sakuzo 吉野作造 & politics of the people 民本主義 (*minpon-shugi*) 168

liberalism, Buddhist 135, 138-42, 148, 174, 179, 241-43, 245, 255 Meiji Buddhist Enlightenment Movement (仏教啓蒙活動 *Bukkyo Keimo-katsudo*) 135-42, 152-53, 174, 183, 188, 204, 242-43, 272 New Buddhist Movement (新仏教運動 *Shin Bukkyo-undo*) 150-53, 157, 163, 174, 272 Hirai Kinzo 平井金三 140-41 Imakita Kosen 今北洪川 139-40 Inoue Enryo 井上円了 133, 139, 141, 142, 164, 174, 205 Kiyozawa Manshi 清沢満之 139, 141, 164-66, 188, 205 Murakami Sensho 村上専精 141-42 Shaku Soen 釈宗演 139-40, 149, 157, 185 Shimaji Mokurai 島地黙雷 133, 135-36, 138, 141, 149, 156, 158, 180, 183, 205 Suzuki Daisetsu 鈴木大拙 139, 153, 157, 165, 186, 191, 226, 257-58, 263 Watanabe Kaikyoku 渡辺海旭 150-52, 256, 272, 275, 283

Lotus Sutra (Skt. *Saddharma Pundarika Sutra* 法華經 *Hokke-kyo*) 39, 47, 49, 77, 71-73, 82, 87, 92, 110, 141, 156, 158, 166-67, 178-181, 186, 205-19, 239-44, 258, 276, 300 recitation of taking refuge in the *Lotus Sutra* (南無妙法蓮華經 *namu-myo-horenge-kyo* or 題目 *daimoku*) 67, 71-73, 104, 206, 211, 216, 240, 242, 292,295

M

Marxism/communism 22, 116, 130, 158, 161-2, 169-78, 181, 184, 187-88, 194-96, 202, 204, 215 n.40, 215, 217-19, 220, 222-25, 227, 229-30, 232, 242, 254, 258-59, 268, 275-76, 278, 280, 297, 301, 303-04, 306-08, 311 Marxist-socialism 171, 181, 184, 187-88, 204, 223-24, 227, 230, 232, 242, 258, 297, 301 Japan Communist Party (JCP) (日本共産党 *Nihon Kyosan-to*) 172, 184, 215, 276 Sano Manabu 佐野学 & socialism-in-one-country (一国社会主義 *ikkoku shakai-shugi*) 172-76, 188 Umemoto Katsumi 梅本克己 227

materialism 146, 173, 196, 215, 227, 278, 297, 301 spiritual materialism 68, 174 trans-materialism (超物質主義 *cho-busshitsu-shugi*) 174-76, 275

modernity 12, 24, 142, 145, 162-64, 169-170, 175, 177, 187, 196, 222-24, 228-29, 234-36, 279-80, 283, 286, 297-99, 302 & the Three Poisons (*tri-visa* 三毒 *san-doku*) 273, 298, 302-03, 309

monasticism & rules (Skt. *vinaya* 戒律 *kairitsu*) 7 n.1, 24, 36-37, 52-54, 79-80, 103, 113, 157, 260 bodhisattva (perfect and immediate) precepts (円頓戒 *endon-kai*) 24, 52-54, 103-05, 132, 186, 260 bodhisattva vows and practice 39, 41, 58, 64, 66, 71, 73, 179, 186, 212, 269, 275, 298, 300, 308-09 five base precepts (Skt. *panca-sila* 五戒 *go-kai*) 90, 157, 180, 186 Four-Part monastic (Dharmagupta) *vinaya* (四分律 *shibun-ritsu*) 52-53, 103-04, 132 home-leaving/becoming a monastic (Skt. *pravrajya* 出家 *shukke*) 14, 36, 276 laicization/secularization of monks/celibacy 7-8, 13-16, 83, 91, 131-34, 146, 185, 221, 256 lay ordination 103-106 meat eating and marriage policy (肉食妻帯 *nikujiki saitai*) 132-34, 205 ordained lay people/samurai (入道 *nyudo* "enterer of the way") 84 ordination platform (戒壇 *kaidan*) 52 non-violence (Skt. *ahimsa* 不害 *fugai*) 49, 97, 104, 156-57, 186-7, 191, 196, 203, 210, 212-16,

222-23, 268, 282, 299 posthumous name (戒名 *kaimyo*) 12, 105, 112 temple family (寺族 *ji-zoku*) 14, 133 violence 54-56, 158
monasteries, state (国分寺 *kokubun-ji*) & nunneries, state (国分尼寺 *kokubun-ni-ji*) 42
monism
 Vedanta 51 True Mind 51, 69-70, 189, 191, 195 Tendai innate enlightenment (本覚 *hongaku*) 70-72
Myanmar 121, 220, 222, 272

N

Nichiren 日蓮 63, 67, 70-73, 87, 94 admonishing the state (国家諫暁 *kokka-kangyo*) 95, 209-11, 214, 292, 295 *Establishing the Right Teaching and Bringing Peace to the Country* (立正安国論 *Rissho Ankoku-ron*) 88, 209 establishment of a secure nation (立正安国 *rissho ankoku*) 178-79 *fuju-fu-se* (不受布施 "to neither receive, nor offer", non-cooperation with other sects) 87, 246 Pure Land of this world/life 166, 210 *shaku-buku* (折伏 "to break and subdue", conversion to the *Lotus Sutra*) 71-72, 87, 179, 207, 216, 244
Nichiren sect 日蓮宗 94-95 Fuju-fu-se sub-sect 不受不施派 101, 204 Hiden sub-sect 悲田派 101, 204 Kenpon Hokke sub-sect 顕本法華宗 95 merchant militias (法華一揆 *hokke-ikki*) 95, 185 Nichiren Sho-shu sub-sect 日蓮正宗 207-08, 240, 244, 246 Tanaka Chigaku 田中智學 & Nichiren-ism movement (日蓮主義 *Nichiren-shugi*) 166, 178, 206-07, 253
Nipponzan Myoho-ji 日本山妙法寺 211-16, 218, 221, 230-32, 244-46, 282, 292, 294-96, 299, 304, 311 Fujii Nichidatsu 藤井日達 211-16, 296 peace marches (平和行 *heiwa-koshin*) 244, 292, 294-95 U.S.-Japan Security Treaty (*Anpo*) & military base counter movement 215
nuclear radiation victims (被爆者 *hibaku-sha*) 35, 134, 286 *see also* rebellion/protest: anti-nuclear movement

O

origin and manifestation (of buddhas and gods) (本地垂迹 *honji-suijaku*) 48, 85, 87, 90, 94, 131, 258

P

peace and pacifism 18, 144, 149, 157, 179-81, 183, 200-04, 208-09, 213-19, 223-24, 226-232, 243-47, 260, 268, 282, 285-86, 289-96 non-alignment & neutralism 217-220, 222-23, 226, 229-32, 246, 260, 274, 289, 304 Discussion Forum on the Problem of Peace (平和問題談話会 *Heiwa-mondai Danwa-kai*) 226
prime ministers of Japan
 Abe Shinzo 安倍晋三 (2012–2020) 9-10, 17, 231, 250-53, 286, 288-91, 294 Kishi Nobusuke 岸信介 (1957-60) 231, 249-50 Koizumi Junichiro 小泉純一郎 (2001–2006) 9, 252, 286, 307-08 Nakasone Yasuhiro 中曽根康弘 (1982-87) 249-50, 252-53, 262, 305
progressives, postwar (戦後革新勢力 *sengo-kakushin seiryoku*) 18-19, 217-18, 224-25, 231-32, 247, 249-50, 289, 307-08 Maruyama Masao 丸山眞男 111, 123-24, 146, 157, 160-61, 193, 202, 225-29, 232-34, 241, 259, 263 Shimizu Ikutaro 清水幾太郎 226-29, 233 Yoshimoto Takaaki 吉本隆明 232-34, 256 Yoshino Genzaburo 吉野源三郎 & *Sekai* (世界 *The World*) 225-26, 307
psychotherapy & Freud 229
Pure Land Buddhism
 abandoning the tainted world and longing for the Pure Land (厭離穢土欣求浄土 *onri-edo gongu-jodo*) 58, 71 attaining Birth in the Pure Land (往生 *ojo*) 62, 66, 76-77 Daochuo 道綽 & *Collection of Passages on the Blissful Land* (安楽集 *Anraku-shu*) 62, 67 Genshin 源信 63, 76 & *Essentials for Birth in the Pure Land* (往生要集 *Ojoyo-shu*) 63, 76 & Twenty-Five Samadhi Group (二十五三昧会 *Nijugo zanmai-e*) 76 hometown *nenbutsu* (郷里念仏 *kyori nenbutsu*) 58 Ji sect 時宗 94 *nenbutsu hijiri* 念

329

仏聖 45, 58 nenbutsu-ko (念仏講 confraternities) 83 other power (他力 tariki) 76, 234 peasant rebellions (一向一揆 ikko-ikki) 67, 88, 93-96, 185, 204 recitation of the Amitabha Buddha's name (南無阿弥陀仏 namu-amida-butsu) or nenbutsu (Skt. buddhasmrti 念仏) 57-58, 66-68, 72, 76-77, 79, 81, 83, 87, 90, 104 Shandao 善導 66 sincere mind (至誠心 shijo-shin) 67, 77 Three Minds (三心 sanjin) 67 unenlightened, common person/fool (Skt. prthag-jana 凡夫 bonbu) 44, 66-68, 76, 210, 234 & icchantika (一闡提 issendai) those who have fallen too far to be redeemed 45, 72 n.124

Jodo Pure Land sect 浄土宗 13, 100, 132-33, 135, 149-50, 262, 264, 270 Honen 法然 13, 63, 65-70, 72-74, 76-78, 81, 87, 93, 152, 180, 204, 209, 254, 302, 312 Seven Article Pledge (七箇条起請文 Shichi-ka-jo kisho-mon) 78 single-minded nenbutsu (專修念仏 senju-nenbutsu) 65-67, 81, 87

Jodo Shin Pure Land sect 浄土真宗 Jodo Shin-shu) 13, 15, 53, 88, 90-95, 110, 112, 116, 132-35, 141, 148-49, 156, 164-66, 183-84, 205, 262, 270, 280-81, 290 Shinran 親鸞 13, 53, 63, 67-70, 72, 74, 77, 81, 88, 90-93, 180, 204, 209, 234, 254, 302, 312 Akamatsu Katsumaro 赤松克麿 Renjo 連城 (son) Shodo 照幢 (grandson) 183 Kakunyo 覺如 90 myoko-nin (妙好人 "wondrous, excellent person") 116 Rennyo 蓮如 93-94, 156 "Revere the Emperor, preserve the Dharma" (尊王護法 sonno-goho) 148-49 social discrimination & Two Truths (真俗二諦 shinzoku nitai) 156 True Body Society (信身 Shinjin-kai) & Oneness Society (一如会 Ichinyo-kai) 184-85, 265 n. 175 Zonkaku 存覺 90

Q
R

rebellion/protest
American, European, Chinese, and Russian revolutions 8, 22, 127, 129, 280 anti-nuclear movement 9-10, 17, 214, 216, 236-37, 244-49, 279-80, 285-86, 293-95 expressive vs. instrumental protest 203, 211, 213, 236, 295, 299 Freedom and Popular Rights Movement (自由民権運動 Jiyu Minken-undo) 138, 143, 155, 160, 202 Hibiya Riot of 1905 159-161, 203 Kamakura Buddhist reformation/revolution 51, 58-59, 63-74, 83, 97, 101, 129, 181, 201, 204, 301, 312 confraternities (講 ko) 82-83, 116 the lower overturning those above (下克 ge-koku-jo) 89 New Left 232-36, 292, 296 & everydayness (Ger. alltäglichkeit 日常性 nichijosei) 192, 194, 228, 233, 236 principled/ideological change 8, 22, 92-93, 127, 129, 151, 157, 159-62, 223, 227, 229, 235, 243, 247, 260, 276, 280, 285-86, 289, 293-300 religious based peasant revolts (宗教一揆 shukyo-ikki) 90, 185 Nichiren merchant militias (法華一揆 hokke-ikki) 95, 185 Pure Land peasant revolts (一向一揆 ikko-ikki) 67, 88, 93-96, 185, 204 residents' movements 1960s-80s (住民運動 jumin undo) 236 marginalization of protest groups 204-05, 211, 214-15, 221, 235-37, 244, 247, 272-73, 277, 282, 294 U.S.-Japan Security Treaty (安保 Anpo) & military base counter movement 214-15, 226, 230-33, 286, 291 student activism & Zengakuren 全学連 159, 204, 215, 224, 226, 231-35, 244, 268, 277, 292, 296, 304 world renewal (世直し yo-naoshi) movement 19th century 116-17

repaying or returning benefits (報恩 ho-on) 40, 83, 102, 150, 152, 276 four types (四恩 shi-on) 40, 102 to all sentient beings (衆生恩 shujo-on) 150, 152, 276

Rissho Kosei-kai 立正佼成会 16-17, 178, 205, 214, 216, 232, 239-42, 244-47, 263, 265, 267, 290, 294-95 Niwano Nikkyo 庭野日敬 246 Niwano Peace Foundation & Prize 16, 246, 267, 295 World Council for Religion and Peace (WCRP, Religions for Peace) 246, 263-64, 267

Ritsu school 律宗 36, 52, 79

S

secularism 8, 11-14, 22, 24, 39-40, 86, 90, 99, 114-116, 130-39, 142-48, 185, 220, 230, 239, 252, 255, 271, 273-74, 276, 282-83, 298, 301-03, 311

Shingon sect 真言宗 44, 47, 49-50, 52-53, 57, 133 Kukai 空海 44-45, 47, 50 Eison 叡尊 79, 133 Ninkan 仁寛 & Tachikawa lineage 立川流 53 Ninsho 忍性 79, 151

Shinto 神道
   after death 75, 115 Amaterasu (Sun Goddess) 天照大神 48, 85 Yamazaki Ansai 山崎闇斎 & Suika Shinto movement 垂加神道 115 ethics/morality 36, 75 fusion with Confucianism (神儒教宗教 shin-jukyo shukyo) 121, 125-26, 136, 142, 146-47, 203, 224, 241, 251, 259, 309, 312 Hirata Atsutane 平田篤胤 & Restoration Shinto (復古神道 Fukko Shinto) 115 Motoori Norinaga 本居宣長 & National Learning movement (国学 koku-gaku) 115, 126, 175 shinkoku 神国 ideology & Kitabatake Chikafusa 北畠親房 79, 83-88, 99 spiritual/ethical power of the gods (神徳 shin-toku) 85 State Shinto (国家神道 Kokka Shinto) 147, 208, 290 Association of Shinto Shrines (神社本庁 Jinja Honcho) 293 Yoshikawa Koretari 吉川惟足 & Yoshikawa Shinto 吉川神道 115

Prince Shotoku 聖徳太子 38-42, 62, 71 n.120, 82-83, 107, 132, 150, 258, 312 Seventeen Article Constitution (十七条憲法 Ju-shichi-jo kenpo) 38-39, 41-42, 107, 258 Commentary on Three Sutras (三経義書 Sangyo-gi-sho) 39, 62

social welfare, Buddhist movement 149-52, 220, 237, 255-56, 269, 274, 283, 308 vs. social transformation as Engaged Buddhism 141-42, 237, 283

social ethics 203, 223, 240, 250
   Buddhist social ethics 40-41, 50, 75, 125, 196, 219, 254, 260, 300, 309-12 apathy, moral & political 11 civilizational ethics 8, 20-24, 27, 34-35, 38-39, 42, 48, 56, 59, 86, 92, 113, 117, 122, 134, 138, 141-42, 148, 177, 179, 183, 201, 210, 215-16, 223, 273, 299, 304, 310 conventional morality (通俗道徳 tsuzoku-dotoku) 241 Neo-Confucian 126, 144, 305 see also autonomy

socialism/anarchism 22, 155, 158-59, 162-63, 172, 174-76, 179, 184, 210, 213, 215, 217, 219, 283, 304 anarchism 158, 166, 180, 188, 192, 258, 297

Socialism, Buddhist 152, 155-58, 174-81, 216-17, 220, 222, 233, 258-59, 273, 280, 308 Buddhadasa Bhikkhu & Dhammic Socialism 121, 177, 222, 259, 278, 283, 310 Ichikawa Hakugen 市川白弦 & sunya-anarchism-communism (空-無政府-共同体論 ku museifu kyodotai-ron) 41, 190-93, 199, 218-19, 254, 257-59, 261-62, 265, 273 Inoue Shuten 井上秀天 157 Sakaino Koyo 境野黄洋 & trans-materialism (超物質主義 cho-busshitsu-shugi) 174 Seno-o Giro 妹尾義郎 & Popular Buddhism (大衆的仏教 Taishu-teki Bukkyo) 178-81, 216-19 Takagi Kenmyo 高木顕明 156-57 Takashima Beiho 高嶋米峰 & union of the material and the spiritual (物心一 busshin ichinyo) 174-75, 188 Uchiyama Gudo 内山愚童 & anarcho-communist revolution (無政府共産革命 mu-seifu kyosan kakumei) 157-58, 166, 178, 187

Socially Engaged Buddhism
   Ambedkar, B.R. 33, 121, 168, 220, 222, 254, 283 Anagarika Dharmapala 121, 138, 140, 157 Arima Jitsujo 有馬実成 & Shanti Volunteer Association (SVA)/ Japan Soto-shu Relief Committee (JSRC) 274-76, 280, 310-11 A.T. Ariyaratne & Sarvodaya movement 19, 220, 222, 254, 275, 279, 293 Buddhadasa Bhikkhu 121,177, 222, 259, 278, 283, 310 Four Noble Truths 11, 20, 73, 158, 180, 192, 196, 237 n.104, 275, 277, 299, 311 inside Japan 7-8, 23-24, 79, 97, 142, 152, 170, 178, 180, 184, 187, 204-05, 223, 237, 244, 246, 256, 272-83, 300-01 International Network of Engaged Buddhists (INEB) 7, 141, 223, 268,

276-77, 279-80, 311 INEB Japan 277, 311 Japan Network of Engaged Buddhists (JNEB) 7, 277 Maruyama Teruo & INEB Japan 丸山照雄 276-77, 311 Nakamura Hisashi & Pacific Asia Resource Center (PARC) 152, 279-81, 283, 299, 311 Nishikawa Jun 西川潤 & Buddhist development (開発 kaihotsu) 277-81, 283, 311 outside of Japan 19, 121, 138, 158, 220, 222-23, 230, 241, 254, 265, 267-68, 271, 275-83, 293 Sulak Sivaraksa 141, 222-23, 237 n.104, 275-76, 278-79, 281, 293 Taixu 太虛大師 121, 157, 185, 223, 267 Thai development monks (開発僧侶 kaihotsu-soryo) 19 n.14, 220-223, 274-76, 278, 281-82 Thich Nhat Hanh 190, 223, 254, 293, 310

Soka Gakkai 創価学会 16-17, 88, 178, 206-08, 210-11, 214, 216, 232, 239-47, 251, 254, 265, 267-68, 289-95, 305 Makiguchi Tsunesaburo 牧口常三郎 206-08, 210-11, 240, 244-45, 249 Toda Josei 戸田城聖 208, 240, 244 Ikeda Daisaku 池田大作 17, 207, 243, 245, 267, 291, 293 Komei-to 公明党 party 12, 17-18, 242-43, 245, 248, 290-93, 296

Sri Lanka 19, 40, 86, 101, 121, 140, 157, 212, 214-15, 218, 220, 220, 268, 275, 275, 282 Anagarika Dharmapala 121, 138, 140, 157 A.T. Ariyaratne & Sarvodaya movement 19, 220, 222, 254, 275, 279, 293

T

Taiwan 7, 172, 176, 220, 223
temple (Buddhist)
burakumin-only (穢多寺 eta-ji) 112, 156, 183, 264 temple labor (作務 samu) 35 local member temple (菩提寺 bodai-ji) 12, 84 temple registration system (寺請制度 tera-uke seido or 檀家制度 danka seido) 101-03, 113, 221-222, 302 temple-shrine complexes (寺社 ji-sha) 85

Tendai sect 天台宗 31, 44, 47, 49, 52, 133 fusion of Lotus Sutra, esotericism, meditation, and precepts (円密禅戒 en-mitsu-zen-kai) 49 identity of this world of suffering with the Buddha's Land of Tranquil Light (娑婆即寂光土 shaba soku jakko-do) 73 Saicho 最澄 44, 47, 49, 52, 63-64, 71 Ennin 圓仁 29 Jien 慈圓 & Gukan-sho (Selected Foolish Opinions 愚管抄) 79, 85

Thailand 19, 121, 220-222, 259, 268-69, 274-75, 278-79, 281 Buddhadasa Bhikkhu 121, 177, 222, 259, 278, 283, 310 development monks (開発僧侶 kaihotsu-soryo) 19 n.14, 220-223, 274-76, 278, 281-82 Sulak Sivaraksa 141, 222-23, 237 n.104, 275-76, 278-79, 281, 293

thaumaturgy (magic, performing of miracles) 43, 49, 57-58, 96

Theravada Buddhism 29 n.11, 37, 40, 44, 46, 52-53, 65, 78, 86, 110, 140, 157, 201, 265, 269, 275 Buddhaghosa & Path of Purity (Visuddhimagga) 110

this-worldly benefit (現世利益 gen-se riyaku) 32, 74, 84-85, 90, 96, 180, 205, 239, 283, 305

Three Trainings (Skt. trisiksa 三学 sangaku) 34, 37, 58, 69, 91 as sila-samadhi-prajna (戒定慧 kai-jo-e) 34, 37, 58, 64-65, 67, 91, 132, 298, 300

traditional Buddhist sects
Funeral Buddhism (葬式仏教 Soshiki Bukkyo) 12-14, 102-07, 221, 255-56, 260, 263, 268, 276, 283, 302 Imperial Way Buddhism (皇道仏教 Kodo Bukkyo) 183-87, 273, 283 Japan Buddhist Federation (JBF) (全日本仏教会 Zen Nihon Bukkyo-kai) 17 n.10, 199, 237, 263, 267-68, 294 post-war shift to peace 200, 203, 217-19, 259 social conservatism 12-13, 16-19, 255-56, 271-72, 293 social discrimination 32, 35, 40 n.35, 51, 77, 109, 134, 183-84, 189-90, 264-65 war responsibility 257-63, 265, 285-86, 289-90, 294-95, 304 Yasukuni Shrine 246, 252, 262

U

utopian/social retreat movements 116-17, 127, 162-67, 183, 204, 228, 272, 297 Garden of One Light (一燈園 Itto-en) 163, 216 n. 42 Garden of Selflessness (無我苑 Muga-en) 163, 165-66 Kiyozawa Manshi 清沢満之 and "spiritualism" (精神主義 seishin-shugi) 139, 141, 164-66, 188, 205 Miyazawa Kenji 宮沢賢治 164-67, 178, 234 Tolstoy, Leo 149, 163, 167, 178

utilitarianism 144-46, 286-88, 297, 303, 309, 312 collective utilitarianism (集団功利主義 shudan kori-shugi) 145-46, 159-60, 225, 247, 251-53, 273, 286-88, 300, 303 Nishi Amane 西周 143-44

V

Vietnam 190, 220, 223, 226-27, 267-68, 310 Thich Nhat Hanh 190, 223, 254, 293, 310

W

war responsibility (戦争責任 senso sekinin) 16-17, 161, 191, 193, 199, 219, 224-26, 229, 230, 247, 249, 257-63, 265, 285-86, 289-90, 294-95, 304

warrior monks/militarized Buddhists (僧兵 sohei) 54-56, 95, 158, 184-85 Benkei 弁慶 55

Way of the Warrior (武士道 bushido) 80, 107, 178, 196, 224, 250, 252, 259, 305, 309

women

Blood Pool Sutra (血盆經 Ketsubon-kyo) 111 eugenics and sterilization 134, 150 gender discrimination 12, 16, 111, 113, 133-34, 265 gender potential in Buddhism 16, 45, 72, 75 feminist movement 236-37 marriage to priests 133-34 state nunneries (国分尼寺 kokubun-ni-ji) 42 public participation 159, 231, 291

X
Y

Yogacara teachings (瑜伽行派 Yuga-gyo-ha) 31, 69, 188-90, 258 *see also* emptiness (shunyata)

Z

Zen Buddhism

Baizhang Huaihai 百丈懷海 & "A day without work is a day without food" 一日不做一日不食 36 Confucian ethics 111, 196, 260 Imperial Way Zen 185-87, 190-96, 252-53, 257-62, 289 koan 公案 69-70, 105 soku-hi (即非 "identity and difference") 191, 193, 257, 259 war 149, 157, 185-87, 191-94 Way of the Warrior (武士道 bushido) 80, 107, 178, 196, 224, 250, 252, 259, 305, 309

Rinzai Zen sect 臨済宗 63 n.105, 71, 77, 80-81, 87, 89, 103, 105, 111, 115, 139-40, 191-92, 196, 199-200, 257-59, 261-62, 265, 269, 290, 294 Eisai 栄西 63 n.105, 80-81 Five Mountains (五山 gozan) system 89, 139 Kono Taitsu 河野太通 199-200, 203, 205 n.16, 257, 261-62, 265, 294, 296 Linji school (China) 63 n.105, 69, 190, 190-92, 258 Wuxue Zuyuan (無学 Mugaku Sogen) 103 Yamamoto Genpo 山本玄峰 252-53 Yanagida Seizan 柳田聖山 200, 203, 219

Soto Zen sect 曹洞宗 31-32, 81, 83-84, 91, 94, 104-06, 110-12, 133, 149, 158, 185, 262-64, 271, 274, 290 Dogen 道元 63, 67, 69-70, 73-74, 77-78, 81, 91, 97, 104-05, 164, 298, 312 *The Treasury of the True Dharma Eye* (正法眼蔵 Shobogen-zo) 69-70, 91 just sitting meditation (只管打坐 shikantaza) 67 Caodong school (China) 70 Gasan 峨山 104 Machida Muneo 町田宗夫 263 Rujing 如淨 70 Sawaki Kodo 澤木興道 185-87, 191 secret initiation documents (kirigami) 31, 91, 110

About IBEC and the Author

The International Buddhist Exchange Center (IBEC) @ Kodosan was formed in 1966 by Rev. Shodo Okano, the first president of Kodosan, also known as the Kodo Kyodan Buddhist Fellowship. Its general goals were to develop modern, international perspectives on Buddhism through study and research, to create opportunities for those interested in Buddhism to learn and study further through lectures and events, and to cooperate with Buddhists inside and outside Japan on various social issues. As such, IBEC has always had a strong focus on social issues and the well-being of society since its earliest programs and the creation in 1986 of the Maitri Movement to bring compassion into practice in the world. In 2006, IBEC formed the Engaged Buddhist Project under the guidance of the third president of Kodosan, Rev. Shojun Okano, by bringing in Jonathan Watts to help him develop the research plan.

Rev. Okano and Watts have unique international and domestic networking competencies that enable them to bring a wide range of perspectives into IBEC work. Watts began working with the International Network of Engaged Buddhists (INEB) in 1990 as the foreign coordinator in the main office in Bangkok. In 1996, he helped form the INEB Think Sangha, an activist-oriented Engaged Buddhist think tank, to develop Buddhist perspectives on contemporary social issues. In 1999, he became a member of INEB's Executive Committee. From 1999 to 2018, he also served as a research fellow at the Jodo Shu Research Institute, editing the volume *Buddhist Care for the Dying and Bereaved* (Boston: Wisdom Publications, 2012). In 2008, he joined the Rinbutsuken Institute for Engaged Buddhism as a consultant and teacher in Buddhist chaplaincy training, and in 2009 began lecturing at Keio University on contemporary Buddhism in Japan and Asia. Living in Japan since 1993, Watts has worked with a wide variety of engaged Buddhists in Japan and together with Rev. Okano, who is an Advisory Board member of INEB.

The core focus of IBEC's Engaged Buddhism Project has been to investigate deeply the activities of Japanese Buddhists, especially from traditional denominations, on social issues and problems—that is, the Engaged Buddhist activities of Japanese Buddhists. The deeper emphasis of the research has been on grassroots activities focused on critical Japanese social issues—such as end-of-life care, suicide prevention, disaster trauma, poverty, and anti-nuclear and sustainable energy temple activism—rather than on some of the more high-profile social welfare activities by Buddhists denominations, especially overseas material aid.

From its inception, the Engaged Buddhist Project focused on practical networking that transcends sectarian divisions, and so created links with the International Network of Engaged Buddhists (INEB) based in Bangkok, Thailand. In 2009, IBEC was the leading force in the creation of an INEB chapter in Japan called the Japan Network of Engaged Buddhists (JNEB), which continues to provide an important non-sectarian platform for Buddhists and civil society groups to create cooperative activities.

www.ingramcontent.com/pod-product-compliance
Lightning Source LLC
Chambersburg PA
CBHW020942230426
43666CB00005B/124